John Eales
THE BIOGRAPHY

To Keith

Happy Birthday

John Eales

John Eales
THE BIOGRAPHY

Peter
FitzSimons

ABC
BOOKS

DEDICATION

*To the late Bob Templeton, OAM, one of the
great men of Australian rugby, who coached thousands
of players over the years, among whom were
John Eales and myself. In his not-so-slender frame,
Tempo embodied the best of the game.*

*Bob Templeton presents John with his award for
being part of the Queensland Team of the Century at the
Brisbane Convention Centre, 1999*

Contents

Brissie Born

Is Brisbane really called Brizzie?
It's frightfully pretty — the Naples of the Southern Hemisphere.

Sir John Betjeman,
Sydney Morning Herald, 30 October 1971

Brisbane is hilly. Walk two hundred metres in almost any direction outside the central city (which has been levelled) and you get a view — a new view. It is all gullies and sudden vistas. Not long views down a street to the horizon — and I am thinking now of cities like Melbourne and Adelaide, or Manchester or Milan, those great flat cities where you look away down endless vistas and the mind is drawn to distance. Wherever the eye turns here it learns restlessness, and variety and possibility, as the body learns efforts. Brisbane is a city that tires the legs and demands a certain sort of breath . . .

David Malouf, *Southerly*, Vol. 45, No. 1, 1985

～

JACK EALES was a good man.

Rosa Garrone knew it from the moment she met him. It was a balmy Brissie Saturday night in early 1964, and Jack and Rosa had arrived with separate groups of friends to Cloudland, a famous dancing club perched on a low hill just north of the tiny town centre. This was the club where for many generations of Queenslanders merry-making had led to marry-making, and on this night it was full to bursting with young singles dancing to the big band.

Around ten o'clock, Jack, dressed in his best shirt and tie, was up on the first-floor balcony looking down upon the throbbing throng, while

Rosa in her best going-out-to-dance dress was standing just to one side. By the warm glow of the chandeliers he had for some time been entranced by her pretty pink form. Beyond her comeliness, there was something about her kind and friendly face that particularly appealed to him. Still — as others of his friends continued to pair off all around — it took some confidence to ask a girl you *really* liked to dance, and Jack just didn't have it. Besides, his ankle, which he'd injured while coaching kids at cricket, was seriously sore. Besides again, maybe she would say no, she didn't want to dance. Finally, he decided to take the whole thing out of his own hands and leave it up to fate. Throughout the evening the band had been playing a particularly catchy new tune. He'd never heard it before, and after that evening would never hear it again, but he loved it.

'If they play that tune again,' he told his closest mate, 'I'm going to ask that girl to dance.' Jack felt pretty sure that they wouldn't, as the band had already played it three times, but just two numbers later its unmistakable chords indeed began. Jack looked at his friend. His friend looked straight back at him. Was he a man or not? It was now or never. With as much confidence as he could muster — still not enough to fill a walnut — Jack hobbled down the stairs, crook ankle'n'all, limped over, bowed, and asked this pretty young woman if he might have the pleasure. Why, with a slight blush, she would be *delighted*.

As they danced and began to talk, Rosa appraised him. Big. Solid. Country boy. Gentle. Polite. Gainfully employed as a schoolteacher. There were six big ticks already. But the biggest tick of all was to come. For not only was this fellow — Jack Eales he said his name was — a Roman Catholic, it turned out that his Catholicism was the very essence of him. For eight years he had been studying and teaching in Sydney as a Christian Brother, and even though he had left the order a year previously to return to his native Queensland because he had decided he wanted to have a wife and a family, his faith had not wavered a jot.

Between foxtrots and waltzes as the room gaily swirled around them, Jack gently assessed Rosa. Lovely. Intelligent. Cairns girl. Warm-hearted. Worked in a bank. Tick. Tick. Tick. Tick. Tick. And she was a devout Roman Catholic, with a faith also so profound that as a younger woman she had seriously considered becoming a nun. TICK. As soon as the big band's traditional music gave to way rock'n'roll numbers they went out on to the verandah to catch the cooling breeze off the Brisbane River and talk some more. Rosa was a little surprised that despite Jack's flecks of grey hair he was in fact three years younger than her own 29 years, but that wasn't a big deal. Sure, he looked a lot older than he was, but then everyone said she looked a lot younger. The main thing was that Jack clearly didn't think it a problem, because before the evening was out he had locked her in for three dates leading up to Easter.

The more the two got to know each other — going ten-pin bowling, day-trips to Noosa, more dances and Mass together — the better they clicked. In an age of protest, pot, promiscuity and times that were a'changing, both were delighted to find someone who rejected all of the above and their common deep faith was the foundation stone on which their romance was laid.

In some ways their Catholic courtship was a classic of the time. For far and away the greatest source of Roman Catholics into Australia came from Ireland and Italy, and Jack Eales and Rosa Garrone were products thereof. Jack's forebears had arrived from the Emerald Isle in the hold of a convict ship many generations previously, while Rosa's father Ernesto had first come to Australia from his native Italy in the 1920s to work as an itinerant canecutter in deep tropical north Queensland, and had brought to *il paese Australiano* an Italian bride, who would later say that the only things in her village were 'the church and work'. Rosa, their first daughter after two sons, had thus taken Catholicism with her mother's milk and her father's every exhalation, while Jack too had learned to count on his rosary beads and to read with his Bible.

They were *made* for each other. Within four months of meeting they were engaged and ten months after that, on 1 May 1965, Jack and Rosa were married, and moved into a tiny stucco brick house with a white picket fence they had bought at 209 Banks Street, Dorrington, in Brisbane's western suburbs, for the princely sum of £6,000. This was only about fifteen minutes' walk from where Jack worked as a primary teacher at Marist Brothers, Ashgrove, while Rosa also kept up her work at the bank. It was a measure of just what sort of a gentle and tolerant man Jack was that, within eleven months of their marriage, both of Rosa's now elderly parents moved in — pretty much just like that. It was essentially an Italian thing, the notion that when the parents were getting on a bit, the married daughter would take them into her home, and this presented no particular problem to Jack and Rosa Eales.

When Jack was asked by amazed friends and colleagues how he coped having, particularly, his mother-in-law so close underfoot he always replied with a laugh that it didn't cause him the slightest worry, 'because we are always in complete agreement — she thinks I'm wonderful, and I agree'.

More mouths to feed came along quickly enough, as Jack and Rosa were blessed with the birth of their first child, Bernadette, in 1967, followed by Carmel in 1969 and John, who arrived just seventeen months later on 27 June 1970. Jack's chook-yard and vegetable patch helped provide the eggs and vegies to feed them, his backyard orchid house kept the house full of flowers, Ernie the sheep helped keep the lawn down, and life was good, but cramped. For by this time, the three-bedroom house was ready to split at the seams, and something had to be done. It was. By going into debt just above their eyeballs, Jack and Rosa managed to buy a bigger block of land at the end of a cul-de-sac in the working-class suburb of Grovely, set in the bush on Brisbane's western edge, just near the new predominantly housing commission suburb of Keperra. It was classic suburban Australia of the 1960s, full of Hills hoists, Holden cars and jacaranda trees dotted all around, with every fifth or sixth street seeming to be directly adjacent to a sports oval.

SLOWLY, slowly, Jack and Rosa started organising to have a house built on their own slice of this heaven. Money was so scarce that Jack and Rosa asked their architect to make the rooms fit the sizes of the cheap carpet offcuts they'd secured. One way or another the house was finally completed, though, and in the winter of 1972, with Rosa again heavily pregnant, the whole family moved in.

John remembers arriving at this brick house as a tearaway toddler and bouncing with unfettered joy around the empty rooms. It seemed like a mansion compared to the tiny cottage they had been living in — and this one had an even bigger backyard.

In fact, it was a modest suburban brick home, but John was not the only one impressed. To both Nonno and Nonna — as the children called their Italian grandparents — it was a mansion of almost unbelievable luxury compared to what they had known all of their lives. Nonno (grandfather) had spent his childhood in a two-room house in his backwater Piedmont village in northern Italy, and the first part of his adult life in the hostel-like shacks provided for canecutters in north Queensland.

He returned to Italy with just eight weeks free to woo and wed a bride and bring her back to Australia. Enter Carolina Imarisio, from the tiny northern Italian farming village of San Giorgio, just ten minutes' walk from his own village, who accepted Ernesto's offer in part because it provided her an escape from an arranged marriage she couldn't bear to go through with. The two came back to Australia and settled for a long time in a boarding house before they had children. Nonna taught herself English by committing to memory the menus on the dining-room blackboards, constantly repeating to herself: 'corned beef and vegetables and roast beef with potatoes'.

By the time Rosa was born, the family had moved into a tiny barrack tenement on the edge of the tiny town of Babinda, and Nonna was able to add to Nonno's meagre wage by running the Italian Club and a sly grog shop on the side. Still, it all added up to little enough. Life was hard and the best of all possible things happened shortly after World War II broke out. With just 24 hours' notice to organise her affairs — and essentially because of her leading role with the Italian Club — the physically tiny Nonna was interned as a danger to Australia! (Nonno's labour in the canefields, on the other hand, was adjudged as being valuable to the war effort, so he remained with his oldest child, Henry.)

For Nonna, the whole exercise was sheer, unadulterated bliss. Together with her two youngest children, she was put in an intern camp on the edge of Melbourne, where there was hot and cold running water, inside toilets, and three square meals a day. Not only that, but the government paid for Rosa and Alf to go off to local Catholic schools. Nonna had every reason to believe her own patron saint of St Anthony of Padua had smiled on her as never before. It was with some regret, then, that she took her leave when the war was over, to return to her former hard life with Nonno and her children.

Not the least of Nonno and Nonna's pleasure in the new house at Grovely was to have their three grandchildren all around them. And make that four grandchildren, for two months later Jack and Rosa's fourth child, Damian, was born. While Rosa was nursing him, Nonna was more indefatigable than ever, doing her bit to help with the housework and cooking, as well as helping to look after the older three children. Though she delighted in playing with the *piccolina* girls, the kindly Nonna always seemed to have a particular affinity for the impish John Anthony Eales

— with the John coming from his father, John Francis, and the Anthony deriving from none other than Nonna's patron saint. For hours on end, Nonna would talk with John, play games with him, read him stories and take him for long walks. Ernesto, her husband, would be on the front porch smoking his pipe when she left, and still there when she got back. A few words in Italian to each other, and then she would lead little John by the hand back inside.

'John is a very good boy,' she would often say in her thick Italian accent, and he probably was that. But also a very shy boy. He was quite happy to run around with his family, but very slow to warm up when in the company of strangers. When, for example, Rosa first walked her four-year-old boy along the quiet leafy streets to the Oxford Park preschool, she couldn't help but notice that when she picked him up late that afternoon he had quite severe blisters on both his hands. Upon inquiry as to what could possibly have caused them, the answer was simple. John had stayed on the swing for the entire day, rocking back and forth, and refusing to talk to the other kids. It wasn't the first time he had been put in the company of other kids whose last name wasn't Eales, but he'd never seen things get out of hand *this* badly before and he wanted it stopped.

John was still on the swing about a week later, when a little boy by the name of Simon Whitehart sat down on the next one. The two looked at each other. John saw a neat boy with a big friendly smile. Simon saw a fairly tall, but still scrawny kid, who was clearly unhappy with his lot. And now the kid was speaking to him.

'If I wanted to,' he said, 'I could break this steel chain with my bare hands.'

And that was it. Simon waited for him to demonstrate his claim, but apparently this kid John didn't want to. Just kept rocking on the swing, kind of glowering, and wouldn't say another word.

For John's shyness and unhappiness at the preschool was not a passing thing. One day, several weeks later, the task of walking him there again fell to Nonna. Being taken there by his mother, as was usual, was one thing. There was really no point in running away from her, because John knew she could run him down and haul him in. But Nonna, now in her early seventies and often perspiring heavily beneath her long thick skirts in the hot Brissie sun, was another thing. Seizing the moment, John broke the grip and ran four blocks, all the way home. He was severely admonished, of course, Nonna calling him *cattivo* for wicked, but he would never see the inside of that preschool again. From then on, when it came to child's play he would muck around in the dirt with Damian, or wait patiently for the girls to get home from the local primary when they might play a game of hide-and-seek in the garden.

The good thing about John no longer attending preschool was that at least this saved Jack and Rosa a little money on the fees, a not inconsiderable advantage. For with so many mouths to feed, and baby number five already on the way, things were financially tighter than a bank manager on a bad day. For the growing Eales family there was no money for luxuries such as movies, shopping at the mall, new clothes, or even something so basic as a *phone*, but they managed, and the presents given to the children were mostly things that Jack fashioned in his garage out of old bits of wood that Rosa would decorate and Nonna would wrap in newspapers. When John was four, for example, he received 'a car' for Christmas — essentially a piece of pine roughly hewn into the shape of a car body with four circular lumps attached for wheels. In gold Texta copperplate it had 'John' written on the top, the cost of the materials involved being probably about four cents — plus Jack and Rosa's elbow grease thrown in for free. John couldn't have been happier.

Other frequent Jack and Rosa toys for their kids were things like butterfly nets, which could be fashioned out of a stick, a coathanger and the mesh bags from the greengrocer that you bought oranges in, and kites made from newspaper and a couple of light bits of wood. Whatever. Though there was not enough money left over for birthday parties — in his whole childhood John would have only one — it didn't really matter. There was a whole lot more to life than money — family and Catholicism for starters — and the Eales were generally more than happy with their lot.

One particularly happy thing was that their new house meant it was easier to accommodate more family members, and this was as well because on occasions Rosa's brother Alf also came to stay for long periods due to an ongoing health problem. He was always welcome in Arnell Street, and always bunked down in the room of the delighted John and Damian. When Antoinette was born in 1975 she was brought home to a house already containing ten people. For Jack and Rosa Eales, the more the merrier, and yet another frequent visitor to the house was the children's grandmother on Jack's side, Nanna Violet, who lived in nearby Nundah and loved coming over to play the card games Rickety Kate and Switch with her grandkids. Jack's other five brothers and sisters, mostly still living around Gympie, would also drop in when they were in town — and every Boxing Day the whole lot of them, with all 27 grandchildren, would gather at Nanna Violet's place for lunch. Young John's extended family too, was tight, his farthest horizons patrolled by people who were blood of his blood, flesh of his flesh.

LACK of money for light amusements probably moved the family further down the line of physical fun. It cost nothing at all, for example, for Jack to suspend a cricket ball in a sock from a piece of string attached to a rafter in the garage, and encourage his kids to hit it with a cricket bat he'd cut down to size, and that's exactly what he did.

While the girls quickly lost interest and returned to their dolls, John had started hitting it from just before school age, under Jack's careful instruction, while Uncle Alf, also very keen on his sports, sometimes lent a hand. Left elbow up, John, step forward into it and *hit*, and step back as the ball swings away, and step forward into it and *hit*, and step back, etc. There were two things about John with a bat in hand that Jack noticed early in the piece. Firstly, his older boy seemed to be naturally gifted with coordination and secondly, that he simply took to it naturally without any need of encouragement. Often when Jack went off to work in the morning, John would give him a cheery wave as he pulled out of the driveway, and when he returned in the late afternoon there was John *again*, still hitting away.

Of course he hadn't been there the whole day long, but he sometimes gave that impression. Before going inside, Jack would often give young John tutelage in various shots, being particularly keen on the leg glance, as it had the capacity to deliver a steady supply of runs with little risk.

'Just like this, John,' he would say, showing him how to turn his wrist at the instant of contact. John tried it a few times and with just a few goes seemed to have mastered the basics. And on he'd go, practising over and over again till dinner-time was called and stumps were drawn at the appropriate time of about 6 p.m. Jack sighed with pleasure. What a wonderful thing if John really did go well at cricket, and what a contrast it would be with the way things had been for him.

For Jack had loved the game from the moment he'd first come across it, and had always aspired to play for his school team at Gympie Christian Brothers. With that in mind the 12-year-old Jack had gone to see Brother O'Dwyer, the coach, who'd reluctantly said he could come down for a trial. On that dusty afternoon, there in the backblocks of deep southern Queensland, the Brother had thrown him a ball to bowl and Jack had done his best . . . for the three balls that the Brother allowed him. Alas, one was a wide, one was so short that it was easily dispatched by the batsman for what would have been a boundary, and the last ball was only fair to middling — that is, it fair hit right in the middle of the bat and roared right back past him and Brother O'Dwyer, who was only just able to get out of the way in time, or it would have clocked him proper.

'Can you bat?' enquired the Brother, dubiously. Not really, was surely his opinion, after young Jack had swung wildly at the two balls allowed him and missed both. And that, more or less, was the end of Jack's school cricketing career. His school had not catered to those who simply wanted to play cricket whatever their ability and it was for that reason that, now he was a schoolteacher and father himself, Jack was keen to encourage all kids, regardless of their innate talent or lack thereof. Little Damian, for example, always had less affinity for cricket than John, but Jack Eales spent every bit as much time with him on the sport.

As to other sports, Jack had an equally less-than-lustrous past. He sort of liked football, but he could never get the passion up for it that others could. At Gympie the game had been rugby league and Jack never felt the coach was playing him out of position by putting him on the bench. Seriously. Unlike in the cricket, the school had a policy in football of rotating players to make sure everyone got a go, and before one particularly important game the coach came to the extremely reluctant realisation that he was going to have to drop the best player in the pack so as to give young Jack Eales his turn.

For his part, Jack wouldn't hear of it.

'Look,' he told the coach. 'It's all very easy, I'm quite happy on the bench. Don't worry about it.'

Delighted, the coach agreed, and that was fine.

Jack's self-view was that he was 'physically strong, but mentally soft'. He simply didn't see too much sense in chasing this ball around with such vigour and took the view it was better to let those keener on this type of thing to get on with it.

With such a background, Jack ever after had a soft spot for giving sporting opportunities to kids who were not necessarily in the front rank, and he always offered his services to coach the lower grade teams at both rugby union and cricket. Some seasons he would have as many as four teams under his wing, and was happy for it. This was not necessarily just for the sport itself, but for what it delivered.

From his earliest teaching days Jack found coaching sport a wonderful way to have influence on the way children developed. When he had them in a physical education environment they were often pretty faceless, just in and out and then they were gone. But when the same kids turned up for training and games every couple of days, it was marvellous to see how they reacted to pressure, to perceived success and failure, to helping team-mates. It was possible to have real influence in guiding them and nurturing their finer instincts. And though winning was not the be-all and end-all, doing the best you could and improving yourself definitely were. One of the many things Rosa admired about Jack was that he was at his happiest as a coach when one year he took a rugby team that had been used to losing 60-0 and by the end of the season had them losing by only 20 points or so.

WHEN John turned five he went to the local Catholic primary school, St William's, just up the road. Most mornings it was his two older sisters, Carmel and Bernadette, who would walk him to the expansive school which stood beside St William's Catholic Church, a place very familiar to the entire Eales family. Sometimes John used to dawdle on the way and his sisters would have to wait for him to make sure he crossed the road safely, mostly though he kept up. For with eight-year-old Bernadette and six-year-old Carmel, there was no point in trying to run away as he had with Nonna.

Besides which, John mostly liked school. The lessons were fine — he quite liked learning all about numbers and letters — while the playtime with all the other kids was nothing short of sensational. For outside of the classroom, the drill was simple. When the school-bell rang to signal play-lunch or lunch, you hustled out the door, had your sandwich on the run, and then picked an oval, any oval. Then you played a sport, any sport. Cricket, touch football, frisbee, soccer, it didn't really matter . . .

Fortuitously, John was growing up on a part of the planet where the grass grew green, the sun shone long and strong, and it was not just he who was imbued with a love of sport. All around, there were many other kids who shared his passion, and sometimes it seemed that formal school lessons were more a break from their sport than the other way round. One of John's fellow students who was every bit as keen on sport was the same Simon Whitehart he'd met on the swings at preschool, and he and John quickly became close friends. It was a friendship strong enough to withstand a few trials along the way.

On the day that Simon turned six he was just about to enthral the class with 'show and tell' of his brand new Lakeland colouring-in pencils, which he had in a shiny new pencil case, when there was a sudden ominous gurgle beside him. It was his best friend, John, who had been green at the gills all morning, but was now feeling a lot better thank you, after . . . after . . . after throwing up right in Simon's new pencil case! Anything so as not to spatter the floor or the desk, because John was also quite a neat boy.

The following year, there was further tension when John and Simon fastened their affection on the same pretty young girl with big brown eyes, by the name of Alison Wrigley. Simon thought he had won the battle after she had spent an entire lunch hour playing catch and kiss with her. Straight after lunch, though, he turned around in class and saw his Alison sitting next to John. The Eales boy was wearing a Kawasaki motor cycle hat and Alison was wearing a black Suzuki cap which, it turned out, John asked her to wear because it made her 'look sexy'.

Still, their friendship survived the contretemps, and overall John did so well at St William's that the teachers often wrote glowing things in his school reports. At the end of Year 2, the teacher R.O. Brien had not held back. '*John's achievements are a just reward for his hard work. I feel he will do extremely well in all he undertakes, because of his industrious attitude towards his work.*' In Year 3 it was noted that '*John is a very keen sports-man*'.

He was that. Nobody in the whole class was as good at sport as John. His play with the ball in the sock had not gone to waste and he was soon able to show how good he was with a bat. Perhaps his most legendary feat was in Grade 3, when he scored an amazing 300 not out, spread over three lunch-hours, which was the talk of the school. The other thing that particularly impressed the school was John's ability to catch footballs. One of the teachers, Mr Aspland, would come down on to the oval and he'd put up these huge towering punt-kick bombs to see if any of the kids could catch them. Most of the kids used to run a mile for fear they'd get hit on the head, but John would catch the ball just about every time.

Not that John didn't have other passions. Despite the atrocity committed on Simon's pencil case, John had a peculiar love of coloured pencils. He accumulated a huge and varied collection of them, and on Sunday nights he would constantly form up new versions of his 'Top Ten pencils', mulling for an hour over whether, for example, he preferred the olive green one to the turquoise beauty he'd swapped Simon for in return for a go at bat. Why he loved these pencils so much no-one can remember, though Bernadette would often afterwards think of it as the first sign of John's highly developed sense of order.

Another passion was going on 'money-hunts'. Out of a clear blue sky on a Saturday afternoon, he would announce that he was off on a money-hunt, and shortly thereafter be seen on his hands and knees in the backyard doing a one-boy emu bob, searching the blades of grass for the tell-tale glint of a five-cent piece. Surprisingly — for money was still very scarce in the Eales household — he was often successful on these hunts, finding the grass beneath the clothes line a particular treasure trove.

Finally, John loved mischief.

Some of Antoinette Eales' first memories as she began to emerge from the state of babydom are of an overpowering smell, so strong it seemed to assault *all* of her senses. It was John, making and letting off 'stink bombs'. To do it, he would gather up nasturtium buds, put them in a jar and let them ferment for a month in a warm place. When he took the lid off and hid the jar behind, say, the couch, even cockroaches dropped dead at 50 paces. All the kids, led by John, would run around like mad things, screaming with laughter and holding their noses while Nonna would shout '*cattivo*' and Jack and Rosa would implore John to take whatever it was outside, usually to no avail in the short term. It was simply too much fun.

Sport remained John's principal passion, however.

By the time he had graduated from hitting a ball in a sock, when not at school John would head out to the brick wall next to the family garage and, in classic Bradman fashion, hold a single stump in his hand and begin hitting a tennis ball against the wall, constantly refining his technique. In the leery summer haze the whole exercise assumed a kind of mesmerising circadian rhythm of its own — *thwack! pffft, pttt, thwack! pffft, pttt, thwack! pffft* . . .

Jack told Rosa proudly that on one occasion he had seen young John hit the ball 500 times in a row cleanly. Sometimes this game would go on for hours, whereupon Rosa would hear the 75-year-old Mr Cevdar from next door call out very politely in his thick Russian accent, 'John, I'm ready for a break now, would you like to have a rest for a couple of hours?'

'Sure, Mr Cevdar,' she would hear John reply cheerily, and then the only sound was the low hum of insects in the beautiful Brissie day. Rosa would look at the clock — say 3.07 p.m. — for from here she knew exactly what would happen. At *precisely* 5.07 pm, it would be back: *thwack! pffft pttt, thwack! pffft pttt, thwack!* . . .

Now returned from his own after-school sport, Jack would also watch John, and once again find himself starting to dream. What if this boy of his could one day wear the baggy green cap . . . one day play for the most esteemed sporting team in the country? After all, the lad clearly had extraordinarily good hand-eye coordination, great talent and determination, so why not? Often, in an effort to nurture this ambition, Jack would save his money to take John and Damian to see a day of Test cricket at the Gabba and, sure enough, John always came away more enthusiastic than before. Eales Snr was never a man to overtly push such a thing, never one to say outright 'I'd love it if you'd play for Australia, and I want you to work hard to do so,' but still . . .

But still the son gave the father every reason to quietly hope. Many times, he wouldn't be content just hitting the ball with the stump, but would have a scorecard with him, recording how much the entire Australian team got in their innings. One after the other then, he would pretend to be Ian Chappell, Greg Chappell, Doug Walters down to his favourite, Dennis Lillee, and dutifully record how many each batsman got, before totalling how many Australia achieved in their innings. (Most days Doug Walters seemed to have absolute blinders, and even Dennis Lillee was known to reel off the odd century before breakfast.)

Another who was impressed was Uncle Alf, who continued to share the room with John and Damian for long stints. 'John,' he would often say, 'Queensland won't win the Shield until you are a part of it.'

'Yes, Uncle Alf.' John batted on.

Even when John watched Australia playing one-day cricket on the Eales' tiny black-and-white television, he was not content to just sit there. Rather, he would often make up a scorecard and notch down the runs as the batsmen made them, always confirming that the Channel 9 statisticians had it right. And when day was done, gone the sun, it was still not over.

While Rosa and Nonna settled into the washing up, Nonno went to bed, the older girls did their homework, Antoinette was put to bed and Jack pursued his favourite relaxation of reading a Louis Lamour novel, John and Damian and Uncle Alf would often retire to their room. Here, the seven-year-old John, with five-year-old Damian listening, would get Uncle Alf to quiz him on the contents of a book he loved which detailed statistics of the Australian Ashes tour of England in 1961.

'How many runs did Colin Cowdrey score in the first innings of the Third Test at Headingly?'

'Ninety-three,' John would reply.

'Correct. And how did he get out?'

'Caught Wally Grout, bowled Graham McKenzie.'

'Correct. And . . . '

And so on . . .

Damian was amazed at just how much John loved sports statistics, but presumed it was just his way of making sport go into the night, when it was too dark to play or practise any more. Alf just loved it that John loved sports so much, and always encouraged him in this direction.

In winter, on Saturdays, Jack would often take John and Damian to Marist Brothers, Ashgrove, to watch the First XV play. Marist Brothers, like many boys private schools, was a fairly self-contained world for a trousered tribe of spirited young men, and in that world the Saturday afternoon football game against the visiting warriors from another tribe was a hugely important event. On the first occasion Jack took the boys there, John sat on the banks of No.1 Oval, set in a natural amphitheatre surrounded by gum trees, completely enthralled as the supporters of both schools cheered their champions on. John and Damian did too, as the young men on the field performed heroic deeds in their wonderful shining gold jerseys, and the game teetered in the balance. Certainly, it was the most noise John had ever heard in what had otherwise been a pretty quiet life, but that was not the reason he lay awake that night reliving it all. What got to him was the excitement of it, the drama, the sheer exhilaration of the game. When he shut his eyes he could see it all again, hear the crowd, see the action, remember the tries and the tackles . . . and when he finally journeyed to the Land of Nod it was complete with 30 footballers dancing around among the sleep fairies.

For many weeks afterwards, when Nonna went to call John for lunch or dinner — '*Mangiare!*' was her habitual cry, for eating time! — he'd be in the backyard, kicking around an old football Jack had given him for one birthday. She would gaze at him quizzically, wondering what on earth he was up to, and ask him just that, without ever quite understanding the answer.

Nonna was more than merely a constant presence in John's life, in the sense of a person who was always simply around. She was active, every day, in every way. From years of hard labour looking after her often invalid husband she had grown into the habit of rising at 5 a.m., whatever the season, whatever the day held, and she was thus, among many other things, the house's alarm clock. Every night, either of the boys who needed to rise early would leave a note out for Nonna detailing what time, what they wanted for breakfast, and their first conscious moment the following morning would be their grandmother gently shaking their shoulder.

By the time the boys were dressed and in the kitchen, their breakfast would be waiting for them, and when they had finished and gone back to their room to get ready for school, their bed was made. Rosa Eales, meanwhile, would be feeding the baby and helping Jack prepare to get away on time, before making the children's lunches, a progressively more major exercise the larger the family got.

While the Eales girls would never remember Nonna being quite so devoted to them, this was for a very simple reason. She wasn't. As a person whose ideas on a woman's place in the world had been formed in deeply provincial Italy just after the turn of the century, there was no doubt these ideas were a lot different from those of her granddaughters, but she did her best to teach them anyway. It drove them to *distraction*, yet Nonna never gave up hope. In the outside world, the feminist ideas of the likes of Germaine Greer and Gloria Steinem were howling like hurricanes through traditional thought processes about the relationship between the sexes, but not one breath of breeze from their direction ever ruffled Nonna's bountiful skirts.

If the boys had an advantage in the family's informal battle of the sexes, because Nonna was always a natural champion for their cause, still they were disadvantaged when the battle abated and democracy would naturally rule again. In all family disputes Jack and Rosa were big on having votes, and often it would be a bloc of Damian and John against the many girls and that was the end of it. Or nearly the end of it. At least in terms of licking their wounds, the boys could retreat to Nonna's corner, have her make them some hot chocolate or the like and they could all glower together at wicked fate that had so overturned the natural order of things by letting girls have their say.

And Nonno?

He too was a constant presence in the wider family's life, though — without putting too fine a point on it — the only thing in the house that equalled the level of energy that Nonna put into domestic activities was the level with which Nonno didn't. Yet there was a good reason for this. Firstly, after long decades cutting cane, while the sun beat down and his arms thrashed till they dropped with exhaustion, his body was racked by osteo-arthritis and he had long been incapable of working. And secondly, as an old-style Italian the way they used to make them, he had formed his own views on such things as domestic duties a good ten years *before* Nonna — and his view was that all that kind of stuff was woman's work anyway. Every morning, Nonna would not only make Nonno's breakfast, his bed and all the rest, but also kneel to tie his shoelaces.

Still, Nonno could be very kind, to the girls particularly, and if his pension had arrived a day or two before he would often, with a twinkle in his eye, give them $20 to get a piece of fruit from a passing fruit van . . . and purposefully never ask for change.

And then Nonno died. It had been clear for a long time that the 86-year-old was ailing and one day, when John was nearly eight, the doctor took Nonno off to hospital. That night the whole family was walking around crying . . . but the following morning Nonna made John breakfast all the same. There was a lot of grief at the funeral, yet life moved on.

ALL good parents are, of course, constant monitors of how their children are getting on in life, just as near neighbours often keep half an eye to windward on how the kids next door are travelling. Rarely, however, do they see exactly the same thing.

A case in point was the Eales' nearest neighbour, Mrs Cevdar, who would often say to Rosa: 'Your girls, Rosa, are beautiful, lovely, gorgeous . . . but your boy, John, he does not look nice to me that skinny, skinny boy. Not beautiful like his sisters at all. I don't understand.'

True, Mrs Cevdar didn't say outright that while beauty was only skin deep, ugly went clear to the bone — but that seemed to be her implication. Rosa always smiled. Her boy, John, she knew, was a beautiful boy, however gangly he might sometimes appear. He had always been the tallest boy in the class, and sometimes looked a little ungainly, but that was just because he hadn't quite grown into himself yet. That, she felt, would come.

And to be fair to Mrs Cevdar, she was not the only one who held the view. Rosa, who in her young days had sometimes been deeply hurt when called a 'wog', was always a close follower of how her children fared at school. When, for example, Damian went through a long bout of ill health, she specifically sought out one of the teachers at St William's, Mrs Lee, to see how he was getting on.

'*Damian?*' this good woman had replied. 'It's *John* who's always worried me. He just never looks quite right to me.'

That was fine! Rosa, like Jack, couldn't care less what their children looked like and was far more concerned with what kind of personalities their children had. Bernadette, for example, was an obedient and conscientious girl, constantly making sure that her younger brothers and sisters were okay. Damian was more bookish than John, with a passion for electronics, while Antoinette was just an adorable toddler. And then there was their second-born, Carmel. Unlike the others, she was feisty, independent, and sometimes outright rebellious. The biggest earthquake that rocked the young Eales family was when, in Year 6, the 11-year-old Carmel was caught smoking in the girls' toilets at school. Neither Jack nor Rosa could understand why their beloved daughter would do such a thing, but there it was. And there it had always been. It was not an uncommon sight in the Eales household for Nonna to tear around after the children with the huge macaroni stick she used to roll the pasta on the kitchen table, threatening to paddle their behinds. But it was probably Carmel who Nonna chased after the most — usually for cheekiness. Carmel was never particularly contrite. She was just like that, and it showed up in many ways.

In the winter of 1979 for example, one of the Eales' neighbours complained that one of the trees near Jack's orchid shack was shedding too many leaves onto their side of the fence, onto their beautiful lawn. Given that the rest of the backyard had plenty of trees in it, and this was the only one causing a problem the decision was reluctantly taken — despite the committed environmentalist Carmel's vehement protests — that it would have to be cut down.

The terrible day came when the tree loppers arrived, and even while they started to warm up their chain-saws and set up their ladders, their attention was drawn to a deeply upset 10-year-old girl yelling out the window at them, 'TREE KILLERS! TREE KILLERS!' and holding up a sign which said the same.

John was probably practising his cricket at the time they cut it down regardless. As to his personality, two features stood out early, and they are features rarely found side by side in the same spirit. Certainly he had a polite nature, but also — and this was the strange thing — he was always extremely competitive, always wanting to do things better than anyone else. If ever he couldn't, he'd just quietly work away with extraordinary resilience, and stamina until he could.

This stamina had first shown up when John was in Grade 3 at St William's and Jack allowed him to come on a 30-kilometre walkathon to raise money for a charity. He told John he could walk along with him for the first part, until he got tired, and then he could get a ride in one of the accompanying cars. As it happens, it was John who went the full distance with reasonable ease, while Jack finally limped in hours afterwards. As he got back to St William's he saw John running around on the oval with some of the older kids, kicking a football around. Jack couldn't believe it.

Sometimes John's sporting drive bordered on outright aggression, most particularly when he and Damian would observe the sacred rite of all young Australian boys of that era by playing backyard cricket. John was bigger than Damian, stronger than Damian, and quite a lot more skilled than his younger brother in the main facets of the game, but the older boy never seemed to ease off because of it. Many a time Jack would look out to see John charging in at full pace to hurl the ball at his younger brother with everything he had in him. In reply, Damian would bravely try to take the hits he could manage, and dodge the ones he couldn't, but he would drop to the ground like a felled steer when John beaned him.

'Steady, John, *steady*,' Jack would expostulate to his older son, 'you've got to take it a bit easier on Damian, he's a lot littler than you.'

In reply John would nod his head as if he understood, and perhaps even express some contrition, but if Jack happened to pass in, say, another ten minutes there John would be charging in every bit as fast as before. It was odd. Mostly the boys got on well together and were so inseparable that Rosa sometimes faltered with their names and referred to them both as 'Jamian', but whenever sport was involved, John suddenly came out with this killer instinct.

Where did he get that sporting aggression from?

On Rosa's side there was Nonno, who had certainly had an aggressive streak — at least when he and Nonna disagreed on something, which was often — while Rosa herself had been the captain of her school basketball team, but that was hardly the answer. And sure, two of Jack's uncles had been national champion bareback riders in the 1920s — one of them good enough to pluck a rose from the ground with his teeth while the brumby was at full gallop — but Jack doubted that their sporting ability had passed on down two generations. For one thing, he knew it would have had to have passed through him, and he was *positive* he hadn't received any.

And none of the other kids had it either. From an early age Jack had pinned numbers on his kids and lined them up at the start-line of Little Athletics 400 M and the like. Yet John was the only one who clearly pushed himself to the edge of exhaustion, and it certainly hadn't been at his father's behest. For Jack's view of the role of sports had never encompassed or encouraged such an obsessive need to win and dominate. Outside of sports, John was very kind — he had been a particularly caring older brother to baby Antoinette — so Jack just didn't understand the *aggression*.

It was directly because of this in-your-face streak of John's and the belief that it would best be channelled into activities in which it would find constructive outlet that Jack — Rosa was not consulted — decided to take him to be a part of the local Ashgrove Emu U/8B rugby team he was coaching that year.

John reluctantly agreed to give it a go, not at all sure whether he wanted to actually take the step from being an enthralled occasional spectator to actively engaged ongoing participant. Still, he'd promised his father he would, and there was nothing for it in those first still hot days of March but to go with Dad after school down to the GPS Oval in

Yoko Road, Ashgrove, where Jack put the lads through their paces and attempted to get them into shape. The endless laughter from the flocks of galahs flying overhead seemed to mock their efforts at organisation, but with a few other fathers helping out they got ready for their opening game regardless.

Illustrating the casual nature of the competition, the boys practised and played in their bare feet. Still, things were at least organised enough that the team was divided up into 'backs' and 'forwards' with each player having a designated position — whatever the natural tendency of the Emus to look like a mob of headless chooks once the ball was thrown amongst them — and Jack decided that, on the basis of his ball skills, young John had the makings of a half-back.

So it was that when John Anthony Eales woke up one Saturday morning in March 1978, he knew that this was the day he was going to set foot on a rugby field for the first time, with intent. And he was not happy about it, not by a long shot. It was one thing to have gone along with his Dad to this point by attending practice and pretending to be 'a half-back', whatever that was, but quite another to take to the field against the mighty Kenmore Bears.

Bottom line: he *didn't* want to play. Playing football was the unknown and he liked the familiar. And so John did what he mostly did when upset about something and wanting to change his father's mind. He told his mother.

The fact that she was in hospital on this morning, having just given birth to her sixth child, Rosaleen, was no problem. When Jack Eales and John went to visit mother and baby in Royal Brisbane Hospital on the way to the ground, John laid it on the line when Jack had gone to the nursery to get the new baby.

'Mum,' John said tearfully, 'you know Dad's going to make me play football this morning and I don't want to play. I really don't want to play.'

His mother, as she so often did when any of her children were upset, stroked John's cheek to wipe away his tears and told him it would be alright. John cried some more, and she stroked his cheek some more. But she didn't speak to Jack.

The new bottom line: he couldn't get out of it. John's hope that his mother would put her foot down and say that he was too upset to play had failed to materialise and he had nowhere else to go. If she wasn't going to stop it, there was no way he could. For if he simply refused to play, he knew his father would not be angry but he would be disappointed, and that was far worse. He had to go through with it.

Game-time. John lined up with all the other seven-year-olds and eyed the mighty Kenmore Bears forming up to run out from the other side of the field. They looked pretty big, like eight-year-olds even, but anyway . . . The last thing his father said to him before he ran out that day was the same thing he had always said to every boy in his care, at whatever level, just before they took the field: 'Make sure you enjoy it.'

Which was easy for Dad to say. *He* didn't have to be out there with them, John noted as the opening whistle blew, *he* didn't have to roll around on the grass like they did, didn't have to try and tackle like they did, didn't have to get the ball . . . got the ball . . . GOT THE BALL . . . HE HAD THE BALL! Somewhere in the opening minutes the ball came to him with room to move and John operated from instinct pure. He ran like a hare towards the daylight. There was a bit of a gap ahead through which he could see the tryline and he ran towards it.

The funny thing about scoring a try, John quickly discovered, is that the ground seems to come right up at you as you dive onto it with the ball safely snuggled into your chest. Right up at you and then kind of knocks the wind out of you, before the full glory of what you've done rushes over you and then all your team-mates are crowding around you and slapping you on the back and saying 'Well done, John!' 'Good on you, John!' and that sort of thing. Maybe this wasn't such a bad game after all. John enjoyed scoring that try so much, he shortly afterwards managed to score another one and the Ashgrove Emus secured a handsome win on the day.

Emus! Three cheers for the Kenmore Bears! *Hip! Ray! Hip! Ray! Hip! Ray!*

It was an entirely different boy, then, who visited Rosa and little Rosaleen the following morning. Yesterday he had been trepidatious, nervous, withdrawn. This one Rosa could hear coming down the hall well before he burst into the room chanting the same mantra he had been driving the house crazy with all morning.

'We slaughtered them, we *slaughtered* them 18-nil, we slaughtered them, we *slaughtered* them 18-nil, we slaughtered them, we *slaughtered* them . . .'

Rosa gathered they'd won.

John's rugby career was away. Every Thursday afternoon and every Saturday morning for the following four months or so the Ashgrove Emus trotted out to do their darndest, with John among them and generally enjoying it. As a sideline father and coach, Jack was always of the circumspect variety. Other fathers and coaches would pace up and down the sidelines endlessly ranting and raving about what their sons should do, but Jack disliked that kind of thing in the extreme. He also reserved rare venom for coaches who used the kids in their team as nothing more than cannon fodder for their own coaching careers. He thought at this age the game should be played above all for the simple fun of it, and never get *too* serious about it.

That said, as the two made their way home after the game Jack loved nothing better than talking to John about particular incidents and they would look at how things might have worked out better if the team had done things differently.

'John,' he would say, 'Do you remember just before half-time when you had the ball in the open? Well, you had a big overlap on your left, but you only looked right. You've got to look around you, son, whenever you have the ball.'

To Jack's mind, passing the ball to team-mates in a better position was a large part of the game of rugby and he always tried to impress that on John and Damian, who had quickly joined John in the rugby ranks. Another theme that Jack warmed to was correct technique, technique defined by Jack as 'a safe way of doing things so neither you nor your opponents get hurt.' Ergo . . .

'You see, John, when you tackled their second-rower, you put your head in front of his legs, whereas you should have put it behind him so that when he fell your head wouldn't get crunched the way it did.'

This concentration on correct and safe technique was something that Rosa, particularly, was always delighted to hear. Enthusiasm for rugby was not one that she ever shared with Jack and John. She only saw John play three games in his first ten years of rugby and her primary concern was that neither he nor his opponents ever got hurt. This concern was shared by Nonna.

By this time, Nonna seemed to have actually focused on what this game of rugby actually consisted of, and was suitably appalled. It seemed incredible to her that John would willingly — and encouraged by Jack! — put himself in the face of such danger. Clearly, it was up to her to make things safer for him. And so she established a ritual that John, and later Damian, were obliged to go through before each game. Always, when they went to say goodbye to her, Nonna would take them by the hand and lead them into the lounge room, where she would place their right hand on the head of the statue of St Anthony, and together they would call on him to grant them safety.

Once John was back through the kitchen door, both Rosa and Nonna would look him up and down, counting one nose, two ears, two arms with ten fingers, and two legs, and once all was present and correct, then and only then could he go and clean up.

BEYOND tackling tuition from his dad, and experience gained with the Emus, John also gained a great grounding in the game — literally — by regularly playing tackle with a bloke called Mick Stower in the Cevdars' backyard. Mrs Cevdar was Mick's mother's great friend, and when he was at her house he usually invited John to come over so they could play. Essentially, the game involved one or other of them tucking a football under his arm, and seeing if he could force its passage across the backyard while the other tried to stop him. Anything went. The only rules were that there weren't any rules. Never mind that Mick was five years older than John and considerably taller and heavier. That just made it more interesting. Because Mick was bigger, the only way to bring him down was to take him low, pretty much exactly the way John's dad had told him.

It was a curious thing that the best way was also the safest way, but there it was. And when John had the ball he found the best way to force his way past Mick was to wait till Mick had committed himself to the tackle and then try and palm him down into the turf, or do a last-instant change of direction. The best thing was to be able to practise all different kinds of techniques, and then try them out on Saturday with the Emus. Often, too, John would go over to Mick's place to play and, among other things, admire all the pennants and gold trophies that Mick and his brothers had won, particularly for their prowess at rugby union.

One of John's dearest wishes at the time was to one day have just one of those pennants or trophies to call his own. He would look at the deep maroon colours of the pennants from the Queensland Junior Rugby Union, lift up the trophies to admire them close-up, and then go out into the backyard to pretend that he was playing to win one of them himself.

Unfortunately Damian was a bit too young and small to inculcate into this particularly rough game, so when Mick wasn't there and John was in the mood for football he had to come up with a new activity. The one facet of football you could do on your own, again and again, was goal-kicking, and it wasn't long before John had developed a fantasy whereby the top of the Hills hoist at the end of the Eales' backyard was the crossbar, and he was the match-winning goal-kicker. From his bedroom, or perhaps on the back verandah where he liked to read, Damian would often hear John do his inevitable self-commentary, in the clipped tones of the ABC announcer describing the final moments of a crucial Test match.

'And here's John Eales,' John would be saying, 'stepping up to the mark. The crowd hushes, in his final moments of concentration. Can he do it? Can he kick the winning goal for Australia?'

John would then move in and kick the ball, and if indeed it passed roughly over the top of the Hills hoist the commentator would be back on the air. 'He's done it! Eales has done it! He's kicked the winning goal for Australia!' There would then be about a minute's break while the match-winner climbed the neighbours' fence to retrieve the ball — the Birtwells were very understanding — and then it would start again . . .

'Eales sets the ball up now, I really don't think he can do it from this distance, Bill . . . '

'No, Murray. Into this wind, at this distance, it just seems incredible to me that he's even attempting it. A moment's pause now, while he focuses on the distant goal-posts. The Test match hangs in the balance . . . '

Damian turned the page.

HELPING to propel John towards those distant fields of dreams were the telecasts of the Five Nations games, which the ABC used to show four times a year on Sunday evenings. England vs France at Twickenham, Ireland vs Wales at Cardiff Arms Park, John watched them all, mesmerised. The player he loved most was the French breakaway and captain Jean-Pierre Rives, a diminutive bloke with untamed blond locks who always seemed to be everywhere at once on the field, always knocking over blokes twice his size. The way he played got to John. He didn't know why. Didn't care. He just liked watching Rives.

He also liked the goal-kickers, but of course. And the final stars in the piece were the stadiums themselves, these extraordinary vaulting cathedrals with their capacity crowds and their classic chants. John soaked it all up, entranced. Twickenham . . . Cardiff Arms Park . . . Lansdowne Road . . . Murrayfield. One day, one day, he thought, he might be able to go to those stadiums himself and watch Australia play a Test match. If he could do that, it would just about be the greatest thing he could do.

Sure, he fantasised in the backyard about actually being one of the players, but that was different. That really was dreaming. In reality, if one day he could see the Wallabies go round, well, life just wouldn't get any better . . .

WHILE viewing rugby games was often a solo pursuit, the one show that received a unanimous vote to watch on the television in the Eales household — apart from the Royal Wedding between Charles and Diana, which entranced the lot of them — was 'M*A*S*H'. But one day an unfortunate thing happened. A thundering editorial in the *Catholic Leader* asserted that M*A*S*H was immoral, and after consideration Jack decided it would have to be turned off — even though he enjoyed it as much as any of them. It took the Eales kids nigh on a month to persuade him to turn it back on again, but finally it was done, and Jack was back in the front row with the best of them — an extremely rare departure for Jack from the dictates of the *Catholic Leader*.

For just as Jack and Rosa had had a Catholic courtship, so too had they raised a family which lived a Catholic life. Every night, after dinner, the entire family, no exceptions, would go into the living room and kneel before the altar on which Nonna's statue of Saint Anthony was placed. And for the next half-hour, essentially led by Jack, they would worship their Lord God and Saviour, Jesus Christ.

Jack would begin: 'Hail Mary, full of grace, the Lord is with thee, blessed art thou amongst women and blessed is the fruit of your womb Jesus.'

All would respond: 'Holy Mary, Mother of God, pray for us sinners now and at the hour of our death, Amen.' This would be repeated ten times over, before moving on to the rosary beads, etc.

After ten Hail Marys with ten responses, Jack would say: 'Glory be to the Father and to the Son and to the Holy Spirit as it was in the beginning and is now and ever shall be, world without end. Amen.'

Then they would pray for various things, perhaps for a sick neighbour to get well, perhaps for those who had lost a loved one in the recent Granville train disaster to receive spiritual comfort from the Lord. Jack might give a reading from one of his favourite books, *The Saints of the Day*.

John used to dislike these sessions immensely. While his faith never wavered, he would later look back and describe their evening worship thus: 'This was more like a ritual for me rather than something that was particularly meaningful. My attention would wander sometimes, even though I would still be saying the words. Mum and Dad and Nonna, as adults who had grown up with this form of worship from the year dot had a much better idea of the significance of all the forms than we ever did and . . . '

And is that the phone ringing in the kitchen? Thank goodness their father had had to put it on when he had become principal of the nearby Brackenridge primary school. Anyone who rang the Eales household when the family was worshipping probably only had to wait half a ring before it was answered by the first Eales child who was able to get there, while the others desperately hoped that the call was for them.

Still, there was no outright revolt against the ritual. They had grown up with it —that was simply what you did — and they pretty much kept at it. And there remained a lot more to do as an Eales to fulfil one's commitment to the Lord. During school holidays, each child had to attend Mass once a day. Whatever else you had on, wherever else you were going, no excuses accepted, once a day. Mass.

There were three options. St William's had a Mass at 6.30 a.m., and if you missed that you could celebrate Mass at nearby Oxford Park Monastery at nine, but if you missed them both then you had to go to the evening Mass at 7.30 at the monastery.

Jack was very clear about the value of such a religious emphasis in the family life. To his mind, when religious belief was the focus of the family, it helped give an understanding of what life was all about. 'But it's not just about praying, and going through the rituals,' he would tell his children, 'it's also about living it.'

Marist Brothers, Ashgrove

Now is the time to show what mettle is in you — and there
shall be a warm seat near the hall fire, and honour and lots of bottled
beer tonight for him who does his duty in the next half hour.
This is worth living for — a half hour worth a year of common life.

THOMAS HUGHES, *Tom Brown's Schooldays*

Rugby rests entirely on the enthusiasm of players and ex-players. Its gate is
microscopic; its monetary return to players and officials is nil; it is fiercely and
uncompromisingly amateur, the cult of free men who love their fellows with
unparalleled ferocity. No other game permits men to plough opponents into the
ground and then cheerfully help them to their feet to suffer like treatment in
reverse. For boys it is the game for the sunshine of their lives, when the world is
full and round and there is health and wonder in the air; a game of the mind as
well as the body, and a test and source of character. Rugby football inspires all
those qualities of skill and courage, magnanimity, cooperation and unselfishness
that gives the games its universal appeal to men of free spirit.'

GERARD PIPER of Manly, letter to *Sydney Morning Herald*, 28 June 1995,
quoting an unknown author

❧

THE GREAT day came. On a sparkling early February morning of
1980, as the eight-year-old Damian watched with awe, John got into
his new school uniform — collared shirt, pleated grey pants, long socks
and shiny black shoes — and climbed with his father and Bernadette into
the Ealesmobile, as they called the family's battered green station-wagon.

'Good luck Johnny, you'll be fine!' Carmel called, as in her own St William's uniform she waved from the driveway. In short order John was dropped at the mighty iron gates of Marist Brothers Ashgrove, while Jack drove off with Bernadette to drop her a kilometre down the road at the Catholic girls' school of Mount St Michael's and then headed off to his own primary school of Brackenridge.

For John, this was it.

Satchel firmly in his hand, heart in his mouth, he crossed the great divide which separated the outside world from the school. He was here to do his final three years of primary education before transferring to the senior school, which was also on the same campus.

For Jack and Rosa, sending John to this school was an obvious choice, and not just because Jack had taught there for fifteen years before leaving the previous year. More importantly, it was a very good Catholic school, with its roots deep in the Marist Brothers tradition which had begun nearly two centuries earlier. It was then that Saint Marcellin Champagnat began his Order in France devoted to establishing schools which would celebrate above all things, Mary. (Hence, from 'Mary', the derivation 'Marist'.) 'Every time I see a child,' Saint Marcellin had written, 'I long to teach him his catechism, to make him realise how much Jesus Christ has loved him.'

With this devotion to establishing education based in the Catholic faith and firm discipline, Saint Marcellin was forty-seven schools to the good when he died in 1840, and since then Marist Brothers schools had spread to over 50 countries, first arriving in Australia in 1872. Marist Brothers Ashgrove had been set up on the western edge of Brisbane in 1940 on 22 verdant hectares which sloped down to Enoggera Creek. Hedged on three sides by thick bushland, it was the perfect kind of place to establish a self-contained world where the values of Catholicism could be instilled into all the young men who passed through its portals, and this was pursued on many levels, not least of which was physically . . .

In the first ten minutes of his first day there, John was called up to the front of the class and asked to put his hand out to receive the cane.

'And *that's* for your father,' the young teacher, Gerard McGuire, said, after swishing down on John's hand with a bit of wood shaped like a cricket bat which he delighted in referring to as 'Killer'. Mr McGuire, it turned out, had been taught and occasionally caned by Jack Eales. John, though initially shocked, could see that 'Sir' was smiling, and given that he hadn't really been hit hard he smiled too. It was the teacher's way of welcoming him, a kind of joke.

What was no joke — and the school made this clear to all newcomers from the beginning — was the need for the boys to have on them at all times a hanky, a comb and rosary beads. If you didn't have those things, it was a guaranteed caning for real. For there was no mere undercurrent of discipline at the school. Rather, it was overt, a constant flood that you fell into at your peril if you ever strayed from the straight and narrow path . . .

In his early days there, for example, John had stuck particularly closely to Simon Whitehart, who had also come to the school that year, and Patrick McGrath, a friend he had made playing with the Emus. One day, when their teacher was momentarily out of the room, John and Patrick were just mucking around, demonstrating to the class with a schoolmate's ruler the interesting way the Brothers used to cane — when the ruler suddenly broke. No big deal, both John and Patrick thought. They apologised to the owner of the ruler and thought that would be the end of it. It wasn't.

The following day they were called into teacher Graham Lawson's office. Mr Lawson was, John knew, a fine fellow, a very good teacher, a long-time friend of Jack Eales, a regular visitor to the Eales family home and no less than godfather to John's little sister, Rosaleen. None of the above saved him, though.

'Can you explain this broken ruler?' Mr Lawson asked the duo.

When they couldn't to his satisfaction, both were caned in the *modern* Ashgrove fashion, for real this time — once each, over the hand. Neither liked it, but neither complained, particularly. Caning, they knew, was simply part of the culture, and if you stepped out of line you figured you probably had it coming. For just as Catholicism came with very strict rules, so too did the school.

In fact, it was never clear where Catholicism ended and the school began. Many of the teachers were actual Marist Brothers and all wore their traditional white cassocks — neck-to-ankle robes, as worn by the original Marist Brothers. Statues of Mother Mary and Jesus abounded. On every bit of written work, not merely during their daily Religious Education classes, the boys were obliged to draw a left-hand margin and neatly write at the top 'JMJ,' short for Jesus, Mary and Joseph. This was intended as a reminder that all of the above were watching over them all the time, including their school work. Most of the school buildings had crucifixes on most walls as well as a crucifix on the highest point of their structures. In the entire school pretty much the only constructions missing the crucifixes — on which the many perpetually cawing crows would so often perch — were the rugby goal-posts on the eight huge ovals which were dotted around the school.

As with most serious Catholic schools across Australia, the passion for football was not a trifling one. One story, no doubt apocryphal, had it that the first students at the school in the early 1940s were told by the Brothers to sit down and memorise the 384 Laws and By-Laws of Rugby Union, as endorsed by the International Rugby Board. 'After that,' the Brothers told them, 'there's another ten rules you should also know about, things called commandments, but make sure you get the rugby ones first . . . '

Theories why rugby union had grown so well in Catholic soil in Australia have abounded, but at least part of it was the notion propounded by Dr Arnold, the famous headmaster of the Church of England Rugby school in England from 1827 to 1842, that the game was ideally suited for building 'muscular Christianity'. That is, just as the teachings of Christianity held that the individual was as nothing to the Holy Spirit, that humility was one of the prime virtues and all were answerable for their actions to a higher power, so did a good rugby player understand all of the same things applied when you simply replaced 'Holy Spirit' and 'higher power' with 'the rugby team,' and 'the coach'.

Within the culture of Marist Brothers Ashgrove and its formal motto of *viriliter age* (act manfully) the view was held that Dr Arnold was absolutely right. Good rugby teams tended to produce good citizens, and the game really was one of the best environments where 'muscular Christians' could be naturally produced. Reading, 'riting, 'rithmetic, religion and rugby just seemed to go well together! To be sure, rugby union was not exclusive in this regard, and other strongly Catholic schools had pursued rugby league for much the same reasons, but at Marist Brothers Ashgrove it was rugby union all the way. The founding father of rugby at the school, the legendary Brother Cyprian, was even reputed to have said that the three greatest scourges the world had to face were 'Communism, Christian Brothers and Rugby League.'

In short, rugby was king and the fifteen students who had had the privilege of wearing the all-gold jersey of the First XV were its princes most revered. From the day that John arrived at the school a key ambition was to one day wear that jersey, but there was a whole lot of rugby to play meantime. When his cricket season was over, right off the bat he was delighted to make the team for the Marist Brothers Ashgrove U/10As rugby side. True, his jersey was the school's standard brand one of blue and gold stripes that all the rest of the school, bar the First XV wore, but it was a start! Although Brother John O'Brien was the coach of this side, he accepted Jack Eales' kind offer to be an assistant coach.

Certainly the Ashgrove boys trained harder than the Emus had, but more importantly John's team had the best of all possible things that any rugby side, anywhere, can have — they had a chemistry. That is, they simply clicked together and had a natural cohesion that other teams found hard to match. For game after game they took on the teams from such schools as Nudgee, St Laurence, Gregory Terrace, St Columban's, Brisbane Boys College and bested most of them.

By the end of the season, though John and Patrick and all the rest could scarcely believe it, the Marist Brothers Ashgrove team found themselves in the Grand Final against the Nudgee Junior School . . . at Ballymore! This was the very same turf where both the *Wallabies* and the *Queensland Maroons* played. It scarcely seemed credible, but sure enough the great day arrived and with Jack Eales' usual encouragement to 'make sure you enjoy it, son,' ringing in his ears, John ran out on to Ballymore for the first time. If they won this day, John knew, he would actually get one of those deep maroon pennants just like Mick Stower had. As a team, they would win a gold cup!

In the middle of the ground, waiting for kick-off, John felt like a mere speck in the swirling greenness of it all and looked around. Ballymore was big alright, and across the halfway line the boys of Nudgee looked a little intimidating. Each and every one of them had put boot polish in two black streaks under their eyes — just like their Rugby League heroes did in the Amco Cup night-time competition which was very popular right then. Still, John instinctively felt that his side would have their measure. The referee blew his whistle, and it was on . . .

Some sixty minutes later, just seconds before the sands in the hour-glass had trickled their way through the gurgle hole of full time, the score stood at 6-4 in Nudgee's favour when Ashgrove was awarded a penalty kick almost directly in front, just 25 metres out. The Ashgrove captain threw the ball to John, the team's kicker. Even as John carefully lined his kick up, he couldn't help thinking this was *exactly* like the scenes he'd seen so many times before on the television. That is, at a famous stadium, with the full-time whistle blown, the ball was in the hands of the goal-kicker who had the power of victory in his hands. Or defeat. Some goal-kickers, he knew, were inclined to buckle under such pressure, but with a great thrill he realised that this was the stuff of his dreams and he loved it. ('Do you think he can do it, Bill?' 'I *certainly* do, Murray.' John thought so, too!)

Who didn't love it were the Nudgee team.

Standing behind the posts that day was the inside centre for Nudgee, Andrew Khoo, and he for one was furious. To his mind the whole game to that point had been just so unfair. Unfair. Unfair. Unfair. Every time there was a line-out, this big stringbean called John had jumped much higher than everyone else and got the ball every time. Then when there was a scrum, their most damaging back was the five-eighth, and that was this kid John too! Ashgrove just moved this kid around wherever he could hurt Nudgee most, and when Andrew found out John was the goal-kicker *too*, he could hardly stand it. Not fair! There oughta be a law. All the Nudgee boys felt the same, and stared balefully at the brute who had done them down to this point, and was about to administer the final blow.

Meanwhile, John was carefully, oh so carefully, lining up the kick and revelling in the attention of everyone on the field and everyone in the stands — including his mum who, extremely rarely for her, had turned up for this game and would be there to see his moment of triumph. It was up to him!

He moved in then, smoothly, rhythmically, with music in his mind and a song in his heart . . . and connected perfectly. Or almost perfectly. To his infinite horror, instead of spinning lazily through the uprights as he had just *known* it would, the ball swung out to the side, well to the right of the upright. Full-time. Marist Brothers had lost. Nudgee had won.

John burst into tears. And wouldn't stop. Most devastating, apart from the fact that he had let the team down, single-handedly lost the game and totally disgraced himself was that he wouldn't be getting one of those pennants like Mick Stower's after all, nor a gold trophy to bless himself with. He really, really wanted that pennant or a gold cup, and nothing could console him. All through the break-up BBQ that afternoon, he was still crying and it took a long time to get over. A long time. On meeting Andrew Khoo again, some twenty years later, John told him that he was mostly okay about it now, and 'really, these days, I only think about it once or twice a week.'

DESPITE such disappointments, it was a notably happy time in John's life. For whatever the many strictures of the school, however pious the parameters that the discipline system snarled at the edges of, the reality was that a fully initiated member of the trousered tribe could find the school a very happy experience indeed. John was one of them. He felt like he belonged there from the beginning, was proud to be a Marist Brothers Ashgrove boy, and eager to do his bit to add to the pride of the school.

One of the key ways of accomplishing that, of course, was winning while wearing the school colours, and by the time John got into the senior school he was probably doing as much as anyone in his age group to achieve just that. He played cricket, rugby and basketball with equal enthusiasm, did well in athletics — particularly the high-jump — and was a stand-out in the playground for his general sporting prowess.

One of the teachers, former Wallaby centre Barry Honan, was on playground duty one day when he noticed young Eales playing muckaround cricket. The lad was a good friend and team-mate of his son Terry, so Honan took particular interest. John was holding a stick no thicker than a stump, and the other students including Terry were hurling this tennis ball at him from about 15 metres away, but no-one could hit the rubbish bin they were using as a wicket. It was rare to see a guy as big as him, as gangly, who was in such amazing control but there it was. Most other kids who got that big that early tended to lose some of their coordination, but John clearly hadn't. Honan was amazed and thought the kid had one of the best eyes he'd ever seen. It seemed to him that young John might one day wear the baggy green. He said as much to his great friend, Jack Eales, a short time later.

'That is music to my ears,' Jack had replied.

In the classroom John was conscientious, and well-mannered without ever giving the impression that he was really pushing himself. At the end of 1982 his main teacher, Brother John Wagner, looked back on the year of John Eales and searched for the words that would sum up for his parents what kind of student their boy was. In his elegant hand, he wrote: '*A very good year for John. His results will continue to be very good, if the effort is kept up. He will have no problem coping. He still tries to find the easiest way out with the least amount of work. This doesn't always work.*'

FOUR years after his beginnings at Kenmore Oval, John was enjoying his rugby as much as ever and was even invited to turn up at the very same field to try his luck in the Queensland U/12 selection trials. Though he didn't like to say it out loud, he felt he must be a good chance of being selected, the more so after he played the game of his life. But, he was not picked.

John was so bitterly disappointed when he found out he cried all day. Not even Nonna could comfort him — which was when the family really knew it was serious. A common solution of many kids to the desire to wear a Queensland jersey was to simply go to Woolworths and buy one, and many of John's friends did exactly that, but John always refused. Certainly, he never had the money to spare on such trifles, but even if he did he didn't want to get a jersey like that, he wanted to earn it.

If sport at Marist Brothers Ashgrove was a world unto itself, passages from the sporting world outside were occasionally forced. As an example, when John was in Year 8, the just retired Wallaby captain Tony Shaw came to present the best and fairest awards for each age group.

For John, the winner in the U/13s, it was a moment suspended in time, a moment when he actually shook the hand of a Wallaby *captain*. As the whole school applauded, John felt if there was an assassin lurking behind the curtain who shot him on the spot, it wouldn't matter, he could die happy. What also impressed John was that Shaw was from the famous Brothers Rugby Club — one of Brisbane's most successful— which he had followed ever since he had once asked his father who he followed and was told 'Brothers, because that's where Ashgrove Old Boys mostly go'.

The Brothers club also figured in the equation later that same year, when John was selected to be a cricketer in the U/12 State Championships in Cairns, representing the North Brisbane Regional XI — provided he could come up with the necessary travel and accommodation money.

This was in fact a lot easier said than done. With a floating population at Arnell Street of between ten and twelve, as sometimes Rosa's other brother Henry stayed over as well, the Eales didn't have the kind of money required. But when Jack Eales mentioned this in passing to one of his teaching colleagues, Pat Burke, who was also the Seniors Fifth Grade coach at Brothers, Burke said, 'no problem'.

'Give me the brochure [detailing the cricket tour],' Pat had said, 'and I'll pass it around the bar at Brothers after training tonight, and we'll see what we can do.'

As good as his word. The following day Burke handed to Jack Eales $110 which he had gathered from the Brethren — as they liked to call themselves — after he'd explained that young John was a great cricketing talent, who needed a bit of a financial hand so as to be able to make the trip. The Cairns tournament proved to be an absolute pleasure, not just because John played cricket all day long, but also because he was able to make friends with boys from other parts of Queensland, including the star of the entire tournament, Jason Little from Toowoomba Grammar. This kid Little could bat and bowl, field and fly around like no other kid John had ever seen. Little was great friends with a bloke called Tim Horan from Downlands College, and long afterwards Horan would remember the moment when they had their first look at John Eales. In the tropical heat of a sweltering summer's day, with the sweat trickling down their legs and into their squelching socks, this enormous kid had wandered onto the field with his bat, a kid so big that the pads he had from the team kit barely came above his knees. Horan was wicket-keeper, Jason Little was the bowler and they followed their usual ritual when a new batsman/victim took his place at the crease.

'Let's put this bloke in the book!' Horan yelled out to Little, which was kid-speak at the time for 'Let's put him in the scoring book as "out".' Little glowered back, trying to look his most intimidating. Usually when Horan called out things like that, the batsmen was unnerved or would look around to see who was talking, but this kid didn't. Horan tried again. 'LET'S PUT THIS KID IN THE BOOK!' Still nothing. He just seemed very relaxed, very controlled, and not at all concerned. And then, in a very calculating fashion — taking almost no risks without being boring about it — John went on to put together a nice 40 runs or so. Horan and Little were both impressed in spite of themselves, and got to know him a bit over the next few days. He turned out to be every bit as obsessed with sport as they were, had a great sense of fun, and was exactly the kind of down-to-earth bloke that they liked most. He in turn liked them.

The main thing for John, however, was that his team had won. It scarcely seemed credible, but of all the twelve-year-olds in Queensland he was a part of the best team there was. In all of Queensland!

This was no small thing. Later, much later, a rugby player by the name of Peter Slattery would famously say, 'It's great to be an Australian, but it's better to be a Queenslander.'

Growing up, John and his friends just felt passionate about Queensland, and cared how the state was going in everything — particularly sport. When it came to rugby, John's heroes were the great Queensland Wallabies of that generation in Paul McLean, Mark Loane and Tony Shaw, and he followed avidly their fortunes. When Paul McLean was dropped in 1982 for an upstart from NSW by the name of Mark Ella, for example, John had been *furious*.

Rugby union's greatest provincial match every year was the annual match at Ballymore between NSW and Queensland and now and then Jack Eales would take his two boys to see such matches. From the stands, John always watched, absorbed. They were playing the game he played, rugby union, and as he often reminded himself, he had actually played on that sacred turf himself. As a matter of fact, he had missed a goal from straight in front of the northern posts, a goal which would have won the game for the U/10As . . . . . . but he didn't want to dwell on that. Always after they returned from Ballymore, John would drag Damian out into the backyard with the football and try to recreate the things they had seen, and they would talk about it for weeks afterwards.

If Damian's passion and abilities at football were no match for John's at this stage — he was far more academically inclined, and in sport was an accomplished volleyball player — still he enjoyed it all well enough that he was a frequent companion to his older brother in these muck-around sessions. Though John's sporting prowess in the school was beginning to earn him a fair measure of localised fame, there was never any sense that Damian was overshadowed because of it.

At home, John's successes pleased the family, but no-one went over-board. When John had received his award for being the best and fairest rugby player of the U/13As, for example, his parents had said, 'Well done, John' but that was that. So too, when Carmel won an art prize, or Bernadette or Damian a scholastic award. From the starting point that all of their children were extremely special to them, making a big deal out of one of their achievements would imply that one was extra special, and that just didn't fit.

None of which stopped John dreaming.

'What are you doing?' Antoinette asked John one day not long after his thirteenth birthday, when he was scribbling something over and over again, as the television broadcast a Wallaby Test.

'Antoinette,' he replied, handing her a few examples of his handiwork with a flourish. 'I am practising signing my autograph. Keep these, and one day they will be worth millions. One day I'm going to be out there, like that. I am going to be a great Wallaby.'

As John moved into his early teenage years, he knew it was time. Time to get a job . . .

He had before him the example of his two older sisters — Bernadette who had gone to work at Myers, Carmel with the local coffee shop. Both had done so without any prompting by their parents. They were never asked to contribute to the still tiny pool of family money that they were all living off — made tighter by the school fees — but still, the fact that they could henceforth buy their own clothes and some of their own school materials helped no end. And now it was John's turn. After a rough stint working as a gardener for a neighbour, he took his decidedly ungreen thumb to see if he could help out the local greengrocer.

His parents had long been faithful customers at Basil's Fruit Shop in Arana Hills, so Basil was more than happy to give the young teenager a go. At the princely sum of two dollars an hour, with the added bonus of a slice of pizza at the end of the day and the opportunity to take quick peeks at the nudie girlie calendar out the back of the shop, John began to help load customers' bags into their cars, bring back errant trolleys, replenish fruit bins, and throw out fruit that had gone past its use-by date and was starting to go off. The job he hated most was sorting the rotten potatoes. The only way to tell whether they had gone off or not was to press them firmly all over, and if they had, then his finger would go right inside, which he found quite *disgusting*. This smell, this horrible putrid smell, would be on his fingers for the rest of the day. What he far preferred was when Basil had him deal directly with the customers, either serving or packing, and for this he seemed to show a greater talent.

'The customers,' Basil would quietly tell John's parents in his thick Greek accent, when they came to pick him up, 'they just love Johnny boy, just love him. "Polite, nice boy," they say. Good boy, Johnny boy.'

This view that John Eales was just about the nicest young man going around was not universal, however. There were even signs in his school report that there was a smidgin of dissatisfaction abroad in his early teen years.

CLASS 8B. Marist College Ashgrove. *'John has not been consistent in showing leadership. He has a great deal of potential, which he should take care not to dissipate.'* P.V. Anderson. This was a view endorsed by the year master, Mr J. Shermann. *'John has been an excellent student for most of the year; but he has tended to become "one of the boys" in recent times.'*

One of the boys? Which boys? In terms of friends at the school, John was very tight with a group of friends which included Pat McGrath, Simon Mammino, Shaun Gelling, Terry Honan and his faithful friend since the days of preschool, Simon Whitehart. Though in the context of the school culture the group could roughly be categorised as the 'sports blokes', John by no means confined himself to that group. He also had a wide range of friends from others in the class, which often included kids who just didn't fit in.

The one guy in John's group who probably surpassed his own passion for sport was Patrick McGrath, whose sport of choice was rugby, as played specifically by the mighty Queensland team and the Wallabies. Patrick, though not big, was a fiery flanker and hooker and he liked players just like that. Chris Roche, who played on the flank for the Wallabies at the time, was a comparatively small man, and Patrick used to constantly cite him as exactly the kind of player he wanted to be. Tommy Lawton, the gargantuan Wallaby hooker? No thank you. Patrick's view was that the reserve hooker, Mark McBain, who had dimensions similar only to Tommy's left leg, was a better player. (True, McBain, was not quite the hero to Patrick that the Queensland premier Joh Bjelke-Petersen was, but he ran him close!)

A favourite activity of the central group of John's friends, though, now that they were old enough for their parents to occasionally allow them out on their own, was to go to see the Queensland rugby league team play State of Origin matches against New South Wales at Lang Park. The lads didn't have the money, of course, but this wasn't an insurmountable problem. At the back of the northern pavilion of the famous ground there was a spot where if one boy stood on the tallest boy's shoulders he could just manage to scramble over the fence and then help the following boys scramble up. It was always a hassle to get the last lad up, of course, but by dangling a rope made up of belts joined together they managed. Inside, some 30,000 people would be in full cry as Queensland took on the lowly 'Cockroaches', as the NSW team was often referred to. Certainly it was a bit naughty to get in like that without paying, but it was worth it just to see Queensland play. The roar of the crowd, the huge hits, the tries, the *atmosphere*. Heaven on a stick.

As to other traditional one-of-the-boys activities, the fact was that Marist Brothers Ashgrove had strict rules against such things as smoking, drinking and swearing. This, of course, did not mean that they did not go on. Like most teenagers, John was exposed to such things and he did not turn his back on them simply because there was a school rule against it. On one occasion when he was about fourteen years old, he attended a party where there was alcohol. What the hey? Feeling deliciously *wicked*, he knocked back five or six small bottles of beer — pretty much hating the taste but it was too good an opportunity to miss — and didn't feel too badly for it. No fool though, he realised that with his father picking him up at 10 o'clock he would have to do something to hide the smell of it on his breath, so took the precaution of having a quick dip in the pool and swilling round a few mouthfuls of the chlorinated water. Ugh. If that didn't do the trick, nothing would. As it turned out, nothing would.

Within one second of John being in the car, and settling back in his seat — strange, he felt rather sleepy — his father said, 'You've been drinking.'

'No I haven't.'

'Well I can smell it.'

'Well . . . I might have had one or two . . .'

A fairly long lecture followed, lasting for the entire trip home, but at the end of it his father said the magic words 'I'm not going to tell your mother about this one, but I'm going to be very wary of whatever parties you go to from here on in.'

And that was the end of it. Jack Eales never made mention of it again and when John went to another party where there was alcohol several weeks later, he stayed clear of it. Somehow it wasn't just that he stood to be busted if he drank, it was, as always, that he didn't want to let his father down. Jack Eales was in fact of a forgiving nature, and had always been so. One of his favourite sayings, both to his children and to students was, 'If you find someone who isn't making mistakes, then go and put them in a box and bury them, because they're dead. It doesn't matter that you make mistakes, so long as you learn something from them.'

On this score, of all the Eales children, it was probably Carmel who was learning more than most, because she continued to get into most of the scrapes with authority, but it was still never anything too serious. It might be for answering back, or wagging school, or failing to put in a required assignment. She was so good-hearted about being in trouble, though, it was hard for her parents to stay upset with her for long. Still, if she could catch her, Nonna would usually take Carmel into the living room for a good prayer session with St Anthony, to see if between them they could work it out. Carmel would oblige, out of love for Nonna, but still might manage to get a wink off to John as he passed.

Going into Year 9, John began to take his rugby even more seriously, and for the first time started doing serious pre-season training. To this point he had been fit as a result of his sport, but it was the first time he had specifically focused on fitness. He decided he needed to run. Long and hard. And he wanted all the Eales kids to do it with him. Plus Simon Whitehart, who was every bit as keen as he was. Just why Carmel and Bernadette, particularly, didn't tell John that if he wanted to run in the early morning he could darn well do it on his own was never clear, but one way or another they were all out there early one morning in January of 1984, as John mapped out their running route. It was a serious exercise, and he had already put a great deal of thought into it.

'Down Arnell Street,' he showed them on the Brisbane Refedex directory, with his finger, 'we'll go right onto Elmstead, right on Crestway Street, then all the way along Samford Road, before we . . . '

And so on. John knew exactly how long it was, having obliged Jack the previous day to take the Ealesmobile, and reminded them that 5.3 kilometres wasn't actually that far. Then they would begin to run.

One by one, as the days turned into weeks, the other kids dropped out of this morning madness, but John and Simon continued, changing the map from time to time and re-measuring to give variety. John tended to up the ante by having more hills, while Simon was more keen on the flatter routes. John usually won. Running with John on these hill-climbs, Damian was often appalled and impressed in equal measure. He was appalled at how hard John had made the route, but impressed that John would never leave him behind until he was sure that he had got every last ounce of effort out of him.

The upshot was the same, that John and Simon went into the rugby season in better shape than ever. Bolstering the Marist Brothers Ashgrove U/15A team further was a new boy who, though solidly built, was very lithe and very fast, and just perfect to play on the wing. His name was Garrick Morgan — son of a famous rugby league Test player from an earlier era, John 'Pogo' Morgan — and John got on well with him from the beginning. This, despite the fact that they were entirely different in personalities. Garrick was the odd combination of being both laid-back and an extrovert, while John was simply what was then known as a 'BP Quiet Achiever', after a television advertisement of the time.

Garrick saw John as a softly-spoken sporty sorta bloke with a lot of loyal mates who was nice to him as the new kid. John saw Garrick as a happy-go-lucky fellow who could run like the wind.

Another new boy that John got on well with that year was Chris White, a lad from Mitchell in deep western Queensland, who had arrived at Ashgrove to board. One of the things that amazed Chris from the beginning was how competitive John was in all things, not just formal sport. The two could be walking down the street and if John saw two pebbles on the ground he'd just as likely pick them up and invent a game where each could see how many times they could hit yonder bin out of twenty throws. And Eales would always win. Darts, basketball, tennis, pingpong, or any invented game he could think of — including an Eales-patented Frisbee Cricket with which he was briefly obsessed — it didn't really matter. John had to win.

All up, there was only one area of life where John's friends were safe from his competitive drive. In the water. Whenever they went to the school swimming pool, John's mates would laugh themselves silly to see him over with all the 'mungos' in the non-swimming class, doing dog-paddle after a tennis ball, while they practised their butterfly stroke. Let them laugh. John always made up the difference back on dry land, and then some . . .

On one occasion, John was with a group of friends on Ashgrove's basketball court playing muck-around basketball when out of the blue he said, 'I bet I can walk on my hands further down the court than any of you.'

For some reason, one kid was convinced he was a great talent at walking on his hands and took the bet. Sure enough, he 'walked' all the way down to the halfway mark before toppling. He turned around glee-fully to Eales in the manner of: 'Beat that!' With which, John got up on his hands, walked down the complete length of the basketball court, and just to make sure the kid got the message, walked back again. He didn't boast about it afterwards either, which impressed his mates even more.

Not that John was entirely a goodie-two-boots for all that.

On one occasion Chris White was selected with John to go to a Marist Brothers Schools Cricket Carnival in Perth during the Christmas holidays. He had to begin his journey with an eight-hour bus trip from Mitchell to Brisbane, where he would stay at the Eales' overnight before catching an early flight to Perth. When he arrived, though, not only had there had been some kind of mix-up — with Jack and Rosa having gone on a camping trip with the three youngest kids — but their usually quiet suburban household had become the site for a full-blown party, chocka with all of Carmel and Bernadette's late-teenager friends. Everyone was drinking or drunk or both, dancing, smoking, the lot. Nonna had bunked down in her room, away from the noise, and the lunatics had taken over the asylum. And John? He was knocking it back with the best of them, and dancing up a *storm*. Very late that night, Chris did in fact get to bed and get some sleep, but seemingly within minutes the alarm went. It was 4.30 a.m. They would have just enough time for a shower before catching a cab to the airport to make the 5.30 a.m flight to Perth, which begged the obvious question. Who was going to pay for the cab?

Chris proposed that they share the fare, but John had what he was pleased to call a better idea. In the pre-dawn light, he had scampered a safe distance to where he wouldn't be recognised even if seen, and then as the first glimpses of the sun's light appeared in the east, taken the milk money from the front step of the residents. And that was their cab fare to the airport.

It would remain on John's conscience for some time to come. At least fifteen years.

SOCRATES is a man. Man is mortal. Therefore, Socrates is mortal. This, John learned, was logic. And he learned about it in a class called Logic, taught by a kindly sort of fellow with a particular ability to make things easy to understand, Austin Skinner. Of all John's subjects, in his whole school career, this was the one he loved most. English was fine, as far as it went. Maths and science were good. But Logic was different. It was kind of clean, structured, orderly, a rough academic equivalent of the coloured pencils he used to love so much. John regularly came near the top of the class and would go on to win the Speech Day Prize for Logic in Year 11.

Going into that second last year, John's greatest rugby dream was to make it into the First XV. Though this was a feat achieved rarely for those not in their senior year, particularly in the forwards, John had every confidence that he would actually make it. In all humility, he believed he was one of the best eight forwards in the school, and so should be selected to wear the beautiful gold jersey to which he had long aspired, the thing he had long regarded as his own version of the Holy Grail.

He felt he had played a cracker-jack season for the U/15As, was feeling even stronger now, and by rights the spot should be his. Alas, it was not to be. When the names were read out, his second-rower team-mate from the U/15As, Chris Kennedy, had made the First XV, while he was relegated to the Seconds. That was no disgrace, to be sure, but he did feel rather hardly done by.

TRADITIONALLY, the boys of Marist Brothers Ashgrove tended to go out with the students from the Catholic girls schools of All Hallows and the nearby Mount St Michaels, where Carmel and Bernadette went. Within John's group of friends, quite a few had steady girlfriends from one or other of those establishments, but when it came to attracting the favourable attention of these young women, John was certainly not Ashgrove's answer to Warren Beatty. The reasons for this were varied, and sometimes discussed among his mates ...

John, they noted, could not dress a salad: sandals and socks, holes in his jeans, shirt out, the whole catastrophe. Clearly, the bloke just had no idea. It was even said that at All Hallows school dances, it was a big joke as to who was going to be unlucky enough to get landed with John Eales. At the very least, he was not what was known in the vernacular of the time as a spunk.

In fact, one of the girls at All Hallows at the time, Karen Walton, could put forth a teenage girl version of what Mrs Cevdar had always told Rosa Eales: 'Your girls are so lovely, so beautiful, but John . . . John . . . he is just not nice.' That is, in discussions with her female friends, she would say, and they would agree, that 'John's one of those tall, gangly guys who's still a bit dorky. He's good as a friend but you wouldn't want to go out with him. You just wouldn't pash him!'

And she told John as much. When at a school dance, John tried to 'win on' to her, Karen replied, 'Oh John, *pluh-eaassse.*'

Still, none of these views prevented Karen from trying to convince her very good friend Amanda Cheetham that, given that she didn't yet have a date for the All Hallows formal, she should ask John. 'Amanda,' she told her, 'he's tall, dark and . . . and . . . very nice.'

Amanda took some convincing, but at last agreed. After all, John was still a very nice guy and it was probably better than going to her school formal alone. Probably.

In the final year of school John was made a prefect, though the treasured prize of the school captaincy went to a young man by the name of Anthony Harding. It was not a close call. Harding was an extroverted leader, and John was not that. In any case, John's ambition did not lie in that direction. His ambitions mostly centred on sport, and he was delighted to be in the First XI for the second year running, keeping at bay — among others — a Year 11 opening batsman by the name of Matthew Hayden in the 2nd XI. John's real focus, however, was to at last make the ranks of the school's First XV.

One day in April 1987, it happened. Before a full school assembly, John Eales was presented with a gold jersey which signified that he was a bona fide member of the Marist Brothers Ashgrove First XV. Following deeply cherished tradition, once the last jersey had been presented, all 1,500 students in the school rose to their feet and applauded the newly anointed, with full-throated roars of acclamation thrown in.

However happy John had been to finally make the First XV, this did not mean he wanted to pursue rugby to the exclusion of all else. Far from it. When, for example, the coach of the First XV that year, Brother Richard Sidorko, tried to institute the system that had been in currency at his old Sydney school — the famous rugby nursery of St Joseph's College — of practising every afternoon after school, the voice in the team that spoke up loudest against it was one *Eales, J.* John was adamant that it should be just two afternoons a week at the most.

Brother Sidorko had support from within the team to train daily, but so did John to keep it the way it was. In the end a compromise was reached of training three afternoons a week. One of the key reasons John had held the line was the simple matter of time. Or lack thereof. He had always loved being busy and never like sitting still. By that measure then, this was probably one of the happiest times in his life. For even allowing for the fact that he was in the final year of school and would face extremely important exams at year's end, he had a lot of other commitments to get through. On a typical weekend he would play in the last stage of the inter-school basketball competition on a Friday night, play cricket all day Saturday, work at an El Taco dine-in establishment on the Saturday night, attend football fitness training at 6 a.m. Sunday morning, then work in the laundry at a nursing home from 11 a.m. to 3 p.m., followed by Mass. Occasionally, he could also fit in a game of golf afterward at Keperra Golf Club with Simon Whitehart. That night, John would study for his final exams.

An interesting sideline as the school rugby season began was the fact that the inaugural Rugby World Cup was on, a gathering in New Zealand and Australia of the sixteen foremost rugby nations to determine who were the world champions. For some reason this contest did not grip John quite the same way that watching the Five Nations matches used to, but the single memory that lingers is wagging school one day to go over to Pat McGrath's place and watch Australia lose to Wales in the consolation final. For the Wallabies this meant that, despite beginning the tournament with high hopes, they had actually finished *fourth*, behind Wales, France and (the ultimate victors) New Zealand.

John felt the way he always felt when an Australian team failed to triumph in any sport: shattered that they hadn't won.

He felt little better, about two months later, when the Marist Brothers Ashgrove First XV took on their greatest rivals, St Laurence's, and lost

19-0 in the grand final of their school competition. It was their biggest
game of the year, and the men in the gold jerseys had blown it. Nearing
the end of John's final rugby season at Marist Brothers Ashgrove, his
biggest excitement was the possibility of being picked in the Queensland
Schoolboys team. To make the side one first had to be selected for one of
the TAS sides — TAS standing for The Associated Schools — which
would take on the GPS teams, the best teams that could be selected from
the General Public School system. Alas, alas, when he turned up for the
trial John had little hope that he would make the side from the moment,
just before running on, he had heard one of the selectors say to another,
'Now, which one is Kennedy?,' referring to his second-row partner.

'Oh no,' John thought, 'here we go again.'

Suddenly though, he felt a renewed will take over. Surely, if he really
played well, they'd have no *choice* but to pick him. Thus, John Anthony
Eales proceeded to play the house down. He won the lineouts, pushed hard
in the scrum, took the ball in the kick-offs and charged upfield with it
many times. At game's end he knew. Knew that he was going to make it.

But they picked Chris Kennedy anyway. John found himself only a
humble reserve for the TAS 2nd XV. Though this time, John didn't cry all
day, as he had five years earlier when he had been left out of the U/12
Queensland side, still he felt pretty miserable.

Unbeknownst to him, John's non-selection had in fact been extremely
contentious. One of the TAS and Queensland Schoolboy selectors who
was also a teacher at Marist Brothers Ashgrove, Dave Robertson, had
been firmly of the view that Eales should have been not only in the TAS
1st XV, but also the Queensland Schoolboys side.

'He's that good, it's *ridiculous*,' he finally shouted at his fellow selectors. 'He has great hands, sensational coordination, a cool head and he's
very fit — what more do you want?'

The answer, as Robertson would ever after remember, was 'more beef'.
For when Robertson finally stormed from the selection meeting the last
words he heard were much the same as the first words he heard when the
subject of Eales came up: 'He's too skinny', 'He's too scrawny.'

As if that was the only thing that counted!

The bottom line was the same. John did not make the first side picked,
and though through injury he did finally get a run in the TAS 2nd XV, he
was no more than a spectator when the Queensland Schoolboy XV ran

out to play against the visiting Irish Schoolboy team. Adding insult to injury to indignity to injustice was that none other than Garrick Morgan had his spot in the second row! Unbelievably, the same lithe winger who had been with John in the U/15As had since gone to Downlands College, grown 15 cm, put on 20 kilograms and was now wearing the maroon jersey that should have been John's!

Sitting beside him at the time was good ol' faithful Simon Whitehart, and though John didn't speak throughout the game, Simon knew. John was burning up inside.

If there was one person who didn't feel *too* bad about the fact that John had missed out on representative rugby selection again, it was his mum, Rosa. Though normally she did not insert herself into the issues of her children's lives — she took the view that the way they lived their life was essentially their business — she did make an exception for rugby. Whatever Jack had to say about it, it always seemed way too dangerous to her, and she looked forward to the day when John gave it up and she wouldn't have to worry herself sick until he returned home safe and sound after each game.

When the orthodontist had fixed John's teeth with braces when he was thirteen, Rosa had said with some feeling, 'Well, at least you won't be playing rugby this year.' And when the orthodontist had said, 'No, that's alright, we can fit him with a special mouthguard,' John had smiled and Rosa had frowned. When John had finished his season with the U/14As and emerged unscathed — Praise the Lord and pass the binoculars — she had said with obvious relief, 'Well, only two years of rugby to go now.'

The following year the same . . . 'Well, just one more year of rugby to go now, John.'

And now, with some force, she said, 'Well John, that's enough now, no more rugby. You won't be playing rugby after school and that's that.'

John let it through to the keeper, as the expression runs, and did not choose to take a stand in the there and then. If he *did* choose to go on with it the following year — and that was far from certain, so wretched did he feel once again about his non-selection — he would talk his mother through it then.

And not even Jack, oddly enough, had been a source of total support when it came to John going ahead with his rugby. On one occasion, Jack had actually sat John down and had a good man-to-man conversation with him about his sporting career and how he had to face the fact that really, he was probably just that little bit too slow to make a big-time impact on rugby, and he would be far better advised — which was why Jack was doing it, incidentally — to really concentrate on his cricket, where there looked to be no limit to how far he could go.

Whatever. John appreciated the sincerity of his parents' views and the fact that they were offered with the best intent, but knew that when it came right down to it, neither parent would seriously stand in the way of John pursuing his passion, wheresoever that passion might lie. For the moment it was time to grind down hard for his final exams, which were now just weeks away . . .

In the constant juggling process between the demands of his sport and his studies, John to this point had managed reasonably well. He was not one to stay up till all hours hitting the books, but nor was he a student incapable of studying for one hour uninterrupted. He had said to Rosa once that the only way he could make it all work for him was to use his class time well and his sport time well and that way he'd be able to fit it all in, and he had pretty well kept to that.

Pretty well . . . Though he continued to excel in the subject of Logic, his final report for Mathematics II in Year 12, where he achieved 58 per cent when the class average was 62 per cent, is a fair indication of how things stood for him in this regard. For as his teacher Bill O'Donnell wrote, *'This result is not commensurate with John's ability. Time lost in study due to sporting demands is probably to blame.'*

Still, it was extraordinary the ground that could be made up when you focused solely on the one thing, and for the weeks leading into those final exams John did not so much as kick a football or lift a bat. His consequent results for his TES — Tertiary Entrance Score — when they came, were excellent, 965 out of a possible 990, putting him in the top 5 per cent in the state. Such a score meant, essentially, that he could study anything he wanted to at Queensland University, apart from Medicine and Veterinary Science, which was all well and good. It had always been assumed that he would head to university or do some form of tertiary education. Bernadette was already studying to be a teacher at McAuley College, while Carmel was doing Architecture at the Queensland Institute of Technology. The problem was he had no real idea of what it was he wanted to study. His calling at this point was not clear to him, though the fact that his last act at the school had been to accept the Des Ridley Sportsman of the Year award on the school's packed speech night gave some clue to his ultimate direction.

He settled on taking a degree in Human Movements at Queensland University, a kind of Physical Education course. This was not, mind, because he planned a career for himself in this field, but basically because he didn't know what else he wanted to do, and Human Movements sounded vaguely interesting. Or maybe he was doing it because Simon Whitehart was doing it too. Whatever.

Of Brothers and Sisters

*I'm pretty sure John Eales knew within himself that he
was something special, but he never sort of pushed it out on you.*

RON PRICE, John's coach at Brothers Colts, 1989

*Australians are Home Lovers to an extent which surpasses that quality
in any other land on Earth. When not following his healthful pursuits on the
beach, racetrack, football grandstand, convivial 'pub', or 'lodge',
the Australian is to be found embraced in the 'bosom of his family'.*

ROBIN BOYD, *The Great Australian Dream*, 1972

⤿

A MONTH AFTER John left school, Carmel suddenly announced
that she was going to move out of the family home. Given that she
was nineteen years old and a fully fledged card-carrying adult who had
already been studying Architecture for a year, this might have seemed a
fairly normal thing for her to want to do, but not in the Eales family it
wasn't. The understanding, at least from Jack and Rosa's point of view, was
that the children would all remain living at home until they were married.

Nonna went further and took it as a family embarrassment that Carmel
was leaving. 'What will people think?' she asked Carmel, sometimes wailing
outright. 'That we don't look after you properly? What sort of a family
will they think we are?'

Carmel didn't particularly care what people thought. She loved her family and they loved her — that wasn't the issue. What counted was that she needed a bit more space and she was going to do what she was going to do, and let the devil take the hindmost. For all the upset it put Jack, Rosa and Nonna through, not one of the children was surprised that Carmel should be the first one to break down that particular barricade. She had always been the most independent-minded of the children and the one who marched to the beat of a different drummer, almost literally. While the rest of the Eales kids were into the music of Simon and Garfunkel, Billy Joel, Elton John and Neil Diamond, Carmel always liked more esoteric bands like the Dead Kennedys, the Electric Pandas and lots of pub bands that no-one had heard of.

Just before Christmas, she moved into her new share-accommodation premises at Red Hill. It was, to John's mind, a 'total dive' and a weird kind of place to visit — with all sorts of people drifting in and out of the always smoky rooms which had mattresses on the floor — but it was interesting to spend time there. His parents were not at all happy about her living in such a place, and really wanted her to come home, but though Carmel remained a constant visitor, that was out of the question.

JOHN, phone for you. It was early March 1988, about a week after he had begun attending lectures at uni. On the blower was a nice kinda rugby bloke called Doug Fraser who John knew a bit from around the traps, a one-time coach of St Laurence's First XV who was now a coach with the Colts teams at the Brothers Rugby Club, and he quickly came to the point. He had long been an admirer of the way John played the game, and was wondering if he would like to come down to the trial games which were going to be held shortly. He couldn't promise John a position in the Firsts, of course, but they'd love to have a look at him, if indeed John hadn't yet committed himself to any other club . . . ?

John hadn't so committed himself — in fact no other club had called — and yes, he would like to come down to the trials thank you. See you next Saturday week, at Brothers. And that was that. (Apart from explaining to his mother, of course, just why she should be happy that he continue playing rugby. It took a while, but finally it was done.)

If John was going to play on, then Brothers was a fairly obvious choice, given the club's previous support of him and the fact that he had always followed their fortunes. Brothers had been formed in 1905 by the side of the famous Orient Hotel, and had originally been the Christian Brothers Old Boys Club before widening its net to include players from Marist Brothers schools. In the modern era anyone could join, and was most welcome. The club remained heavily Catholic, however, and large annual Masses were held in the club rooms for players and supporters. In short, though Brothers' motto was not 'the club that prays together and plays together stays together', it could have been.

John played a few trials on Brothers' No. 1 oval at Albion and decided he liked both the club and the feel of the place. The Brothers blokes seemed friendly enough, and he was particularly taken with the sheer beauty of their No. 1 oval, with its green banks and surrounding Moreton Bay figs and gum trees. More to the point, Brothers was also reasonably taken with him. This kid Eales was certainly no stand-out, but in the view of Doug Fraser and the experienced former A Grade coach he had assisting, Ron Price, he had *something*. At the first trial game Eales took the ball from the base of the scrum and had been knocked nearly senseless by both opposing flankers — he was that slow and cumbersome — but still. But still he had something. At the very least he was an extremely good lineout jumper, and after some discussion Fraser and Price offered him a position in Brothers Colts Firsts.

It was at this point that John met the most important Brothers man of all. For every rugby club has someone who is, at least figuratively, the keeper of the torch. Usually an older man, he is the person who most cares about the club, whose bone marrow oozes the club colours, who can tell you the story of what happened in the '64 grand final, who remembers the fellow who once played third grade for a couple of years back in the late seventies and has now turned up at the bar looking to catch up. He often has done some coaching in the past, and either helps out with a bit more here and there, or does other things like that. The keeper of the torch is a touchstone for all others in the club, the rock, who doesn't drift from club to club, but stays, year after year, decade after decade.

At Brothers that man was Merv Hazell, the oldest Brothers life member, and it was he who had signed up every player in the club once they had committed themselves to be one of the Brethren. John met Merv on the night of his first training session. A soberly dressed man in a pork-pie hat, as he presented John with the form to sign that would commit him to Brothers, he asked him his name.

'John Eales . . . '

Merv started. Looked up. Looked John fully up and down, then looked him up and down once more.

'John Eales, eh? Let's have a look at you,' he said in the slightly qua-vering voice of an elderly man. 'I've already *heard* a lot about you, and even seen you play once or twice. I've got a bit of a feeling you'll be the Brothers' next Wallaby . . . '

It was an extremely kind thing of Merv Hazell to have said, and John was not a little pleased about it, albeit quietly. If only he had stayed quiet about it . . . But when he happened to mention what a very kind thing Merv Hazell had said to him to a few of the other Colts a couple of weeks later, his team-mates fell about laughing.

'John!' they said. 'Don't you get it? Merv said that to us too, and they reckon he's said it to just about every Brothers colt since 1966!'

THE 1988 Brothers Colts Firsts did not prove to be a vintage for the ages, but they were capable enough and won their fair share of games. For John, the Colts was simply one of the many things he did, from attending Mass (though now less regularly than before), going to university, studying, going out with friends, the lot. He enjoyed the whole thing, but not one of his team-mates or coaches would later remember him playing like a German band in that year.

Never mind. John was just happy to be playing, without taking it all too seriously. The few blokes from Marist Brothers Ashgrove who'd also joined Brothers took much the same approach.

One who'd joined with John was Simon Whitehart, and though their friendship was as tight as ever, the bearded Simon was now only half John's size. In one of the early trial games, Simon was out on the wing when a barracker called out, 'Hey mate, this is Colts. It goes by age, not height!' Everyone, including Simon, had laughed, but his lack of size really was a problem and he was not long in the Colts Firsts. Others, like Terry Honan, Simon Best and Stephen Fleming, stuck, and they were John's initial friends within the team, though he soon made plenty of others.

One who would become a friend from the day they met was a fellow by the name of Rupert McCall, playing in the position of half-back. Rupert was with John when they went on their first Brothers pub crawl — a characteristically raucous affair. Traditional dress at such events could be best described as 'rough casual', as in something that could variously be spilled over and even thrown upon without serious problem, and as that described exactly what John wore most days anyway, he observed this form correctly. But he also had an extraordinary accompanying accoutrement. That is, he had his school lunch-box with him. Not as a joke. Because he had his lunch in it. Sandwiches made by his mum.

All the blokes on the crawl, including Rupert, laughed uproariously when they saw it, but John didn't see what the joke was. For him it was absolutely normal that when he was having lunch away from home then he'd bring his with him, pub crawl or no pub crawl. His mum used to make great sandwiches, so why wouldn't he bring his lunchbox?

The difference between John and the others in the team didn't stop there. When after about the tenth pub the lads began to stand on their chairs and sing ribald rugby songs to the order of 'The Hairs on her Dicky-Didle' and 'The Ringi Rangi Do', John decided to proffer an alternative. He too stood on his chair and — eager to make the point that there was no reason why the devil should have all the good tunes — began to regale the pub with a selection of his favourite hymns, led off by 'Peace is Flowing Like a River'.

Meanwhile, the rugby continued pleasurably enough. Not once, however, did John take it so seriously that he decided to stay in on a Friday night before an important game and get a good night's sleep. In fact, quite the reverse. His attitude was that if he didn't go out the night before a match he would be missing out.

So he did go out. Sometimes with his fellow Brethren, sometimes with friends from uni. In such drinking rambles others might have set their compass by the coolest pubs in town, but John's compass only ever pointed in one direction: *where was cheapest?* From 4 to 5 p.m. on a Friday after-noon, Her Majesty's offered jugs of beer for three dollars. And from 6 until 7 p.m., spirits for one dollar at the Wintergarden Tavern were just too good for a struggling student to knock back. With all that on board, John might then head off to one of the many balls around which campus social life revolved. If he was staying at a friend's place he could grog on to the wee hours; if staying at home, midnight was more like it — as he knew Rosa Eales never went to sleep until all of her children were accounted for.

As to his studies, the Human Movements course had its moments, and he particularly liked some of the academic aspects of such subjects as Biomechanics, learning how the human body worked. But by the end of the second semester, when they got to 'practical examination' of that same human body. things changed quickly. The day he found himself in the university's 'cadaver room' — invited to dissect the limbs of various poor souls who had donated their bodies to science — he had the strong feeling it was time for a re-think. Simon Whitehart was with him at the time and the look of distaste on John's face was something he would never forget. The bottom line was that you had to have a lot more passion for the course than John did to really get into something like that, and though he did not drop out, he at least began to cast around for other possible directions.

Beyond the odd worry about his studies, though, life seemed sunny and pleasant, not unlike a lazy Brissie afternoon in the suburbs . . .

Then, the first crack of lightning. One Tuesday about halfway through the '88 season, John came home to find Damian in tears and the whole house strangely empty. What on earth was going on?

Damian told him. Carmel had called up Mum and Dad, coughing horribly, and had said she wanted to go to the doctor but was too weak to get there. Could her parents come? All of them knew how crook the fiercely independent Carmel would have to be to have made such a call, and of course both Rosa and Jack Eales had rushed to their daughter immediately, fearing a bad case of bronchitis. But it was worse. Forget the doctor, just one look at their daughter and they had rushed her straight to the hospital, where she had undergone an immediate X-ray. There, to their horror, they saw a large shadow over her heart and lungs. It looked a lot like a tumour, but would need further tests . . .

The thing was, Damian finished into John's completely shocked silence, Carmel was right then and there in hospital, with their parents and their sisters at her bedside. The rumbling mumble John had heard in the next room was Nonna, on her knees before St Anthony, imploring his intervention.

Holy Mary, Mother of God. This was something that happened to other people, to the neighbours' cousin, or someone you heard about on the news. It *couldn't* be happening to their Carmel. When Jack and Rosa finally returned much later that evening, with the eyes of those who had exchanged sleep for tears, they filled John and Damian in a bit more. Yes it was extremely serious, but they would have to wait until the biopsy on Friday before they knew more. The entire family joined Nonna in the living room to pray.

Alas, Friday brought only worse news. Following minor exploratory surgery, Carmel had suffered serious complications with a great deal of swelling around the tumour pressuring her airway down to 2 millimetres and causing her to be put onto life support. The family was told to expect the worst that night and that Carmel's best hope was to undergo emergency radiotherapy to try to shrink the tumour, and if that did not work then she would undergo emergency surgery.

It was a long night, but, led by Carmel, they all got through it. On the Saturday, she remained in a coma, but was at least breathing more easily. Diagnosis showed that it was Hodgkin's lymphoma, a particularly virulent kind of cancer, which attacked the lymph gland and was potentially fatal in its own right.

By the middle of the following week, however — after a marathon of prayers by the Eales family, and superb medical care by the hospital staff — Carmel slowly emerged from the coma and was able to speak to the family. Best of all, they now had hope that she could make a recovery. She was already undergoing intense sessions of both radiotherapy and chemotherapy and, sure enough, the signs were good. A fortnight after the diagnosis she was progressing well, getting good reports, and seemed quite upbeat. Through all the chemotherapy, Carmel had been one of the very few, for some reason, who had not lost any of her hair. Within six weeks, things had improved enough for Carmel to resume her studies in Architecture, albeit with a lighter load of lectures.

All up, the feeling was that although Carmel had been through a terribly rough trot, at least the worst of it was over, and it was time for everyone in the family to pick up their own scattered reins and get on with their lives. Although John had not missed any rugby games because of Carmel's illness, he did hit the second half of the season with a little more vigour than the first.

That year, the powerhouse team in the Colts competition was Souths, led by the same Tim Horan whom John had met at the Cairns cricket carnival. His friend Jason Little had turned out to be so good at rugby that he had gone straight into A grade, but Horan decided to have a year of

Colts and had gone so well he was well on his way to being Brisbane's Colt Player of the Year. Horan led Souths to win the competition, though John at least had the satisfaction of being in the team that beat them 6-3 just before the finals began.

With rugby over for the season, John now focused on three things: exams, cricket and girls . . . though not necessarily in that order. For the rather callow youth of schooldays had now at last managed to 'grow into himself', and apparently was more of a catch than he had previously been. One of the first to notice, oddly enough, was Mrs Cevdar, next door. John was just about to depart for a university formal in his father's tux — which Rosa had spent a couple of nights altering, so it wouldn't float on him — when he knocked on Mrs Cevdar's door to borrow some sugar for Nonna. This good woman opened the door, gazed up at him, blinked, and then gaped.

'Your ugly duckling,' she had marvelled to Rosa shortly afterwards, 'has turned into a beautiful swan!'

While that might have been going a bit far, Mrs Cevdar was not the only one to notice that the young man's form had changed. For in terms of girls, he was also now starting to have some success. Sometimes, more than was good for him . . .

On one occasion around this time, he was out on a date with a young woman called Jenny, and after a visit to a nightclub things were going so well and getting soooo amorous, there in Brisbane's Royal Botanical Gardens, that they decided they needed a little more privacy. (They didn't need total privacy, mind, just enough to get away from the prying eyes of late-night passers-by.)

John suddenly had a stroke of genius. Right across the road stood the Brisbane Park Royal, and he happened to know that this far into the evening their gym would be all but empty. Why not try their luck in there for a little more high-powered canoodling? Why not indeed? Sure enough, the gym was entirely abandoned, and they thought it quite safe to fully get to grips.

It wasn't.

Suddenly the door opened, and there stood a very angry manager — with eyes like lasers and a bristling moustache which quivered with outrage — who promptly hauled them both down to his office to give them a dressing down neither would ever forget. And speaking of dressing down, will you please TUCK YOUR SHIRT IN, young man, and DO YOUR BUTTONS UP, young lady! Just who did they think they were, he asked? This time he wasn't going to call the police and have them arrested for trespassing, but if he EVER saw them set foot in the Park Royal, there would be trouble, are we clear?

Crystal.

Infinitely glad that the police hadn't been called, and with their passion now stone motherless dead, the two slunk off into the night, each going their separate embarrassed ways. Apart from this young woman, there were quite a few others John went out with from time to time and took to university formals and parties and the like. But if a relationship can be defined as exclusivity of affection for a single other, then he was never really in one. Rather in the realms of romance he simply drifted around — completely rudderless in Simon Whitehart's affectionate view — but was not at all unhappy about that. As the months passed his lack of romantic rudder meant that he washed up on a large number of exotic shores, and he always viewed that as no bad thing.

WITH summer came exams, and despite his lack of passion for his course John passed, but he had decided that the following year he would change over to get an Arts degree. With still no idea of what career he wanted to pursue, except that he knew it wasn't within the field of Human Movements — he decided Arts was better to broaden his range of knowledge.

In the meantime, to Jack's infinite satisfaction, John went to the Queensland University cricket trials and was immediately adjudged a good enough all-rounder to make the First Grade side. As a batsman, a slogger he wasn't. His former school-mate Chris White was also in the club and with others would good-naturedly call out to Eales at the crease, 'Go on, *have a go!*' but as ever Eales would only hit the loose balls as he patiently compiled his innings. Which was just the way Jack, who never missed a game, liked it.

John was also a useful medium fast bowler, and had the particular thrill of bowling to such former Test cricketers as Greg Ritchie and Trevor Hohns. Hohns, who was turning out for the Sandgate-Redcliffe club and who would go on to be the Chairman of Selectors for the Australian cricket side, was impressed with the bounce Eales generated with his high action. The kid obviously had a great deal of potential, he

Above: John aged four.
Eales family collection

Left: John aged seven,
endlessly practising his
kicking in the back yard.
Eales family collection

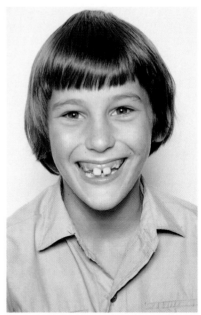

Damian readies to tackle a rampaging John at a picnic, 1980. *Eales family collection*

John, aged eight, in Year 3. *Eales family collection*

In the driveway of the house at Arnell Street. *Left to right:* Bernadette, Carmel, Rosaleen, John, Damian and Antoinette. *Eales family collection*

The Marist Brothers, Ashgrove, U/10 team at Ballymore immediately after John, the boy in the centre back row, failed to kick what would have been the winning goal. *Eales family collection*

Left: Carmel Eales at the end of 1988, just four months before she died. *Eales family collection*

On the cricket trip to Cairns in 1982. John is in the middle of the back row. His life-long friend, Stephen Fleming, is second from the left at the front. *Eales family collection*

On the last day at Marist Brothers Ashgrove, November 1987. *Eales family collection*

With the trophy that identified him as the best sportsman in the school, November 1987. *Eales family collection*

The folk at Arnell Street, Grovely, late 1988. *Eales family collection*

John being borne from the field after leading the Brothers Colts Firsts to victory in the 1989 Grand Final. Rupert McCall is second on the left from John. *Eales family collection*

Above: Receiving the highly coveted Rothman's Medal from All Black coach Grizz Wyllie, August 1990.
Eales family collection

Right: 'How sweet it is'. After making his Test debut against Wales, July 1991. Tim Horan is on the right.
Photo: Col Whelan
© *Action Photographics*

Making Test debut vs Wales, Ballymore, July 1991. *Photo: Col Whelan © Action Photographics*

With his partner in the 'engine room', Rod McCall, on the evening after the Wallabies won the 1991 World Cup. *Eales family collection*

At the dinner after the 1991 World Cup, the best second-rowers in the world join in a toast: To second-rowers! *From left:* Paul Ackford, Rod McCall (obscured), Ian Jones, John Eales, Steve Cutler, Gary Whetton and Doddie Weir. *Eales family collection*

noted, and might just possibly be able to deliver something to the elite level of the game that was in short supply.

LIFE was not all salad days of summer, however. At this time, John had two significant worries, one serious the other trivial but pressing.

Though she continued to pursue her Architecture studies, Carmel remained ill and the family remained on constant alert as to her health. In the one bathroom they shared, John would clean his teeth in the morning with one eye on an enormous ice-cream container full of the pills Carmel had to take every day, and it constantly amazed him that she could keep track of which pills she had to take when. Then, often, John would become the family driver, often dropping Antoinette and Rosaleen off to friends' houses to keep them occupied for the day before taking Rosa and Carmel to the hospital where his sister was booked in for a full day of treatment.

John's other ongoing concern — though nothing by comparison — was his chronic lack of money, despite trying many ways to alleviate the problem. One was to continue to work in the laundry of the nursing home, another to regularly mow the neighbours' lawns, as well as Nana Violet's over in Nundah and some of her neighbours'. At best he had ten lawns he was keeping in trim, but still he couldn't make ends meet. Finally, in January '89 he and his old school-friend Stephen Fleming were desperate enough to embark on a new and quite surprising money-making venture, at John's earnest behest. That is, they would join the Queensland University Army Reserve, going on two fortnight-long camps where they would be trained and paid in equal measure — hard but fair. For a fortnight they would be paid about $600 each, not inconsiderable when you added in the fact that they would be spending no money at all meantime.

IT was a disaster. There were many things that got John's goat about the whole experience, but a large part of it was what he saw as the sheer *mindlessness* of it all, the pursuit of things without visible purpose other than that the commanding officer thought it was a good idea. In John's view the Reserve had a 'hurry up and wait' mentality where he and his platoon would go flat out hurrying, hurrying, hurrying and then you would wait for half a day until anything else happened. But there was more, much more. Despite his impressive level of sports coordination, he found marching in time with all the other soldiers a near impossible task, and beyond that there were nearly enough final straws to make a bale of hay.

For starters, a wretched corporal and the platoon sergeant — fellow students playing dress-up soldiers in John's view — delighted in nick-naming him Private Stretch, something he absolutely hated but was powerless to stop.

Then, as the biggest bloke there it fell to him to carry the heavy machine-gun, and on the first night of their bivouac he was further assigned to stand guard with that same machine-gun, and look out for raiding parties until someone relieved him at midnight. John woke up at around 11 p.m., to the sound of gunfire coming from the machine-gun he was meant to be manning! The raiding party — actually another platoon of recruits — had chosen that night to attack, and their forward scouts had found John asleep and nicked his machine-gun. When the sergeant found out what had happened, Private Stretch was forced to find out how many push-ups he could do: not that many. He was given 400 to do as punishment, but was eventually obliged to do them in instalments over several days, because he was simply incapable of it.

Adding to his woes was that Stephen Fleming was every bit as unhappy with the whole thing as John was, and didn't mind reminding his friend why he'd signed up for it in the first place.

'*You* told me this would be like a holiday camp!' he said through gritted teeth one evening as they did push-ups, directly after peeling a couple of hundred potatoes, some of which were rotten. '*You* said we'd be playing touch football every afternoon, and doing a lot of fun fitness work! Well here's a newsflash mate: it ain't quite a holiday camp . . . '

With every wretched push-up, John resolved that he was never going to go on another one of these camps, that he would resign as soon as he was able. And that's exactly what he did. So did Stephen Fleming.

ON 17 February 1989, the entire Eales family, together with some of her closest friends, went to an Indian restaurant for Carmel's twentieth birthday. Because of the ongoing chemotherapy, she never had any appetite at all, but turning twenty was something special to celebrate, given what she had come through. At times it had seemed Carmel was well on the way to winning the battle against the cancer, at others it was obvious that she was falling back, losing weight and feeling weaker. Then she would rally . . . then she would fade again. But on this night Carmel was in fine form, looking almost a picture of health and laughing gaily, much as she ever had. It was easy to imagine that there was no problem whatsoever, and if weren't for her occasional racking cough — which reminded everyone of her real situation — they might have been able to. There were no speeches, as Jack and Rosa were never ones for formality like that, but there were at least a few toasts to 'good health', a 'good year' and 'happy birthday!'

THE 1989 rugby season dawned on a rather impatient John Eales. Already, he had half an eye on the Queensland U/19 team, which he thought he might be a rough chance of making. Given how absurd this would surely seem to some, since he had never been picked for any other representative rugby team, ever, and he had hardly set the world alight the previous season, he really only mentioned that ambition to one fellow. In February, he and Luke Steel were playing a game of golf, and when the subject came up John decided to confide how much he would really love to, *for once*, be picked in a genuine Queensland side. Once, just once.

'Yesss, Luke reflected with him, 'realistically, it is probably the last chance you've got to ever make a Queensland team. After you get out of the under/this and under/that age groups, you really get lost in the big stuff . . . '

'Yeah, you're right,' John said, agreeing quietly, if a little bleakly.

There were two key differences with the Brothers Colts Firsts of 1989, compared with the previous year. Firstly, more of John's friends from school had arrived, including Pat McGrath, who had repeated his final year, Luke Steel, Shaun Gelling, Brendan Williamson and Simon Best. It wasn't quite 'the gang's all here' but it was close. They were a tight group of friends, this lot, and when some of them occasionally slept over at the Eales' house after a big night out, John used to amuse them at the breakfast table the following morning in curious fashion. That is, he would demonstrate the code he had developed with Nonna in the kitchen. One tap on the table meant more fried eggs and bacon, please, two taps for coffee, three taps for toast. Nonna would play along with a big smile, and all would laugh heartily when she emerged with what John had ordered.

The second difference was that whereas the previous year Ron Price had been more of a background figure, this season he took the reins as sole coach. This was as Price himself preferred it, and as a five-time A-Grade Premiership winning coach with Brothers in the early eighties, he certainly knew what he was doing. One interesting move was to make John captain, after a succession of other captains in the trial games had only worked out so-so.

'I just had a hunch,' he would later tell people who asked, 'that the other players respected him so much, and he was playing so well, that he would make a good captain.'

The Price was right — and the fact that John found he enjoyed being skipper further cemented the bond between him and the coach. The other players were similarly well disposed to the older man.

For whatever his barking on the field might have been, it was softened by the beer he had with them after training, and all of his team knew that they were welcome at all times to call on him at home and help themselves to a beer. The players availed themselves of this hospitality, not least John, and many were the nights in that early part of the season when Price and his wife Judy would wake at 2 a.m. on a Sunday to the sound of singing, and blearily look out the window to see John, Patrick, Luke, Rupert and a few of the others lying on his lilos in the pool and drinking their beer.

Judy was sometimes less than impressed, and expressed her views forcefully out the window at them. This could then prompt the players to sing the opening lines of the famous Beatles song: 'Hey, Jude'.

Price, though, was more understanding, and in an effort to quieten them would promise to come down and have a beer with them. Often, Rupert would amuse the others by reciting poetry that he had made up. He'd been doing it since he was fourteen, putting together a kind of clever verse that had a beat of its own, and the reaction he got was amazing. At a moment's notice he could jot down a few lines about any situation or person, and the others would be enthralled. When, for example, the team had gone down to the trots one night and won an absolute motza on a trotter called Fiery Tooth, Rupert used that as the base for a poem which included the following lines:

> But who's the one that's letting loose with 'Go the fiery tooth!'
> In voice that we respected for its wisdom and its truth?

Who's the one that's dishing out this valuable advice?
It's the baldy headed bastard that we like to call 'the Price'.

We weren't a team of champions, but we were a team of mates,
And when you're under pressure that's a formula that rates,
For champions will rise today but next week they will tumble.
But mateship has a certain strength that rarely ever crumbles
And at the helm was Pricey, standing strong and giving call.
He might have been the coach but he was best mates with us all.

Price was, in short, a great rugby man, imbued with the spirit of the game — the belief that the point of the exercise was not merely exercise itself, but camaraderie, bonhomie and fun. Beyond all that, though, he was a very capable coach in terms of getting a team to win, and John could sense from the beginning of the season that the team would go better this year.

CARMEL was crook again. And this time there seemed to be no bouncing back. Late one night in March, lying in his room downstairs, John was conscious that his sister in the bedroom next door just kept coughing without any break. Concerned, he knocked softly and went in. In between her coughs, they talked.

At one point she said, and he would never forget it — as it was the only time in her whole illness she had shown fear to him — 'I don't want to die, John.'

John and she had never been particularly tactile, but at this moment he hugged her, held her and assured her there was no chance of that happening. In his deepest self, however, he wondered. In the last few weeks, John had on a couple of occasions taken Carmel for day trips into the country just to get away from it all. Such trips soon became out of the question, as her illness worsened.

Never had the Eales' family faith in their Lord been so tested, never had they called on Him so much. All prayed nightly for Carmel's recovery, and outside of her constant duties in the house, Nonna did little else but call on St Anthony to intervene on her beloved grand-daughter's behalf. As to Carmel, she had stopped going to Mass and was pursuing Zen Buddhism with a friend from university. As Carmel explained it to Bernadette, she was developing her own version of spirituality, away from the lectures, rituals and formulas. This was partly for the nourishment of her soul, but also because she felt that it might help restore her health.

Still, nothing seemed to turn her around, and in early April Carmel returned to hospital. It was not dramatic, like she was on her actual last legs or anything, just a decision that hospital was the best place for her to receive the constant treatment she needed. John, with all of his siblings, went to visit her most days — Jack and Rosa were there all day, every day — always hoping that she would be just a little better than she was the day before. Instead, it was usually the other way around.

On his way to visit Carmel one night after football training on 17 April 1989, John was passing the ward where a friend was recovering from an operation on the tendons in his hand. The two were chatting when a nurse from the Oncology Unit came in, saw John, and stiffened slightly . . .

'Have you been to see Carmel tonight?' she asked, a little awkwardly.

'Not yet,' replied John, a little mystified at her manner. 'I'll be going up shortly.'

The nurse quickly made her excuses and left, but a few minutes later a phone call told John it would be a good idea if he came to see Carmel right away. John raced upstairs to be told that his sister was likely to die at any time, and all of the family had been called. He went into her room, to see Carmel with her eyes closed, far paler and more haggard than the previous day, and her breathing was a lot, lot shallower. In knots and in singles, including Nonna, the family arrived to gather around her bedside, hold each other, weep and pray. They were joined by a priest who administered the last rites. Usually priests on such occasions are an island of calm amidst the distress all around, but this one was not. Father Leo Bourke was a wonderful man who had formed a close bond with Carmel over her weeks in hospital — despite her flirtation with Zen Buddhism — and was visibly moved as he performed the ritual, the tears rolling down his cheeks. He would later tell Bernadette that this was 'the worst night of my entire life'.

The last rites completed, they waited. While they watched, each lost in their thoughts and their prayers, even as they held each other, Carmel's breathing got progressively shallower. Each one of them, Nonna, Jack, Rosa, Bernadette, John, Damian, Antoinette and Rosaleen, placed a hand upon her, as Jack led the family in prayers, telling his daughter to 'go towards the light, Carmel, go towards the light . . . '

A single tear came out of her left eye and rolled down her cheek. For John, that was the moment that she died, and he would ever afterward think she was crying because she was saying goodbye to the family.

The funeral was three days later, and John was back at training two days after that. As he arrived in the dressing room, each of his team-mates and Ron Price — many of whom had gone to the funeral on his account — wordlessly came up and shook his hand.

And then they got on with it. Scrums, lineouts, sprints.

THINGS would change for John in rugby, dramatically, from this point on — and if he could pinpoint a time when he became *totally* committed to doing as well as he possibly could in the game, it was when Carmel died. For though the game itself was trivial beside the tragedy of her death, it was perhaps for that very reason that the one could have so great an effect on the other. Out of the enormity of what had happened, John wanted to take something good and make it live. Who knows what Carmel might have achieved had she lived? They would never know, but somehow it seemed right that those left behind achieved whatever they could on her behalf. Something . . . anything . . . something from her . . . his thinking was not absolutely clear and logical on the subject. He just knew there was a hardening of his resolve. At a bare minimum, Carmel's death made him realise that nothing in life could be taken for granted and if your place in the world could be snuffed out in a moment it was as well to make the most of whatever opportunities come your way. For John, rugby was one. He had always wanted to do well at it. Now was the time. And, however odd it might sound, he felt he was going to play with her strength as well. That much at least was clear.

With which, he began to train harder, and play harder, than ever before, *throwing* himself into rucks and mauls almost as if angry — and there was probably something of that, too. Added to all of this, in terms of John beginning to achieve his potential, was that now that he was just entering his twentieth year, nature had given him that last little surge of strength that he had previously lacked. From the middle of 1989 — the same time as the Lions were playing the Wallabies in a three-Test series, which he followed more closely than ever before — he seemed able to jump higher, run faster, and make more of an impact on a game than ever before.

Jack, who went to see every game John played in Brisbane, noticed it too. In the devastation he and Rosa had suffered at Carmel's death, John's growing rugby prowess was in no way any comfort. But it was a distraction, and Jack looked forward more than ever to seeing him play. John's team reeled off four successive wins before two events intervened to interrupt John's Colts career. The first was blessed in that he actually did get selected for the Queensland U/19 team. John was so delighted to pull on a maroon jersey for the first time he slept in it that night and felt like he never wanted to take it off. Beside his old mate Garrick Morgan, who had also been selected, he played a solid game against the Yorkshire Colts, but before he could back up to play the climactic game of the season — Queensland vs NSW — fate intervened.

John broke his arm. In a typically willing game between Brothers and Souths, John had charged through from the kick-off only to find his arm coming into contact with reputedly the hardest head in Brisbane — Garrick Morgan's! Morgan was building a reputation as one of the most promising forwards in the competition, and with John gone from the field he proceeded to dominate the lineout, meaning that John — with his throbbing arm in a sling — had to suffer the indignity of watching the mighty Souths side putting Brothers to the sword.

Rosa and Nonna were horrified at John suffering such an injury, but after X-rays it was clear that it would not take long to repair. After just a six-week lay-off, John made his comeback to the Brothers Colts side on 5 August 1989 — the date remembered so precisely because it was the day of the one Bledisloe Cup match of that year, in Auckland. The Brothers boys decided to watch it at Ron Price's house and then, because of the time difference with New Zealand, they could hustle to the game against University. John had always watched rugby Tests with great interest, but on this occasion he was mesmerised.

Watching him. Tim Horan. Making his debut for Australia that day, plucked out of a clear blue sky before he had even played for Queensland. The same Tim Horan he had played cricket with and against so many times. More to the point, the same Tim Horan who was playing Colts football for Souths just the previous year. John sat there, stunned, recalling that it was only twelve months ago that he had been playing against him. And now there he was at Eden Park playing a Test for the Wallabies against the All Blacks! Australia went down on the day, 24-12, but somehow the loss didn't resonate with John on this occasion. What gripped him was that someone he knew, someone he had played with, had actually made the Wallabies!

For the first time, the feeling grew that if he did kick on and keep playing well, *and* there were a few injuries, *and* he played for long enough, *and* there was no-one else, he just might get a run for Queensland or Brisbane maybe, and maybe after that Australia. Who knows?

As soon as the following day, John received some amazing encouragement for this line of thinking. The scene was set when he went out to Ballymore to see the Queensland vs Waikato game. The team were just returning from their warm-up on an outside oval when John ran into, almost literally, the Queensland coach John Connolly. Eales knew who he was, of course, but it never would have occurred to him in a month of Sundays, a millennium of Masses, that Connolly would also know who he was. And yet Connolly shook his hand and said, 'I've been watching a few Colts games and you've gone really well. I thought you'd like to know you'll be in the state squad next year . . . '

'Really?' John said, a little awkwardly.

'Yes, really,' Connolly replied, a little amused. 'We'll be announcing the squad in a few weeks' time.' Then he moved off.

John's flabber had never been more gasted. In response to the extraordinary news — he hadn't even played a grade game for Brothers, and was going to be in the state squad — John sealed his lips tighter than a tomb. If he told anyone it would be bragging, and if he told everyone and it didn't happen he would look like a complete fool.

So he kept mum, even from his own mum and dad, and played on. He knuckled down hard to playing as well as he could and keeping alive the hopes of Brothers Colts Firsts. The team had finished the regular season in fifth position, meaning the only way they could make the grand final was to play a series of sudden-death games against the teams that had finished higher places. Thus, in four closely fought encounters in the next four weeks, Eales continued to lead from the front, in the process playing what team-mate Pat McGrath would later describe as 'blinder, after blinder, after blinder'.

So it was that somewhere in the late winter of 1989, Harry Shaw, another club stalwart of the Merv Hazell ilk, was playing a game of golf at the Victoria Park Golf Club with former Wallaby captain and current

Brothers President, Paul McLean, as he often did. One might have expected ol' Harry would spend more time playing golf with his son Tony — who was also a distinguished former Wallaby captain — but as McLean would note to other Brothers blokes of their vintage, 'Tony has a philosophical objection to any sport where there is a semblance of non-violence'.

Either way, he was an astute judge of rugby was old Harry, and an inveterate watcher of the game at all levels. Somewhere on the fifth fairway he mentioned to Paul that this young lad John Eales was starting to tear them up in Colts and he really thought the club president should go and have a look at him. He said he'd been to every one of the games of the Colts Final series, where they had survived sudden death victories over Wests, Easts and University, and every time it was Eales who had taken the lead and kept them afloat whenever the team seemed likely to sink beneath the waves.

'I think,' finished Harry, 'he might be *very* good.'

McLean took pause. He had heard of Eales' efforts in recent weeks, but this was the first time he'd heard a detailed report, and given that Shaw had never spoken with such enthusiasm about a player before, he thought he'd better keep a particular eye on young Eales when he attended the Colts Final the following Sunday at Ballymore, where Brothers were taking on the highly fancied Souths.

Souths had beaten Brothers four times out of four over the course of the season and had something like six Queensland U/19 players, while Brothers only had one in Eales. So it was unlikely they would be able to win, but it would still be worth it to have a look at the young player they were talking about.

THE following Saturday Paul McLean paid particular attention to the match-up between Eales and his direct opponent in the lineout that day, Garrick Morgan — who the previous week had won the coveted Colt of the Year award. Which was great for Garrick, but as far as McLean could see Eales was all over Morgan like a cheap suit, constantly snaffling the ball even on Souths' throw-in.

Another who was there on the day was the captain of the Grand Slam winning Wallaby side of 1984, Souths player, Andrew Slack. He parked in the Ballymore car park and, as he approached the oval all he could hear, he later told journalist Mike Colman, 'were these Brothers voices screaming out, "Givvitta Ealzie, givvitta Ealzie". So they gaveitta Ealzie, and needless to say he'd boot it 50 metres downfield or run right through our pack. I looked at this long stringbean second-rower who could do just about everything and it was obvious this was not your stock standard second-rower.'

At least in part because of Eales' prodigious feats on the day, with twenty minutes to go Brothers were leading a Souths team that out-gunned them in strength, pace and talent by the princely margin of 3-0. It was a terrific effort against a side that was unbeaten the whole year. And then it happened.

The five-eighth for Souths, a bloke they called Dancing Dave Marriot, shimmied left, stepped right, broke through a tackle and went clean through the Brothers defence down the blind-side of the scrum. Ovaaah, for a try. Suddenly Brothers Colts Firsts were losing 4-3 to a team that everyone thought was going to win anyway, and it was almost like all the wind went out of them at once. Eales gathered the little graveyard group under the goalposts as the surprisingly cold wind whipped around and set about turning things around.

'It was amazing,' Rupert McCall later recounted, 'and I'll never forget it. It wasn't so much what John said as the way he said it. The feeling in the team was that it was all over, once Dancing Dave had scored — like we half-thought Souths were always going to win, and now they had proved it by going to the lead. But what John did was just say very calmly and clearly that we are going to win this game, and all we've got to do is play the game down their end of the field and wait for an opportunity and . . . '

And pause, while the Souths fullback makes the conversion attempt. Mercifully, it hit the upright and bounced back. You bah-yooty! With new resolution the Brothers boys kicked off, and focused simply on the task at hand, every player concentrating on beating his opposite number. And just as John said, the break really did come. Or at least sort of one . . .

With just six minutes left, referee Bernie Fienberg awarded Brothers a penalty after spying Souths' 'hands in the ruck' from perhaps 30 metres out on an angle. Eales called for the ball and signalled to the referee that they would kick for goal. More specifically, *he* would kick for goal. John was even then lost in a very strong sense of *déjà vu*, for he actually had been there before. A decade earlier, for the Ashgrove U/10s, he had faced just such a kick for victory and blown it.

Somewhere lost in his 'zone', Eales took three deep breaths to steady himself, ran four steps in, and brought his swinging right boot into contact with the pumped up bit of leather. As Pat McGrath would tell the story for at least the next decade, 'It went through the bloody posts, three-quarters of the way up Ballymore, and never looked liked missing!'

Brothers now led 6-4 and had only to keep Souths scoreless in the next five minutes to make their way into the holy land. With Eales leading the way, bringing off two particularly massive tackles in that time, and the Brothers boys hurling themselves into it like never before, they managed to hold on . . . HOLD ON! . . . hold on . . . until at last referee Fienberg blew his blessed whistle.

For John, it was the best feeling he had known on a rugby field to that point, so good it almost made up for having missed the kick from straight in front to lose the game for the U/10A Emus. Almost, but not quite.

THAT night, back at the Brothers clubhouse, the drinking and singing went long and strong. When the Colts' own meagre funds had run out, two of the club's former Wallabies, Chris Handy and Pat Burke, the same man who'd passed the hat around the club so John could go on the cricket tour, put $100 on the bar between them and the young men had availed themselves in full. And when, at 2 a.m., the bar had to close because of licensing laws, still that did not present a problem. With Handy and Burke in tow, the lads simply grabbed several cartons of beer and removed themselves 50 metres to the dressing sheds.

Like many rugby clubs, Brothers had at least its fair share of testosterone-fuelled activities, and then some. A favourite practice at such celebratory times as this was to sink 'torpedoes'. That is, take a can of beer, hold it upside down on your mouth, and then use a can opener to make a hole at the top. This means that when you pull open the lid, the air pressure forces the beer down your throat in something like three seconds flat. John had always been hopeless at it — in his whole rugby career he would only ever meet one player more hopeless, and that was Tim Horan — but he at least did the obligatory one, and everyone cheered.

It was at this point that Chris Handy stepped up to the plate. Scooping up one of the full beer cans on the table, he took a can and the can opener, and before their very eyes, *stood on his head*. Without then so much as a by-your-leave, he accomplished an Upside Down Torpedo, righted himself, burped to wake the dead, and bowed. With full throat the Colts roared their approval, and on into the rollicking night they went . . .

THE following Sunday, Ron Price held a barbecue at his home. It was the same day that, in Sydney, Canberra played Balmain in the era's most famous rugby league grand final, scoring a stunning victory in extra time with a celebrated try by Raiders winger Chicka Ferguson. (They might have been lads of rugby union, but one simply didn't miss rugby league grand finals — they were too huge, one of the most important days on the sporting calendar.)

With the league game over, the barbecue again moved into full swing, and the speeches began. After both John and Ron had thanked each other and the players for their efforts, it was the turn of Merv Hazell, the keeper of the club torch, to speak.

'Just a word, lads, if I could,' he said, while standing with one hand on a table for support. 'There is one presentation I'd like to make . . . and that is to your wonderful captain, John.'

All eyes turned to the blushing skipper, as Merv continued in his quavering voice.

'John,' he said, 'I have seen a lot of players come through Brothers over the years, but I can honestly say I don't think I've seen one with more talent than you. I honestly believe you will become one of this country's greatest players, and in honour of that I would like you to accept my Brothers tie-pin, which I have worn to every Brothers grand final since 1966 . . . '

With which, Merv took it off and presented it to John. This time, none of the players laughed, but simply applauded warmly. No joke, they'd never heard of Merv doing that for any other Colt, ever, and everyone knew how much he treasured that tie-pin. The keeper of the Brothers torch had practically knighted one of them before their very eyes.

John was humbled and said so. A little later, though, it looked to Pat McGrath like John was about to meet Humble's ugly cousin, Humiliated, when the two of them came to the end of their cab ride back from the coach's house. It was John's turn to pay and he clearly didn't have the fare. Not to worry, though!

'Tell you what, mate,' John said. 'I'll give you the six bucks I've got, plus these four avocados, and we'll call it quits, okay?'

The taxi driver looked carefully at John, poked and prodded the avocados a little to test their freshness, much as John used to test for rotten potatoes, and grinned . . .

'Okay, mate, you've got a deal.'

Only John, Pat thought with a ruefully amused shake of his head, would ever have had the idea to trade the avocados one of the other players had brought as an end-of-season gift for a taxi fare. All up, the grand final win and the news that he was in the Queensland squad confirmed more than ever for John that rugby was the game he wanted to pursue with everything he had in him, at the expense of cricket if necessary.

Which was fine for John. But cricket, it seems, would not go quietly. One night driving home from work about two months later, Uncle Alf heard Jack Potter, the esteemed head of the newly established Cricket Academy in Adelaide, being interviewed. And when he was asked which prospects around the country most excited him as future members of the Academy, one of three names mentioned was John Eales from Brisbane.

Alf got home and excitedly called up his sister Rosa, who told Jack who equally excitedly told John that night. John was pleased, after a fashion, but . . .

But by this time he had played two games for Queensland University at the beginning of the new season — one of which had been in the company of a rising young fast bowler by the name of Michael Kasprowicz — and it had already become obvious that there was simply no way he could fulfil his cricket training and playing commitments and his rugby commitments. Besides which, he didn't enjoy cricket as much as rugby. Fullstop. He loved the batting and the bowling and even liked it when the other team was in and he could sit around chatting with his team-mates, but then the rest of the day was just a bit of a drag, out there fielding. Not enough to do. Too little *action*. Rugby, he knew, would never pose that problem.

He had made his decision to leave cricket, was happy with it, and had already informed the Queensland University Cricket Club that he would not be turning out with them after all that season.

His captain at Queensland University, the former Sheffield Shield player Andrew Courtice, was most shocked when he heard.

'Everyone thought his future was in cricket,' he later recounted, 'and a big future we thought it was, too!'

Which was kind, but nothing changed the personal stockmarket of John Eales' life: cricket futures were down, university futures were steady, and rugby futures were starting to soar . . .

Queenslander!

There is a tide in the affairs of men
Which, taken at the flood, leads on to fortune . . .
And we must take the current where it serves,
Or lose our ventures.

WILLIAM SHAKESPEARE, Julius Caesar,
Act IV, Scene 3

～

J OHN EALES' introduction to the Queensland squad in mid-October
of 1989 was a little underwhelming only in the sense that all of the
Queensland Wallabies were away on the two Test tour of France — meaning
that he wouldn't be palling around with the likes of Michael Lynagh and
Anthony Herbert. But it didn't really matter. The main thing was that he
was being given an opportunity to show what he could do in rugby, and
he intended to pursue it with everything he had in him. Every Tuesday
and Thursday for the next four months, those in the Queensland squad
would gather in the confines of Ballymore and train. At this early stage,
before they even saw a ball or John Connolly himself, most of the focus
was on increasing fitness and strength through regular heavy training.

To be able to do that effectively, it was first necessary to establish
what levels of strength the squad members possessed, by doing such
things as progressively heavier bench-presses. Supervising the procedure

was Ian King, a strength conditioner who took his work very seriously indeed. The way he talked about strength as it pertained to rugby players — and indeed most everybody — was that if it wasn't a crime against nature not to be as strong as you could be, it was almost *certainly* a crime against reason.

Ten minutes later he had his answer and shook his head.

'All you can manage is a 62 kilogram bench-press, with one repetition . . . ' he said doubtfully. 'I don't think John Connolly is going to be too happy with that.'

Somehow, King said it in a manner which made John think Coach Connolly would fall to his knees and weep at the futility of trying to make an elite rugby player out of a bloke who was built like a thermometer and lifted weights like a pansy with the flu — but there was nowt that John could do on the instant other than feel miserable. Clearly, upper-body strength was highly prized by the rugby powers, and the simple fact was that Eales didn't have any . . .

'And so what you'll have to do,' King was saying, 'is follow the program I'm about to give you. You'll have to come in here and lift four times a week, and we'll see if we can fill you out a bit more. Then we'll give you another test in six weeks to see if there's been some improvement . . . ' (Again, the tone seemed to say, '*on the very off chance* that there's been some improvement . . . ')

And so it began. Under the supervision of King, John Eales began to lift weights at the Toowong Village gym — often going to or coming from uni lectures — each time straining to expand his limits just that little bit. Oddly enough, he found he enjoyed heaving heavy metal, even if it was humiliating to be starting off with the low figure of ten repetitions at 35 kilograms. Still, he kept at it, put his head down, and did all the running training as well, a combination of distance and sprints. By the time of his next bench-press test he had the satisfaction of being able to do three repetitions at 89 kilograms. (While this meant that John was, as the expression of the time ran, still not strong enough to knock a sick girl off a chair, it at least showed progress.)

To come down from such strenuous sessions and relax, John would often go home, retire to his room for a while and crank up his pride and joy, the one luxury item he possessed, a CD player. Damian, often trying to study for his Speech Pathology degree at Queensland Uni, would have to suffer listening to John playing too loudly an eclectic combination of Joe Cocker, Rolling Stones, Cat Stevens, REM and Indigo Girls.

CHRISTMAS in the Eales household that year was the bleakest John had known, as all were acutely aware of the aching absence of Carmel, but somehow with many prayers, tears and fond reminiscences of their favourite Carmel stories, they struggled through. In some measure, training hard for rugby remained therapeutic for John. When you were lying on your back trying to push 95 kilograms towards the ceiling — getting stronger now — there was no room for any emotion in the soul other than *nnnnnNNNNNNGGGGhhhh,* and in a way he enjoyed the pure emptiness of it. Plus he liked the simple fact of feeling stronger. He liked looking at a biggish bloke on a bus on the way to Queensland Uni and realising that if somehow that fellow could sit on an iron bar, the amazing thing was he, John Anthony Eales, would be able to lift him off his chest! By early January, all of the Wallabies had rejoined the squad and John was able to get to know the more senior members of the team, including of course the coach, John Connolly.

The Queensland coach was known to one and all as Knuckles — because that was the part of his body that he was reputed to have used most when he was a player, and perhaps even afterwards when he worked as a bouncer. And he had a surprisingly similar pedigree to John's. That is, he was not only raised a devout Catholic, but had also attended Marist Brothers Ashgrove and gone on to the Brothers Rugby Club, where he had made the most classic of all journeys for a rugby player, from the position of centre, to breakaway to front-row. He had a long background in the game, and no small amount of technical knowledge. In John's first lineout training session, for example, Connolly took him aside and told him that he would go better in the lineout if he began with his feet together, as that would give him half-a-second start when the time came to manoeuvre his body to the optimum position to win the ball. John tried it, and immediately found it a better way to make the jump. Connolly, in turn, was impressed with John, noting that you only had to tell him something once and he'd usually get it. Certainly he'd want to understand *why* something was a good idea, but once he believed in it he'd go with it.

For all that, Ian King had been right when he said that Connolly was likely to be underwhelmed when it came to John's seeming physical fragility. One day Connolly was watching John and the Queensland captain that year, Wallaby second-rower Bill Campbell, running across the field together, and shook his head in wonder. Campbell was always known as a beanpole, but when he ran beside Eales he fair dinkum looked like Arnold Schwarzenegger.

All up, John greatly enjoyed the squad training, both for the knowledge he felt he was gaining, and the camaraderie of the other players. Two players in the squad with whom he immediately felt comfortable were Tim Horan and Jason Little, both as new to the Queensland caper as he was, even though at this stage they were the Wallabies' latest stars. In a strange beginning to their representative rugby careers, each had made his debut for Australia before he had sighted Queensland squad training, with Horan's first Test match against the All Blacks in August being closely followed by Little's sterling debut against the French in Strasbourg two months later.

John was one of the quietest members of the squad in those early days, though as he warmed up Horan and Little were probably the two players he spent most time with. At a purely footballing level, the two young backs were amazed at what they saw from John when the squad played touch before training proper began. Often these games were backs vs forwards and the backs expected the forwards to be their usual lumbering selves, without particular ball skills, but from the beginning John was different. Not only did he know the difference between a flick pass and a ham sandwich, but he could actually execute the pass! There was some admiring banter among the squad that the new fellow was in the sad position of being a back horribly trapped inside a forward's body.

John also gravitated towards the Brothers and Wallaby second-rower Rod McCall, with the older man effectively taking John under his wing. However, a squad member John kept at arm's length was Garrick Morgan. There was no open animosity between them and away from a rugby field they got on well, but both were keenly aware that in all likelihood only one of them would be taken on the upcoming Queensland tour to Western Samoa, and it was as well to not get too close to someone you were so openly competing against. As it happened, both John and Garrick had already been selected for an Australian U/21 camp in Canberra — the coach was none other than Ron Price — but by this time the contours of John's ambitions had changed. Having the opportunity to wear an

Australian U/21 jersey was delightful, but now that he was right on the edge of senior representative football, that was the forum he wanted to make it in, and Garrick clearly felt the same.

John enjoyed training with the squad immensely, and loved learning the ways of Queensland rugby as it was played at its highest level.

For if it can be accepted that the rugby game grows in an entirely different fashion depending on the kind of soil in which its seed is sown — with obvious differences in styles of play between, say, the free-form French and the ever-orthodox English — then let it be said that the plant in Queensland was a very particular one indeed. Maroon to its very core, part venom, part flower, part *win*-whatever-way-you-can, it was covered in proud prickles and its most notable characteristic was that it grew a good foot taller whenever placed anywhere near the hated New South Wales weed that grew south of the Tweed.

Though over the decades the Reds had rarely boasted as much talent pound for pound as the Waratahs from the south, they had traditionally always played above themselves whenever the two teams had clashed. At the time John made the squad, the Reds were at a particularly high point in their cycle, having won 16 of their previous 22 games and the representative calendar that year offered them the chance to have even more scalps hanging from their belts. But the one they most wanted that year — as the coach made clear from the beginning — was NSW.

When John Connolly had taken the coaching reins of Queensland from Bob Templeton a year before, one of key rugby power-brokers in the state, Norbert Byrne, had said to him, 'John, you can lose every other game of the season, but if you beat NSW it will be a great year.' And Connolly had never forgotten it. Beating NSW not only gave you bragging rights, not only gave you the supreme satisfaction of beating NSW in *anything*, it gave your team a more secure mortgage on getting the coveted Wallaby jerseys when the national team was formed.

The men of Queensland trained on, under the late afternoon sun, and on into the evening, throwing it up a couple of gears more as the season got closer. John continued to edge up his bench-press weight and the first chance he had to take his newly strong body out for a run was in the trial matches at the end of February — with the entire squad broken into two teams. Garrick Morgan was in John's team and the *Courier-Mail*, at least, thought that John put in a better performance, saying 'Eales could have done no more than he did. His coverage of the field demonstrated an amazing knowledge of rugby short-cuts for a player of only 19.'

John left shortly afterwards for the U/21 camp at the Australian Institute of Sport in Canberra, confident that he had shown enough to secure a prized berth in the Queensland side that would shortly be touring Western Samoa. Sure, Rod McCall and Bill Campbell had the second-row positions locked in, but there was still a spot in the squad for a player who could play in either the second-row or back-row, and John had every confidence — as always — that that would go to him and not Garrick, based on how they had gone in the trials.

And now, praise the Lord and pass the passport, the head of the AIS rugby unit, David Clarke, was going to tell them just that. He had called both John and Garrick into his office on the promise that he had news on that subject. After a little maddening preliminary chit-chat — the way rugby officials always bloody well do in such situations — Clarke got to the point.

'Guys,' he said, looking at them both evenly, 'I've been asked to advise you what is happening with the Queensland team. You have probably both worked out that there isn't room in the squad to take both of you. I've been asked to tell you that it was very close, and to convey how impressed the selectors were with both of you. But . . . '

Here he paused in what had been a fairly ponderous delivery, and finished the last of it in a rush.

'John, they thought you probably needed a bit more time and Garrick is the one who is going. John, they at least want you to play with the Queensland B team next week, against the Russians at Ballymore.'

Got him again. How many times, dear Lord, how many times? How many times was he going to be done down from his rightful spot in a representative rugby side — this time with the chance to wear the maroon jersey of the full Queensland team in battle? Not that he held it against Garrick, much, and to give him his due Garrick was very good-natured about it and never once crowed, but still it hurt.

At least the consolation prize wasn't a bad one. While yet to play a senior game of rugby, John would still be wearing a senior Maroon jersey, even if it was the B variety. His appointment attracted some press attention, with the *Courier-Mail* noting that 'few forwards have generated such excitement so early in their careers as Eales, and if he is able to handle the

Soviet's bear-like No. 8 Alexander Tikhonov, it is unlikely he will encounter many more formidable rivals in years to come . . . '

If that really were true, Eales thought after the game, then he really *might* be able to handle representative rugby! In fact, most of the Russians had been sunburnt to a crisp in their previous port of call in Cairns, and had been treated by their inexperienced doctor with sticking plaster put over the worst affected parts (!), meaning they were in little shape to play serious rugby. What John had seen of Tikhonov resembled a boiled lobster, and the Queensland B side enjoyed a handsome 40-17 victory. The reviews for John's performance were generally good and he held his position in the side for the game against NSW B. That game went well, too, with a big win for the men in the maroon jerseys, and on a whim John decided to stay for a few days with a friend living in Sydney for a few days, so as to get a good look at Australia's biggest city.

On a Wednesday evening in late April then he called home from a phone booth in Kings Cross, just to touch base, when his mother told him the extraordinary news. John Connolly had called. *Eales, J.*, had been picked on the bench for the game against Wellington and was due at training that night. John looked at his watch. Training started in twenty minutes. He was an unlikely starter. His first thought was that he had very likely blown his big chance.

Actually Connolly was more than understanding, and though John didn't actually get off the Queensland bench for the game against Wellington, there was now no doubt he was getting closer to the mark. For the tour to Western Samoa had gone badly for Garrick from the moment, during his first game, that the young man had unburdened himself of the opinion that Bill Campbell was a 'wanker' for not having called him more in the lineout. Both captain and coach had taken a very dim view of this opinion, and the word was that Garrick should be hung out to dry for a good spell until he matured more.

In the meantime, John had also made his debut for Brothers A Grade under the coaching of Mark Nightingale, a long-time Brethren stalwart who took an extremely no-nonsense approach to the task. In some ways it was a strange thing for John to be playing his first game for Brothers in the senior side after he had already played for Queensland B side. Brothers had good players who had never had such an opportunity in their careers, but he was warmly welcomed. It helped that the man he would usually be slotting into the second row beside was Rod McCall, who took on the same mentor role there that he had with the Queensland squad. Still, for young Eales, McCall was not to prove the most influential person in the club that year, and therein lay a tale . . .

Just as all true rugby clubs need a keeper of the torch, so too do all clubs worthy of the name need at least one eccentric — a bloke who no-one really understands, but everyone likes anyway, a bloke who will do things and say things that the whole club can have a good-natured laugh about. In 1990 Brothers had, by most measures, the Prince of all Eccentrics in their corner. His name was Ben Perkins and he was the A Grade side's fitness conditioner. As a player he had been the *Courier-Mail*'s Club Rugby Player of the Year in 1978, had once sat on the bench for Queensland, and his knowledge of the game was wide. When John met him, Ben was 31 years old, with wispy blond hair, a slight paunch, piercing blue eyes, and a slightly other-worldly manner.

As a matter of fact, he was from another world, he told John and anyone else who would listen. As a follower of the only one and true religion, called Eckankar, he was able to project his soul through astral travel. Yesterday he had been to Mars, tomorrow he thought he might go for another burn around Jupiter. They could do it too, he said, if they wanted to read the books he had, or listen to his tapes.

What was his actual job? The card he gave John contained a few clues. 'Ben Perkins,' it read. '*Freelance Development Consultant*.' Beneath was listed his accomplishments:

Horse racing tipster. Sports journalist. Short Story Writer.
Goal Kicking Coach. Rugby Coach. Cricket Coach. Movie & Theatre Critic.
Be Grateful Instructor. True Religion Raconteur.
Poetry and Satire Recitals. Golf Caddie and Mentor. Eventual Ballet Film
Maker. Speed Reading Teacher. Horse Racing and Football Confidante.
Gambling Commission Agent. Part time Palm Reader, Eventual TV Presenter.

NO FIXED RATES. RING WHEN YOU'RE READY,
RING WHEN YOU'RE NOT READY.

STILL, most of that clearly wasn't how he paid the rent. As a matter of fact it wasn't clear to anyone how Ben did that, although it was known that his family in South Australia were monied. What was known was that he was a mad-keen punter. The way he told the always amused Brothers boys, the force of Eckankar could also help him pick the right horses. That is, of course, so long as they went about it the right way by making sure that when they placed their bet the toilet seats in the house were all down and every bathroom door in the house was closed. Sure, a lot of people thought this sort of stuff was mere superstition, but as Ben told them, in his view it was 'superstitious not to be superstitious' . . . And it could help them win rugby games.

It all depended on 'HUUUUUU'.

This was the chant that released the energy within. For all of life, Ben explained, was a constant battle between *kal*, the negative force, and *eck*, the positive, good force. Chanting 'HUUUUUU' helped release the *eck*. No, really.

Hey, some of the Brothers were prepared to try anything', and sometimes in games Ben Perkins could be seen on the hill getting some of the crowd to, as one, take up the chant.

'HUUUU,' they would intone at Ben's signal. 'HUUUUUU.'

Somewhere, surely, Merv Hazell was wondering what on earth things were coming to, but as a good rugby man would probably have also understood the club's need for an eccentric.

'HUUUUU.'

For many of the other players, Perkins was a lovable fruit loop, a bloke who clearly had a couple of kangaroos loose in the top paddock, but John never took him like that. He liked him a lot and the two simply hit it off. A long and significant friendship in John's life had just begun.

Often, after training, they would often go and get a bite to eat together and have a drink. Without exception, Ben always ordered an orange juice with three ice cubes please. Not two, or four, or five . . . just three. That was the way he wanted it, and he would not drink it otherwise. And late into the night the two would talk. Perkins, in his turn, was delighted with his friendship with Eales. This was not just because John was an engaging companion and good fellow. It was something way more than that. Rarely had Ben met someone so full of *eck* as John, and it got him to thinking. Before long, he *had* it. John was *clearly* the reincarnation of John the Baptist. He was sure of it. The sense of calm, he had. The way he treated people. Just the way he was. Why, their first names were even the same! John the Baptist, for sure. On the subject of religion, the two had many long discussions, each exploring the outer boundaries of the other's beliefs, but neither seriously tempted to change sides, it was just very interesting to talk about.

Not everyone understood the friendship between Eales and Perkins. Many just didn't understand Perkins, fullstop.

John Connolly, who was a frequent visitor at his old club, was one who used to have a good-natured laugh at Perkins' expense.

'What sort of a #$!&-ing idiot,' he would say to Rod McCall, 'would have a bloke like that on their team? You wouldn't let him within two *miles* of your football team. What does he know about rugby?'

The answer, for John, was 'quite a bit', and the two used to discuss tactics and strategies of the game along with everything else. One thing that Ben was a great advocate of, and that John followed for the rest of his rugby career, was the need to go off on your own on the morning of the match and engage in some light physical activity while you thought about the match. Ben thought it helped minimise kal and maximise eck; John found it helped clear his head and maximise his focus. Whatever.

For John, the rugby went on, as did his studies, his family life, his club life, his jobs — now including regular work in the bottle shop of the Albany Creek Tavern — and his attendance at Mass, albeit on a less regular basis than before. True, it was sometimes difficult to meet his study commitments, and he sometimes had to miss lectures, but with the help of his friends — a young woman called Peta Dee was particularly gracious in handing over her lecture notes — he was able to get by. At least mostly. His lecturer in Economics, an American, Amelia Preece, was very nice but less understanding than others when rugby commitments took him away from her lectures. John managed to get extensions from her for his assignments, but it was always touch and go.

The main thing was, nothing was allowed to interfere with John's focus on rugby. He had played well for Brothers from the first games of the season, and as the most assiduous observer of all, Jack Eales, noted, he seemed to be increasing his abilities exponentially from game to game. Damian too — who by this time was turning out for Brothers Colts — also watched every game of John's that he could and was amazed at what he saw, and *heard*.

'Your brother,' people would tell him everywhere he went, 'is just killing 'em!'

Not that everyone was convinced for all that. On one notable occasion when John was playing fast and loose in a grade game against Souths, a number of the Souths supporters singled him out for special attention because he was dropping back to play almost like a second full-back, fielding bombs himself, prompting the Souths supporters to yell in high hilarity, 'Don't worry, no. 5 will get it!' and 'What are you doing in the back-line, Eales, you're meant to be a FORWARD!' Haw-de-haw-haw-haw. Mostly, though, the accolades for his play were warm and getting warmer, and articles in the press noted that representative honours must be just around the corner. At least whatever lingering concerns selectors might have had about John's toughness to withstand the rigours of rep-resentative rugby must have begun to dissipate. In March, for example, when Brothers won a closely fought match with Souths, the climactic moment of the game had been ten minutes before half time, when a full-on brawl broke out. Eales was pinpointed as one of the catalysts for the fight.

'It was his no-holds-barred fist fight with state second-row rival, Garrick Morgan, which put the flame to the fuse of the explosive brawl,' the *Courier-Mail* reported. 'While Morgan may have taken a narrow decision in the fight, partially because Eales had had his jersey pulled half over his shoulders, the skilful Brothers back-rower won when it counted, outpointing Morgan 13-9 in the line-outs and generally having the greater impact on proceedings.' So cop that, Garrick.

John's education in the seamier side of life also continued apace. One Saturday night after playing and winning a game against Easts, John, Rupert McCall, Patrick McGrath, Simon Whitehart and a couple of others went to a house-warming in Brisbane's outer suburbs where somehow or other things got out of hand. Awash in youth, alcohol, testosterone and a little more alcohol, one of their number was accused of breaking a window, and nearing midnight they found themselves out on the street. All they had to their names were their high spirits, a couple of eskies full of beer, no money to speak of for a cab, and a 10-kilometre walk back to down-town Brisbane.

They set off, pausing every now and again to lighten their load by drinking what was in the eskies, and to joyously dance around those eskies in the middle of the road, singing 'She'll be comin' round the mountain when she comes'.

In such a fashion did they at last make their way into the infamously seedy Valley section of downtown Brisbane, to go into the first bar they saw. They still had no money, but thought it might be nice to drink some of their esky beer in a real bar for a change. And a funny sort of bar it was, too. Very dimly lit. Strange kind of atmosphere. Lots of patrons looking at them kind of *intently*. Lots of blokes, actually. Saaaay, can you see any women here? Any women *at all*? Oh muh goodness. Oh muh very goodness. As soon as the Brothers boys realised they had happened upon a gay bar they hit the road, eskies in frantic tow. About 100 metres down the road, they realised. Where was John? In their haste they had forgotten that John had gone off to the loo and they had inadvertently left him there. They had just turned back in force, on a mission to get their man out, when they saw John running down the road towards them, 'dancing neath the diamond sky, with one hand waving free, silhouetted by the sea . . .' and shouting in a kind of shocked, strangled, high-pitched screech they had never heard from him before.

'He *touched* it!' John was shouting. 'He TOUCHED it!'

After a while the Brothers boys gathered that 'he', a bloke standing next to John at the urinal, had suddenly reached out and touched it, and John was not happy about it, not by a long shot.

IF there was a single event that helped galvanise the growing word buzzing around about young Eales and turn it into a full-blown wave of acclamation travelling up and down the eastern seaboard, it occurred one night in mid-April 1990, at the Brothers home ground of Crosby Park.

Because of severe wet weather, the Brothers game against Teachers-Norths had been postponed — there were too many cane toads hopping around on the field — and it was now taking place on an unseasonally cold and wet Monday night with little more than the three men and a dog of popular mythology watching. Eales was enjoying the encounter as little as everyone else, but one of his team-mates, the loose-head prop Mick Crank, kept trying to rev his fellow forwards up. Now, Mick was a special case. Known as The Garbo, on the simple reckoning that he only turned up once a week, he was nothing if not enthusiastic come the time of the game — any game, even horrible games in stinking mud — and this night he was at his persuasive best.

'*John*,' he kept exhorting the young second-rower, while tapping him in the chest by way of emphasis, 'come on, *you've* got to do something here, got to *try* something, got to make an *impression*.'

The Garbo was not actually specific about what he had in mind, but the second-rower knew exactly what he was getting at. It was pointless to merely turn up and go through the motions, even if on this particular evening that was going to be good enough to secure a win — Brothers were leading by twenty points with as many minutes to go. Sure he was wet and stinking, but it would be good to do something that would make that fact worthwhile beyond merely two competition points and . . .

And *hulloa*! Right then the Teachers-Norths five-eighth Richard Herring drop-kicked a clearing kick from his 22-metre line and it landed right in the hands of one John Eales, who had just been exhorted by a respected team-mate to do something. He did something. Almost in the manner of Mick Dundee famously saying to the New York mugger, 'Call that a knife? *This* is a knife', Eales was figuratively able to say to the opposing five-eighth, 'Call that a drop-kick? . . . *This* is a drop-kick!'

With which, from 45 metres out, on a severe angle and in the middle of a swirling wind, John dropped the ball onto his swinging right boot and sent it soaring — up through the at-mos-phere, up where the air is clear — right through the middle of the far uprights. The stunned silence, for no-one could quite believe it, least of all John himself, was pierced by the sound of the referee's whistle — field goal to *Eales, J.*, and another three points to the total. It was something that was talked about for years afterwards with, by one reckoning, the number of people claiming to have been there on the night about ten times the actual ground attendance. The key in determining whether people actually saw it, Rupert McCall claims — and he was playing in the centres when it happened — is whether they say the ball only began to drop once it was over the dead-ball line. Because that is what it was doing.

In the there and then, the headline in the Brisbane *Sun* the following day — 'EALES BOOTS FREAK FIELD GOAL' — and the accompanying story set the rugby community abuzz.

I T was on the strength of such a buzz that Eales graduated to the Queensland bench. He was soon on his way to New Zealand, to act as back-up to Rod McCall and Bill Campbell when the Maroons took on Canterbury at Lancaster Park, Christchurch, in early May. On the way over there one of the veteran smartie-pants in the team advised John that he should turn his clock forward two hours and back twenty years. The young second-rower thought that a bit harsh, but at the movies that night he was amused to note that the fifteen minutes of intermission were filled with '101 great Cantabrian tries' . . . as called by radio announcers, with no vision!

The day before the game, journalist Wayne Smith — who had made the trip across the Tasman for his paper — thought it might be a good idea to have a few words with the up-and-coming Eales, and found him standing under the goalposts retrieving balls for Michael Lynagh as he practised his goal kicks. John was happy to talk, but Smith couldn't help but notice a couple of things.

The first was the manner in which Eales would simply reach out a massive hand and pluck Lynagh's kicks out of the sky, all without interrupting their conversation. Ditto, when he kicked the ball back to Lynagh. Smith was amazed. Eales continued to give him answers, catch the ball and kick it back to Lynagh 50 metres away, all in the one movement. These were among the longest punts he'd ever *seen*, and yet Eales didn't even seem to notice he was doing them!

As he would tell people afterwards, 'I was thinking, "What have we got here? Who *is* this guy?"'

The following day, it was exciting enough for John to be a reserve for Queensland, but centre Dominic McGuire advised him not to get too carried away. Dominic had been on the bench for the last seven games, he told John, and had never so much as got a minute on the field. The other reserves nodded in agreement. They were professional bench-warmers and the firm message to the young 'un was: you could have a bit of a wait here. But not to worry, John was happy enough, and amazed enough to even be this close to the action, as out on the field the men of the maroon seemed to be in singularly good form, getting the better of the Cantabrians.

Then it happened. With fifteen minutes remaining Bill Campbell was not only prone on the ground, but also gingerly feeling his left arm around the biceps even as he shook his head in the classic tut-tut manner of a doctor who did not like his own grave diagnosis. (He *was* a doctor, as it happened.) John Eales suddenly felt a bolt of electricity shoot up his spine and . . .

And now Knuckles Connolly was looming over him, looking purposeful. 'John, he said, 'Bill's hurt, I want you to go on.'

. . .

'John, Bill's hurt, I want you to go on.'

. . .

'JOHN, BILL'S HURT, I WANT YOU TO GO ON.'

. . .

John Connolly did not say those words three times over, but that's at least how many times they echoed around John's head, getting louder every time before he fully comprehended their meaning. Somehow the words came to him in a disorientating fashion. It seemed incredible that his long-held dream of donning, just once, the Queensland jersey in battle was about to be realised. He trotted out onto the green, green grass of Lancaster Park, aware that this was a moment he would always remember, but all he could truly focus on was the upcoming lineout.

Rod McCall called it to him. John leaped high, secured it, and came down hard on a rising fist from the All Black's notorious hard-man-to-beat-all-hard-men, his opposing second-rower on the day, Andy Earl. The force of the fist crunched him back, and as he landed his head hit the ground hard, effectively doubling the whammy. From the stands, John Connolly watched closely. All young footballers have to pass tests before they are considered worthy of going to the next level, and this was John's first test. If he got up from a hit like that, it would be a good sign.

John not only got up, but also caught the next throw in the lineout—and this is what staggered Connolly the most — without looking around to see whether another Andy Earl fist was coming at him. Connolly shook his head in amazement. The kid really did have it.

From there, for John, the game went quickly to the ensuing ruck and-then-a-lineout-and-a-ruck-and-another-ruck-and-two-more-scrums-and-on-and-on-like-this . . . His most powerful impression was the sheer *pace* of the game. Even though by this time he'd seen a fair bit of provincial rugby, it was extraordinary how fast it was when you were actually out on the field. For, asquicklyasthat, the game was over. The referee blew the final whistle on a surprising Queensland victory in which young Eales was adjudged to have acquitted himself well. Having taken all of the four line-out balls directed to him, as well as securing three kick-offs without spilling them, plus two runs upfield with the ball in hand, he left the field walking a good six inches taller than he'd entered it.

'I thought I could die happy,' he later recalled, 'just for having worn the Queensland jersey in a game once.'

One who was more than somewhat impressed was Wallaby coach Bob Dwyer, who had made the trip to New Zealand to check on the form most particularly of Bill Campbell and Rod McCall, as he tried to sort out who was going to be in the Wallaby second-row that year. In his view both Bill and Rod had fairly quiet games— with just about no tackles between them, and no charges with the ball — and Eales' performance had been nothing less than a revelation. Beyond just his work rate, he had had a poise and a presence out on the field rarely seen in one so young . . .

In the Queensland dressing room afterwards, Dwyer's first words to Connolly were reflective of that high estimation.

'That young Eales looks pretty good . . . ' he said quietly, as they stood in the detritus, with exhausted players, discarded ankle strappings and boots all around.

'I think he's going to be very good,' Connolly agreed. 'And it's a great pity the World Cup is next year, and not a year later, because I think he could be a great help to the Wallabies.'

'And I was thinking,' Dwyer recalls, "Gee, he looks pretty good to me *right now!*"

Perhaps an hour after the game, the two teams engaged in rugby's traditional post-match function whereby both captains and various officials make speeches, congratulate the other on the game and exchange ties. This function was much the same as most — beer, bonhomie and back-slapping — with one thing out of the ordinary. That is that when Bill Campbell made his captain's speech, he not only gave John an official Queensland tie — a prized possession accorded all those who'd worn the proud maroon jersey in action — but said something else others would recall years later.

'John Eales made his debut today,' said the skipper, 'and I want to both congratulate him and make a prediction. I reckon that in ten years' time he will be coming back to Christchurch, he will be Captain of the Queensland team and he will be earning $100,000 a year.'

Everyone laughed.

A short while after the function in New Zealand had finished, the phone in the kitchen back at Arnell Street had only got through half a ring before Rosa Eales snatched it up.

'Mum . . . it's John, I played for Queensland, and I'm okay.'

As he would do through his entire rugby career, the second-rower always made a quick call at some time soon after playing a game away from home to tell his parents that he was uninjured — at least when that was the case. When he was injured he'd tell them there was every reason to think the injury wasn't that serious.

Queensland did not have a game on the following weekend, meaning John was back in the Brothers side. He turned up at training on the Tuesday night with no little nervousness, on the grounds that while he had been delighted to take his place in the Queensland team, the fellow whose spot he had taken in the touring squad was another Brothers forward, Tim Dodson. Dodson was a very popular guy in the club, very much John's senior, and here was John, just out of Colts, taking his spot. Frankly, John didn't feel worthy, and was concerned about how others would perceive it and . . .

And there was Dodson coming right towards him.

'Congratulations,' Dodson said with a big grin, and his hand outstretched. 'You were great . . . you *bastard.*'

Everyone laughed, crowded round and added their own congratulations.

A WEEK later, and it was back to the Queensland side. Fortunately for John, Bill Campbell had not recovered and John was selected for the first time in the run-on team to play the Australian Capital Territory team in Canberra. Nonna insisted he have an extra-long session with St Anthony before leaving the house, but finally she was satisfied. Still wide-eyed at the thrill of it all, John caught the flight to Canberra, and sat in the economy section beside Jason Little, who was reading a book. In a little under 72 hours he would be running on for Queensland, a huge step up, the way he saw it, from coming on from the bench. What if he blew it? What if he'd just been lucky last time? What if, what if, what if . . . ?

'What's your book like?' John asked, to try and take his mind off things, as on the far horizon to the east Sydney town glinted small against the sea.

'Some of it's very good,' Jason replied quite seriously, 'but the plot seems to jump around all over the place and sometimes I can't follow it.'

John had a sticky-beak to see what the book was called: *Great Short Stories.*

On the morning of the match, John received a disheartening jolt when he picked up the copy of the *Canberra Times* and saw a back-page headline reading: 'LOSS OF CAMPBELL WILL LIMIT QLD'S LINEOUT DOMINANCE AGAINST KOOKAS'. What? If there was one part of John's game he felt was up to speed at this level it was lineouts! With deep disappointment and his confidence already bruised, Eales read on . . .

'The loss of international rugby second-rower Bill Campbell will limit Qld's lineout dominance against the Canberra Kookaburras in their clash at 2.30 pm at Bruce Stadium today. That is the concern of Qld coach John Connolly who [related] that Campbell's replacement is the relatively inexperienced and short John Eales . . .'

Then, the killer quote from Connolly: 'I'm sure this will make the teams a lot closer because we won't be able to dominate the lineouts and possession as perhaps we would have.'

Eales was still shaking his head in confusion when Rod McCall explained it all to him over breakfast. This was just Knuckles playing his tricks, he said, trying to take some pressure off the new boy and play mind games with the Kookaburras, as well as having a bit of innocent fun. John would get used to his way of doing things. As to the game itself, Queensland won well, and Eales consolidated his position by winning his fair share of clean lineout ball. As Wayne Smith reported, 'While McCall was always the man Queensland threw to in crisis, Eales gave a memorable account of himself in his first full game for Queensland, supplementing his eight catches with a high work rate.'

His career in representative rugby was at last on its way, and with it came activities that simply went with the territory. When for example St Edmond's Christian Brothers School at Ipswich asked for a speaker for their Saturday night old boys rugby dinner and none of the other Queensland players wanted to make the trip, the QRU's PR man Michael Blucher asked John if he wanted to go. He was a bit young and anonymous, and totally inexperienced, but there was simply no-one else. John agreed he would give it a go.

The following Monday morning, Blucher received a phone call from St Edmond's principal.

'Thank you for sending that lovely boy John Eales,' he said.

'Oh,' replied Blucher, amazed at such a positive tone for one who had never really spoken in public before, 'that's great! Did he speak well? '

'No,' the principal replied, 'he was absolutely *dreadful*, had no idea, but such a nice fellow nobody particularly cared. They all liked him a lot. I really think he's going to go far. '

From John's point of view, while he was aware he was not close to receiving a standing ovation when he finished his speech, he enjoyed it regardless, and told Blucher that he was happy to do whatever other speaking jobs arose.

THOUGH John's opportunities to play for Queensland dried up as the representative season wound down, he at least had the wonderful privilege of pulling on an Australian jersey for the first time with the Australian U/21 side to play the New Zealand U/21 team as the curtain-raiser to the First Test, Wallabies vs France, at the Sydney Football Stadium in June 1990.

While it was a great thrill to represent Australia for the first time, and play at the Sydney Football Stadium, it proved to be also a great agony for John when they lost. In fact, although the junior Wallabies had gone down fighting, 24-21, to a strong New Zealand side coached by John Hart and including three All Blacks in V'aiga Tuigamala, Craig Innes and Jason Goldsmith, Eales received rave reviews.

'Although NZ deserved their victory,' the *Daily Telegraph* reported, 'the outstanding individual performance of the match came from Brothers lineout ace John Eales who was responsible for more than half of Australia's overall 21-14 lineout advantage and supplemented his jumping with an extraordinary work-rate.'

IF having worn the Queensland and Australian U/21 jumper in battle was a great delight for John, Providence had many more pleasures in store for him that year. At that time in both Sydney and Brisbane, the biggest night of the year in the club rugby calendar was the Rothmans Medal dinner, a black-tie function at a big city hotel when the Club Player of the Year was announced — based on previously unrevealed best-and-fairest points awarded by the referees. In 1990 it was held at the Mayfair Crest Hotel, and John had been extended an invitation to go. Again, it took Rosa many hours sewing to take in Jack's oversize black-tie outfit to make sure it fitted John, but at last it was done. As John was dropped off at the hotel by his father the thought occurred to the twenty-year-old that he might be a rough sort of chance to go well at it, but he never thought . . . he never thought . . .

'And the winner is, John Eales!'

You mean like ME? The crowd, some 500 strong, roared its approval after John's name was called out, and still in a rather dazed state he made his way to the podium, where the All Black coach Grizz Wyllie presented him with the medal as the flashbulbs went off and he was given the microphone to mumble a speech of thanks.

Ron Price had tears in his eyes. John was the youngest Rothmans winner in the history of the competition, and the first second-rower. One of the most heartening things about the whole exercise was how happy everyone seemed for him. All evening long people were slapping him on the back, shaking his hand and buying him drinks. And buying him drinks. And buying him more drinks. And . . . can that be the *time*? It was 4.30 in the morning, in a God-forsaken and seedy bar called Wall Street in downtown Brissie. One tequila, two tequila, three tequila, floor. Or very nearly. With his last tenuous grip on sobriety, and his very last dollars, the Rothmans medallist caught a cab for home.

Softly, softly, catchee monkey — and softly, softly, keepee family sleepee — John slipped off his shoes on the porch and turned the key in the front door before gently, gently opening it.

THWACK!

'And what sort of time do you call this to be coming home? University today, and you're expecting to learn anything on two hours' sleep? Is this what rugby does for you? Do you think you can just treat this place like a motel coming home any time you please? This is a *disgrace*.'

It was his mother, and it was almost as if her Italian roots could be traced all the way back deep down into Mount Vesuvius because she was clearly on course for a major eruption, a rant as severe as it was rare. She was seriously angry and the rant continued all the way down the stairs as John staggered his way down to his room. Rosa never slept a wink until all of her children were home, and she did indeed have legitimate cause for her anger. John could have tried to explain, but thought it better to simply try and escape the worst of it . . .

Still she kept going. John at last got his hand on the doorknob to escape, but she had one last communication, and she would not be put off.

'And John, one more thing.'

'Yes, Mum?'

'Congratulations on winning the medal,' she said softly, 'we're very proud of you . . . '

'Thanks, Mum, g'night.'

'G'night, son.'

For John, it was strange to see his photo on the back page of the *Courier-Mail* the following day, but also kinda nice. And he wasn't the only one impressed. Uncle Alf thought John looked so good with his big beaming smile that he cut the photo out and sent it to Colgate, manufacturers of a famous toothpaste, with a covering letter introducing himself and saying 'you've got to sponsor my nephew'.

Nothing came of it of course, and John was more than a smidgin embarrassed when he found out, but it was very nice for Uncle Alf to have been thinking of him.

ONE of the oldest and most vulgar sayings in rugby is that 'the distance from the penthouse to the s---house is only a very short distance', and John had first-hand experience of that just a fortnight later when in the grand final of the Brisbane competition, Brothers went down to University, 19-10. John felt completely gutted, both with the loss and the feeling that he had not had the impact on the game he felt he was capable of, but some news the following day perked him up. He had been selected to go on an Emerging Wallaby tour through five countries in Europe, starting in October, under the coaching guidance of the ACT's Bob Hitchcock — an affable man with a strong rugby background. He was backed up by forwards coach, Jake Howard. The Emerging Wallabies was a new concept for the ARU, essentially an idea to form a team which would be a bridge between the games at Australian U/21 level and the senior Wallabies. With the second World Cup being held a year hence in Britain and Ireland, it was a last chance to see if some new talent could be unearthed.

While John was excited at the opportunity, the one down-side was that he would miss all his university lectures and therefore have to take his exams the following January. At least most of his lecturers were understanding, but his Economics lecturer Amelia Preece had by this time just about had enough.

'Who *are* these rugby people?' she asked him pointedly. 'They are @#$!ing up your life. You want to get a grip on yourself and take control of the situation.' Though Ms Preece eventually agreed that John could take his exams in January, she was far from happy about it.

FOR John, it was his first time away from home for longer than a fortnight, and when he arrived in London to begin the tour the sense of homesickness he felt was almost debilitating. He wouldn't be home for another three months. Still, things quickly got better from there as he got into the rhythm of the rugby ramble across Europe. It was an arduous tour with many long training sessions, and many much longer train trips, staying in mostly low-rent hotels with rooms not big enough to swing a dead cat, but most of it pleased him greatly regardless. The essence of its impact can be boiled down to one conversation John had with another player on the tour, David Williams, of the Queensland University Club. Williams and John were sitting together on the bus in Shakespeare's home-town of Stratford-upon-Avon, on the way to yet one more training session. The team had been in the town for a week, training twice a day in preparation for their game against English Students. And Williams, for one, was seriously jack of it. Usually a quietly spoken sort of fellow, he confided to John with some venom that he wasn't enjoying the tour at all, that he couldn't stand the constant training, that he couldn't *wait* to get home, and once he got there he didn't plan on leaving it any time soon.

John knew exactly what Dave was talking about. But he felt otherwise and told him as much as they pulled up — *once more unto the breach dear friends, once more* — to the training ground. His own thoughts were that while it was going to be tough playing ten years of the game with anything like this level of intensity, on the other hand they were travelling all over Europe for free with good people, and they got to play some high-level rugby games, which was what it was all about. To their east, the Berlin Wall had come down just a year before and the two Germanys were coming together. The Soviet Union was dismantling itself before their eyes. Margaret Thatcher was fighting a furious rearguard action to keep her prime ministership intact. And they were there! Too, there was a sense of history about Europe that John had never quite felt in Australia. Everywhere they went there were castles, museums, famous battle sites, extraordinary things he'd never seen before on heaven and earth. They'd already been to see the famous Rugby school, where their whole game had originated, and John had wandered around fascinated.

Certainly the training was hard, but they were representing their country, and getting to see an extremely interesting part of the world. It was definitely something John felt he wanted to do a lot more of. Other players on the tour felt the same, though for some of them this was the one and only major representative tour they would go on. Part of the reason for the whole exercise was to sort out who was capable of going up to the next step, and who wasn't cut out for elite rugby. Eales was most definitely one of the former.

When interviewed over the telephone by the *Courier-Mail*, coach Bob Hitchcock laid it on with a trowel. 'Eales is one of the most talented footballers I have ever seen,' he told Wayne Smith. 'He has beautiful hands, runs powerfully with the ball, and is one of those truly great players who can reach the top without any nastiness in his game.'

All up, the tour was a great success for Eales, at least at a footballing and tourist level. On the study level, he had taken all his textbooks with him but it was hopeless. He had not opened a book even once, and although the university had allowed him to defer his exams he felt he would still be up against it when he got back.

But when would he get back?

Six months previously, when Peter Slattery was asked to fill out his occupation for the QRU he put down, 'full-time rugby tourist'. At the time, everyone had laughed, and it had been something of a running gag with the team. Now though, John knew exactly what he meant. For no sooner was the Emerging Wallabies tour over than another tour in Europe was about to begin, this one with Queensland playing in the World Provincial Championships in Toulouse. John had one week's delightful R&R in London — sightseeing and drinking and reading about Margaret Thatcher's resignation as Prime Minister of Great Britain — and then flew to join the team in France. After three weeks of the tournament, Queensland lost in the final, with John once again replacing the injured Bill Campbell in the second half. It was sad to have lost, of course, but wonderful to be heading home.

John arrived back in Brisbane on Christmas morning, and instituted a tradition that would continue for almost as long as his rugby career. That is, after catching up with everyone in the family, he particularly sought out Nonna — for some reason the person in the family he seemed to miss most, while away — and that night when she went to bed lay on top of the blankets talking to her and singing hymns until she dropped off to sleep.

He gently kissed her cheek and left the room. Long year. Good year, but long year.

The Season to End Reason

I believe John Eales, this year, will launch himself
into a rugby career up there among the best we have produced.

MICHAEL LYNAGH, in his *Courier-Mail* column,
'Talking Rugby', 10 March 1991

⌐

'JOHN . . . Nick Farr-Jones, pleased to meet you . . . '

It was late January 1991, in one of Queensland University's residential colleges, and the Australian rugby captain of the last three years was proffering John his hand. This was not just as a fellow rugby player, but as a *fellow member* of the Wallaby World Cup Squad which had gathered to begin serious preparations to secure the William Webb Ellis Trophy. While on tour with the Emerging Wallabies, John had received the extraordinary news that he had been adjudged as one of the best 45 players in the country who had been invited to gather for the three day camp, and now, here he was.

Plenty of the other Wallabies were happy to get a look at young Eales, close up. For the previous six months or so, the word had been circulating in representative ranks: 'Wait till you see this kid'; 'This bloke is the goods'; 'This is the bloke who kicked the field goal'. Funny, for a bloke of whom there had been so much talk, in person he didn't have an ounce of swagger about him. Rather, John seemed just a softly spoken sort of bloke who remained very quiet for the duration of the camp.

Helping to ease the passage of the youngster into this new fraternity was the redoubtable Bob Templeton, a legendary figure in both Australian and Queensland rugby, who was then the assistant coach of the Wallaby side, predominantly responsible for the forward pack. His role, however, went a lot deeper than mere technical advice. As a deeply respected elder of the Wallaby tribe, Tempo was always just *around*, raising a laugh, telling a story of the great Wallaby teams of the past with which he was the most tangible link, or pounding away on a particular point of his rugby passion — like the need for forwards to stay *low* when they hit the ruck.

Speaking of which . . .

Just as training with Queensland had been an enormous step-up from Brothers Colts, so too was being in the environs of the Australian team a good sized step-up again from the state side. Back at Brothers, the training regimen pursued had simply steered by the star of No Pain, No Gain! At Queensland level things had been about three gears higher than that, with a specific kind of pain for a specific kind of gain, and at Australian level an array of Bob Dwyer-appointed experts told them that not only should their exercise be undergone at specific times of the season so that the players would be at absolute maximum power on the day of the most important games— but there were also optimum amounts of recovery time, before you started again. All gains had to be precisely measured to determine just what sort of pain it was best to go to next. Add buckets of sweat, and mix. A sports psychologist lectured them long about the ideal 'arousal level' prior to the game; a dietitian told them all about eating to maximise their power/weight ratio; a biomechanical expert taught them exercises that would help reduce the incidence of injury. On and on it went. John had made it into the Wallaby squad at almost the exact instant that elite rugby in Australia had gone techno — and generally there was a clear difference in the way the senior and junior members of the squad responded to it. At one point during a particularly long lecture by strength trainer Brian Hopley, Farr-Jones looked over and saw young Eales taking copious notes, clearly hanging on every word. As an older, established player, Farr-Jones was taking all of this new-fangled stuff with a pinch of salt, but Eales was eating the whole meal, as was young Phil Kearns beside him.

Beyond such sessions, a significant part of the camp was filled with Australian coach Bob Dwyer talking to them. One of the most effective lines he used, and his moustache bristled as he said it, was: 'I don't want players who want to win — I want players who want to *prepare* to win.'

He went on, his hand jabbing the air for emphasis . . .

'I don't want players who want to be the best in their position in Australia, I want players who are trying to be the best in their position in the *world*. To win the World Cup we need at least five players who are automatic selections in a World XV, and each of you has to work towards that goal, and I do mean work.'

Mere talent was not going to be enough to get anyone a place in the team — there had to be a work ethic to embrace the new way of doing things. And make no mistake, Dwyer continued, if you are not prepared to make winning the World Cup in 241 days' time your NUMBER ONE PRIORITY, then you simply had no place being here. No excuses! Not your job, not your family, not your girlfriend, nothing. You will have to work harder than ever before if you want to be a part of the World Cup team in October.

'If you have to give up your jobs to do this, then *fine*,' Dwyer said, 'I couldn't be happier! I'd be delighted!'

This particular remark occasioned a fair amount of quiet grumbling. The running gag among the players at a scrum session later that afternoon was that for the rest of the year if you wanted something to eat, you'd have to put your Wallaby jersey in the oven. John didn't laugh because he didn't dare. Wallaby Test second-rower Bill Campbell didn't laugh because to him it was no joke. He could see that Dwyer was serious. The 29-year-old Campbell, a doctor who was married and the father of three children, was on the edge of beginning further heavyweight studies to become a surgeon. There were only so many hours in the day to be a doctor, husband, father and football player, and with Dwyer wanting this extra commitment, something was going to have to give. He knew for sure it was not going to be his marriage, his parenting, or his profession. It would have to be the rugby itself. On the spot — though he forestalled announcing it for a week — he decided to retire.

Without Campbell around, the queue of second-rowers lining up to get into the Test team was suddenly a lot thinner. To get into that Australian side, John would first have to secure a spot in the Queensland Reds and perform well there, but in that regard he felt a growing confidence. Just twelve months previously, John had been naught but a knock on the door of the state side, with no senior representative experience to his credit. Now, though, he was the Rothmans Medal winner, the star of the just-returned Emerging Wallabies and already a member of the World Cup squad — meaning he was the obvious successor to Campbell. Plus, as a single twenty-year-old still living at home, and able to live by the seat of his pants, John was almost ideally suited to follow Dwyer's dictum to 'always put rugby first'. There wasn't a whole lot competing for second. Not much, anyway . . .

For once the camp was over, John had to return immediately to the only other thing that had been occupying him of late — getting through the exams which the university had allowed him to delay sitting because of his rugby commitments. Feeling sick at heart that he was very likely going to fail, John studied night and day for three weeks, trying to get up to speed. When it came time to do the Social Psychology exam, the still desperate John played a hunch. Having heard somewhere that his lecturer was a devout Roman Catholic, he very neatly drew a red line down the left hand side of the page and up in the top left-hand corner wrote 'JMJ'. If she wasn't a devout Catholic it would mean nothing to her, and if she was it certainly wouldn't hurt.

He passed. Whether through direct help from the lecturer, or indirect help from above, he was never sure. Nothing, however, could get him through Amelia Preece's Economics exam, and for the first and only time in his life he failed the exam. He would have to do just one more semester to finish.

AND so back to the rugby. Always back to the rugby. The poet T.S. Eliot had once penned the immortal line, 'I have measured out my life with coffee spoons'. Now, it wasn't going too far to say that John measured his life in rugby practices and games, as his day-to-day existence began to move to the rhythms of the rugby calendar. If the state squad was training at Ballymore at 6 o'clock on a Wednesday evening, then that was where he was. If they determined that the squad would be doing fitness tests on a wet Monday morning at 7 o'clock, then that was where he was too. If they said the side was playing Auckland at Eden Park for the opening game of the season, then it was Eales, J., present again, including for the three days leading up to it.

And even then he was not done! For being a part of the Queensland

Reds meant more of a time commitment than merely attending training and games. Just like Brothers, being a Queensland Red was almost a lifestyle, which included regular social events at the homes of the other players and coaching staff, charity affairs where John would turn up in team blazer representing the team, attending functions for sponsors, golf days and coaching seminars at various schools around Brisbane.

And, just as had happened at Brothers, as time went by the rest of the Queensland team and management got to know him better and became aware of just how much he had to offer.

On one occasion in mid-February of 1991, for example, the Reds team were involved in a social cricket match against Marist Brothers Ashgrove, with John standing at first slip and John Connolly at second slip. At one point a tearaway bowler hurled down an absolute *scorcher*, which the Marist opener snicked. It was going so fast Connolly barely saw it, but Eales did and hurled himself like a soccer goalkeeper far to his right to catch it about an inch off the ground. Connolly was still shaking his head at the extraordinary reflexes and athleticism of the lad, when three balls later John did it again — a pearler caught at much the same level, this to his left. On top of the fact that Eales had also top-scored and opened the bowling to great effect, the whole episode set Connolly to thinking.

The Queensland coach was a long-time cricket aficionado, they were two of the most extraordinary slips catches he'd ever seen, and he was staggered at John's coordination and reflexes.

'Mate,' he said to John at the end of the over, 'with coordination like that you're going to be our goal-kicker . . . '

Eales barely gave it another thought — he was after all in a team that boasted Michael Lynagh, one of the two greatest goal-kickers in the world at that time, but Connolly was as good as his word. Just three weeks later the Reds were on a brief tour of Japan, and playing a Japanese representative side when the ball was thrown to John to kick for goal. Under normal circumstances Michael Lynagh would have obliged himself, but because the Queensland five-eighth was then sitting on a total of 992 points for the Maroons, the decision had been taken to have him break Paul McLean's 1000 points record at the game against Canterbury at Ballymore on the following weekend. (Such was the growing consciousness of the importance of marketing, in Australian rugby in the early 1990s.) So it was that while in the first half Tim Horan slotted none out of four kicks, John was asked to do the honours in the second half and nailed seven goals out of eight.

Far more important from the team's point of view was the fact that John's mobility around the field had improved, as had his strength in the scrum, while his magisterial ability in the lineout was as strong as ever. Armed with his new-found knowledge and greater experience, Eales played some very fine rugby for Queensland over the next three months, perhaps a little too fine on some occasions. When, for example, Auckland beat Queensland late in March by the score of 34-26, a controversy blew up over the way the referee Fred Thomson had run the game.

'While reluctant to make an issue of Thompson's refereeing,' the *Courier-Mail* reported, 'John Connolly was bewildered by five penalties awarded against Queensland in the lineout, four of them for the alleged lifting of John Eales. "He apparently could not believe that Eales could jump that high on his own," Connolly said.'

A constant confidant and adviser to John in this heady time was Ben Perkins, who by this time was a frequent visitor to Arnell Street. Jack and Rosa Eales had never been quite sure what to make of Ben, but the fact that John was so clearly taken with him was good enough for them, and he was always most welcome. With Nonna, that welcome was always particularly warm. Her own eccentricity at the age of 86 was that she liked drinking Guinness, and whenever Ben came over he always brought her a few cans. Though he did not drink alcohol himself, he would some-times sit down on the front porch with Nonna while she had half a glass and they could have a good chat about Eckankar, among other things. Exactly where they found their common ground was never clear, but some-how it worked between them. Ben never got Nonna to sing 'HUUUUU' but they had a fine old time regardless.

Ben and John would talk rugby. Tactics, strategies, techniques, John never ceased to be amazed at the depths of Ben's technical knowledge, and though some might have taken him as a kind of Eales-acolyte he was not that. In fact Ben was an honest critic about areas where he thought John could improve, and they would discuss them. Somehow, Ben managed to be a critic without being critical, and he managed to give John a lot of confidence. Ben clearly had so much faith in how talented the young second-rower was that John's own quiet belief in himself and how good he *could* be would soar. And of course they would discuss a hundred other things. 'Ben is just one of those people,' John would later say. 'He makes me feel good about myself. I don't have to be anything or anyone, I can just be myself.'

The exciting thing for John at this point was not just that more and more commentators were saying he would make the first announced Wallaby side of the season, but that the portents for a triumphant Wallaby performance at the World Cup were also very good. Queensland had a very good team that year, and NSW, under the stewardship of their new coach Rod Macqueen, was undefeated. The expectations for a great series were high, and no-one was disappointed. For the first time in memory at the end of an interstate game at Ballymore, the crowd rose as one and applauded both teams as they left the field. Rightly so. A week later the NSW crowd accorded the teams much the same acclaim. In front of record crowds in both Sydney and Brisbane, the games were technically excellent, played at furious pace and without spite.

Certainly it was disappointing that Queensland had narrowly lost both games, 24-18 and 21-12. Jack Eales had been so nervous in the final twenty minutes of the Sydney game he was seen to eat half of a cardboard video container, but it had no impact on the perception that John was the coming thing. Most notably he had bested the legendary Wallaby second-rower of the 1980s, Stephen Cutler, in both games . . .

If that was something to celebrate, so too was the fact that John turned 21 and graduated with a Bachelor of Arts from Queensland University, all in the last week of June. Not that he celebrated much. Typical of this time of his life, if it wasn't wearing football boots or blowing a whistle at him, John could barely give it any attention at all. So his 21st passed with just a quiet, specially made Nonna dinner of pasta at home, while he didn't actually get around to making his graduation ceremony. He was happy to have an Arts degree, but there was a much bigger game in town . . .

TIMING. Of all sporting attributes, including drive, tenacity, coordination and skills, timing is one of the key prerequisites of success. Throughout his sporting career to that point, John Eales had always exhibited extraordinary timing from the sweet way he hit a cover drive seemingly without effort, to casual 280 metre golf drives, to the way he could kick a ball from a tiny pile of sand through wooden uprights 45 metres distant. Now, though, he was showing an even more acute sense of timing and in an entirely different sense. That is, he was rising to the top of Wallaby second-row contention just when a huge void was opening above him. In the previous two years the Wallabies had lived on the services of Rod McCall and Bill Campbell from Queensland and Peter FitzSimons and Stephen Cutler from New South Wales.

At the beginning of 1991, though McCall was still in the swim and as keen as ever, Campbell had retired and Cutler was in the deepening twilight of a magnificent career. FitzSimons, meanwhile, was on the crest of a slump, essentially through an unfortunate propensity for giving away needless penalties and his own lack of drive this late in his career to put in month after month of the kind of disciplined focus necessary. Eales, by contrast, was fresh, focused, and not only inordinately talented, but possessing a demonstrated ability to withstand the blows of foes keen to do him down. The *Sydney Morning Herald* rugby correspondent Greg Growden was one who espoused the virtues of selecting Eales for the opening Test, even though many thought he was still too green to throw into the national engine room.

'As Australia is certain to go into the contest with many members of the Emerging Wallabies contingent,' Growden wrote, 'now is the time to find out whether young second-rowers like Warwick Waugh and John Eales are capable of negotiating the large step between interstate and international football. If it works, we will see the blossoming of one of the most exciting Australian second-row combinations. If it doesn't work, there is always Steve Cutler, Rod McCall and Peter FitzSimons to call on for the more tense England and All Black encounters.'

Despite such media support, John was in little danger of losing focus because of getting big-headed. When, for example, Brothers just managed to beat Easts three weeks before the Test side was announced, their coach Mark Nightingale gave his view to the press on just what the problem was. 'I thought Eales could have made a few more two-handed takes, instead of tapping down to the half-back,' he fulminated. 'And for a player who earns rave reviews for his ball skills, he knocked on three times.'

Not to worry. The coach was quite right, John *had* knocked on three times, and knew he would have to do better if he made the Test side. Everywhere he went in early July 1991, people seemed to be wishing him luck for his probable selection, and it was so taken for granted in some sections of the rugby world that Queensland Rugby Union's PR manager

Michael Blucher asked John to sign a Wallaby jersey as part of a fund-raising drive. John refused, politely but firmly. John had not been selected to the Wallabies yet, and thought it would be a great arrogance to sign a jersey beforehand — not to mention bad karma — and a little embarrassing if it didn't actually happen.

The old proverb that 'there is many a slip 'twixt cup and lip' might well have been invented for football players of promise who somehow just missed out on fulfilling everyone's predictions. The first real test of whether Eales had what it took to play Tests — at least in the selectors' eyes — would come when Queensland played the touring Welsh and English sides on successive Saturdays. See, the traditional rugby reckoning has it, while it's one thing to have gone well against provincial teams, you never really know how a bloke is going to go until you put him up against internationals.

The following Sunday, the remaining doubters had their initial answer when Queensland ripped through a hapless Welsh side by 35-24, in no small part thanks to John's domination in the lineouts. Ahhhhh yes, but what about England then, the current Grand Slam Champions of the Five Nations? That would be the acid test of his abilities. For in the engine room of the English pack were Paul Ackford and Wade Dooley — the most highly acclaimed second-row pairing in world rugby. If Eales could cut it against them, then he really was a good chance to be named in the Wallaby side. At the conclusion of the game the selectors had their answer. Not only had Queensland recorded a handsome win, but Eales and McCall had beaten Ackford and Dooley in the lineouts by the margin of 20-17, out of which John had snaffled 13 clean takes! In the stands, Jack and Rosa sitting with Bernadette and Damian, quietly thrilled to every successful leap.

Some six of John's snatches had come in the first twenty minutes, when he repeatedly out-leapt Dooley, despite the veteran trying every-thing he knew to thwart the youngster. When at one point Dooley found Eales at the bottom of a ruck, he took a swing and said, 'Take that, you @$#%-ing Arts student.' Still Eales proceeded to outjump him, and even when Ackford tried his luck to stop Eales in the middle of the lineout nothing appeared to work.

'What impressed me,' Ackford noted in a newspaper column years later, 'even in those old days of the lineout which could be claustrophobic and intense, was that Eales was still able to make space for himself. We were always closer in those days, what with trying to lift the jumpers when it was still illegal to do so and it was easier to get to grips with an opponent. But not Eales. He somehow managed to evade the opposition's clutches. He seemed to hang out of the line and come in when the ball was thrown in.'

This was an astute technical analysis of what was essentially the natural Eales style. Somewhere in the course of his lineout jumping career, Eales had established that the best way to secure the ball was to soar high a split second after the collision between the two lines, not allowing himself in any way to be caught in the car-smash, and leaving himself free to pluck the plums that were so often waiting there. Not for nothing had his team-mates continued to liken John to a praying mantis, all arms and legs leaning just out of the line and ready to attack.

Immediately after the match Wade Dooley, Paul Ackford and the great English no. 8 Dean Richards — all three of them members of the English constabulary — were in a corner of the dressing room discussing the new lad Eales and just how he might be stopped, when they realised they had been joined by another. With a big smile and an outstretched hand, John said, 'Wade, we weren't properly introduced. John Eales. Any chance you'd like to swap jerseys with a #$%!ing Arts student?'

Dooley would be delighted, and the four of them shared a couple of beers together before attending the post-match function upstairs. It was near the end of this function that there was a call for quiet, as a very important announcement was to be made: the Australian team to play Wales at Ballymore the following Saturday. Appropriately, the highest ranking Wallaby official on site, Bob Templeton, stepped to the microphone. John stood at the back of the room, not moving, hanging on every word.

'And the Australian team to play against Wales,' Tempo said, in maddeningly neutral tones, is . . . Tony Daly, Phil Kearns, Ewen McKenzie . . . John Eales . . . '

MADE IT. *Made it!* MADE IT! Correct form on such occasions is for the crowd to keep calm until the announcement of the team is completed, and this was observed, but the instant Templeton read out the last name, John was awash in handshakes and congratulations. Simon Whitehart, who had come along as John's guest, chuckled quietly as he watched John closely. Just about everyone else he knew would have given themselves the luxury of a couple of air-punches or a few cartwheels around the room from joy. Not John. That would have been showing off.

There was another good reason John did not seem to be the Jumpin' Jack Flash of Joy at that very moment. For although during the last year Ben Perkins had preached to him the virtues of astral travel, all to no avail, John confided to him later that at the moment of the announcement . . . be darned if it didn't feel a bit like an out-of-body-experience.

That is, in some kind of surreal way, John strongly felt like he was watching someone else being so warmly congratulated, not him. *Him*, John Eales, the Australian Test second-rower, in only his second year of senior rugby? It couldn't be right, could it?

Too right. Both Jack and Rosa were delighted for John, as were of course the rest of the family, and they congratulated him warmly on his achievement . . . without going over the top. Still, it's just possible that Jack was a lot more bursting with pride than he let on.

The following day, Basil the fruiterer was in his shop at Arana Hills when his regular customer, the man he called 'Uncle Jack' because of his avuncular ways, arrived. Basil did what he always did, which was to ask after the family, with particular reference to his former employee and 'best boy', John. In response, Jack looked left, looked right, made absolutely sure no-one was listening, and then put his mouth conspiratorially close to Basil's ear.

'He's been picked to play for AUSTRALIA,' Jack whispered, his voice breaking with excitement.

Basil himself was thrilled with the news, and extremely quietly, the two did something of a jig of joy around the cumquats before order was restored.

'It was the way Jack told me,' Basil would tell the story ever afterwards. 'He was just bursting with happiness and pride.'

As was Rosa Eales, in her own fashion. Though delighted at her son's achievement, she could still be a little vague about it. When Shaun Gelling, one of John's friends, called in on the following Tuesday afternoon, mistakenly thinking John wouldn't have gone into camp with the Wallabies yet, Rosa informed him, 'no, he's off practising with that new team he's in.'

THOUGH nominally under the rules of the International Rugby Board no home team was allowed to go into camp more than 72 hours before the kick-off of a Test match, Bob Dwyer had found a good way to play fast and loose with this was to have the Wallabies attend some kind of function on the Tuesday lunchtime, and then have them squeeze in a training session in the afternoon. They weren't thus quite 'in camp' — they all just happened to be in the same spot at the same time and decided, what the hey, let's train! (John was particularly delighted with this arrangement, as he found out that the players would all get $50 a day allowance for every day in camp, meaning he would clear the very tidy sum of $250 for the week.)

For the four days leading into the Test against Wales, the Wallabies moved into Brisbane's Park Royal, the same establishment where he had been in a spot of bother with a young woman a couple of years previously. For the first couple of days John kept an eye out for the manager who had threatened to have him arrested if ever he set foot on the premises again, but when no shrill whistle was blown in his ear while eating breakfast he was able to relax a little.

John settled in well with the other Wallabies and noted that they appeared to have a lot of confidence in him. At lineout training, for example, it was clear that he was expected to be the chief ball-winner and there would be no easing him into international rugby. He was a *Test* player now, and they were confident he would produce.

If only John shared their confidence. On the morning of the Test match, after a restless night's sleep, John woke just after dawn and stared at the cracks in the ceiling, while Rod McCall in the next bed continued to sleep soundly. He returned to the same question. Was he was up to it? A TEST match! Him! Was it possible they had made a terrible mistake? Or was he the one going to be making terrible mistakes, giving away penalties in front of the posts perhaps, or knocking on from the kick-off as the cameras broadcast his blunders across the continent? Was this going to be not only his first match, but also his last, as he was dreadfully exposed for the fraud that he was? His nervousness was so bad now, how was he going to be at 3 p.m.? Would he even be able to take the field?

'Of course you will John, and you'll be fine.' They were not Carmel's words, per se, because she of course was no longer physically there with him, but they were the words he knew she *would* have said to him had she been there, and in a funny kind of way he felt like she almost was. These days, whenever he felt stressed he tended to think about her and somehow it calmed him, nurtured him, nourished him. He liked thinking about Carmel, and he was still thinking about her at about 1.30 p.m. when slowly, slowly, the bus carrying the Wallabies made its way into the back of the Ballymore car park and began nosing through the crowd gathering outside the stadium. John was about four seats back on the left, in the hazy territory between the jungle seats up the back where the hard men of the forwards were wont to bump heads, and the front seats where the likes of Dwyer, Campese, Farr-Jones and Lynagh liked to preside.

Looking out the window to where all the people were gathered, many of them having barbecues, eating hot dogs and chatting to each other, John couldn't help but catch something of the spirit of these people who'd come out to see them play. Somewhere out there his entire family had likely just arrived, and though he didn't see them, he saw plenty of others. John recognised blokes he'd gone to school with, people he'd sat beside in church, played football with and against, an old fellow who'd come up to him out of the blue on the street and warmly congratulated him on his selection. And to a man, woman and child, when they saw that the bus carried the Wallabies they rose and cheered, clapped and carried on.

Hooray! Go get 'em! Go you Wallabies. Good luck! We're with you.

It was a moment where John Anthony Eales suddenly realised the magnitude of the privilege that had been afforded him to play for his country. He'd felt very emotional an hour earlier when in front of the team at the hotel Nick Farr-Jones had presented him with his Wallaby jersey, but this was more powerful still. It was all he could do to stop himself bawling.

In the dressing room — just before kick-off — Phil Kearns came up to where John was sitting on the bench, shook his hand, and put his mouth close to his ear so no-one else could hear.

'I think I know what you're feeling,' he said, 'but don't worry about it, enjoy it. Just remember that we've all been through what you're going through now, and, whatever happens out there, we are all with you.'

And then it began. The knock on the door. The lining up of the team in any order you liked between the two book-ends of Farr-Jones at the front because he was captain, and Campese at the back because he was Campese — and they started to file out the door. Down the darkened tunnel. Into the light. Another massive roar from the crowd. GO YOU WALLABIES!

On the field, the Australians gathered together in a huddle to sing the national anthem, though John had problems from the first moments of *'Australians all let us rejoice, for we are young and . . .'*

Surreal. Choked up. Out-of-body. Carmel. Calmer. *'Our land abounds in nature's gifts'.* John kept gurgling it out, best he could, while instinctively beginning a practice that would stay with him for the rest of his career. That is, as he kept going . . . *'in joyful strains then let us sing'* . . . he focused on a single face in the crowd, a particular bloke who seemed to be in raptures as he too roared out the words of *'Advance Australia Fair'* with the Wallabies. In a strange sort of way, John drew even more strength from the bloke's enthusiasm, and was reminded once again that apart from playing for himself and for the Wallabies, he was also playing for that bloke and for so many like him who desperately wanted Australia to win on the day, who in all likelihood would cut off his little finger to don the Wallaby jersey but once. That bloke couldn't do it, but he, John, could. And by God he was gunna! The opening whistle blew . . .

. . . Closely followed by the final whistle. Just like it had been for his first game for Queensland against Canterbury, it almost seemed that quick to the debutante, unbelievable that the game was already over. This may have been because while time flies when you're having fun, as the cliché runs, it positively blinks by when you're enjoying yourself hugely and putting an ancient enemy to the sword in extraordinary fashion. John had a stunning Test debut, whereby he made several charges upfield, pulled off many tackles and entirely dominated the lineouts to the tune of 13 clean takes in an overall lineout margin of 20-5, Most importantly, Australia had registered an extraordinary win, scoring twelve tries on their way to running up a record margin against Wales of 63-6.

Some guys finish their first Test simply relieved that they have at least fulfilled their life's dream by playing for their country on at least one occasion; most guys finish totally exhausted, astounded by the step up in physical commitment required at that level. John Eales finished his first Test wildly enthused. Going into it his ambition had been to just play *one* Test — at least that one Test — but after it was over, all he wanted to do was play fifty!

His ebullience for the game was matched by the rugby wise-heads' delight at his performance. In one corner of the dressing room, Bob Dwyer quietly mentioned to his fellow selectors that their next meeting would be very quick when it came to discussing who would fill the No. 5 jersey. The Wallaby coach's views were fully endorsed by the rugby press with the Australian Society of Rugby Writers voting John the Man of the Match. Read all about it, read all about it . . . Eales, in his first Test, playing alongside such luminaries as Farr-Jones, Michael Lynagh and David Campese — the Holy Trinity, as they were known — and against a Five Nations side, had been adjudged the best player on the field. It was as close to cricket's celebrated century on debut as Eales could possibly have mustered, even if it was against an opposition that was notably below strength.

So just where was the manpower to stop the Wallabies so humiliating Wales? The answer: somewhere in the English north, preparing for the coming Rugby League season. In the previous five years, no fewer than seventeen Welsh Test players had defected to League. They went because, in the words of one defector Mark Jones, the Welsh No. 8 of 1989: 'Rugby Union doesn't pay the mortgage.' Closer to home, the previous year one of the Brothers' best players, and John's good friend from school, Simon Best, had 'defected' to League to play for the Broncos. John and his friends decided to get for Simon's 21st birthday present Simon Poidevin's famously titled book *For Love Not Money*. In the end — or so the running gag had it — they just couldn't afford to buy it. Elsewhere, the demise of the unfortunate Welsh at that time had given rise to a joke circulating in the Australian rugby community.

Q: What is the difference between Cinderella and the Welsh side?

A: At least Cinderella got to the ball.

When John returned to Arnell Street after the Test there were piles of congratulatory mail waiting for him and he delighted in reading it all, though he was bemused by one letter that wasn't congratulatory at all. It was from the Life Be In It Association, and began . . . 'Dear John, We are concerned about your general health and fitness . . . ' Charmed, he was sure! (Somehow the fact that John had been attending the gyms provided by the QRU and the ARU, and had thus let his membership at another gym wane, had generated this automatic mailing list response.)

THERE is an enormous difference between the approach taken by a player going into his first Test and into his second. Though only 80 minutes of action separates the former from the latter, there is a world of difference in terms of feel. Going into the second Test, no longer is the player quite the new boy, the untested one he once was. Now, he has earned his spurs; has travelled in the mystical land known as Test Match Rugby, and returned to tell the tale. This does not give him any rights to swagger, mind — and p's and q's must still be minded — but still there is a greater level of comfort all around.

Having made his Test debut, John was now that little bit freer to enjoy a lot of what was going on around him, to get to know his fellow players better, to get into the rhythms of Wallaby life. For there were indeed many things to learn about the Wallabies and how they worked, which went a long way beyond scrum moves and lineout calls . . .

In the lead-up to the next Test, against England in Sydney, the Wallaby squad went to another Park Royal hotel, this time in Wollongong, about an hour south of Sydney, to prepare. On their first night there, the team had their traditional Happy Hour, which follows every Wallaby game at the soonest opportune moment. A long-standing tradition, the Happy Hour is a brief drinking session in a closed room where the power imbalance between management and the team is momentarily redressed. For this is a session run exclusively by the players, where various rites and rituals that have evolved over the years are performed, songs sung, stories told and awards awarded. One of the traditions was that Test debutants had to serve the others drinks, and John, together with fullback Marty Roebuck and winger Bobby Egerton, was happy to do so.

Though the Happy Hour was fun, there was still a serious purpose to it. Essentially, it was the method whereby the Wallabies ensured that their rigid code of conduct was enforced. A small example was the code of correct dress, it being deemed that whenever the team was gathered in a public hotel, no-one was allowed to come to breakfast unless they were wearing a shirt with a collar, pants with a crease in them, and leather shoes. Every Wallaby had to ensure that every other Wallaby observed this rule — and those who breached it not only had to go back upstairs and dress correctly, but were obliged to answer to the team in the Happy Hour. If, on a show of hands, a player was found guilty, he might have to skol a schooner of beer in under ten seconds, to uproarious laughter all round, but the point was still made.

Certainly, the Wallaby coach and manager were a part of this code of behaviour — though not as enforcers but as participants. For as other players had told John, Bob Dwyer was no stranger to being told by one or other of his players that a polo-neck sweater did not qualify as 'a shirt with collar' and he too must return to his room to change it. Correct dress, though, was just the beginning. The bottom line was that all players inducted into the Wallabies were made to understand that, when representing their country, a singularly high standard of comportment was required. As John had observed, the same code applied when the Wallabies were out and about in public, whatever revelries might be going on. Any player deviating from the code was soon told by the other players to lift his game, and that they would have to answer to the team later. No-one missed the point: if they were slovenly or misbehaved it didn't just reflect badly on them, but on Australia, and it was important that they get it right.

This point was always driven home. At the end of the Happy Hour that night, for example — as with all Happy Hours — all the players stood, put their drinks down, and their blazers back on, and sang the national anthem with their hands by their side. Any new player who did not know the words would be quickly detected and obliged to learn it by the next Happy Hour, on pain of having to drink two schooners, or the like, next time. All up, this system of internal pride as opposed to external policing, worked wonderfully well.

In the days leading up to his second Test, John looked around at the happiness of the team, the tight sense of community they had, and had a strong sense of privilege that he was playing with such a terrific bunch of guys.

But to work. In the face of England, there was an even greater urgency to their training than the week before as Dwyer put them through their paces, at pace. Again and again and again.

HIT! CLEAN 'EM OUT! GET YOUR SHOULDER ON, JOHN! DRIVE INTO THE BAG WITH YOUR WHOLE BODY WEIGHT BEHIND IT! GO! GO! GOOOO!

Bob could be like that, perpetually speaking in capitals during training sessions, as if he had swallowed a megaphone when he was a young man and had delighted in taking advantage of it ever since. His intensity prior to a Test match tended to rub off on the team. And yet the happiest of all things about Dwyer was that as intense as he might be at a training session, he was an equable if loquacious fellow around the dinner table and hence there was a good deal of respite.

As Rod McCall said to John once, 'Bob's got his faults, but he's actually an interesting bloke who is worth listening to.' As with a lot of things Rod had told him, John found that to be true, and he was of the opinion that one of the reasons Dwyer was such a good coach was because he cared about so much more than just rugby.

The relationship between Eales and McCall was a curious one. It would not have been at all unusual for the older, established player to resent the younger hard-rising one, to perhaps down-play his talents to others, but there seemed never to be any sign of this. Most of what John had been going through — bar Man of the Match awards — McCall had already experienced, and there were many things on which he was able to give John cogent tips. For the Test against England, McCall's advice was to just stick to his guns, whatever happened. The English would be all over him, McCall said, trying to put him off his game, but no matter what, no matter what, John had to keep doing what he was out there to do. Win the ball in the lineout. Push in the scrum. Take the ball up in attack. Tackle on suspicion in defence.

Game time. At a jam-packed Sydney Football Stadium on the last Saturday of July 1991, the English visitors were savaged, torn apart and swallowed by the Australians with all the ceremony of a junkyard dog who finds a stray bit of sausage. The Wallabies that day played technically excellent rugby to beat England 40-15, in what Bob Dwyer later described as 'the best 80 minutes of rugby I have ever seen an Australian team play . . .'

Again John was at the very least one-fifteenth of that success. In the lineouts, in the absence of Wade Dooley who had been injured in the previous game and was prevented from taking the field, meaning that Eales went up in the lineouts against all 6 feet 10 inches of Martin Bayfield. This was the first time in John's adult years he found himself jumping against someone significantly bigger than him — but still it presented no problem. Again, the youngster dominated the lineouts; again he was extraordinarily active around the field both in terms of making and breaking tackles.

John had in fact been so outstanding that the legendary All Black second-rower Colin Meads, who had seen the game, was moved to predict:

'[Eales] could be anything, and a force at this level for ten years.'

The post-Test function that night with the English team was at the Manly Pacific Hotel, and was as good as the one with Wales at Ballymore had been bad. On that occasion the Welsh had started fighting between themselves as to who was most to blame for the debacle — even to the point that a glass had been broken in the fracas — but here, with the English, it was all good friends and jolly good comp-a-ny until very late that night. In classic fashion, John sat next to Brian Moore, the English forward who had been the most aggressive on the field, but who was now charm itself. In the ongoing celebrations, members of both sides smoked the cigars with pink ribbons around them that Nick Farr-Jones had brought with him to celebrate his wife Angela giving birth to their first baby, Jessica, just three days previously.

Sitting at midnight, drinking and smoking the cigars in a hugely convivial atmosphere with men from the other side of the world he had just hours previously been going at hammer and tongs, beside countrymen and friends whom he deeply respected, John felt a strong sense that if this was international rugby, give him more of it.

JACK Eales could hear them talking sometimes. Now installed as principal of St William's school which all his children had attended, every now and then he would overhear one or other of his students point him out in awed tones as he passed. 'The principal is John Eales' *father.*' Often as not, the wonder in their voice was enough to make Jack laugh in spite of himself. Even some of his teachers were not immune, bringing John up in conversation, wondering how he was getting on, and so on. For the first time in his life, Jack was asked questions as if his opinions on rugby were worth listening to. Did Jack think the Wallabies would win the Bledisloe Cup? The World Cup?

Jack, frankly, didn't know, but was honoured to be asked.

BACK. Way back. Way back when, in the Land of the Long White Cloud, a fearsome race of warriors had developed a war-cry designed to turn their opponents to water even before the battle had begun, a thing known as the haka. Time and again the raiding parties of the warrior chief Te Rauparaha had used the haka to singular effect, most particularly when challenging the Maori tribes of the South Island.

While those warriors had long since departed, the spirit of their cry had been passed on, from generation to generation until in the latter part of the twentieth century, the rights to use it before battle had arrived in the souls of the land's then greatest warriors — the All Blacks.

And now, at the SFS, on 10 August, John Eales was finally facing them . . .

The mighty All Black no. 8, Zinzan Brooke, led the cry, the veins in his neck seeming to pulsate in unison with his bulging eyes as he screamed it out: '*Ka mate! / Ka mate! / Ka Ora / Ka Ora / Tenei te tangata puhuruhuru / Nana nei i tiki mai / I whakawhite te ra / Upane / Upane / Upane / Ka Upane / Whiti te ra!*'(It is death / It is death / It is life / It is life / This is the hairy person / Who caused the sun to shine / Abreast / Keep abreast / The rank / Hold fast / Into the sun that shines.)

It was as powerful a feeling as he'd known before a match to that point — the air all around John seemed to *vibrate* — but he followed the advice of the other Wallabies and simply stared evenly back at the New Zealanders, using their cry to build his own adrenalin. It worked, and as he lined up for the kick-off it felt like he had more adrenalin than blood in his veins. John's crash course in the ways of international rugby were continuing apace. A month previously, in his first Test, he had been dipping his toe into the waters of international rugby. Against the English he had gone in boots and all. Here, though, his body and soul were being hurled around in the unending rugby storm.

By some measures, one of the cruellest places on earth is at the bottom of an All Black ruck, described by one of John's predecessors in the Australian second-row as 'like having a multi-Adidased centipede dancing a jig on your back', and John knew what he meant. Round and round in a washing machine with a thousand boots was another way of looking at it, but any way you described it, nothing could quite convey the sheer physical toughness of a collective All Black pack. On this day, John in particular had something of a point to prove up against the All Blacks. For clearly, not everyone in New Zealand had acknowledged his arrival on the representative rugby scene with respect.

'Against me,' the great All Black second-rower Andy Haden had been quoted as saying, when Eales had first started to attract attention in New Zealand earlier in the season, 'he would last three lineouts.'

If Haden meant that someone built like John was always going to be vulnerable to a little well-placed nefariousness — and he had — well, it was hardly surprising. Playing each rugby nation offers different challenges, and against the All Blacks of that era, mere survival was one of them. Against a forward pack composed of such characters as Richard Loe, Steve McDowell and Alan Whetton, young Eales was always going to be tested. As it happened, he turned in his finest game for the Wallabies to that point, constantly outleaping his more experienced opponent, Ian Jones, and being equally busy around the field, particularly in terms of tackling. Around and about John, the Wallabies also turned in a singularly fine performance.

Opposing them that day was five-eighth Grant Fox, who would ever afterwards retain a clear memory of this Test. For in his entire career, it was the only time he felt powerless on a football field. To him, that day, everything the Wallabies did was so precise, so clinical, so strong, he had a strange kind of feeling that there was nothing the All Blacks could do to stop them. At its worst, it felt like they were a bunch of corks being hurled around on the Wallabies' storming ocean.

When the smoke had cleared the Wallabies were the victors by the singularly handsome score of 21-10 and they did a victory lap of the SFS, where their every step was cheered to the echo by the tightly packed crowd. More than merely the score, though, it was the way the Wallabies had played, the variety of skills they brought to the party and the way these skills so neatly dovetailed with each other that had so thrilled their supporters. For sheer toughness, the front-row of Ewen McKenzie, Phil Kearns and Tony Daly was rightly receiving rave reviews from around the world. They were the foundation stone on which the whole forward pack was built and had never buckled. Beyond that there was the extraordinary athleticism of Eales, the explosiveness of Willie Ofahengaue (sometimes nicknamed 'Often-Has-A-Go' by the Wallabies), the leadership of Farr-Jones, the precision of Lynagh, combination of Horan 'n' Little, sheer genius of Campese and so on. Even allowing for that, the sum of the parts was greater than the whole.

Up in Brisbane, John's old friend and team-mate Rupert McCall switched off the set, still shaking his head in wonder. For the last few weeks everyone had been raving about what a world-class player John was, and somehow he hadn't quite believed it. After all, only two years previously John had just been a kid playing Colts with them, and now they were saying he was a *world-beater*!?

It wasn't that familiarity bred contempt, just that it seemed odd when people spoke so breathlessly about John when Rupert knew him so well. Sure he was good, but was he *that* good? So Rupert watched him very closely. Yes he was that good. Up against one of the best teams in the world, he had dominated, all at the age of 21. That said, the happy thing for Rupert and their shared group of friends was that the Wallaby second-rower didn't seem to change at all with his new-found stardom. They kept telling him he did, of course. And telling him he was getting a big head, but as far as they could see, there was simply no change at all. He was the same bloke sharing a room with brother Damian at Arnell St as he'd always been, and though he'd been terrific in helping them get Test tickets, he didn't seem to have any tickets on himself.

AND so to the Wallabies' last Test before heading off to the World Cup in Britain and Ireland. A fortnight after the first Bledisloe Cup encounter of the year, the Australians played a wretchedly muddy international against the All Blacks at Auckland's Eden Park. With just a minute to go and New Zealand holding a 6-3 lead, the Wallabies were awarded a penalty. The game to that point had been miserable, marked by the worst refereeing John had experienced, with Scottish referee Ken McCartney constantly making both teams dance to his whistle. (It would later be worked out that once time for lineouts, scrums and goal-kicks were taken out, there had only been just a little over twelve minutes of unencumbered rugby played in each half.)

All that could be forgotten, though, if Australia could at least salvage a draw.

Alas Lynagh missed, and was predictably devastated. John knew how he felt. As he told Lynagh later, exactly the same thing had happened to him for the Ashgrove U/10As. Still for the first time, just four Tests into his career, Eales now knew what it was like to lose one. Bad. Awful. Gnawing.

Hopefully it wouldn't happen again that year.

The 1991
World Cup

*The Wallabies brought charm, class and
natural humour to the 1991 World Cup. They were not
unsmiling giants, nor noisome braggarts.*

DON CAMERON, *New Zealand Herald*,
November 1991

*It's a bit sad. Our quaint little old game played in the
corner paddock is now gone forever.*

BOB DWYER, Swansea, 30 September 1991, at the
beginning of the Rugby World Cup

⤳

NICK FARR-JONES plopped himself on the seat beside John in
the bus and they chatted briefly about the dinner they were heading
to which would mark the formal opening of the 1991 World Cup.

'The alicadoos will be everywhere,' Nick said, 'more alicadoos than
you've ever seen in your life, and one or two citrons, but it should be a
great jowl at least, and a great occasion. Still, I don't think we should be
out too late. Everyone is going to need as much kippage as we can get
after the trip, even the dirties and dirty-dirties . . . '

Just four months ago John would have understood very little of such
a conversation, but now, after three months with the Wallabies, he comprehended most of the special language they used. 'Alicadoos', he now knew

were also called the 'blazer brigade', as in the rugby officials who abounded at such rugby occasions, often outnumbering the players. 'Citrons' was French for lemons and Wallaby English for rugby bores who wanted to tell you about the try they scored back in 1956 in the north-west corner of Eden Park. 'A great jowl' was a good feed, 'kippage' was sleep, 'the dirties' were the reserves for the first game, and the 'dirty-dirties' were those players who weren't even on the bench. He was getting there!

A few nights before the opening game of the tournament, the World Cup Organising Committee were hosting a dinner for all sixteen international teams at London's Royal Lancaster Hotel, together with all their alicadoos, sponsors, etc. When they got there, John looked around in amazement. In the glittering vast ballroom there were 1300 people, all resplendent in their finest formal wear, while each of the 130 tables had a veritable bushfire of candles throwing up a gentle flickering light towards the equally soft glow coming from the dripping crystal chandeliers above.

The set-up was in microcosm typical of the kind of *looxury* they'd experienced since first settling into their magnificent estate set on 100 hectares of greenery at Middlesex, owned by the Shell Oil Company. Clearly, there was a lot of money swirling around for this tournament. Already the projections were that this World Cup would generate ten times more money than the inaugural Cup four years previously. In terms of Australian currency, roughly $83 million would be flowing into rugby's coffers, by virtue of some $30 million in ticket sales, $24 million in world television and subsequent video rights, and a whopping $16 million in sponsorship with seven major sponsors paying between $1.6 million and $2 million each. The rest was made up through merchandising and licensing agreements, corporate hospitality, and travel and tours. No, the players weren't receiving a single cent of the proceeds — apart from the $50 a day travel allowance that each was allowed, *yippee!* — but that wasn't really an issue. It was still terrific to be part of such a world-class event, so praise the Lord and pass the wine. And a very fine wine it was too . . .

With that many people in the one room, and that many candles, it was a very hot, very closed atmosphere, and a lot of the teams had taken their coats off and loosened their ties. Yet for the first part of the evening the Wallabies to a man kept their navy blazers on and ties done up. Again, as John had come to understand, they were observing yet another unwritten law of the way the Wallabies functioned. On this occasion the unwritten law that applied was that on such formal occasions as this no-one was to remove their coat until the captain gave the nod by removing his. Farr-Jones had decided to keep his on and that was that. Nary a word from anyone in complaint. Besides, at the beginning of the dinner at least there was too much chortling to be done to bother complaining anyway. On the bus the Wallabies had each put five pounds into a collective pot, to have a bet on how many alicadoos there would be on the top table. When it was finally totted up, there no fewer than 44 — a post-war record!

And so it began . . .

By this time Eales felt an increasing sense of comfort in the Wallaby pack — almost as if he belonged there. However, before the first game of the World Cup, against Argentina at Llanelli, Bob Dwyer took him aside and explained he wanted to change all that. He and the selectors had decided they wanted to play him at No. 8. Since Tim Gavin had got injured just before the World Cup, the Wallabies had been searching for an effective replacement for him and Bob thought that John might be the answer.

What could John say? Though the idea didn't fill him with enthusiasm, he was very clearly still a Junior Burger in a team of mostly Big Macs, and the Quarter-Pounder with double cheese had just told him the way it was going to be, however politely he had put it.

'Yes, Bob, that should be fine,' he said.

In fact John wasn't fine. For the first time in his Wallaby career, John struggled in his position, occasionally fumbling the ball at the base of the scrum, and mixing up the calls at crucial moments — even though, happily, the Wallabies came away with a reasonably solid 32-19 win.

Though Farr-Jones had given young Eales a bit of a hard time out on the field on a couple of occasions, lambasting him when the ball went astray, he sympathised with his plight. Trying to take the place of a vastly experienced no. 8 like Tim Gavin — and executing a complicated series of moves in a Test match for the first time — was too much to ask him to try to get his head around in a few days.

In the second of the Wallabies' pool games against, Western Samoa at Pontypool just five days later and played in driving rain, howling wind and horribly gluey mud, the same thing happened. The Wallabies came away with a slim 9-3 win and Dwyer had no choice but to acknowledge the bleeding obvious. 'We recognise the change in the second-row has not

Right: John Eales and
Tim Horan with a
golfer who insisted on
having his photo-
graph taken with
them at a sportsmen's
dinner in 1992.
Eales family collection

Below: With Tim
Gavin and Phil Kearns
after beating South
Africa in Cape
Town, 1992.
Eales family collection

Showing what might have been, when playing in a testimonial match for Carl Rackemann at ANZ Stadium in 1994. Ray Phillips is behind the stumps. *Eales family collection*

John with Wallaby manager Peter Falk and coach Bob Dwyer in Sydney, July 1995.
Photo: Col Whelan © Action Photographics

All present and correct. For the first time as captain John Eales runs an eye over his troops during the National Anthem. Australia vs Wales 1st Test, Ballymore, June 8th 1996. Garrick Morgan is second on John's left. *Photo: Colin Whelan © Action Photographics*

With Chris White, Brian Lara and Rupert McCall at a function to welcome the West Indies cricket team to Brisbane in 1996. *Eales family collection*

Right: Accepting an award from Merv Hazell, the 'keeper of the Brothers' torch', in 1996. *Eales family collection*

Below: John and Wallaby manager Peter Falk meet the Queen at Buckingham Palace, October 1996. *Eales family collection*

Singing 'Advance Australia Fair' before playing the second Test against Wales at Sydney Football Stadium, 1996. *Photo: Adrian Short*

John touches down for his disallowed (double movement) try. during Australia vs NZ Bledisloe Cup at the MCG, July 1997. *Photo: Colin Whelan © Action Photographics*

Right: Nonna with the famous statuette of Saint Anthony.
Photo: Rene Marcel, Impulse Images

Below: John with his mother Rosa, 1997.
Photo: David Kapernick © Courier Mail

Six-year-old leukaemia patient, Haylea Sargeant, helps kick off the 1997 Leukaemia Doorknock Appeal with Olympic gold medallist Duncan Armstrong. *Photo courtesty Leukaemia Foundation*

John makes a break from Canterbury Crusaders Paula Bale in the Super 12 match at Lancaster Park, Christchurch, May 1997. *Photo: Ross Setford ©Fotopress / Action Photographics*

Wallaby coach Greg Smith with his captain in 1996. © *Duif du Toit / Touchline Photo / Action Photographics*

been positive for the team,' the coach told the Australian rugby press. 'We want to get back to the form we had in Australia.'

In short, John would be returned to his favourite position of second-rower. For the record, and though unbeknown to John at the time, the one person who thought he'd had a couple of *amazingly* good games was Nonna back in Australia, who stayed up with the family each night to watch the action. This was probably because she used a different measuring stick as to what a 'good game' consisted of.

Her own ready-reckoner was how many times her John showed up on screen in close-up. She particularly liked national anthems, because that was where it was guaranteed that they'd show John in all his glory. Tries? Wasn't interested, unless John scored them and the camera would swoop in close. Great tackles? No interest unless John was the one making them — and *outrage* if he was the one being tackled. And for her, the best thing about him playing at No. 8 was that every time the Wallabies set a scrum she could see him, right there at the back, instead of being lost somewhere in the forest of thighs.

In his time away from training and playing, John tended to stick close to his fellow Queensland forward, Bobby Nasser. Bobby attended Queensland Uni, where he was studying dentistry and at all times, bar when he had football boots on, had a gentle nature similar to John's. Both were very popular members of the team, while also a bit off-centre from the rest. When many of the Wallabies went out to nightclubs, John and Bobby would go off to play pool. When a group was being formed up to go and have a drink, John and Bobby might instead go to see a local tourist attraction.

Everywhere the Wallabies travelled during that World Cup, as with most tours, the locals put things on, offering to take players to local cultural attractions and the like, but most players dropped out of such activities after a while. John Eales and Bobby Nasser used to go. If there was a 7 a.m. call to be on the bus if you wanted to go and see the local cardigan factory, they'd be on it. Another two who'd often be on that same bus were the team doctor, John Moulton, and Bob Dwyer, who was always interested in what rugby tours had to offer beyond mere rugby.

So it was that the Australian coach happened to be with John when they went to see the Pontarddulais Male Choir singing a special session to welcome the Wallabies in Swansea. For an hour they sang as one, and their haunting hymns completely spellbound their audience. Dwyer noticed John had tears in his eyes throughout. As they left, John turned to the coach and said with some feeling, 'That was one of the best experiences of my life.'

THE final of the pool games was in Cardiff, against Wales, and John was impatient for the kick-off to the point where he was practically counting the hours. Three days before the match, on the day they arrived in the Welsh capital, the Wallaby second-rower could practically sense it before he actually saw it . . .

Cardiff Arms Park. It was close, he knew. And when the Wallaby bus took a left on Ninian Park Road, the famous brooding contours of the world's most famous rugby ground revealed themselves. For a few moments, John was something very close to awe-struck.

As they walked around to familiarise themselves with the ground, John went a little off on his own, soaking it all up. The green, green grass seemed to have a dreamy, silky quality to it, while the towering walls of the rugby cathedral which crowded all around appeared to reach to the heavens. The atmosphere of the place was simply stunning.

One of the problems in the 48 hours before truly big matches was to know quite what to do with yourself in the time between training, eating and sleeping. Totally frivolous pursuits were out, as was anything too physically tiring, which tended to cut down one's options. On this occasion, John passed a fair measure of his down-time in his room, reading. One of the things that fascinated him was the British press and the amount of coverage they were giving to this World Cup. Back in Brisbane, rugby coverage was consigned to the sports pages, squeezed in behind the myriad articles on rugby league, but here, for this occasion, rugby seemed to be all through the papers all the time, even on things that had *nothing* to do with the game itself.

In the lead-up to the Welsh Test, for example, John was amused to read a two page feature article in London's *Daily Mail*, 'Will Carling ever find a girl to make him happy?' The lantern-jawed English captain Will Carling told the paper that the bane of his life was being stalked by females and that his 'sack load of raunchy fan mail was a sick joke'. (Welllll, for John's part, he had at least recently received an enormous G-string sent to him anonymously in the post, but he always suspected that was from

Patrick McGrath so it didn't really count.) An unidentified team-mate of Carling's was quoted: 'Of course, after a big match we let our hair down, Will included, but he actually doesn't really like to drink, and as for women, he's too intelligent and conscious of press interest in him to be caught with some old boiler of a barmaid in his hotel bedroom.'

DIANA, Princess of Wales. The word spread around the Wallabies quick-smart. The rumour was correct. She really *was* going to be there at their game against Wales, and the team was to be presented to her beforehand. She was said to have had a growing interest in rugby, and the entire team was delighted. For if she wasn't necessarily the most beautiful woman in the world, she was certainly the most celebrated, and it was yet another example for John of the extraordinary kinds of things that rugby turned up for you. Come the game proper, it was all just as he had imagined, if even a little better. As the Wallabies ran out onto the ground, some 60,000 Welsh sang in heart-breaking unison their amazing hymns.

The team was indeed presented to Princess Diana, introduced to her by Farr-Jones one by one as they were lined up and it all left at least one Wallaby feeling overwhelmed. John. This was someone whom he had seen hundreds of times on television and covers of magazines his sisters bought, without really having thought a whole lot about her. She had looked quite attractive, but no more than that. Now, though, he thought she was far and away the most beautiful woman he had ever seen.

Down, Tiger. Further impressing John, and surprising him, was Princess Diana's firm handshake. He had expected a dainty little pressing of the flesh, but instead she gave a very firm grip and looked him right in the eyes, nearly half a foot above her. He in turned looked her right in the eyes — about the bluest he'd ever seen — and also noted her extraordinary peaches and cream complexion. He could barely speak, but got out something along the lines of 'Pleased to meet you, ma'am'. As he later told the boys back in Brisbane, 'She was just so *amazingly* stunning'.

Down, Tiger!

ALL up, John was in the mood to play rugby as never before, and proceeded to do exactly that. Back in the familiar territory of the second-row on such a stage as this, he exploded. Apart from an extraordinarily high work rate, with many charging runs and crashing tackles, he and Rod

McCall won the lineouts by the unheard of margin of 28-2, including 18-1 in the first half. International rugby had never seen the like, never witnessed such total domination by one team over another in one facet of play — at least not against a major rugby nation.

The Wallabies ran out easy winners, 38-3 — ensuring that their next game would be in the World Cup quarter-finals against Ireland at Dublin's Lansdowne Road. In the dressing room afterwards, the euphoria was near total, with one notable exception. Amid all the cheering, *whoop-de-whoop* and carrying on, the president of the Australian Rugby Union, 'Smoking' Joe French, was to be seen huddled away in a corner, furiously sucking on a succession of Benson & Hedges cigarettes. As the famously wizened Joe had been sitting next to the Princess of Wales in the Royal Box throughout the match, it had been out of the question for him to smoke for the previous two hours, and he was now endeavouring to catch up.

'Did you enjoy the game, Joe?' the Wallabies' assistant forward coach Jake Howard enquired of him.

'Yes,' Joe growled after another long drag on his cigarette.

'Was it nice to sit next to as beautiful a woman as Princess Di?'

'Yeahhhh,' Joe finally conceded after one more long draw, 'but she knows f--- all about rugby.'

IN all the accolades that landed on the Wallabies in the wake of their performance, no-one received more plaudits than the young Australian second-rower. Bob Dwyer was quoted in the British press describing Eales as 'close to being the most significant person in world rugby'. This was less because of his performance in that one Test than the body of his play throughout the year, but Eales could barely believe such extravagant praise. Naturally though, the British press took aim at Dwyer's statement. The most influential and respected rugby journalist in Britain was Stephen Jones of the *Sunday Times* and typically, he did not mince words. 'The Australian John Eales,' he wrote, 'has recently been described by his coach Bob Dwyer as "close to being the most significant person in world rugby." In my view Dwyer is wrong. There is nothing close about it. Eales will win the World Cup for Australia unless he is neutralised in the lineout and . . . in the quarter-final in Dublin, Francis and his minders have the first try.'

The aforementioned Neil Francis was a likeable sort of rugby troubadour who had played all over the world, but was now back in the home country to stiffen up the Irish pack and jump against the likes of Eales. For his part, he was in no doubt about the prospects for the quarter-final against Australia, and he let everyone know it.

'What we need,' he was quoted in the press as saying, 'is 50,000 Paddys, dressed in green and singing their heads off. And rain. Anything can happen if it lashes down. We're capable of doing something really stupid. Like winning.'

Funny he should say that. For in the lead-up to the game the rain had indeed pelted down, making the ground very slippery, and with just six minutes to go Australia was tenuously holding onto a 15-12 lead when the Irish flanker Gordon Hamilton broke through a David Campese tackle and ran 60 metres to score in the corner. The situation, as General Custer once remarked, was looking pretty grim. On the edge of the abyss, against an Irish team just minutes from an historic victory in front of 50,000 of their own, the only way out for the Wallabies was to score again themselves and . . .

And it is absurd the thoughts that can pop into your head at the damnedest of times. Despite the seriousness of the situation, John had the passing trivial thought that if they really were on a plane back to Australia as soon as the following morning — as Dwyer had warned them would happen if they lost — he would be unable to retrieve a favourite shirt that he had just put through the hotel's laundry system. For some reason it was the first thing that came to mind.

Others were having entirely different thoughts. For the Eales clan at that time, gathered around the television back in Arnell Street, it seemed just possible that Nonna had been right all along. She had *always* pin-pointed Ireland as the most likely side to beat the Wallabies, on the simple reckoning that as they and their family and friends were strongly Roman Catholic, the Irish would have the full power of prayer behind them. Nonna had done everything she could to match this power — praying night and day for John's team to win — but at this moment the look on her face said that she thought the game was up. Meanwhile Patrick McGrath, who had returned to Marist Brothers Ashgrove as a boarding master, was so sure that the Wallabies would lose he told his fellow masters crowded close to the TV set that he would do a nude lap of the school if Australia won from here.

Back at Lansdowne Road, Michael Lynagh was taking command. Nick Farr-Jones had been injured early in the game, so it was the Wallaby five-eighth who now lay down the law. Leading the team away from the scene of the tragedy — the spot where Hamilton had put the ball down — he gathered his thoughts.

'How long to go?' he asked the referee. 'Four minutes, after the conversion,' came the reply. Easily long enough to work a miracle if the whole team kept together and stuck to it. In a calm voice, Lynagh then spoke to the Wallaby huddle in concise, clear terms: 'Be calm and controlled. There's still plenty of time left. From the kick-off we will kick the ball long and to the left. The forwards must secure clean possession and we'll go from there. If ever in doubt about what to do with the ball, just hold it tightly and head towards their line. We *will win* this game.'

To a 't'. Two minutes later, from a Wallaby scrum in Ireland's half, Lynagh called to his backs to execute a move by the name of Cut Two Loop. Then, from halfback Peter Slattery's pass, the Wallaby pivot sent the ball out on its appointed course before doubling around in support. The ball found its way through the hands of Tim Horan, Marty Roebuck and Jason Little to David Campese on the wing. The last, though hit by two Irish defenders, managed to bounce back inside a Hail Mary pass to keep the ball alive. Hovering right there for just such a ball was Lynagh, who gathered and burrowed his way forward . . .

TRY! They say you could hear the silence from three kilometres away, in the all-but-deserted streets of downtown Dublin. Such was the momentary stunned shock that a dog barking in the park beside Lansdowne Road was clearly audible. Up in the ABC broadcasting box, commentators Gordon Bray, Gary Pearce and Chris Handy said absolutely nothing, allowing the eloquence of the stillness full play.

Shortly afterwards, the full-time whistle came like the water to a man in the desert who was on the edge of extinction. As one, the Wallabies simply sagged, weak with relief, but if they thought they had done it tough out on the field, the tearful white faces of the reserves bench and the injured Farr-Jones awaiting them was a clear indication that it was the dirties and the dirty-dirties who had done it the toughest.

All of them, John noted, looked like they had just seen a ghost, and were hugging the players coming off the field with thanks that they'd finished the job. Most passionate in his gratitude to John was the back-up five-eighth, David Knox, who was one of only two Wallabies not to take the field during the tournament and who had been availing himself of other nocturnal pleasures meantime.

'For a moment,' he told John, as he warmly pumped his hand, 'I thought my night-club tour of Ireland and Britain was over!'

All of the Wallabies were knocked out in the immediate aftermath of the match by how good-hearted the Irish were in defeat. Everywhere they went that night — and they did indeed go everywhere — men and women were coming up to them and wishing them well. Part of this, as they admitted, was because if the Wallabies won the World Cup they might still claim to be the second best team in the world, but there also seemed to be a natural affinity between the Australians and the Irish, as there has been since the Wallabies first began to tour there.

The happiest of all things for the Wallabies was that they didn't have to jump straight onto a plane and go to another city, but could stay there among such terrific people. This was a great luxury, because so much of rugby touring is the actual physical 'touring' part, which can be so exhausting when all you really want to do is stop in the one spot. For all of them there was nowhere that they would rather have stopped than in Dublin. And for the Irish, it seemed, there was no team they would have rather had stay there. At the very least, it certainly wasn't the All Blacks . . .

An article in the *Irish Independent*, in the week leading up to their semi-final against the All Blacks set the tone. 'MEN OF STONE, HEARTS OF STEEL' ran the headline, above a byline of the well-known local rugby writer Vincent Hogan.

'Reassuringly,' he began, 'they rolled into town with all the charm-lessness of old . . . Frowns of stone, eyes glazed with frosty indifference, All Black teams have never been known for courting niceties. They carry themselves with all the gaiety of gravediggers . . . What is it about these doleful souls from the southern hemisphere? How can they be so dour, so cold, so colourless when their Australian neighbours survive just as imperiously by extending the hand of friendship? New Zealand's rugger men strut and scowl and generally imply a superior presence. It is as though, in their hostile silence, they are reminding you that God wears a black shirt.'

This contrast between the open and friendly approach of the Wallabies and the more closed approach of other teams was one that was oft remarked.

Whatever the reasons for it, at least some credit can go to Bob Dwyer. Typical of the tone he helped to set was his frequent reminder to the players that, 'while it might be your 200th autograph for the day, never forget that for the kid in front of you, it's his first'.

In fact, for John it never really was a chore to sign autographs, and he still couldn't get over the fact that people considered his signature worth having. Generally, he loved being out and about among the Dubliners, with one notable exception . . .

As John had learned, on every Wallaby tour between training, travelling and playing commitments, each player was expected to spend time among the public selling such things as Wallaby T-shirts, signed programs and match tickets drawn from the team's allocation to contribute to a tour fund which was divvied up between the players at the end of the tour. To that purpose, John regularly found himself out on Grafton Street, the busy pedestrian mall which neatly bisects the very heart of Dublin, trying to hustle up business. Some guys were very good at this kind of caper, while other guys were like John. Hopeless.

He hated it. He found standing there, raising his eyebrows expectantly at all the hurrying throng as he asked them if they wanted tickets or T-shirts, excruciatingly embarrassing. If they said no, he felt like a loser, and if they said yes he felt grubby, handing over merchandise for money on a busy mall. Never mind. It still had to be done, and there were a lot of Wallabies for whom such money was a lot more than mere cream. It was more like the meat and potatoes with which they could help pay the rent when they got home. On top of the tour allowance, the whole thing could turn into quite a tidy sum.

BUT to the football itself. A sure sign that the Wallaby pack was in the right mood for the coming encounter came on the Tuesday afternoon scrum training session at Trinity College. At one point in the proceedings the selected Test forwards came together with the reserve pack with the usual crashing thump, wrestled with each other for a moment, and then suddenly split apart. From the morass, Rod McCall exploded, shaking with rage and pointing a furious finger at the reserve prop Dan Crowley, accusing him of having gouged his eyes.

Crowley, equally outraged at the accusation, nevertheless made a very telling reply.

'Get !#$&* Slaughter, if I was going to gouge anyone it'd be one of the props! Do you think I'd waste my time gouging *you*?'

It was a fair point, by any measure. McCall had to acknowledge the logic of it, and before long the two packs went back to their practice. The thunder was over, but there was still plenty of lightning around — Simon Poidevin and Phil Kearns narrowly avoiding fisticuffs a short time later — and Bob Templeton loved it. Jake Howard loved it. While John Eales seemed his normal mild-mannered self, there were signs that deep within his psyche he too was building for a big one ...

About 3 o'clock on the following morning, McCall suddenly woke to the sound of shouting and a serious physical struggle going on about one metre from him.

'NGGGGH ... get away ... get ...BACK ... bastard.'

McCall sat bolt upright, switched on the light, and saw a scene he would never forget. It was his room-mate, young Eales, in his jim-jams, standing on the bed engaged in a life and death struggle with the drapes that the old-style hotel had hanging above every bed. From the look of things, Eales was marginally winning the battle, all arms and legs, battering into the heavy fabric, but the proud drapes seemed capable of absorbing his worst punishment and were not falling to his blows. Eales in any case was taking no chances and was now working in tight, wrapping his arms around and squeezing the life out of them, as he even unleashed the odd head-butt.

'Get down ... nnnnngh ... go ... DOWN ... '

And the drapes really might have gone down, but at this point McCall threw in the towel on their behalf.

'John! John! What are you doing?' he shouted. Without a word, John let go of the curtains, looked at Rod a little blankly, climbed back into bed and went to sleep. McCall turned off the light and did likewise.

The following night, it wasn't noise that awoke McCall, it was just a strange presentiment that something was awry. At much the same time, he awoke, fumbled in the darkness for the light switch and turned it on. There was John standing above him and staring intently down, an aggressive look on his face that looked, for all the world, like a lion who was about to leap on a wounded buffalo. The buffalo shouted: 'JOHN!' and it did the trick. Again, the young man got back into bed and went to sleep.

Enough was enough. The following morning McCall tackled him about it. *'What the hell is going on?'*

'Yes,' John replied very mildly, 'apparently I do sleep walk.'

'Apparently!?!?' McCall spluttered. 'You want to go and see someone about it.'

IMMEDIATELY before every Test match in the dressing room, it is usual for each player to be allowed some time to do his own thing. After all the warm-ups are over, the game-plan given a last going-over, the vaseline applied to foreheads so punches are more likely to slide off, and mouth-guards checked, a kind of silence falls upon the team, usually in the period that goes from about ten minutes to five minutes before kick-off. Players fill this time with different things, and it is often an unchanging ritual. Over there in the corner, John saw, David Campese was reading a dog-eared copy of a poem about 'Winners' that his mother had given him years before. In another corner, Tim Horan and Jason Little were in deep consultation, their heads close together, whispering their last-minute plans. There was Tony Daly, disappearing to the toilets for the last of all last-minute ablutions. Phil Kearns was carefully removing from his bag his Australian jersey which he always elaborately folded with the crest facing up. Willie Ofahengaue was praying. On this afternoon before playing the All Blacks, John did what he always did. That is, took off the sandshoes that had sufficed to this point and put on his boots, always the left boot first. In all the nerves and tearing tension, this was for John, as were the rituals of the other players, a kind of sanctuary — the familiar thing you cling to in the rising floodwaters of midnight when the unknown is pressing in from all around. John had begun putting on his left boot first when he had read in a cricket magazine at the age of seven that that is what Greg Chappell did — which was good enough for him — and he had done it ever since.

Left boot on. Right boot on. Double knots for both. Then he took his tiny statue of St Anthony out of his kitbag and held it tightly while he did a little more praying himself.

This practice of carrying a statuette of St Anthony given to him by his mother had begun when John started to go on rugby tours and could no longer observe his ritual at home with Nonna. And for much the same reasons as with the left boot first, it somehow helped focus his mind. In this World Cup semi-final against the All Blacks, he knew he would need every ounce of both his energy and his concentration to get things right.

The knock came on the door, and then they were out there and into it. The massive roar from the Lansdowne Road crowd confirmed their view that the Irish would be fully behind them and not the New Zealanders, something that they all found curiously heartening, and in short order it was *on*.

None was more powerful for the Wallabies that day than David Campese. Six minutes before half-time, from the base of a ruck, Farr-Jones passed the ball to Michael Lynagh, who angled a narrow chip-kick just over the defence, and Campese burst behind the All Black lines in an effort to retrieve it. It was a day when he seemed to have the ball entirely at his command. The leather could have gone anywhere, but instead came swinging back right to the winger as a baby monkey might to its mother's arms — *phwooooomp!* Still the try was far from scored at that stage, as the All Blacks moved quickly to block off the threat. Roaring down the right touchline with the centre Tim Horan inside him, Campese first darted left, then right, then left again, and just at the last possible moment when the New Zealand defence had turned themselves so far inside out that they were ready to tackle him again and were about to do so, he hurled an absolutely impossible pass over his right shoulder, completely blind, to where he assumed Horan was.

Another *phwooooomp!* Another baby monkey. John, following up hard in a desperate effort to get to Campese in support, was momentarily confused as to where the ball had gone. Campo had it, and was covered, and then suddenly Tim had it, but at that instant John couldn't understand how the ball had gone from one to the other. Neither could the New Zealand defence, meaning Horan crossed the line without an All Black hand being laid upon him. TRY! Back home in Australia, at the moment that Horan scored, there was an instantaneous explosion of joy. Not just in the Horan family home or even in the Eales living room where the entire family including St Anthony were glorying in every moment, but far wider than that. In pubs and clubs, family homes and offices across the continent and in many nooks and crannies where rugby had never been seen before, the Wallabies had attracted an enormous following, in much the same way that *Australia II*'s fortunes in the America's Cup eight years earlier had also attracted nationwide joy far beyond normal sailing circles. When the final bell tolled, the Australians were worthy 16-6 victors. It was only the third time the All Blacks had lost a Test match since 1987, and the Wallabies had booked themselves an appearance in the World Cup Final at Twickenham in six days' time. Their opponents would be England, who had near bored Scotland to death in the other semi-final, but they would get to that. First, there was some celebrating to do.

THAT night at the conclusion of a particularly joyous Happy Hour, Bob Dwyer asked permission to say a few words. Permission was reluctantly granted, so long as he kept it brief. His central message was congratulations, but the job wasn't done. 'In six days, you'll be in the final of your lives, a day you will remember forever, and be remembered for forever. We have to prepare professionally for it. We're going to be travelling tomorrow, and training hard for the next five days, so it is very important that you all get a good night's sleep tonight.'

It was a fair point, a good point, a sensible point . . . and ultimately, totally ignored. One didn't thump the All Blacks in a World Cup semi-final every day of the week, and if you couldn't celebrate that wildly, what *could* you celebrate wildly? So it was that, despite Dwyer's words, most of the Wallabies hit Dublin town hard that night, and stuck particularly close to David Campese. This was not because of Campese's sunny personality so much as because wherever Campo was these days, people were buying him champagne, and after the game he had played his bottle never emptied.

WAITER! More Bollinger!

On and on they went, John Eales and Rod McCall included, until the wee-est of all wee hours.

ON their way to England for the lead-up to the final, feeling very seedy, the Wallabies did what they often did on such trips. That is, they read the reviews of their last performance in the papers, handing them around as they went along. After this game it was rightfully — and thankfully, the way John saw it — David Campese who received all the accolades. The *Independent* quoted former Irish five-eighth Tony Ward saying: 'He is the Maradona, the Pele of international rugby all rolled into one. You can't put a value on his importance to the game. He's a breath of fresh air and I think perhaps the greatest player of all time. Without being too soppy, it was an honour to be at Lansdowne Road just to see him perform.'

And that was just one of Campo's more ordinary reviews!

FROM Heathrow International Airport the Wallabies moved to Weybridge in Surrey, where the luxurious Oatlands Park Hotel — once the hunting lodge of King Henry VIII — was situated. Surrounded by woods, gardens and a golf course, it provided exactly the kind of space and fresh air that the Wallabies needed to clear their heads. For, of pressure, there would be plenty.

When the Wallabies turned up for their training session on the Tuesday, they were amazed to see an absolute forest of cameras, microphones and antennae coming from above the heads of what were surely 100 members of the international rugby press. Whereas only nine days previously the attention of the press had been divided between the surviving eight teams, and then three days later between the four survivors, the Wallabies were getting at least 50 per cent of the attention and possibly more.

Nor was it just the press that were showing an interest. At their hotel the faxes of support from Australia were so bountiful that staff had to connect up six specifically devoted machines and all of them were spitting out messages around the clock. In the days leading up to the final, these machines delivered no fewer than 45,000 faxes. Prior to the win over Ireland, the faxes had predominantly been coming from the main rugby communities, but now they were coming from everywhere. On one fax, a woman from Adelaide promised to give her body to the first Wallaby to score a try in the World Cup Final. Another fax informed them that a baby girl who had been born in Melbourne on the day the Wallabies had beaten the All Blacks had been named, quite seriously, Harriet Elizabeth Nicola Farr-Jones Davina Campese Wallaby Geddes.

Beyond those kinds of general faxes, though, John was touched by how many people he hadn't heard from in years were sending him best wishes — some former teachers, an old neighbour, an early coach — and, as with all the other Wallabies, he started to get the sense of how big the whole thing was becoming in Australia. Prime Minister Bob Hawke took a little time out from a fight-to-the-political-death with his former Treasurer Paul Keating to send the team his warmest congratulations on their performance thus far, and his hope that they would do Australia proud by securing the ultimate triumph.

The Eales family also felt the growing excitement in their own understated way. On most occasions, wild horses could not have made any of them claim kinship to the Australian second-rower unless the person they were talking to already knew — for it would have been immodest — but there was at least one exception.

On the Wednesday before the Cup Final, Damian Eales was working at the main Myer store in Brisbane — he was on the lower rungs of a ladder that would take him to high managerial ranks of the retailing business— when he decided to duck down to the television department, where they were showing an edited highlights package of the World Cup, mixed with scenes from training sessions. Up on the screen at the moment he arrived, John was leaping high in the lineout. Bursting with pride, Damian couldn't help himself.

Turning to a female customer who was also standing there, Damian pointed John out and said, 'That's my *brother*.'

In response, the attractive young woman smiled, pointed out the short blond-headed prop standing next to John in the lineouts and said, 'That's my *husband*.'

It was Lisa Crowley, wife of Dan.

At the training session the following day, Crowley also featured large. The media had once again turned out in full force, including around 50 photographers. Just before the training proper began, Crowley took a boomerang from his bag and proceeded to throw it, to the delight of the world press. Just as he caught the first whirring blade, in extremis, the reserve Wallaby hooker David Nucifora called out, 'Hey, Dan, tell them the story of how one of those cut your legs off!'

ON the eve of the World Cup Final, the manager of the Wallabies, John Breen, called John to his room. Breen was a good man, a Brothers Rugby Club man, a Catholic man, and he and Eales had grown close over the course of the year, among other things frequently attending Mass together. On one occasion, Breen had even organised for a priest to come and say Mass for all the Catholic Wallabies including John, Jake Howard and Bobby Nasser. Bob Templeton, though not a Catholic, had also attended, telling the others he thought it a good idea to have all his bases covered. On this occasion, though, John Breen had something else on his mind.

'I thought you might like to call your parents, John,' he said, waving the young man towards the phone, even as he moved towards the door.

It was a typically thoughtful gesture from Breen, as John simply had not had the money to keep in regular telephone contact with home.

In 30 seconds he was through, and even at a distances of 15,000 kilometres, the excitement from Arnell Street buzzed clearly out of the handpiece. The phone has been ringing off the hook from everyone wishing you well, John, it's just been amazing, they said. After talking to Bernadette, Damian, Rosaleen and Antoinette, the phone was passed to Rosa, Nonna and Jack. As John would always remember it, the last words of each were . . .

Rosa: 'Good night, make sure you say your prayers tonight, John. St Anthony will look after you.'

Nonna. 'Oh, John, John, bring home the world, John. Win. Win. Win.'

Jack: 'Make sure you *enjoy* it, John.'

IT was the afternoon of 2 November 1991. And Twickenham was in their cross-hairs. The mood on the Wallaby bus was one of steely resolution. All the training had been done, all the fine points worked on, all the moves calibrated and checked one last time, all the speeches made and faxes read. Now it was time to get on with it, as the bus nosed its way into the famous Twickenham Western Car Park, past the literally thousands of people lunching out of the boots of their Jaguars, Daimlers and Rolls-Royces, nibbling their chicken drumsticks, sipping their wine and chatting merrily away beneath gaily flapping English flags showing the Cross of St George.

Before the game, John once again felt slightly unreal walking out on to the hallowed turf of his childhood dreams. It was as well, too, that he felt Carmel there with him, to calm him.

Somehow, the fact that the team was to be presented to the Queen had almost been lost in the lead-up to the game — there hadn't been nearly as much discussion about it as there had been about Princess Di, for some reason — but fifteen minutes before the game, there she was, walking along the line and being introduced by Nick Farr-Jones to each team member.

When it came John's turn, he simply reached a long way down to shake her hand and said, 'Pleased to meet you, Ma'am,' but his mind was already whirring on the task at hand. He was actually thinking of the words of Bob Dwyer six days previously: 'Whatever happens, this is a day you will remember forever, and be remembered for *forever*'.

Too true. John's own thoughts, just ten minutes before kick-off, were that this was a moment of destiny, a turn in the road where the team had to go either one way or the other. Either they would be 'World Champions!' or 'the guys who made the World Cup Final but couldn't cut it . . . '

As the Wallabies ran out onto the field for the game proper, John looked around, saw the pressing crowd, the television cameras, the colour; heard all the cheering, soaked up all the atmosphere, and thought, 'This, *this* is a World Cup Final. I really will remember this all my life.'

Just before the whistle blew, he looked at Nick Farr-Jones, who was smiling. John smiled too. This really was what it was all about.

The whistle blew. At the Brothers Club, where so many of John's rugby mates were gathered, a mighty cheer went up. They were minus one Patrick McGrath, who was watching the game from his hospital bed, having caught his near death of cold a fortnight previously while completing his nude run around Marist Brothers Ashgrove. Meanwhile, far, far to their north, at a goldmine called Camel Creek in deep north Queensland, John's old backyard rugby opponent, Mick Stower, now a surveyor, was still adjusting the rabbit ears on the old television set, trying to squeeze out the best possible image from the grainy reception.

'I *know* John Eales,' he told the disbelieving miners. 'I used to play football with him in the backyard!' Yes, Mick, shut up, Mick, let us watch the bloody game!

AND there was a turn-up for the books. Instead of the English grinding out their usual stultifyingly safe game — constantly angling for field position through a kicking game, and hoping to win through penalty goals — they spread the ball wide, tried to *run* their way to the line. Conversely, through sterling English tackling, the Wallabies were not able to spread the ball wide nearly as much as they had hoped. It was 24 minutes before David Campese was even able to get his hands on the ball and go for a bit of a run and even then the English, to their credit, were all over him.

A few minutes later, though, the breakthrough. After a wonderful Tim Horan kick and chase, the ball had been carried over the sideline by the English fullback Jonathan Webb, giving Australia the throw only five metres out. To this point, much of the lineout ball had been directed to John and he had been gaining his usual bountiful supply. Clearly, he was the most obvious candidate to get it again in such a pressure situation, so the Australian pack tried a variation. The plan was that John would jump forward bringing all the scrabbling English hands with him, while for the first time in the entire tournament the ball would be called to Willie Ofahengaue standing in the line-up just behind John. If it all went according to plan, Willie would be substantially alone, unmarked and the surprise recipient of the ball.

It worked. John went forward, right in the middle of a mobile cat-fight, while Willie leaped high and safely brought the ball down into the middle of the driving Australian pack. *Heave-ho me hearties*, for treasure is near at hand, and so it proved. In the middle of the maul, the Wallaby props Tony Daly and Ewen McKenzie had control of the ball and when they were safely over the line fell down upon it for a try. (And the afore-mentioned woman from Adelaide who had promised her body to the first Wallaby try-scorer? No-one ever heard from her again.)

The try was converted by Michael Lynagh and, added to his previous penalty goal, it gave Australia a 9-0 lead at half-time.

To John as for all the Wallabies, half-time was a chance to have a rest, catch your breath, and then go again. The mood was fairly confident, but wary of the English who had played very well . . . and it proved to be a wariness well-placed. For straight after the break it seemed as if someone had thrown the switch to send the English forwards into high gear, so quickly did they begin to dominate proceedings, and the Wallabies sud-denly had to move into continuous tackle mode. John and Rod McCall attracted a slew of penalties against them in the lineouts, even though to their mind they weren't doing anything that the English weren't doing. A penalty apiece for Michael Lynagh and Jonathan Webb brought the scores to 12-3. With another English penalty goal to make it 12-6, and precious little time to go, it seemed to many as if the match must surely go into overtime, for the English forwards were now winning so much ball that a try seemed a probability.

For John, the fog of total exhaustion was rolling in, starting to cloud his perceptions. It was seriously hard to think straight, to understand everything that was happening when all you could feel was that you needed more air in your lungs and more blood in your legs. Through it all though, while in the middle of broken play, he could still perceive that something had happened. Something urgent!

Right under the bristling guns of the English defensive line, Michael Lynagh tried an entirely uncharacteristic loop-de-loop with David Campese and the ball spilled loose. Jeremy Guscott swooped like a vulture on a stray baby rabbit, plucked it and raced towards the line. In cover defence, the Wallaby full-back Marty Roebuck hurled himself at Guscott to bring him down, but not before the English centre was able to hoik a pass inside to his five-eighth, Rob Andrew, who had only daylight between him and the line just 25 metres away.

This looked like a job for . . . Super John!

Operating in the realms of desperate instinct rather than conscious thought, Eales set off after Rob Andrew, in these, the last exhausting minutes of his 40th match of the year. What chance he, of catching him? For Phil Kearns, running about fifteen metres behind John, it never occurred to him that he could. From the moment he saw Rob Andrew get through, and saw where John was, he thought, 'That's it, we're back to 12-all.'

Somehow though, impossibly, before Kearns' very eyes, Eales — who was once told by his father that he was probably too slow for international rugby — ate up the ground between him and the English five-eighth. He ran as fast as his legs could fly, faster than he'd once run away from Nonna on his way back from preschool, faster than the time he stole the neighbours' milk money, faster than he'd run away from the Army Reserve, quite possibly faster than he'd ever run before. He hurled himself at Rob Andrew's ankles, *just* managing to bring him down about five metres from the line. The rest of the Wallaby cavalry closed in and the day was saved.

Only a couple of minutes later, it was over. The whistle blew and they had won. Oddly enough, the overwhelming feeling John experienced was not joy, not rhapsody, not rapture. It was relief. Simple, sweet relief, that after everything they had been through, they hadn't blown it. He threw his arms in the air in triumph and then hugged the closest Wallaby to him, Tony Daly, before the team gathered in a kind of freewheeling communal hug. The English were swift and gracious in their own congratulations, including Rob Andrew, who shook John's hand with a grin and a mock rueful shake of his head.

From there, the Wallabies finally formed a single file to climb up into the stands where Farr-Jones received the World Cup from the Queen.

Following on, each of them received a medallion before lifting the Cup themselves and acknowledging the endless cheers. See, Mick Stower, old tackling play-mate in the backyard at Arnell Street? John did get to lift a gold cup, after all!

The Wallabies then deliriously made their way back to the dressing room. John sank to the benches in sheer exhaustion, but was not allowed to stay off his feet long, as he was summoned by his team-mates to stand and do a loud, proud rendition of 'Advance Australia Fair' as the World Cup was passed from hand to hand and filled with champagne, with at least as much again going down their jerseys. After much back-slapping, warm hugs and pumping handshakes, there was a spontaneous cry taken up of 'Phil Kearns, world champion! Tony Daly, world champion! John Eales, world champion!' as they all pointed to the various players one after the other.

In the corner, a beaming Bob Dwyer was holding court with the few Australian pressmen allowed into the room before the general news conference was held later.

'You tell me,' Dwyer was saying, his head shaking with much the same resonance as the rest of him, 'how does a 6 foot 7 inch second-rower run down a fleet-of-foot fly-half like Rob Andrew? As long as I live, I'll never know.'

In far off Athens, meantime, a man was dancing on the rooftops, crying out his joy, for reasons unknown to the neighbours. It was Basil the fruiterer, back home in Greece for a brief visit — and he had just heard the news over the Greek radio. He was a very, very happy man, saying joyously to his bemused, elderly father in Greek: '*E omatha Rugby apo tin Australia kerthise to pankosmio kipelo, kai o kaliteros pehtis ergazotan yia mena! Xero poly kala ti mana kai ton patera tou. Einai eva poly kalo pai-the o Tzionis!*' (The rugby team from Australia has won the World Cup, and their best player used to work for me! I know his mother and father very well! He is a very good boy, Johnny-boy!)

Meanwhile, equally excited was thirteen-year-old Rosaleen Eales, still struggling to get to sleep back in Arnell Street two hours after the victory.

'The whole family was just so happy,' she told her schoolfriends and teachers on Monday morning, 'and the phone never stopped ringing. It took John about an hour before he could get through to us, and we all had a few words with him. Dad kept saying, "Well done, John".'

At the World Cup dinner that night, John received many handshakes, congratulations and slaps on the back from the rugby people gathered from all over the world who were genuinely delighted at both the Wallabies' success and the part that John had played in it. One gesture, though, touched him particularly. Nearing the end of the dinner, the co-coach of the All Blacks, John Hart, came up to John, shook his hand, took off his treasured All Black tie and gave it to him.

'I gave him the All Black tie as a gesture for what I saw him do that day,' Hart later explained. 'He is one of the greatest players of all time.'

Somewhere around midnight, John found himself in a corner of the hotel ballroom, with ten of the biggest men there, to a man international second-rowers. Their doyen was the All Black captain Gary Whetton, and together with the likes of Ian Jones, Rod McCall, Wade Dooley, Paul Ackford, Doddie Weir and Damian Cronin they drank two toasts: To rugby! And to second-rowers around the world! John knocked back both toasts with the best of them, of whom he was now one. 1991 had been a very good year.

Two days later, Jack Eales was walking down Queen Street, Brisbane, when he ran into one of his old school-mates, a man who had been an accomplished footballer and who had raised his son with high hopes that he might go all the way. Though he was good-hearted about it, this fellow quickly enough came to the point.

'What I can't understand, Jack,' the cove said frankly, 'is how *you*, of all people, have a son who is so damn good!'

Frankly, Jack didn't understand it either, but he was happy enough for all that.

The Aftermath

Dearest John,
I am so proud of you, please St Anthony and our lady of St Carmel,
all my saints hear my prayer for my adorable John,
Love, Nonna xx

Card from John's grandmother after the World Cup win.

I'm still not happy. Queensland lost to NSW, Brothers didn't win the
A Grade premiership and Australia didn't win the Bledisloe Cup last season.
I would feel unfulfilled much as I have enjoyed the experience . . .
I can't see myself playing into my thirties and I won't be playing golden
oldies, you can be sure of that.

JOHN EALES, quoted in the *Courier-Mail*, 15 December 1991

❧

THE ACCOLADES John had been receiving in Britain widened and deepened when he got home to Brisbane. Everywhere he went people wanted to shake his hand, slap his back, get his autograph, talk to him about the Rob Andrew tackle or just be around him. He seemed to deal with it well. 'Unflappable and unfailingly polite,' the *Courier-Mail* opined, 'John Eales represents everything that is good about the Wallaby game. He has "future Australian captain" stamped all over him.'

Did John change with such praise and his new-found stature as a member of the World Cup Winning Wallabies, as they quickly became known? Did he, *hell.* This was the same John they had always known. Soon after the young Wallaby returned from the World Cup, he and his closest rugby mates were heading down for a drink and catch-up chat at the Brothers club in a soft-top convertible. They'd just gone over the Albion overpass and were in *thick* peak-hour traffic, when John suddenly jumped out of the car, dodged a couple of the cars that were screaming through, and made his way to the gutter on the other side of the road. When he got there, he lifted up the grate on the drain, reached in and came up holding a five dollar note! As Rupert McCall joyously described it to friends later on, 'John was holding up this five buck note with a huge satisfied grin like it was the World Cup!'

Therein lay something of a tale. That is, for all the glory of winning the World Cup, all the warm congratulations and tickertape parades, none of it actually *paid the bills* — bills that were totting up, now that John had moved from teenagerdom to adulthood and was developing more expensive tastes, going out to restaurants, etc. And yet Australian rugby which he had worked so hard towards making successful was starting to see money flow into its coffers as never before. Commercial interest didn't simply take the form of sponsors writing big cheques. Far more importantly, the greatest sugar-daddy of them all in the world of sports — commercial television — had been tickling the ARU under the chin and make cooing noises. Immediately prior to the World Cup, the television rights to broadcast an Australian rugby union season had been going for $250,000 a year, to the ABC. However, even before the World Cup was over, Channel Ten had come in over the top and put their signature to a contract guaranteeing the ARU just under $1 million per annum over the next three years.

Since the World Cup, at least one Wallaby had been able to capitalise on all this money sloshing around. David Campese had no sooner made some well-timed comments that he might very well retire now that he'd achieved everything he wanted to, than he emerged with a $300,000 contract over three years to do work for Channel Ten in a commentary/ reporting role — on the express condition that he not retire from the Wallabies. It was a deal which had nothing at all to do with the other players, but it was certainly a sign of the riches which might come if rugby were to get serious about pursuing the corporate dollar . . .

Though on an infinitely lesser scale, John, too, was able to garner some commercial benefit from the increased prestige of being a Wallaby. In a conversation with Rod McCall over lunch a week or so after they returned to Brisbane, John mentioned that while the glory of it all was very nice, he could actually do with having a job. After the lunch, McCall made a single phone call to a mate by the name of John Nugent. He called his brother Tracy, a rugby bloke, who called *another* rugby bloke and in short order everything was organised.

A press conference was held on 21 November announcing that G & E Hotels had employed the young Wallaby second-rower to do promotional work for them, as well as be trained in various facets of the hotel business. G & E Hotels were a Japanese based company whose owner, Miyuki Inoue, was a big supporter of sportspeople in Japan and was seeking to do a similar thing in Australia. For John, it meant a very basic salary — around $400 a week — while still allowing him time to do all the rugby training and playing he needed.

In honour of his new job, the Brothers club gave John a briefcase in which was nestled a lunchbox and a newspaper, on the reckoning that that was all he would need to do his job properly. John laughed with all the rest, but not even he had any clear idea what the job would entail. An irony in his appointment was that his principal workplace was the Park Royal Hotel where three years previously the manager had threatened to call the police if he trespassed there again . . . but not to worry. The work itself consisted of a bit more than the Brothers Club had implied with their gift — variously, taking reservations, working at the reception desk, dining with key clients, etc. — but the main thing was he arrived and left at his own whim. This job, thus fitted in superbly well with John's plans, because beyond paying the bills and doing as well as he could at rugby, he didn't really have any. He had a vague feeling that he would like to play for Australia for the next ten years, but that was about it. Still aged only 21, he didn't actually need any other plans.

Further helping to ease the financial burden on John and the other Wallabies — and to give them a share of the massive spoils of their win — was the formation shortly after their return of Wallabies Promotions and Marketing (WPM). Run by a corporate concern allied with the ARU, its charter was to turn the Wallabies' fame into money, then put the profits into a discretionary trust fund which could distribute cheques to the players. Though the proceeds John would receive from WPM — around

$20,000 over the first year of its creation, and a little more each year for the next three years— were undoubtedly contrary to rugby union's supposed strict ethos of amateurism, there was a let-out clause. In the middle of 1991 the International Rugby Board, realising that they could hardly be making money hand over fist while still keeping the players in the poorhouse, had loosened their strict amateur regulations to the point where players were allowed to be paid for speaking at corporate functions, writing books and doing promotions. Therefore, by maintaining that WPM's payments to the players were for promotions, it was nominally okay. The bottom line for John was that, financially at least, things were starting to look up.

They seemed so rosy, in fact, that he decided that by going halves with Bernadette (who had qualified as a teacher), he could afford to buy a house at the cheaper end of Brisbane's property market, and the two began to spend their weekends casting around for an appropriate place. Of course, Jack, Rosa and Nonna would have preferred that the two oldest Eales siblings stay home until they were married, but when these same siblings argued that it would be a good investment and forced way of saving money for both of them — and crucially, that they would get a better rate from the bank if the house was owner-occupied — Jack and Rosa's resistance faded. Nonna, however, held the line.

In early 1992, John and Bernadette found and moved into just the kind of place they'd been looking for. The house was a three-bedroom terrace on Carberry Street in the aspiring middle-class suburb of Grange that they were able to buy for $130,000. Certainly there was a minor problem when — in John's absence on a trip to play for a World XV against the All Blacks — Chris White had lent a hand to move John's bed from Arnell Street. Nonna kept wailing and hurling herself on the mattress in an effort to put a stop to this madness, but finally it was done. Chris, with Rosa Eales' help, assured Nonna that John still loved her and would return often, and she finally allowed the mattress to leave. John returned to the house where Bernadette and Terry Honan, who had rented a room to help defray their costs, had already settled in.

Though John and Bernadette were frequent visitors back at Arnell Street, the independence of having their own house proved to be desirable for both, given that each was now embarked on a relationship. Bernadette had for some time been seeing a young schoolteacher, Tony Byrne, who

John got on well with at least partly because he was knockabout and unaffected in the Eales fashion. That he had also been a good enough rugby player to keep Bill Campbell out of the Queensland U/21 side many years before didn't hurt either. In fact the whole family liked him. When he had first showed up at the door to take Bernadette to a formal, Nonna had made his acquaintance for all of one minute before she remarked that the suit he was wearing would be excellent to wear on the day he married her oldest grand-daughter.

As to John's relationship — the first serious one of his life — it was with the same attractive brunette, Peta Dee, whom he had met in Human Movements and Arts lectures, and who had been kind enough to share her notes with him. They had started out as part of the same wide group of friends and become progressively closer from there until shortly after John returned from the World Cup, when they had started going out. At least, sort of . . .

One problem was John was not really a 'going out together' kind of guy. That is, he was not a bloke to line up dates, pick young women up at 8 p.m. sharp and kiss them hello before showing off the *surprise!* flowers and chocolates he had brought with him. This was partly born of the fact that being a chocolate'n'flowers'n'theatre sort of boyfriend went with territory of not having cobwebs in your wallet, and up until the last couple of months John had been on first name terms with every spider in there. Still, Peta and he had a lot of fun together, going to parties and movies together as well as the occasional Japanese restaurant, and it was exactly the kind of casual relationship John wanted to be in at that time. So too, for Peta. She got on extremely well with John, and as the 1992 season progressed, particularly enjoyed going to Ballymore to watch him play, as well as socialise with the wives and girlfriends of the players. But she also had a career which was starting to take off in the world of marketing and had many things occupying her energies besides John. Nonna would say to John and Peta on occasion what a wonderful married couple they would make, but both laughed it off without trouble.

MOVING out of home is of course a seminal time in anyone's life, and perhaps because John seemed to be having so many of those kinds of moments lately, he decided to start keeping a diary —after his own fashion. On stray bits of paper which he would then shove into a bottom drawer, he started jotting down notes recording his thoughts. One such piece of paper in early March 1992 read as follows.

Things I may possibly fit in my rugby career:
Many Tests / QLD games / Club games
Season or two in Italy
Season and study in England
A couple of months in U.S.A.
Season in South Africa

This year, for the first time, Queensland's rugby games were shown between commercial breaks, on Channel Ten, and — specifically for the purposes of television — instead of an *ad hoc* series of games against other provinces, the provinces had formed into a regular competition called the Super Six. So the reckoning ran, this was likely to get the television public more interested, and it more or less seemed to work. When Queensland won the inaugural Super Six championship by beating NSW 23-18 in the deciding encounter, the ratings set a new record for a provincial rugby match in Australia.

As to the international season, rugby's newly dedicated dynamic to making itself a better television spectacle for the consumers (formally known as the rugby community), saw something else that was new under the sun. In June 1992, the International Rugby Board introduced 40 rule changes to ye olde game, designed to make it less prone to stoppages and to have more tries scored. Many rugby players, of course, only knew about five rules in the first place — 'don't tackle someone without the ball', 'don't pass forward', 'don't knock on', etc. — but at least everyone understood that with tries now worth five points instead of only four, it would be a good idea to score more of them. Though the changes had their critics, there is no doubt that the two Test series against Scotland, played under the old rules, had been dour, while the three Test series against the All Blacks, under the new rules, had 'fast-flowing rugby' — something of a buzz phrase at the time — bursting forth like Niagara on a good day. Best of all, for the Wallabies, were the results.

On the pointy end of the Australian spear, John was voted the Chivas Regal Man of the Series after Australia beat Scotland for the second time, and thus ensured the Wallabies' ninth successive Test win. Not everyone was happy with that statistic, and that included fifteen men dressed in black who arrived at Sydney airport mid-July, and thereafter assiduously devoted themselves to putting a stop to it.

In Sydney, the All Blacks were just shaded by the Wallabies 16-15 in a thriller, while in a double thriller in Brisbane it was the Australians who again emerged triumphant, 19-17. That Test was the cause of high public outrage over a particularly bloody incident involving the notorious All Black prop Richard Loe. Immediately after the diminutive Wallaby winger Paul Carozza had scored a crucial try just before half-time, Loe brought his swinging forearm hard down on the Queenslander's nose, smashing it. Eales was about fifteen metres away when it happened, and cites it as one of the most appalling things he has seen on a rugby field. Increasing the general outrage at the ground was that this was the first time Ballymore had the use of a huge video screen at the northern end of the ground and everyone there bar Loe and the still felled Carozza was able to watch the after-effects of the Loe blow over and over. Blood sprayed everywhere and though the flow was eventually stemmed, nothing would quell the calls for the New Zealander's scalp.

Entirely unmoved, the CEO of the NZRU, George Very, explained two days later that, after carefully spooling through the tape of the incident, he and his colleagues had been able to conclusively establish that Loe was innocent. 'Loe had slid on his knees and pinned Carozza on his back in an endeavour to smother the ball and prevent it from being grounded,' Very explained. (No, really.)

On the following Thursday night, the situation was superbly summed up by the Channel Ten weatherman, Brian Bury, who pointed to a low-pressure system between Australia and New Zealand and said: 'And there you see a low heading east across the Tasman, but unfortunately it is the wrong low!'

Loe took his place, then, in the All Blacks line-up which took on the Wallabies in the Third Test in Sydney to try and prevent an historic 3-0 sweep at the hands of their ancient foes. It was a predictably torrid encounter. Just before half-time, with the score locked at 13-13, John was tackled awkwardly and felt a sudden terrible pain in his hip. From the moment it happened, he knew he had to come off, as much as he hated to. Coming out to replace him, and they gave each other an acknowledging touch of hands as they passed, was none other than Garrick Morgan making his debut in a Test match.

It would be going too far to say that the Wallaby pack struggled without Eales in the engine-room, but the constant torrent of ball that John had provided from the lineout in the first half was greatly reduced. In the final wash-up, the All Blacks weren't all washed up as so many in the Australian rugby community had hoped and the New Zealanders emerged as 26-23 victors.

However satisfying the series result, everyone in the Wallabies knew that the summit of the season had not yet been reached. Because right there before them, on a now not-so-distant hilltop, lay one of the biggest challenges that Australian rugby had faced in the last two decades. Over there, now clearly visible for the first time in eons, the craggy peaks of . . . the Springboks.

After two decades of international isolation due to their apartheid policies, South Africa were now to be allowed back into international rugby with Nelson Mandela's blessing. Both the Wallabies and the All Blacks were due to travel there in late August to play Tests on successive weekends. No-one knew what to expect, either politically or in terms of the football. Politically the situation remained unstable. As the republic struggled early to make the transition from white rule to democratic rule, there had been throughout 1992 sporadic outbreaks of rioting and random violence and, in late June, the ARU had warned that if the absolute security of the Wallabies could not be guaranteed then they would cancel the tour.

By early August, though, the word came through: Thunderbirds are *go*. All Blacks are *go*. Wallabies are GO!

John, newly recovered from his badly bruised hip, was as delighted as all the rest of his team-mates. This was a Test match the entire side was particularly keen to play. For whereas in the rest of the rugby world no-one had questioned the legitimacy of Australia's right to the title of World Champions, the same could not be said of South Africa. Since 2 November 1991, there had been a strong feeling from the Limpopo River all the way down to the Cape of Good Hope that the Wallabies couldn't claim that title until they had also beaten the Springboks. In their supporters' eyes, at least, such a Test would be the true World Cup Final.

At Brisbane airport, Tim Horan was farewelled by his wife Katrina and their young baby Lucy. Tim, as John noted, was clearly doing it very tough to be leaving his young family behind, prompting another diary entry for John shortly afterwards.

As a result of what I have seen and how I would envisage myself in certain circumstances, I have come to the conclusion that I would be preferably retired before got married but definitely retired before I have children. The marriage part is not set in stone, as I don't foresee too many problems. With child I think I could really struggle especially when you consider 2 things.

You may not even be home for the birth of your child.

You could feasibly be away for all of your baby's life up to some point eg

3 week tours left when baby 1 week old. This would *torture me.*

OUT of a clear blue sky on a Sunday morning in mid-August 1992 then, Africa suddenly stretched before them, the first such sighting by a Wallaby team for two generations — and as the coast was crossed, champagne was broken out all round by the players and the myriad Australian rugby identities who had come along for the historic trip. On the long flight the mood on the plane had been at a surface level boisterously upbeat, though tinged with an unspoken tension. Not only were they flying into a still delicate political situation, but also the lair of notoriously hard opponents. John had heard all the stories. Some of the props were so 'built' it was said, that on those rare occasions when they smiled, they did so using the muscles on the back of their necks. There were second-rowers with arms as thick as another man's thighs, and back-rowers who ate bolts for breakfast, lamp-posts for lunch.

The truth was that the Wallabies didn't really know what to expect, but the reputation of the South African rugby players was that they were probably going to be more enormous and certainly tougher than any they'd ever come up against. John had seen a few of them in action earlier in the year when he played in two Tests for the World XV against the All Blacks to celebrate the latter's centenary and had been impressed with their abilities.

Waiting for the Australians at Pretoria's Jan Smuts airport when they came through customs were more alicadoos than they had seen at any previous reception committee. No fewer than twenty-three — count 'em, *twenty-three!* — South African rugby officials awaited them, of whom the legendary SARFU co-president, the 82-year-old Dr Danie Craven, was first and foremost. A former Springbok and long-time charismatic figure in the international game, Dr Craven appeared to be close to tears as he shook each and every Australian player by the hand.

'This is so wonderful,' the old man told them and the gathered press, 'I really cannot describe my feelings. I waited up all night for this, so I could greet the Australians. I was always very hopeful and optimistic that this tour would eventually happen. That is why we have worked so hard to make certain it did happen.'

Craven was joined by his co-president, Ebrahim Patel. This gentleman was far more circumspect in his welcome, though his mere presence — and the fact that he was black — was hugely significant. Just three years previously it would have been unthinkable that a black man could ever have co-control of such a proudly 'white' institution as SARFU had been. Old attitudes still prevailed, though. On the way to training that afternoon, John was sitting just behind Nick Farr-Jones when the Wallaby skipper asked one of the South African officials how many people lived in Pretoria.

'Oh, about three hundred thousand,' came the reply.

'Only three hundred thousand? Gee, it looks a lot bigger than that somehow.'

'Well, it's a million . . . if you count the blacks.'

Not for nothing would the running gag among the Wallabies for that tour be that the white South Africans liked to watch the famous American slave film *Roots* backwards — so it had a happy ending. That night, carousing in downtown Pretoria, the team's education in the South African way continued. For if the welcome at the airport had been quite touching, the welcome from South African rugby supporters was something else again. While genuinely delighted to see the Wallabies, there was always a rider. 'Just wait till our boys get a hold of you.' 'You'll never beat the Boks.' 'You're not true world champions yet.' 'Naas will kick your arse!' 'The Boks will be all over you!'

On and on and on. Everywhere. Highlighting the sense that they were in an alien and often hostile environment, was that wherever the Wallabies went, either individually or collectively, they were accompanied by men of the South African Army who, though not in uniform, were armed to the teeth and constantly vigilant against any possible terrorist attack. These men, at least, did not participate in the constant goading about what the Springboks were going to do to the Wallabies when they got a hold of them, but they were just about the only ones. It became extremely wearing after a while, but also had the effect of binding the Wallabies even more tightly together as a team. As the tour went on, it started to get very personal, and there was a lot of talk about how good it was going to feel to beat the Springboks, just so the Wallabies could shut their supporters up.

A nice contrast for John from the high tension and high security of South Africa was what was happening at home. When he called home and no one was there, he decided to leave a message on the answering machine. 'Hi,' the greeting message came on, in a voice that sounded suspiciously like new house-mate Patrick McGrath's. 'I'm John Eales, World Cup Champion, Bledisloe Cup champion, Possibly the greatest rugby player since World War II. I'm not home at the moment, I'm over in South Africa covering myself, my family and my country in glory. In the meantime, please leave a message after the beep.'

This was not entirely untypical of McGrath. The previous year when John had been otherwise engaged, 'representing the little people' while many of their friends were having 21st birthday parties, McGrath had gotten into the habit of signing collective cards on John's behalf, faking his signature. Usually, he would sign something like HAPPY 21st DICK-HEAD, I NEVER LIKED YOU — JOHN EALES. But on one occasion, for an Italian friend, when John was off playing the All Blacks, McGrath had signed, 'Happy birthday, James, you wog pr --- John Eales.' The extended family read the card the following day and were less than impressed, though all of John's friends had laughed themselves sick.

BUT to the summit! The first chance the Wallabies had to show what they could do came just days after arriving when they played Western Transvaal at Potchefstroom. The bus had charged down the highway from Pretoria at 150 km/h under police escort — partly for reasons of security and partly because they were late — but the players could see for the first time the famous black township of Soweto flash past on their right. It was only the briefest view of row upon row of grim-looking tenements, but it was another reminder of the sort of place they were in and contributed to the feeling they shared of being in a really *different* sort of country.

The ground itself, at Olen Stadium, was another revelation. Described by Tony Daly as 'looking like that part of the paddock where the shearer lets his sheep go down the chute after he's shorn them', it was pretty much the most uninviting ground they'd seen, anywhere. As a matter of fact its uninvitingness was matched only by the rudeness of the Western

Transvaal supporters, as the Wallabies warmed up. In thick Afrikaaner accents: 'We're going to get you!' 'Wait till the Boks get a hold of you lot, you won't be so smart then!' 'Remember now, don't get on the bottom of any rucks, boys!'

Some of them were even wearing a T-shirt that was selling out all over South Africa which showed a leaping Springbok engaged in coitus with a bedraggled Wallaby, above the words: 'You can't say you are world champions until you beat the Boks.'

They could, though, by God, say they were better than Western Transvaal by beating them right then and there, and did so with alacrity, putting them to the sword 46-13. Typical of what John and many of the Wallabies saw as the prevailing South African arrogance was that in the speeches afterwards the president of Western Transvaal spoke entirely in Afrikaans, even though he spoke English perfectly well.

While the Wallabies were astonished, the episode had one upside in that it prompted another story from Tempo. As John had learnt by now, most things that happened on a Wallaby tour reminded Tempo of something that had happened on a previous one, and the story the Wallaby assistant coach told on this occasion had particular resonance for John. Back in '69, Tempo recounted, the Wallaby captain Des Connor had faced a similar problem when the Australians were on tour through the republic. When the after-match speech was delivered in entirely incomprehensible Afrikaans, Connor, also a graduate of Marist Brothers Ashgrove, had simply stood up and spoken in what he purported was Aboriginal, but was in fact the Marist Brothers Ashgrove war cry, combined with a few Australian place names.

'*Gungalora , hootiora, Ashgrovina, Erigamora . . .*' he began.

'On behalf of the Australian team, I would like to say,' Wallaby prop Roy Prosser translated.

'*Karikaruka, bidjigong, bubragundi . . .*'

'That it was a wonderful game today.'

'*Gungalong, hoo, hoo, Coolangatta, Woolloomoloo, Wagga, Wagga.*'

'And we thank you very much for it!'

Both the Wallabies then sat down to a standing ovation from their team-mates and the puzzled looks of their hosts.

Five days later, in the high altitude of Pretoria's Loftus Versfeld's stadium, the Australians again triumphed, this time 24-17 over the Blue

Bulls of Northern Transvaal. It was a difficult game, given that the lack of oxygen often made it feel like they had plastic bags over their heads, but a supremely satisfying win. Given that the constant rant that the Wallabies were not the real world champions was starting to get to them, it would have been unthinkable to lose. At least the president of Northern Transvaal was more charming in defeat than his Western Transvaal counterpart. For not only did he address them in English, but he also had quite a nice line.

'Congratulations to the Wallabies,' he said at the after-match function, 'but I really think we made a tactical error today in that we didn't cover the ground in paper as I suggested.' At this point he paused, as both the Australians and the Northern Transvaal players looked at each other quizzically to try and discern his meaning. With perfect timing, he then resumed. 'Yes . . . this year we've been a whole lot better on paper than on grass.'

IT was a crazy kind of thing to be at a Test match where they were mere spectators — 'a little like being in Switzerland during the Second World War,' someone commented at the time — but on Saturday, 15 August, the Wallabies attended Ellis Park in Johannesburg to watch the All Blacks play the Springboks. From the moment they arrived, perhaps an hour before the match began, there was a hint of madness in the air. On the field, bands of supporters kept invading the pitch waving South African flags. Elsewhere, the Afrikaaner extremist leader Eugene Terre' Blanche arrived for the game brandishing a Boer flag. Were they at a rugby game, or at a mass political rally? Around the ground, 50,000 spectators seemed to be roaring a kind of primal collective bellow of joy that after two decades on the outer, South African rugby was back in business. The Springboks would *again* be playing the All Blacks as in days of yore, and could *again* demonstrate their rugby supremacy to the rest of the rugby world. But first . . .

But first, just after the teams ran out onto the ground to an even more guttural roar, a one-minute silence was scheduled to commemorate the 42 people who had been killed at the Boipatong massacre three months previously. This one-minute silence, in place of the anthems, had been one of the conditions laid down by the African National Congress for allowing the tour to go ahead. But the static had not even faded from the announcement when the crowd began to sing the Afrikaaner anthem

'*Die Stem*' in full voice. They were barely a quarter-way through the spirited rendition when the loudspeaker again crackled to life. This was not to rebuke the crowd for failing to observe even a few seconds of the minute's silence but, amazingly, to add official sanction to the singing of the anthem by piping through the musical accompaniment to 'Die Stem'.

Around the stadium thousands of voices took up the song with even greater vigour, complete with clenched-fist salutes, and on the field many of the Springboks openly cried at the emotion of it all.

All anthems are emotional, of course, but 'Die Stem' in this context was something else again. In the words of the South African-born novelist Bryce Courtenay, 'It is an anthem which celebrates the White Tribe and its love of a land it believes it won from the Black Tribes and for which it is willing to die. Make no mistake, "Die Stem" is a war cry.'

John, sitting next to fellow Wallaby Tim Kelaher, was appalled, saying to the fullback as he looked around in great agitation. 'What are they doing? This is a *disgrace*.'

At least the Wallabies were glad, as their bus took them back to Pretoria, that the All Blacks had won the game 26-23, silencing the uppity Afrikaaners for a bit. But they were sure they could do better the following week. It was with relief that the Wallabies escaped to Port Elizabeth on the South African coast the following morning. They were leaving, they thought, most of the fuss about the anthem behind them, but actually it followed them. For several tense days — as the outcry over the singing of the anthem continued to reverberate— there was every chance that the African National Congress would withdraw permission for the Wallaby Test to be played and they would fly home. Citing the non-observance of the minute's silence, the playing of the anthems and the flying of the flags as a general breach of conditions agreed upon, the ANC maintained they were quite within their rights to withdraw their support.

In a conversation with Rod McCall, John sounded out the older man on the issue.

'They wouldn't really send us home without playing the Test would they, Rod?'

'Mate,' McCall replied, 'if the ANC withdraw their support, we couldn't get out of here quick enough. It would be way too dangerous to stay.'

Sure enough, on the Tuesday morning before training, ARU president Joe French informed the Wallabies that the ANC were meeting in an hour's time to decide on whether the tour would proceed. If they said 'no', then the Wallabies would be on a flight out that afternoon. To London. There would be no waiting for the Saturday flight to Perth. It was out, out, out. In the meantime, French told them, they should train that morning as if the Test was still on, as hard as he felt they might find it.

A definitive answer still hadn't come through by the end of training, but when they returned to the hotel French reported that the first noises out of the ANC had been unexpectedly tolerant, and it had been decided to keep to the original tour schedule until further notice. All well and good. After lunch, Wallaby manager John Breen announced that he wanted some volunteers to go out to a nearby black township to teach some of the kids about rugby. Of course there was no question really of raising the standard of rugby in the township, but if there was one thing the Wallabies had gained from their time in South Africa, it was a greater affinity for the country's black people, as opposed to the whites, and there were many volunteers.

The minibus set off from the genteel confines of their four-star hotel in Port Elizabeth at 2 p.m. with sixteen Wallabies and Bob Dwyer on board. Through the window, the scenery passed them by like a long, panning shot in a movie. Concrete buildings, white faces, paved streets, expensive suits, parking meters, white, white, black, white, Mercedes, brick houses, gardens, black, white, black, fields, more fields, black, black, black, black, dirt tracks, tin shacks, hessian walls, wooden tables laden with meat, flies, flies, flies, lots of black faces now. Seeing so many people packed into such a small space and comparing it with the spacious 'white areas' that they'd come from reminded John of something he'd heard Desmond Tutu had once said: 'When the white man came here, they had the Bible and we had the land. They said close your eyes and let us pray. When we opened our eyes we had the Bible and they had the land.' The thing was, the blacks certainly didn't have a lot of land now. John was stunned, as they kept driving, to see, for mile after mile after wretched mile, corrugated-iron shacks densely packed together. It seemed amazing that so many people could live without even the most basic of modern accoutrements such as electricity or sewerage systems. Finally, though, they came to a field, in a poor state of repair on the edge of the township, but it was at least basically flat, with a stark concrete stand on its western edge.

As they pulled up and got out of the minibus, hundreds and hundreds of black kids crowded around the Australians, with smiles every bit as wide as their heads, welcoming them, touching them and just as quickly running away. The more shy of them would only dare touch Willie Ofahengaue, the only black man among the visitors. So began a wonderful afternoon, where the Wallabies divided up and nominally took a training session for the fifty kids each one had in his care.

John tried for a lineout session, Tim Horan (*bizarrely!*) took his lot for a road-run, Farr-Jones tried to teach some basic passing skills and so on. Mostly everyone laughed and fell about, and it wasn't long before everyone came together for a splendid game of mob touch football.

John loved it. Certainly part of him wondered whether the kids had the first idea of why they were there, or even what rugby was, but in the end it didn't really matter. For the Wallabies it was a wonderful break from the travails of tour life and the deadly serious business of preparing for a Test they weren't even sure was going to take place, while for the kids it was simply a chance to run with their friends in the sunlight with a ball in their hands and the added oddity of being guided by friendly white people.

As the sun started to sink and the time came to leave, all of the children — together with their parents, grandparents, aunts and uncles — gathered with the Wallabies for a sit-down singalong of African songs, with speeches of thanks from all sides. As the haunting African voices mixed, mingled and soared into the twilight, there in the African back-of-beyond John reflected on what an extraordinary passport international rugby was, when it could take you from rubbing elbows with Princess Diana one year, to a wonderful but totally different scene like this the next. He felt privileged to be there.

THE following day the Wallabies beat Eastern Province without trouble, and then headed down to Cape Town for the climactic Test match of the year. Though there had been no official proclamation yet that it was on, both Joe French and the Australian ambassador to South Africa, Colin McDonald, had received private assurances from the ANC that they would not prevent the match taking place.

Coming out of Cape Town airport, the Wallabies received a shock. There were about thirty black protesters holding up an assortment of placards: 'Disgusting Aussies', 'Go Home Racist Aussies', 'Australians have no conscience', 'You Have a Vote, We Don't'. A fair point, that last one, but hell, if it was all right with Nelson Mandela that they come, surely it was all right with them? For at least two kilometres out of the airport, groups of protesters stood by the road, silent sentinels to the fact that the Wallabies were not there with unanimous support.

At least some guys could see the bright side, though.

'Look at it this way, you blokes,' the long-time Wallaby hooker Tommy Lawton called out to the rest of the bus as they passed a particularly big group. 'That's a whole bunch of people we won't have to sign autographs for!'

The bus rocked with laughter as they made their way to the hotel.

ON the morning of the Test, John awoke to find an envelope under the door. He opened it, and read a personal note from Simon Poidevin who had retired the year before, but had come over as a television commentator.

22.8.92

Dear John,

No second-rower in the world has your athletic ability. The opposition today underestimate it — after 80 minutes they will realise why one so young is without peer in the Rugby World.

Regards,

Poido

It was a nice gesture, John appreciated it, and though he never would have put it in Poidevin's words, his steely resolve to prove that he was just that went up a notch. That afternoon, with anthems banned, the Australians linked arms before leaving the dressing room and sang 'Advance Australia Fair' in the lustiest possible manner. Renditions of the anthem when representing your country abroad are always particularly emotive, but this one more than most. Do or die. Were they the true World Champions or not?

'*In joyful strains then let us sing,*
Advance Australia Fair!'

Then out, and into it. Though the Wallabies did not dominate the scoreboard early, they did dominate their opposition. John jumped in the middle of the lineout against a South African by the name of Adolf Malan, and did as well as he could in muddy conditions which turned many of the lineouts into something only a couple of stray fists away from being a dockyard brawl. Still, five minutes before half-time, John managed to soar above Malan for a perfect two-handed take and brought the ball down to set up a maul. Willie Ofahengaue ripped it, charged up the blind side, and from there the ball passed through the hands of Nick Farr-Jones and Michael Lynagh before it got to Paul Carozza who went over for a superb try in the corner. It remained a torrid battle for the rest of the game, and with six minutes to go the Springboks still had a sniff of coming back from an 11-3 deficit.

It was then that Tim Horan pulled off what John still describes as 'the most all-encompassing bit of rugby I have ever seen'. Having hauled in a kick by South African fullback Theo van Rensburg some 35 metres from the Wallabies' line, Horan tucked the ball under his left arm and set off upfield, slicing and sidestepping all the way before sending a kick behind the South African defence. The Springbok centre Danie Gerber fielded the ball just inside his own quarter, but Horan just as quickly tackled him, got back to his knees and somehow, amid all the churning feet and arms, picked the ball cleanly out of the muddy maelstrom without knocking on and got away a perfectly timed pass to . . . to . . . the man with the cleanest jersey on the field, shining out there like a flashing orange beacon, David Campese on the burst for a try!

The South Africans were now comprehensively broken, meaning the Wallabies were soon afterwards able to score again when Paul Carozza crashed over — once more courtesy of Tim Horan — and when the final whistle blew, the Springboks had gone down to their biggest defeat in a hundred years, 26-3. The previous Wallaby record over the South Africans was a 21-6 win by Alec Ross's side in Durban in 1933, while the 23 point difference eclipsed South Africa's 28-9 loss to the 1974 Lions.

In the muck, the Australians had handed to the Boks the biggest hiding in their history. At least that's what the Australians thought. Just as the Wallabies were getting onto the bus to take them back to their hotel, a supporter started banging beneath the windows on one side: 'You might have beaten the Springboks, but you'll never beat Transvaal!'

Which was just about typical. It was nice to be heading home, and nicer still that when they left for Australia the following day, many of the Wallabies took souvenir copies of Cape Town's *Weekend Argus*, which had a massive headline on its front page, 'SJAMBOKKED! BIGGEST DEFEAT IN 100 YEARS.'

Let the South African rugby supporters stick that one in their pipe and smoke it!

At home, John was honoured by being voted the Australian Society of Rugby Writers' Player of the Year. He had finished second behind David Campese in 1991, but this year was not to be denied. The announcement was made at a convivial lunch at a Sydney golf club, and afterwards, what the hey, three of the rugby writers invited Eales to play a round with them. One of them, Greg Growden, is a more than competent golfer and it would have been nice to say he had beaten the great Eales in something. The first hole at the club was a tight 300-metre par four. The three journos hit off fairly and well, putting their drives about two-thirds of the way down the fairway. Eales pulled out Big Bertha and belted the ball on to the front fringe of the green. The journalists looked at the shot, looked at each other, and decided they'd rather be drinking beer back in the clubhouse.

Despite John being acknowledged as the finest rugby player in the land for that year, there remained a lot of rugby for him to play — as the Wallabies were scheduled to fit in a two Test tour of Ireland and Wales before Christmas.

Contemplating it with some fatigue, John realised how much rugby had changed his perspective. As a kid, adolescent, and then young adult, he had always looked forward to Christmas for the presents and family time that went with it. Now, there was something far more important than both of those. It was the break. For six glorious weeks, once this tour was over, he would be able to loaf around the house, not go to training, not catch a plane, not look across the 50-metre line before kick-off and see fifteen guys who for the next 80 minutes would be coming at him hard.

In the meantime, there was a lot of work to do. Freshly landed in Ireland, Bob Dwyer worked the side particularly hard, warming to the theme — some would have said over-heating — that 'if you want to be the No. 1 team in the world, you have to work as if you're No. 2.'

Though the tour got off to a shaky start when the Wallabies lost to the club side of Munster, this was in no way John's fault, as his 'answering machine message' at home made clear. 'Hi, John Eales speaking. I'm not home at the moment, I'm over in Ireland and Wales representing you the average Australian. Yes, the team just lost to Munster, but if the Australian selectors aren't going to pick me how do we expect to win?'

The main thing was John was in the Test side when the Wallabies played Ireland at Lansdowne Road on 31 October and they proceeded to rack up 42 points while the men in green could only manage 17. For Bob Dwyer's 50th Test at the helm, he had guided the Wallabies to their second successive record win.

On to Wales. The Wallabies had just settled into their hotel in Cardiff when Ewen McKenzie, an inveterate reader, approached John in the hotel restaurant over breakfast. Had John seen the autobiography of the Scottish rugby captain, David Sole? When John replied in the negative, Ewen showed him a passage on page 23 which he felt would interest him.

'There is probably nothing I can say about Campo that he hasn't already said himself! Or even as the Wallaby lock John Eales said: "David fell in love with himself ten years ago and has remained faithful ever since!"'

John felt sick. Sick at heart, sick of stomach, sick-sick. During the two Tests John had played for the World XV against the All Blacks earlier in the year, he had repeated to Sole one of the Wallabies' favourite lines of the time, but he never thought it would show up in a book! And so John spent the rest of the day acutely aware that he was on dangerous ground. Sure, Sole had put the line in for some light relief, but here was John, one of the youngest members of the team, seen to be publicly taking a shot at the most revered member of the Wallabies and an icon of the game. What to do?

There was only one thing to do. Go and see Campo and apologise. At about 10 p.m. he knocked on his door.

Campo, as impeccably dressed as ever — funny, he always looked as if he was just going to, or coming from, an opening night somewhere — opened the door and looked at the youngster quizzically. Yes?

'Campo,' John faltered. 'I . . . I just thought I'd have a chat if I could.'

Sure, John, come in. After ten minutes of idle chit-chat over this and that and nothing in particular, with Campo obviously waiting for him to get to the point, John finally took a deep breath and began walking towards the abyss.

'Campo . . . have you . . . uh, have you seen David Sole's autobiography which has just come out?'

'Naaaah, mate, I haven't,' the greatest of all Wallaby wingers replied, 'I wouldn't read something like that if you paid me. Who *cares*?'

'Good,' John replied, barely bothering to hide his relief. 'You're-not-missing-anything-at-all-it's-really terrrible-I-better-get-to-bed-goo'night.'

John went to bed with the relief of a Test batsmen who has just had his wicket shattered while still on a duck, only to find it was a no-ball! The following morning at breakfast, John mentioned to Tony Daly what had happened, and was happy that the prop reassured him.

'You needn't have bothered speaking to Campo about it in the first place,' Daly said. 'He hasn't even read his own book yet so there's no chance he would have read David Sole's.'

Two days later, it was on. If rugby really was the game they play in heaven, then hell probably looked a lot like playing fifteen rampaging rugga-buggas from Llanelli on a muddily sodden sod of a day. Famous for their fight, the men of the Welsh valleys simply refused to be abashed by the superior pedigree of their Australian opponents. Whipped to a frenzy of ferocity by the 25,000 locals, they just kept on coming. To John it looked like they were playing the game of their lives, and they probably were. At one point in the first half, the ball found its way to the Llanelli five-eighth, Colin Stephens, who shaped to kick. John, charging through hard, raised his arms to block it and ended up diving at Stephens' feet in a movement somewhere between a charge down and a tackle. What happened precisely at this point would never be quite clear, but the upshot was that despite the Wallaby second-rower's best efforts, the kick went over his outstretched hands and Stephens then landed with the full weight of his body on John's left shoulder . . . and somewhere deep inside, something broke. The Wallabies' long-time physio, Greg Craig, was by John's side within seconds and immediately insisted that he leave the field. The injured second-rower was still on the sideline just before the final whistle, watching as Stephens slotted his second field-goal to consolidate Llanelli's slim winning margin, and shortly thereafter the final whistle blew. The hard men of Llanelli had won. Hell indeed.

As the Wallabies started to dejectedly troop from the field, and the Llanelli captain, one Rupert Henry St John Barker Moon, was hoisted upon the shoulders of the local fans and carried around in a triumphal lap as he played to the crowd by blowing them kisses, the local supporters unleashed their famous chant: 'Who beat the Walla-Walla-bies? Who beat the Walla-Walla-bies? Who beat the Walla-Walla-bies? We did! We did! We did!'

Add alcohol, mix, and repeat a thousand times before dawn the following day, making particularly sure to be at your loudest when around anyone who looks like they might be an Australian. Extra points awarded if you sing it around an actual Wallaby.

Over the next few days Greg Craig worked hard on John's shoulder, desperately trying to get it in shape in time for Saturday's Test at Cardiff Arms Park, but when John awoke on the Saturday morning and it was clear that a miracle had not occurred overnight, he was forced to tell Bob Dwyer that it was out of the question even to give him a fitness test.

'I just won't be able to play,' John told the Australian coach, thus ensuring that he would miss his first Test for the Wallabies in two years.

One who wasn't too devastated at the news was Garrick Morgan, who now slotted into the second-row beside Rod McCall for his first selection in the run-on Test side, after twice having come on as Test reserve. John warmly congratulated him, though was careful to keep his distance over the next few days, acutely aware that there is a real borderline between the Test team and the rest. Garrick was in it. He wasn't. Simple. Hard, but simple.

Still, though it was a strange thing to be in the stands watching the Wallabies beat Wales by 23-6, it wasn't as if it would be long before he was back out there with the team. The preliminary prognosis with his shoulder was that it was nothing that a good Australian summer of rest and a bit more physio treatment couldn't fix, and John intended to follow those instructions to the hilt — particularly the 'rest' part.

The Long
Haul Back

*This elevation in philosophy, physique and fascination in Wallaby
second-row play can be directly attributed to the odd phenomenon of
Australia producing possibly the two greatest locks
of all time at the one time — John Eales and Garrick Morgan.*

GREG GROWDEN, *Sydney Morning Herald*, 26 April 1994

∽

'HUUUUU ...'
'No, Ben.'

'Go on, John, give it a go! Help the orange healing light! Do it with an open, loving heart!'

By February of 1993, chanting HUUUU with an open loving heart was just about the only thing John *hadn't* tried in his long quest to get his shoulder in working order again. A summer in the sun had done nothing for it. Nor had massage. Nor constant physiotherapy. Nor acupuncture. Nor Nonna's prayers. The doctors had said it was nerve damage and the only healer would be the passage of time, and that was that. Good ol' Ben Perkins, as faithful a friend as ever, had done a lot of HUUUing on his behalf, but was firmly of the belief that *John* really needed to be the one doing it. John maybe gave it one or two bursts while shaving one morning, but never had his heart in it. Even a friendship as strong as John and Ben's had its limits. But now, the problem was pressing. By mid-March, with the representative season fast approaching, John's shoulder still dully ached all the time and he lacked strength in it.

John Connolly at least was understanding, giving him a Get out of Jail Free for all serious contact work — tackling, rucking and the like. The coach assured John it wouldn't be long before his shoulder came good, but John had serious doubts about whether he would make it and for the first time began to voice them. Connolly wouldn't hear of it. You'll be fine, he said. You've got to have confidence, he said. Seen plenty of injuries like this, he said, and they always come good with a rush. In the old days, he said, we'd rub something like this out, it would hurt like hell but the next day it would be fine. Eales went along with it, still trying to steer clear of taking any hard hits, but on the Thursday night before the first Queensland game of the season in late March he made his decision. He simply could not play, knew it, and told Connolly.

'No, John, you'll be right . . . ' Connolly had begun.

'No, I'm *not* playing,' John had replied with uncharacteristic force. And he meant it.

From there, things moved quickly. In some ways it was like a dam bursting. Now that John was actually missing out on games because of injury it was impossible to pretend it wasn't serious and he thus did what he probably should have done as soon as he returned from Wales. That is he went to see Brisbane's leading orthopaedic specialist Peter Myers, and underwent a battery of tests.

After a week, Dr Myers told him. 'Your rotator cuff has completely ruptured,' he said. 'I think we can probably fix it with an operation and a long rehabilitation, but before doing something like that I really think you should get a second opinion.'

Ugh. In John's anatomy studies from Human Movements he had learnt just how crucial the rotator cuff was — it controlled the movement of the whole arm — and so was suitably apprised of the gravity of the injury. The specialist he was guided towards worked in rooms in western Sydney, and in short order John was in his office gazing quizzically up at him as this expert also prepared to give his verdict. Rubbing his chin and having one last thoughtful look at the X-rays and test results John had brought with him, this gentleman began his appraisal:

'No,' he said, 'No, I really don't think just one operation is going to get you back out on the field. You'll definitely need two operations, and even then you won't be right. All that will do is help you with the pain and enable you to live a more normal life, but as far as rugby goes, the nerve damage you've suffered is too extensive and that simply cannot be repaired. I hate to tell you this, but I think playing any kind of rugby is out of the question.'

Out of the question . . .

Out of the question . . .

Out of the question . . .

Was there an echo, or was that just his heart beating like a drum and trying to pound the last words of the specialist into some other kind of meaning? They wouldn't go. The specialist meant what he said, and said what he meant. Rugby was over for John. He'd had a wonderful go of it, been privileged to represent Australia in a World Cup, but the injury he had sustained was so serious there was simply nothing that could be done. Sorry.

Dazed, John thanked the surgeon and left. For about half an hour he wandered the unfamiliar streets, not talking to anyone, and going over the conversation time and again in his head before he caught a taxi to the airport to head back to Brisbane. He was shocked and disbelieving. Still, by the time he had landed at Brisbane an hour and a half later he had decided on his course. With a second opinion like that, he had no choice but to go with the first opinion! In the interim, he told absolutely no-one that at least one specialist thought his career was over — not his parents, not his friends, not his coaches, not Peta — and just got on with it, without dramas.

In mid-April, Dr Myers conducted a four-hour operation on John, and he emerged with a curious contraption under his arm, designed to hold his shoulder rigid while the damage was repaired. At first his arm up to his elbow was locked at a 90 degree angle out from his body. If all went according to plan, after three weeks that would be changed to 45 degrees, and four weeks after that he could be free of the damn thing and begin the long rehabilitation program. Playing any rugby that year was out of the question, but if things went well there was a chance he could make it back in time for pre-season training in 1994. First up, there would be some adjusting to do in coping with the wretched sling, and the fact that he was now no longer part of a team. His new nickname for starters among friends and acquaintances was 'Wazza' . . . as in 'Was a Wallaby'.

Then there were footie friends at Ballymore, who whenever they saw him heading up into the stands with what looked uncannily like an ice-cream tray under his right arm would hold up a couple of fingers and shout out 'coupla cornettos, please, son!'

No, really, they were a riot. Still, John could not blame them, because that's what it looked like. When he was going into a restaurant with Peta and Ben Perkins about a fortnight after the operation, the waiter came up to him and attempted to take away the support, thinking it was a BYO bag.

In some ways the whole thing reminded him of John Connolly's famous reply when he was asked what he had felt when he had once had a mild heart attack. 'The pain,' he said, 'was like the pain you get when you lose to NSW though not quite as bad.'

John's pain was something similar, he decided. It was there, gnawing away, but it wasn't as if you couldn't have a bit of a laugh about it along the way.

As a partial cripple, it was as well, all things considered, that he had moved home to Arnell Street, as, among other things, it was extremely helpful to have Nonna there ready to help him with everything. The household in Carberry Street had amicably dissolved earlier in the year when Bernadette announced that she and Tony were going to get married in December, and she was moving home to save money. John — on the strength of his ongoing job with the hotel chain, and payments from WPM — had bought her half of the house and rented it out to tenants. John and Bernadette's younger siblings were still at home, all still students, and it was nice to be back in the bosom of the family.

Nonna's delight in having them back was second only to her delight that Bernadette was getting married to Tony. It was rare for Nonna to leave the house on shopping expeditions, but for Tony, Nonna made an exception. For three days solid, she scoured Brisbane to find what she was looking for, the perfect wedding present for the happy couple: a plaster statue of St Anthony which was almost a metre tall.

WHILE it was frustrating to not be able to take the field in this time of rehabilitation, there were at least plenty of other outlets for John's energies. In terms of his competitive drive, he spent hour after hour at home, playing yahtzee and backgammon with either Jack or the frequent and welcome visitor, Peta, and he never seemed to tire of it. YAHTZEE!

As to his professional life, this was the first time John was actually able to start turning up at the Park Royal Hotel on a day by day basis and do some real work. Much of it was receiving basic training in the hospitality industry by spending some time in all the different sections of the hotel, from the front desk to the back laundry, to ordering the food for the kitchen from the markets. While he remained glad to have the job, the best thing it did for John was encourage him to work hard on his rehabilitation to get back on the field as soon as possible. The thought of having to do that kind of thing for a living, like everyone else, was not a pleasurable one.

Beyond that, John also became the QRU's player of choice to send out to rugby clubs who wanted speakers for their functions, and this vastly increased John's capacities in the art of speech-making. He found he loved the thrill of holding an audience's attention, and came to understand the virtue of polishing several well-honed stories that he could use as the basis for his address, as well as a couple of guaranteed one-liners. Often, for example, John would steer his speech towards comparisons between rugby union and rugby league and note that the amount of money being offered to rugby union players to switch over seemed to be increasing every year.

'Still,' he said, 'I don't care how much they offer Garrick Morgan to go to league . . . whatever it is, I'll add to it. That might be the only way I'll get back in the side.' Ah, how they laughed, and John along with them. The joke turned on how well Garrick was going in John's position for Queensland, earning constant man-of-the-match awards. Already he was a certainty to keep his Test spot, and he was regarded as the most in-form player in Australia.

Hey that reminds me, let's have a cornetto!

To further broaden his range of experience, John began writing a weekly column in the *Courier-Mail* at $150 dollars a pop, as well as contributing the occasional column to such magazines as *Australian Rugby News*. Journalism had sometimes vaguely interested him as a career path — in the days before rugby had completely swallowed everything else — and after two years of solid physical focus it was a pleasure to get back to the intellectual stimulation offered by writing. Most satisfying was when he wrote something that provoked a lot of comment. One column he wrote in the middle of May for *Rugby News* sparked much debate in both the media and the wider rugby community.

The background to the column was John's strong and firmly held view that the game was unsustainable at the elite level unless the increasingly professional demands placed on the players were rewarded with professional returns to their bank balances.

In articulate and well-reasoned fashion, John promoted the revolutionary idea that the way forward for elite rugby was to start paying top players, no richer than the dirt they played on, a fairer recompense for their efforts. Outright. He even went so far as to put figures on it.

'The top 15 players,' he wrote, 'would be contracted on about $40,000 a year. And the next 15 players about $20,000-30,000 a year. This would total about $1.05 million. On top of this, coaching and support staff need consideration as well. Further players would be contracted to their state unions for lesser amounts. This would certainly give players greater incentive to stay in Australia all year round.'

All well and good John, but would the unions come up with the money to pay for it? John had thought of that too . . .

'Maybe we could add an extra Test at home and drop off two or three of the additional (non-Test) matches on an overseas tour. Therefore there is actually less football being played. The one match could be against one of the Five Nations sides or even a selection XV. It would be realistic to pack the Sydney Football Stadium for such an event.'

Just five years previously, such views would have been nothing less than heretical, but not in Queensland in the middle of 1993. For if there was one place in the world that was pushing the view that rugby had to change and become more professional, it was right there, right then.

For the previous three years, the executive director of the QRU Terry Doyle and its chairman, Dick McGruther, had done all possible to set their union up on as commercial a basis as possible — looking to maximise income by virtue of sponsorships, increased ticket prices, etc. — and Eales' views meshed perfectly with their own. That said, there remained problems with the union heading down this path while the players themselves remained substantially amateur. During that year, for example, a number of dinners and lunches were held where wealthy companies with rugby affiliations were invited to buy tables at prices ranging from $400 to $1000 a head. Each table would have a Queensland player on it, to mix and mingle

Left: Flashpoint! John and ACT's Argentine international Patricio Noriega are pulled apart during a flare up during the Brumbies' defeat of Queensland in the opening round of the Super 12 at Ballymore, March 1997.
Photo: Colin Whelan
© *Action Photographics*

Below: John signs a new contract with the ARU in August 1997 under the watchful eye of ARU CEO John O'Neill and fellow Wallaby Ben Tune.
Photo: Paul Seiser
© *Action Photographics*

John Eales winning the lineout for Australia during the Australia vs New Zealand Bledisloe Cup Test at the MCG in July, 1998. *Photo: Rob Cox © Action Photographics*

Left: Prime Minister John Howard and John talk shop after the Wallabies defeat of the All Blacks at the SFS, 1998. *Photo: Rob Cox © Action Photographics*

Below: 'This is what we are going to do'. Against the Springboks, August 1998, just days after John had become a father for the first time. *Photo: Col Whelan ©Action Photographics*

Above: John walks with
the cup. NZ vs Australia
Bledisloe Cup match in
Christchurch, August 1998.
Photo: Rob Cox
© Action Photographics

Right: Wallaby coach
Rod Macqueen at the
Australian training
session at Cardiff
University ahead of the
World Cup Final against
France at the
Millennium Stadium,
Cardiff, November 1999.
Photo: Nick Wilson
© Allsport

Left: John with Wallaby hooker Michael Foley after the Wallabies beat South Africa in the World Cup semi-final at Twickenham, October 1999. © AFP

Below: John with fellow members of the newly selected 'Queensland Team of the Century', May 1999. *Photo: Anthony Weate* © *Courier Mail*

The Eales family on the wedding day of John and Lara, January 1999. *From left:* Bernadette, Jack, Antoinette, John, Elijah, Lara, Nonna, Rosa, Damian, Rosaleen. *Eales family collection*

On his wedding day, January 1999 with Lara, Nonna and Elijah. *Eales family collection*

Left: Nonna in the front yard wearing John's uniform circa 1993
Eales family collection

Below: John with his nearest and dearest when he received the Order of Australia at Queensland's Government House in 1999.
Eales family collection

The things we do. John dresses as a spider for an ARU television promotion, 1998. *Photo: Rob Cox*
©Action Photographics

with the guests, a wonderful lunch and guest speaker provided, etc. More cash was raised at the end of the function where Queensland Rugby memorabilia such as jerseys signed by all the players were auctioned.

As John wrote in his diary, though, 'sometimes it makes players feel like beggars at a banquet. Players dislike attending, and often feel embarrassed by the situation. We realise the intentions of the dinners and oblige because we see this as our only means of being compensated. Yet in some ways we feel embarrassed at the same people being asked to throw in money all the time.'

BY the end of June when his sling was at last removed, all John could do was lie face down on the bed with his arm hanging loosely, and concentrate on making his hand swing back and forth just a few centimetres at a time. Every extra centimetre hurt and he had to be careful not to overdo it, but each week saw a slight gain in his control and his strength until in a few weeks he was able to do exercises using his body weight to strengthen his shoulder.

While working towards his rehabilitation, John often recalled a brief conversation he'd once had with the Australian swimming coach, Don Talbot at a celebrity golf tournament. 'The biggest problem with people making comebacks,' the coach had said, 'is they often forget how hard they had to work in the first place to get their outstanding results. They instead tend to remember all the good times without all the sacrifices they had to make on the way.'

Bearing that in mind, Eales continued to push himself hard in the rehabilitative process, while always being careful not to go too far.

In the meantime, it wasn't as if John couldn't do some work on those skills that didn't involve hard physical contact. One day, while down at Ballymore, he noticed an odd thing. There was the famous All Black five-eighth, Grant Fox, holding a training session for coaches on the finer points of goal-kicking. John wondered if Grant would mind if he tagged along. Not at all . . . and seeing as he was here, why didn't he stand in as a kind of guinea pig? He'd heard somewhere that John had done a bit of goal-kicking, so why didn't he have a few kicks and then Grant could correct his technique, bit by bit, and see if they couldn't improve his success rate. Excellent idea! The amiable All Black's generosity in sharing his knowledge with an opposing Test player was a key indicator of two things.

Firstly, that the ancient enmity between Australian and New Zealand rugby players, by some reckoning as natural as that between sharks and barracudas, was starting to dissipate as the men from both side of the 'ditch' got to know each other better through increased contact. And secondly, just as there was such a thing in world rugby as the front-rowers club — wherein generally shortish rotund men with cauliflower ears delight in discussing the finer features of the dark nether-world that exists at the point where two worlds collide — so too is there a natural affinity between men who love kicking pumped up bits of leather through a couple of bits of wood.

This was a goal-kicking guru talking to a goal-kicking go-getter and their loyalty was to their art and not merely their teams. Eales would ever afterwards remember the session in great detail, perhaps born of the fact that he concentrated so fiercely during it to soak up everything he could. Sure, at this point Eales already had a solid goal-kicking technique, but even after five minutes it was obvious that Fox had forgotten more than John ever knew.

The most important thing, Fox told him, was that the swinging boot had to connect with the ball's sweet spot — a one inch square located just below its central point. Not a smidgin to the left, not a smidgin to the right, above or below, but right *there*. Look at it as you get yourself set. Focus on hitting it properly, as you line your hips and shoulders up with the target. Now, concentrate as you take your steps in, on bringing your leg through on a perfect straight arc, so the end of your boot connects right on it. Got that?

The other extremely important point is where your non-kicking boot lands. It must land a hip's width to the side of the ball — and be pointing directly at the target — or you're wasting your time. That's why you begin the process by having your non-kicking foot beside the ball and then stepping back from there.

One more thing. Mentally, Fox said, empty your mind of everything but the aforementioned routine. All thoughts of 'this has gotta go over, this has gotta go over' are a waste. The *ball* doesn't know the situation, and doesn't care! It just wants to be hit sweetly, and you're not going to be able to oblige unless you are relaxed. Get the rhythm of the routine right, and everything else will follow. Eales listened, learned, tried it all out, with Fox improving his technique a little each time. Though John would modify and refine to his own needs a lot of the New Zealander's teachings, the foundation stones were being laid for a fine goal-kicking career in its own right.

Both rugby players finished the session equally impressed with the other. Fox, because Eales seemed to absorb everything he said and only had to be told once. To him, the Australian looked like a great, raw natural talent, who just needed some polish to realise his potential.

And Eales was impressed with Fox, not just because of his obvious knowledge and willingness to share it, but his ability to make it simple and teach it.

John was excited enough by what he'd learned to shortly resume serious goal-kicking training down at West Mitchelton Oval, about ten minutes' drive from where he lived. It wasn't always easy to find someone to retrieve the balls when he kicked them on the lost and lonely field, but his mum was one who helped. This far into John's international career, Rosa had dropped all resistance to rugby, and by 1992 would never miss a game he played in Queensland. So for hours at a time, John would slot goals through the posts from all angles — using Fox's technique — and Rosa would gather them in, walking them back to her boy. At the age of 56, it wasn't really her kind of thing, but she was happy to help.

AND there was at least one further compensation in not playing rugby: to actually take pause long enough to watch it closely. It meant John could begin to understand the tactical and deeper side of the game better, a side not often explored by those of his ilk.

For example, one of John's predecessors in the Australian second row, while playing club rugby in France, once expressed a forceful view to the captain of the backs just where he thought the backline was going wrong: how they had to straighten their angle of attack, do shorter passes, and run around each other doing loop-de-loop passes like he had long seen the Ella brothers do, thus giving the centre the full benefit of every ounce of backline knowledge he had in him, until ... until ... until ...

Until he was forcefully interrupted by his team-mate, who said derisively, '*Mais Fizzee, qu'est-ce qu tu sais? T'es un avant et vois le match avec ton cul.*' (But what would you know, Fitzy, you are a *forward* and see the match through your arse.)

It was a fair point by any measure, and could be equally applied to most forwards of the era, including Eales. Head down, bum up, forwards traditionally travelled from ruck to ruck, hit it with the back feet spinning like the back wheel of a motorbike and then moved on to the next ruck, before doing the same . . . and so on. It was not an existence designed to assist understanding a lot of the patterns of a rugby game. And this is why, in 1993, John found it so refreshing to be watching rugby games with his real eyes for a change.

For the first time he really began to see patterns of play, and understood more about what the coaches had been on about. Sometimes, from the stands, he could see glaring weaknesses in the opposition's defences that he never would have seen if he had been out on the field. The time away from actual participation gave him a whole different way of looking at the game. To this point he had seen it as primarily a physical contest, but now started to see that the intellectual side was just as important. Tactically, the game was to move oppositions around the field until a weakness was created, at which point it had to be exploited immediately.

ALL of that aside, however, once the international season was in full swing all the advantages of not being out on the field were long gone, and it was simply frustrating. Wild horses could not have propelled John to hang around the Wallabies now that he wasn't playing with them — he was simply not the dressing-room-afterwards type — but he still wanted to see every game they played, live. From the terraces. Usually he just went along with a couple of mates and watched the game with everyone else.

Rupert McCall was amazed when, accompanying John to the first of the South African Tests at the Sydney Football Stadium that year, they walked back from the stadium to the city afterwards, following Australia's 19-12 loss. As they walked along, people were constantly coming up to John saying, 'If we'd had you, we would have won it.' 'They need you, John.' 'Can you hurry up on your comeback?' The whole way back to the city, it kept going.

'They just *love* him,' Rupert told their wider circle of friends. 'He's a superstar, even when he's injured.'

Which was as maybe. For there was still no getting around an old saying among the rugby wise-heads to the effect that when a player drops out of a team for any particular reason it is 'like taking your finger out of a glass of water, so quickly is the vacuum filled. And there is some truth in it. However much John might have been missing the Wallabies, it was not absolutely sure and certain that the Wallabies were missing him equally. Garrick Morgan had sustained his early season form with Queensland and been even more impressive with the Wallabies. John had to admit it, Garrick was tearing them up. A devastating runner with the ball in his hands, while a still competent lineout jumper and scrummager, he was rightly receiving rave reviews for his efforts.

And when the Wallabies beat the Springboks in the Second Test at Ballymore a fortnight later, the tone of the fans' support for John had changed. 'Weren't they *good?*' the supporters asked him on the way out of Ballymore. 'You'll be lucky to get back into the side.' 'Did you ever think Garrick Morgan could play like that?' A lot of it was said with very friendly jocularity, of course, but there was no getting around it: John was no longer *the man*, and there was a new one in town.

Throughout the international season, Morgan was at the forefront of the Wallaby forwards' attack, and at the year's end the prestigious French rugby newspaper *Midi-Olympique* gave him its International Rugby Player of the Year award. By the time the Wallabies arrived home after a victorious tour, quite a few people weren't saying anything to John, other than hello.

While he was happy enough for Garrick, John was often reminded of one of John Paul Young's earliest hits: 'Take a look at me, I'm yesterday's hero.'

All together sing: *Haven't I seen that face before? Weren't you the boy who used to live next door? Weren't you on television every night . . . ? Didn't you used to be John Eales?*

There remained some evidence, however, that in certain sections of the community his name endured, if not his face, and Garrick had not taken over the world completely. On a flight from Sydney to Brisbane late in the year, for example, John found himself sitting next to a Sri Lankan-born man by the name of Michael. The two were chatting, when Michael asked whether John played any sport.

'Yes, rugby . . . '

'Union or league?'

'Union for the Brothers club.'

'Would you like to play for the Reds one day?'

'One day, yes I would,' John replied, a little uncomfortably, trapped by his own humility.

'You would have to beat John Eales or Rod McCall . . . '

'Mmmmm.'

'By the way, what is your name? I will look out for you . . . '

(No way out).

'John Eales . . . '

Michael looked very sheepish, but John didn't blame him. And at least yesterday's hero was occasionally acknowledged in the present day. A case in point was a function at Sydney's Regent Hotel. John and the rest of the World Cup Winning Wallabies were belatedly presented by the ARU with crystal decanters emblazoned with a likeness of the William Webb Ellis Trophy to commemorate their achievement eighteen months earlier.

'Give this to the woman you love,' President Joe French said to him quietly in a voice raspy with the onset of a cancer that would sadly kill him within months, 'and she'll be yours forever.'

John smiled and told Joe he would do just that. He took it home and put it in a cupboard, against the day . . .

Things were going well enough with Peta, but not *that* well. In fact under the strains of John's continued touring the couple had already broken up once and were really just struggling along. John had been away on so many tours, then had been seriously injured, then constantly concentrating on his rehabilitation, while also keeping up with all his friends . . . which meant there was very little time left over for Peta. So it was. John simply kept on keeping on, continuing with his rehabilitation, his work with G & E Hotels, going out with his friends, seeing a bit of his girlfriend, and hoping that next year would be a better one. At least there were real signs that the shoulder was getting better . . .

When Bernadette and Tony were married on 18 December 1993 in the Marist Brothers Ashgrove Chapel, John was able to hurl confetti every bit as hard as Peta and all the rest, and raise the champagne high as he called on everyone to toast the happy couple. He wasn't over the line by any means, but Peter Myers was extremely happy with how everything was coming along and told him there seemed to be no reason why he wouldn't be able to resume his rugby the following year.

This was not missed by the international rugby community, where news of Eales' forthcoming return spread quickly.

In this first week of February 1994, the All Blacks were doing serious squad training under the tutelage of coach Laurie Mains at scenic Taupo on the North Island. In fact, New Zealand's finest had little time to admire the scenery as Mains flogged them through hard fitness sessions, and no-one more than the veteran All Black second-rower Ian Jones, known to the team as 'Kamo'. When Jones seemed to be flagging at one point in a series of 150 metre sprints — he had after all started training at 7 a.m. and it was now 3.30 p.m. — Laurie Mains zeroed in without mercy.

'Do you think John Eales is doing this, Kamo?!' he shouted. 'Do you think he's driving himself like this?'

Jones was incapable of answering, but was thinking that John probably was soaking up the sun on the Gold Coast this early in the season, and maybe going for a gentle run before breakfast each morning.

In fact, John too was working as hard as ever, not just with ongoing shoulder exercises, but more to the point getting physically fit enough for what he hoped would be a full international season. Beyond the regular Queensland training sessions, he was also going on long runs three to four times a week, sometimes along the old routes he used to take with Damian, with Simon Whitehart, and with his sisters.

ONE of the first real tests of how well John's shoulder had recovered came, oddly enough, in the form of a cricket testimonial for the Queensland and Australian fast bowler Carl Rackemann. With other sports celebrities and great cricketers, John played a one-day game at the ANZ Stadium and remembers being in seventh heaven, most of the time. Certainly he was bowling with his right arm, which was uninjured, but still . . .

But still on a day like that he was unlikely to be feeling any pain anyway. At one point he was running in to bowl to Greg Chappell, with Dennis Lillee at mid-off and Viv Richards at mid-on. After each ball Mr Lillee, make that 'Dennis', would give him some advice as to what to do on the next ball, Viv would wink, and he'd run in again.

When the time came to bat, John only scored a meagre ten runs, but one of the shots that notched a superb single was an absolute beauty. 'I did that leg-glance for you, Dad,' he told his delighted father afterwards.

But the main thing was that, through all the movement of a one-day cricket game, his shoulder had caused him no pain at all. The tests conducted by Peter Myers showed it was almost back to 100 per cent strength.

BY the beginning of the Queensland season proper, there were two lots of good news and one lot of bad. The first good news was that John's shoulder had indeed recovered to the point that he had made his way back into the Queensland squad and successfully completed the pre-season training without breaking down. Also, Ben Perkins had been appointed by John Connolly as the team's goal-kicking coach, meaning that John could spend a lot more time with his close friend. Certainly Ben's approach to goal-kicking was not completely orthodox. He was legendary in his own kicking days for telling a ball boy who brought him the sand that the ball was too flat and he should immediately put precisely three pumps in it — but it seemed he really knew what he was doing when it came to technique. John felt he was of invaluable assistance when it came to refining his own. The way Peta saw it, and she was often around when Ben and John were in long discussions, Ben had a deep technical knowledge which John really enjoyed plumbing. Ben was also absolutely straight with John about everything to do with rugby — telling him when he thought he had a bad or good game, and most particularly how he could improve his game. And of course they could both still talk till the wee hours about matters of philosophy, spirituality, etc.

The bad news was right there in the headlines:

'EALES SPOT NO SURE THING.' *Sunday Telegraph.* 'There is a very real possibility Wallaby ace John Eales will be left in the grandstand when the Queensland team christens the Ballymore lights against N Transvaal.'

'WALLABY ACE STUCK IN LIMBO.' *Sunday Mail.*

'EALES NOT CERTAIN OF REDS SPOT.' *Sun-Herald.*

Typically, Nonna loved these headlines — rarely comprehending the purport of the accompanying words — content merely that 'my John' was in his rightful place with his name in big letters at the top of the page.

The problem was that Rod McCall was in possibly the finest form of his career, while according to *Midi-Olympique* Garrick Morgan was nothing less than the finest rugby player in the world. All of which meant that the Queensland second-row was a hard nut to crack. As to the back-row, it too had specialist players of the calibre of David Wilson, Sam Scott-Young and Ilie Tabua.

And so, for several games of the subsequent Queensland domestic season, the once-mighty Eales was reduced to entering the field from the bench. He did not find it easy but simply had to accept it, and play so well that they just couldn't leave him out.

IN June, good news. Whatever John Connolly's seeming ambivalence about John's worth at that time — for the Super 10 Final against Natal in Durban, he had only made it on to the field for the last twenty minutes — it was not shared by the national coach. When the time came to pick the Wallaby side to play Ireland in Brisbane, Bob Dwyer made it known that 'John Eales was the first one we picked'.

True, there was a certain poignancy in the move, given that the Test second-rower who was axed to make way for Eales was John's long-time mentor, Rod McCall, but ultimately this was naught but an observation of one of sport's strongest laws — the son always rises. John had a certain sympathy for Rod, and commiserated with him, but it was hard to hide his joy at being back in the side after eighteen months away.

Plus, John's second-row partner was Garrick Morgan. By this time, the relationship between the two was very close, and both felt like some kind of destiny had been fulfilled when they packed down together in their first Test scrum. Happily, Dwyer's faith in Eales was rewarded when John played as well as ever in Australia's demolition of Ireland and then of Italy in two one-off Tests.

There were two new faces of note in the Wallabies since John had last graced their presence. One was Daniel Herbert, a fellow Queenslander playing in the centres, both Tim Horan and Jason Little having severely injured their knees in the Super 10 Final at Kings Park, Durban, within ten minutes of each other. The other was young George Gregan from Canberra who had taken over the half-back position from Nick Farr-Jones when he had definitively retired at the end of the previous year.

Only 21 years old, George Musarurwa Gregan had been born in Zambia of an Australian father and Zambian mother. Quietly spoken, almost in the Eales mould, he was a superb athlete who was naturally aggressive and the two got on well from the start.

The wins over Ireland and Italy, while welcome, were hardly satisfying, and provided almost no clue as to how the Wallabies were travelling for the 1995 World Cup to be held in South Africa, starting in May of the following year.

The first *real* test of the Wallabies' capabilities came only in early August when, during a night game at the Sydney Football Stadium, they played Western Samoa. This was a team that only a few months previously had beaten an entirely rebuilt Wales side — good enough to win the Five

Nations — by 34-9. But on this night, the Wallabies were in fine form indeed and smacked them, smoked 'em, rolled 'em up and poked them, and comprehensively beat them 73-3.

The climax of the year, as always, was the clash with the All Blacks — this particular Bledisloe Cup being a one-off Test at the Sydney Football Stadium under lights. Despite their fine win over Western Samoa the week before, the Wallabies' level of confidence going into this Test was not sky-high. The All Blacks had been going through a difficult period of late where they had lost Tests they were expected to win, and they would be desperate to win. In the team-room before the squad got on the bus, John noticed Tony Daly earnestly and obviously looking for something, under chairs, behind the pot plants, under the carpet.

'What are you doing, Dales?' John asked, a little quizzically.

'Looking for it,' Daly replied.

'Looking for what?'

'The Panic Button. It's time to press it.'

So occurred a game of legend that would stay long in the memory of the Australian rugby public — including all the members of the Grand Slam Wallabies of 1984 who were gathered together for a ten-year reunion and had been presented to the crowd before the game. After a massive high kick from the Wallaby five-eighth David Knox was fumbled by the New Zealand fullback, Jason Little scored for Australia after only 16 seconds (!) and 25 minutes later the Wallabies had skipped to a handsome 17-3 lead. But, as All Blacks are wont to do, they simply refused to die and kept coming back hard. With just four minutes to go in the game, Australia was clinging to a 20-16 lead when it happened. After a long New Zealand movement, the ball came into the hands of All Black winger Jeff Wilson about 25 metres from the Wallaby try-line. John scrambled towards him, but was no hope from the start. Wilson, one of the finest wingers New Zealand has produced, jinked inside his opposing winger, Damian Smith, outside the first of the despairing Australian cover defence and set sail for the line. At stake was not only the Bledisloe Cup, but history. Fifteen metres to go. If he scored, this All Black side would escape the ignominy of being the first New Zealand side since 1949 to post a losing season. If he didn't, the 1994 Wallabies would be the first Australian side to have an unbeaten season. Two metres to go. The line yawned before him.

Still about twenty metres away from any possibility of stopping him — short of hurling a football boot at his head and hoping for the best — Eales had an instant of total despair. Then along came George!

Georgie Gregan on the fly, coming from nowhere and hurtling towards a Jeff Wilson who seemed to have only the barest idea Gregan was there. At the last possible instant and in total exocet missile mode, Gregan launched himself the last two metres into Wilson and hit him hard. So hard, that even as Wilson was in the process of scoring the try, the ball was jarred loose from his hands and . . . the game was gone for New Zealand. The final score was 20-16 to Australia, and the Bledisloe Cup was back on the national mantelpiece. It was a fitting climax to a marvellous game which displayed Test rugby at its very best and installed Australia as favourites for the World Cup. The Wallabies had won six out of six Tests, and you couldn't ask for better than that. Apart, of course, from a fair share of the tremendous spoils that their endeavours had helped generate, but there appeared to be little chance of that.

Just two days after the Wallabies' sterling victory, the chairman of the International Rugby Board, Vernon Pugh, visited Australia and issued an extremely blunt warning, which appeared beneath a headline in the *Sydney Morning Herald*: 'WALLABIES MAY FACE WORLD CUP AXE.'

'If a national union is in breach of the [amateurism] regulations,' he fumed, 'then someone can lodge a complaint in response to that union, and you could achieve a position whereby under disciplinary procedures, that union could be expelled . . . '

When asked if he could ever actually see that happening, Pugh was forthright.

'Yes,' he replied simply. 'I honestly can see the possibility of action being taken in respect of some unions if there is a continuance of non-conformity to the regulations.'

He cited particularly the fact 'both Australia and New Zealand are currently in breach of regulation 7 concerning the readmittance of rugby league players', but their lack of strict adherence to amateurism was also a pressing problem. In a statement made earlier the same month, the chairman had made clear his attitudes on amateurism when he said that 'the traditional ethos of the game sits very uneasily with it becoming a fully professional sport . . . The introduction of professionalism would bring attitudes, practices and personalities into the game which are currently wholly alien to it.'

In his interview, Pugh affirmed that position saying that the possibility of rugby going professional was 'extremely unlikely. I do not think rugby has any chance at all of sustaining a professional game.'

And the IRB's likely stance if confronted with proof of a union flouting the amateur regulations?

'The same as I've said before. The rules have to be complied with. There is no option for any country or club to proceed independently.'

An assiduous reader of the Sydney papers, it all made rather sober reading for John. What chance that his own published views of the year before — that rugby had to embrace quasi-professionalism — would actually come to fruition?

Zero. That certainly was the view of Garrick Morgan who, as soon as the international season was over, announced that he was finished with rugby and would henceforth be playing rugby league for the South Queensland Crushers for the unbelievable sum of around $200,000 a season. Which was fine for Garrick. His block-busting skills of making and breaking tackles were transferable to the professional game. John's skills on the other hand, most notably in the lineout, clearly were not — and in his whole life he knew he would never be offered that kind of money. Unless, of course, he could come up with some kind of genius idea totally removed from rugby and make the big bucks himself.

At this time, John recalled a line from Virgin founder, Richard Branson, which he'd read in the UK while on the Emerging Wallabies tour in 1990. 'The secret [to getting rich],' Branson had said, 'is to find out what you absolutely love doing and then to work out how to make money out of it.'

John knew what he absolutely loved doing: playing rugby. The problem was there was no obvious way to make big money out of it.

The Times
They are
a'Changing!

*There seems to be an awful lot of things the union now does to
make money out of the sport, but there is still this feeling that the players
should not make out any money out of it. Everyone seems to do
very well out of Rugby Union except the players. It has become more than
a fun game. You do not have a World Cup for fun and recreation.*

English rugby captain WILL CARLING, May 1995

*We believe we are running a sport as a recreation for
players to play in their spare time. I think money is a corrosive influence.*

Secretary of the English Rugby Union, DUDLEY WOOD, in reply

⌐

STRANGE DAYS indeed, most peculiar, mama.
On the late afternoon of Friday, 1 April 1995, just a couple of
months after beginning his new job as a trainee manager for Qantas —
flitting between the check-in counter, the reservations desk and the
baggage carousel — John was driving to Ballymore for a training run. He
was listening to the car radio with half an ear when some extraordinary
news bulletins started coming, one after the other. Something called
Super League had been launched. Financed by the forces of Rampagin'
Rupert Murdoch, rugby league players in their droves were defecting

from the establishment Australian Rugby League and signing up to play in this new competition, to be launched some time in the near future. They were doing so in return for an amount of dollars which had an uncanny resemblance to their own telephone numbers. Players who had been on $150,000 dollars a year were signing for $500,000. Players on $250,000 were going for $800,000 a year for three years, plus a sign-on fee of $200,000. The word was that the Kerry Packer-backed ARL would soon reply by opening its own coffers, but for the moment all the league establishment had done was express its outrage.

Super League was discussed at training that night, but not dwelt upon. It was interesting from a rugby league point of view, and certainly significant for guys like Garrick who had just joined their ranks, but it didn't really seem to be something that affected the Queensland players.

In fact, the most seminal year in the history of both rugby league and rugby union had just begun, and the rumbling in the near distance was the seismic plates of the international rugby football landscape beginning to shift, propelled by unstoppable forces that had been slowly building up for years. After that first crazy Friday, open warfare had been declared by the forces of Packer on those of Murdoch, which is to say — in this situation — the forces of the Establishment and the Rebels. The principal ammunition used by both sides was huge wads of cash, aimed at any player not already bolted down, and it quickly became obvious to the administrators of rugby union that the Wallaby ranks would be completely decimated unless they acted quickly. The defection of Morgan to rugby league the previous year had not sat well with the rugby union authorities, but that would be as nothing compared to what might happen now. The administrators had to move to prevent the same happening again.

They did so. Just a little over a week later, both the Queensland and the NSW Rugby Unions put out a joint statement, momentous in its implications. 'RUGBY IS NO LONGER AMATEUR,' ran the bold heading. It went on to assert that the 'rugby world has been remunerating players and coaches in various ways for a very long time . . . Amateurism as a concept is outmoded and should be dispensed with in the modern game.' Interestingly, it didn't go on to boldly state the even more bleeding obvious, that 'rugby is now professional', but the effect was exactly the same. For the first time in the history of the game, two rugby union institutions had broken ranks and declared that the first article of faith on which the code had been built worldwide — amateurism — was no longer valid.

They had formalised what had been previously an informal understanding, brought out into the open what had been previously undercover,
saluted what formerly had only been surreptitiously nodded at — but it
was clear to all at the time that this was the day the dam broke. None,
however, had even the vaguest idea just how big the flood would be . . .

For from the moment of that announcement, rugby union at the top
level would never be the same. Beyond matters of rugby *realpolitik*, though,
the most pressing aim of the announcement had already been accomplished — to send a cogent message to the code's elite players. That message
ran: 'DON'T GO! Maintain the faith, don't depart for Super League and
you'll be taken care of financially. You'll stay with the game and the people
you know, and you'll get rich.' Within days the national ruling body, the
Australian Rugby Union, had followed suit and endorsed the statement.
Although rugby had lived on a diet of fresh air and love for well over a
century, it was clear that something far more fragrant would shortly be
added to the mix — though just when was anyone's guess.

John Eales was fascinated by the latest development, but like all of
his Queensland team-mates, not totally convinced that it would make a
difference to him in the short term. For while it was one thing to say 'we
are no longer amateur', it was obviously quite another to actually have
the money to pay the players.

In fact, from the beginning of 1995, eleven of the Wallabies, including
John, had been put on a payment of $75,000 a season, nominally to
'ensure their endorsement of ARU sponsors and to make promotional
appearances'. That kind of money was as nothing compared to the kind
of money rugby league was hurling around, but the problem of where to
get the big money required was being worked on, right then and there, in
two separate camps.

The first camp was within the hallowed halls of the rugby establishment, where it had been decided that the only way to counter the great
gravitational pull of Murdoch's Super League — a creation of Rampaging's
newly established Australian pay television network's voracious appetite
for product — was to go to Murdoch themselves. The deal was to try and
sell him on the idea that rugby was an even better game for his purposes
because of its global nature. If they could come up with what they called
a Perfect Rugby Product — a regular competition made for TV purposes,

spanning Australia, New Zealand and South Africa — they felt confident they could generate the money for rugby to go fully professional.

It was with that in mind that for two days in late April, even while John and his team-mates were coming to and going from rugby training at Ballymore, the QRU CEO Terry Doyle sat in an office of the administrative block with his NSWRU and ARU counterparts, David Moffett and Bruce Hayman, secretly working out just what the Perfect Rugby Product they were hoping to sell actually consisted of.

The model they came up with was, at the provincial level, a Super 12 competition consisting of five sides from New Zealand, four from South Africa and three from Australia. Ideally, that competition would start in early March and go through till the finals in mid-May, whereupon each nation would have six weeks to host the usual incoming tours from the northern hemisphere. Then in July, the model called for each nation to play in a Tri-Series — two Tests apiece against the other two. With minor overlapping, the schedule also allowed for South Africa's Currie Cup and New Zealand's National Provincial Championships to be played out in full at the conclusion of the series. With a touch more tinkering, Moffett, Hayman and Doyle felt they would have the proposal in shape to take it to Rupert Murdoch's lieutenants, who had already expressed provisional interest in it.

IN the meantime, down in Sydney, another independent group was pursuing a similar path, albeit on a far more grandiose scale. Sydney lawyer Geoff Levy and his friend, the former-Wallaby-now-businessman Ross Turnbull had, together with Newcastle solicitor Michael Hill, secretly formed the grandly named World Rugby Corporation. Their idea was also to totally professionalise rugby by forming business franchises all over the world which would run the teams and reap the enormous profits which these men of the WRC were sure would result. Their central idea was that, instead of the international rugby status quo, which was a mosaic of hotchpotch matches played between nations around the world — coming together only once every four years for the World Cup — the game would be properly internationalised, with a veritable World Cup being held throughout the year, every year. Ideally, the rugby unions of the establishment would have half-ownership of these franchises, but if not, that was their pigeon — a dead one.

Turnbull's plan was to sign players up on the quiet, and only unveil that fact to rugby authorities when a critical mass had been reached, at which time the unions would simply have no choice but to embrace the concept. They would need money to get the players signed up around the world, but negotiations with such Sydney businessmen as advertising's John Singleton and Hungry Jack's owner Jack Cowin provided the necessary capital. At a later point, the Australian media mogul Kerry Packer's lieutenants indicated they would also contribute just under $3 million to the exercise, in return for a handsome percentage of ownership should the project actually get up.

THOUGH John and all the other Wallabies were still entirely unaware of it, the battle lines were being drawn for a genuine Rugby Civil War, where no quarter would be asked for or given. At the time however, far more interesting to the Wallabies was the ongoing Super League war where nearly all were seen as potential targets. Regularly, the names of the entire Wallaby team would be listed in the papers with figures as to what they would likely be worth to Super League. Tim Horan and Jason Little, for example, were reputed to be worth as much as $400-500,000 each per year. Though gangly forwards were regarded as being worth a lot less, John was amazed that Rod McCall was listed in the paper as being worth $100,000 dollars.

'But Rod,' Eales enquired of his second-row partner, completely mystified, 'would [Super League boss] John Ribot really pay that much for an *office boy?*'

McCall had his revenge about a week later when one of the Sydney papers listed Rod McCall at admittedly a measly $10,000, but John Eales was merely marked down as 'not considered suitable'.

McCall laughed until he could laugh no more.

IN fact with the World Cup looming, not one Wallaby had jumped across to Super League, though there was no telling how many would hang around once the cup was over. In the meantime, there were many spin-off opportunities for the Wallabies. In the weeks prior to their departure to South Africa, a businessman friend of John's by the name of Terry Jackman organised a $10,000 deal with Triple M radio network for the second-rower to do World Cup previews. John also signed a similar contract with

Channel Seven's *Today Tonight* program. The network — which had just taken over the rugby union broadcasting rights from Channel Ten — would provide a producer and script, and all John had to do was stare down the barrel of the camera and read the autocue, as well as occasionally interview one of his team-mates.

'The network is very pleased with the work of John Eales,' a Seven spokesman was quoted as saying in *TV Scene* shortly after John began. 'He was adept at the role when he started, but his delivery and his confidence have been improving dramatically every week. The best part about using rugby players is that, unlike a lot of footballers from other codes, they can string together sentences that don't start with "mate" and end with "you know".'

All well and good . . .

For John, apart from the money, it was also a much-hoped-for-chance to learn new skills, as the injury to his shoulder had highlighted for him the fact that rugby wouldn't last forever and he would be needing something to fall back upon when it was all over. He still had no idea what he wanted to do when that time came, but in the meantime was eager to use all the leverage that rugby gave him to best effect. Significantly, the deal with Channel Seven was organised and negotiated by his old school and university friend Chris White, who had set up his own sports marketing company. Two of White's first clients had been John and Rupert McCall, who since their days back in Ron Price's swimming pool had continued to explore his poetry skills. Back in 1993, John had invited Rupert to accompany him to speak at an enormous function before South Africa had played the Wallabies at Ballymore, and promised he would try and get him to the podium to recite a poem he'd written about the Wallaby back-rower Ilie Tabua. When the moment came, Rupert had recited the poem and neither he nor John could help but notice that a fair proportion of the room were standing on their feet and cheering as they got into the rhythm of it all.

Lookadim go! The Human Skewer.
Lookadim! Lookadim! Ilie Tabua.
Lookadim running low to the ground.
Lookadim hammer! Lookadim pound!
Lookadim poised like a heavyweight punch.
Lookadim launch! Lookadim crunch!

A career was born, and it wasn't just Ilie Tabua's, who proceeded to play a magnificent match for the Wallabies ...

While the war between Super League and the Australian Rugby League hurtled on, the Wallabies began their international campaign. Two quick Test wins over Argentina proved nothing one way or another, other than that the Wallabies were at least a better chance of winning the World Cup starting in three weeks time than the Argentinians. As defending champions the Wallabies were due to play against hosts South Africa in Cape Town immediately after the Opening Ceremony on 25 May. Because of that, both Tests against Argentina had the feel of trial matches about them. The ultimate nightmare for all players concerned was to get knocked out with an injury when they already had one foot on the plane, so it was two rather careful teams that went into battle.

No damage, no drama. no delays, the Wallabies flew to South Africa on 15 May, leaving Sydney just a few hours after Geoff Levy of the World Rugby Corporation flew in. He had just returned from a week's trip overseas where, with Ross Turnbull and Michael Hill, there had been a frantic scramble to test the amount of international television interest in WRC's vision, and whether key rugby identities in Britain and France were willing to come on board. The short answer was 'yes' on every count — there really was a lot of interest. The World Rugby Corporation was all systems go from that point on, and moved on to the next, very delicate, covert step of trying to sign up the players in total secrecy.

The only clue the Wallabies had of any of this came when the ARU President Phil Harry addressed them all at the hotel just before getting on the plane, informing them that they should be aware that Ross Turnbull was going around with some crazy 'rugby circus' venture, and if they saw him in South Africa they should steer clear of him. Harry told them that the ARU was doing their own negotiations with a couple of very powerful business people and he should have some very good news for everyone shortly.

You beaut. John, with the rest of the Wallabies, had little idea of what Harry was talking about in regard to Turnbull and flew westward ho. It was a curious circumstance that the South African Airways flight taking the Wallabies to the World Cup also bore the team presumed to be their greatest rivals to take home the William Webb Ellis trophy — the All Blacks. The two sides sat side by side up the front of the plane with a bare minimum of restrained chit-chat and a maximum of getting as much sleep as possible. A fierce five week campaign awaited.

At this time, the Wallabies were quite confident. Undefeated the previous year, they had just embarked upon the last and most crucial stage of what the ARU had, the previous year, dubbed Mission: REPEAT. Translated, this meant 'Mission: Reach Ellis Park and Ensure Another Twickenham'.

Certainly, Mission: REPEAT had in many ways been a marketing exercise designed to heighten the interest of the public and potential sponsors alike in the Wallabies venture, and serious resources had been put into the campaign. In the lead-up to the cup no fewer than 30 appointed experts around Australia and the world had been feeding information to Dwyer regarding the physical capacities of his players, the tactics and strategies used by other teams, the effects that playing at altitude would likely have, the time they would need to acclimatise, etc.

Not all nations had been so assiduous in their preparation. During a welcoming function for the World Cup at Stellenbosch, John chatted to Ireland's Neil Francis, the fellow who had jumped against him during the 1991 World Cup quarter-final.

'I see that you Australians have gone to all lengths preparing for the World Cup '95, leaving no stone unturned with acclimatisation and so forth,' Francis told him. 'We Irish play all our pool matches at altitude and in our infinite wisdom had our major World Cup training camp at Kilkenny, a place that's actually 27 feet below sea level.'

JUST two days after the Wallabies arrived in Johannesburg, another key meeting took place in London which, again, though unbeknown to John and the rest of the Wallabies, would ultimately have an enormous effect on all of their lives. It was a meeting between key representatives of the Australian, New Zealand and South African Rugby Unions and Sam Chisholm, Rupert Murdoch's right-hand man for all things concerning television outside America. In the weeks since Super League had been launched and rugby union had tried to organise itself to keep the Hun from the gate, things had progressed quickly. The unions had fine-tuned their Perfect Rugby Product to the point where they were ready to present it to the key News Corp decision-maker. Overseeing the process would be the man the unions had hired to put the deal together, Ian Frykberg, the CEO of TV brokerage firm Communication Services International.

'Now remember,' Frykberg said, as he briefed his companions before they made their way into Chisholm's apartment, opposite a particularly well manicured green park. 'Don't waste Chisholm's time, don't say anything obvious, and keep whatever points you've got to make concise. He's always bloody busy, and he likes to get to the point.'

It was 11 o'clock on the morning of 16 May 1995, a wonderful warm day of late spring, and NSWRU chief executive officer David Moffett, in the company of a bevy of leading southern hemisphere rugby officials in ARU director Dick McGruther, NZ Rugby Football Union chairman Richie Guy, and his deputy Rob Fisher, followed Frykberg through the door, ready to talk turkey . . .

ON the morning of Thursday 25 May, the day the Wallabies were due to fire the opening salvo of their World Cup campaign against the Springboks, John awoke early with the strange presentiment that something was different. What was it? It wasn't just the slightly tight feeling he always had in his belly on match morning, it was a sound.

Hub-bub-bub-bub-bubba-bubba-bubba. People. Lots of them. Where?

He put his head out his window at the Newlands Holiday Inn, just down the road from Newlands Stadium where they were to play that afternoon, looked down, and there they were. It was only 8 a.m., but people were already streaming down that street heading towards the stadium, carrying their flags, their picnic baskets and whatnots. There was an extraordinary atmosphere, almost as if after a long build-up the storm was going to break and these people were going to be there to soak up every moment of it. The previous morning John had read that no fewer than 6 million South Africans would be taking the day off so as to properly enjoy the occasion and he could believe it. It felt like he'd just seen half of them walking by the hotel. This was going to be some match all right.

IN his own Johannesburg hotel room later that day, the captain and hooker of the All Blacks, Sean Fitzpatrick, watched the television set intently as the live transmission showed the Wallabies alighting from their bus for the opening game. Just one look at them, and Fitzpatrick felt the Australians would lose. When asked by an Australian interviewer a short time later just why he had felt that so strongly, Fitzpatrick waved a dismissive hand . . .

'Well, you know,' he said, 'the sunnies, the *attitude*. It was exactly like we All Blacks were four years ago. We thought all we had to do was turn up and put the black jerseys on and we would win. I say that with the greatest respect for the Wallabies . . . but it is funny drawing the analogy from 1991 and seeing it so clearly now. You don't put in the same preparation as you did before, and you keep on telling yourself that everything is all right, even when you know it isn't.'

In the dressing room just prior to the match, John Eales also felt that things weren't right. It wasn't necessarily the Wallaby attitude that was the problem, though, so much as the bandages, and he didn't mean just the ones going around his shoulder. Dan Crowley had them pressed tightly around his lower back, Phil Kearns around his ankle trying to give support to an Achilles tendon that was hanging by a thread, Willie O had them around his knee, Ewen McKenzie around most of his joints, Rod McCall around his ankle, Tim Gavin around both knees and David Wilson also around his ankle. This was, of course, just the pack, while the Australian backline had an almost equally long roll-call of those feeling seriously rucked and far from home. As one Australian writer would shortly note, 'there is some argument that if the injuries carried collectively by them were put together in one player, a near-cripple would be created'.

However, if the Wallabies were feeling tired and jaded on that sunny Thursday afternoon, it was more apparent than ever that their opponents would be feeling quite the reverse. For, having gone for the traditional walk on the pitch to get the feel of the stadium about 45 minutes before the opening whistle, it had become clearer now to the Wallabies that what they would shortly be up against was a lot more than merely fifteen members of a football team. Under the hazy pale blue sky, more than 50,000 passionate rugby supporters were crammed into Newlands stadium, and the vast majority of them were South Africans. Television cameras were everywhere, ready to beam the vision to a potential worldwide audience of two billion, and President Nelson Mandela *himself* was about to open the World Cup only a few skinny kilometres from Roben Island, where he had been imprisoned for more than two decades. The atmosphere was genuinely, joyously, explosive. Banners proclaiming the Springboks slogan of choice for the tournament — 'One Team, One Country' — were everywhere.

As John looked around, he felt very strongly that this was one of the most powerful atmospheres he had experienced in a stadium before a match.

Nor did any of that electric atmosphere dissipate while the Wallabies were making their final preparations. As deep in the bowels of Newlands stadium as their dressing room was, the noises from outside still made their way to them. At the Opening Ceremony, President Mandela, his every sentence greeted with loud and almost hysterical cheering, sounded a theme of how the 'young democracy and rainbow nation is very proud to greet you here today, before the eyes of the world. South Africa opens its arms and heart to embrace you all!'

Jets flew overhead, battalions of tribesmen performed traditional dances, as around and about the President, the mixed races of South Africa roared their approval and waved thousands of the new multi-coloured national flag. Filling out the rugby kaleidoscope were a sprinkling of Australian supporters, bedecked in green and gold as they waved their own flags. It was terrific to have them there, but as was abundantly clear to the Wallabies as soon as they ran out, it was the Springboks who would have the advantage of tapping into that extraordinary atmosphere, and powering their way through 80 minutes of high-octane play.

Having lost the toss, Wallaby captain Michael Lynagh was forced to kick off and the Rugby World Cup 1995 had indeed begun. Thundering across the veldt, the Springbok forwards had marginally the better of their world champion counterparts in the early battle, while the South African backs also played a strong kicking game singularly designed to thwart and frustrate the Australians at every turn. Time and again, the Bok backs kicked the ball over the dead-ball line, meaning that Australia was constantly on the back foot, doing kickoffs from their 22 in the face of a Springbok forward pack that had rarely played better. The pressure on the Wallabies was constant. It seemed that whatever they tried, the swarming Springboks had an answer. This was not surprising given that their captain Francois Pienaar later revealed that for the previous year his team had focused heavily on winning this game, endlessly analysing and working out ways to counter everything the Wallabies had in their armoury.

At half-time the score stood at 14-13 in South Africa's favour, with both sides having scored a try. In the second half the Springboks consolidated their tiny lead with a successful penalty kick and drop goal to go to a 20-13 lead. They then assured their victory with a try to five-eighth Joel Stransky seventeen minutes from full-time. The Wallabies at least scored a late try to Phil Kearns to make the score more respectable at 27-18, but as everyone on the field knew, this was no more than a little window-dressing on what was in fact a gallingly heavy defeat. For John, it was the first Test loss he'd experienced with the Wallabies since late July 1992, nearly three years previously, and the first against a side other than the All Blacks — to whom he had twice lost by a margin of three points only.

As the Wallabies dragged their weary way back to their hotel for one of the unhappiest Happy Hours in their recent history, two other men also made their way back to their hotel rooms and got back to work. They were Ian Frykberg, and one of his associates from CSI, Jim Fitzmaurice. They had taken just a short break from working sun-up to sun-down, trying to calculate to the nearest lazy ten million dollars or so, a particular figure. That was, just how much News Corporation could be convinced to pay the rugby unions of Australia, New Zealand and South Africa for the now fully developed Perfect Rugby Product which, it was estimated, would annually generate 750 hours of hopefully absorbing television in three nations. The first meeting in Chisholm's apartment had gone well, and now the rugby unions were trying to work out just how much money they could ask for.

The two men worked late into the night, as in another part of the country at exactly the same time Ross Turnbull and Michael Hill of the newly formed World Rugby Corporation began to move around and open lines of communication with the various international teams. Though unknown to most of the Wallabies at the time, these men of the WRC had already talked extensively with Bob Dwyer, who had shown some interest. The Australian coach had in turn talked to Michael Lynagh to signal that, should he be thinking of retirement, he should at least be aware that there was a good chance that there would be money in the game the following year. When he had asked Lynagh whether he thought the other players would be interested in the whole concept, Lynagh had replied: 'I would like to wait until after the World Cup. This is our objective now, let's do this, win the cup, and then get on to that.'

After more discussion, Dwyer and Lynagh agreed that there were a couple of guys in the team under pressure from Super League, most notably Jason Little and Tim Horan, and they should at least be told that there was going to be an alternative available within rugby union where they could also be handsomely paid.

As a man 'not considered suitable' for League, John was not one of those so informed. His focus remained exclusively on the task at hand of getting to, and winning the World Cup Final. For all was not completely lost. Despite the *Cape Times* headline after Australia's opening defeat: 'CAMPO AND CO ARE NOW WORLD CHUMPS', it didn't have to be like that. The Springboks' victory merely meant that while the home-boys were set to cruise along the high road towards a possible finals berth — via likely encounters with Argentina in the quarter-finals and perhaps France in the semis — the Wallabies would be forced to fight their way along the low road, with a probable clash with England in the quarter-finals and the All Blacks in the semis. It was difficult, but manageable, they felt.

AFTER South Africa, the Wallabies' next Test was against Canada, where two young players, Joe Roff and Michael Foley, made significant debuts, and a single moment in the match proved symbolic of the Australian campaign. With ten minutes to go, David Campese pulled one of his classic goosesteps from out of his very top drawer and tried it on his Canadian opponent. It was clever, it was intricate, it was infinitely skilled and the opposing Canadian winger was no doubt impressed — but he dropped Campese like a sack of spuds all the same. So it went . . . The Wallabies finally won, but only by the meagre score of 27-11. The portents for the Wallabies successfully defending their World Cup remained poor.

The next game was against Romania at Stellenbosch, and it was significant for one key thing in the life and rugby career of John Eales. The Wallabies kicker, Matt Burke, had a rare off day with the boot — succeeding in only two of six penalty kicks — and the Wallaby captain of the day, Rod McCall, threw John the ball and said, 'Have a kick, John.'

Was Rod serious? He was serious. John was nervous. It was one thing to have occasionally kicked for Queensland in provincial games, but quite another to be lining the ball up in a Test match for Australia in a World Cup game. What if he missed?

He didn't miss. Not once. In the next 40 minutes he slotted all four of the possible conversions presented to him — each one from near the sideline — and finished the day with eight points next to his name. Not that he was particularly enthused by it.

'I'd be very happy if I never have to kick in a Test match again,' he told the press conference afterwards. 'I'd be happy to sit on that record.'

An openly admiring Bob Dwyer wouldn't hear of it. 'It is obvious goal-kicking is something John shouldn't practise, either — because he didn't have a kick all week!'

While John had been reasonably happy with his form throughout this World Cup, there was no question who the star, make that STAR of the tournament was. That honour went to a young New Zealander by the name of Jonah Lomu. His name and image were plastered all over front and back page across the country, in much the same fashion as in person he had been plastering opponents all over the field. Having grown up on the mean streets of a down-trodden part of Auckland, Lomu exploded in this World Cup. In the All Blacks' first game, against Ireland, for example, he had scored two tries and set up another by virtue of simply bumping off the five Irishmen — count 'em, *five!* — who hit him amidships.

WITH the conclusion of the pool games at least Australia had made it into the quarter-finals, up against England, but things just weren't right. For John's part, it was clear that the Wallabies weren't playing well. What was less obvious was how they could play better.

On the evening before the Test against England, Bob Dwyer addressed the Wallabies at the team-meeting, just as he always did. In the past, he would get so emotionally worked up at such meetings that it was not at all uncommon for him to be in tears as he exhorted his charges of the NEED to win, of the WAY they were going to accomplish it, on what it would MEAN to the supporters at home when they had done it, but on this evening he was curiously downbeat. Not resigned to defeat, per se, but to John's mind he at least seemed to be making oblique references to the fact that defeat was not out of the question.

Shocked and disappointed, John did not quite understand. It sounded like Bob was basically saying, 'Look, whatever happens tomorrow, we've been a great team and no-one can take that away from us.' At the very least, the Wallaby coach made it absolutely clear that he thought England was a very, very strong team.

Which was, to be fair, true enough. Unfortunately for the Wallabies, there seemed to be little sign in the English side of the kind of chaos that had been predicted after the terrible upheaval they had gone through a month previously. That had come about after their captain, Will Carling, had commented on a British television program: 'What gets me and a lot of players now is the hypocrisy of the situation. Why are we not just honest and say there is a lot of money in the game? If the game is run properly, as a professional game, you do not need 57 old farts running Rugby.' For Carling's trouble, the 57 'old farts' had combined and blown him clean out of the captaincy. He had regained it shortly afterwards — in response to a huge player outcry — but the pundits had predicted that their wheels would wobble throughout the campaign because of it.

WITH just two minutes to go in the quarter-final itself, the score was locked at 22-all. It had been a blazing battle of a Test with both sides having played themselves to exhaustion. A particularly notable clash had been in the backs, where Will Carling had a particularly fine game, despite David Campese prior to the match having unburdened himself of the view in a World Cup program that 'Carling himself epitomises England's lack of skills. He has speed and bulk, but plays like a castrated bull.' Which was as may be, but he was a bull who did a lot of damage, and the Englishman had been instrumental in setting up the key English try, in the first half, which had taken them to a 13-6 lead. The Australians had rallied magnificently to bring the scores level again, none more than Eales, who, as reported by Bruce Wilson of the *Daily Telegraph* 'played one of the best forward matches I have ever seen'.

Now, in those final minutes, both sides were hurling the very last ounces of energy they had in them to win the day. From an English line-out about 45 metres out from the Australian line, John's opposite number, Martin Bayfield, jumped just a fraction earlier — forewarned, as he was, that the ball was to him — and brought it down on the English side. From there, the English launched a forward drive some ten metres downfield, whereupon the ball was released to the English five-eighth Rob Andrew — the one and the same who John had brought down four years previously to ensure a Wallaby victory in the World Cup Final of 1991.

Shockingly, even from some 45 metres out, Andrew suddenly shaped to kick a field goal, and then *connected*. WHOOOOOOOOSHKA!

At that very instant, Bob Dwyer was making his way from the stands to the touch-line, ready to issue instructions on what to do in the extra time that would have to be played, when he looked up and saw it. The ball had left Andrew's boot straight and true, burnt past just above Michael Lynagh's desperately up-stretched fingers and looked to be sailing straight between the cross-bars. No, no, no, NOOOOOOOOOO! Yes. The ball went through. Scoreline: England 25, Australia 22.

Of all the Wallabies, Eales was the first back to the kick-off line, desperate to squeeze as much football into the final minute as possible in the vain hope of snatching victory from the jaws of defeat — just as they had so famously done in their last World Cup quarter-final against Ireland — but it was to no avail. The blast of the referee's shrill whistle to signal the end of the game and the Wallabies' campaign shattered more than just the air around. John felt completely gutted. For all their high hopes, all their impressive credentials, all their Mission: REPEATs, they simply hadn't played that well in the tournament, so there was always a chance they were going to lose. But after that kick came the realisation that they no longer had their title as world champions. John had only cried after a few games in his life but this was one. His overwhelming feeling was they had let Australia down. The rugby public's expectations had been high, certainly, but no higher than the Wallabies'. They expected nothing less than to get into the final and to win it. They had a good team which was capable of it . . . and yet somehow they had failed.

That night at the team hotel, Eales was more than merely morose when rugby journalist Greg Growden ran into him in the hotel restaurant, quietly having a meal. Other Wallabies had started to pick themselves up and start partying, but to Growden it seemed almost like Eales didn't want it to be that easy. The second-rower was inconsolable over the loss and didn't really want to talk about it, though he did say to Growden that he had no doubt that he had just experienced the low point of his career.

On a personal level, Eales had little to reproach himself for in terms of the way he had performed, a fact acknowledged by his fellow Wallabies when they voted him Player's Player. This high opinion was not restricted to just the Australian players. The coach of the Springboks, Kitch Christie, put himself at the front of the queue of admirers when he was quoted in Sydney's *Daily Telegraph*, 'If I could have any player in the world, I would pick John Eales.'

SUCH awards and comments were very nice, but they were no equal of having the gleaming Rugby World Cup sitting with the Wallabies in the business class section of a Qantas jet heading back to Australia. Instead, when the Wallaby team headed for home four days later, they had pretty much naught but horrible hangovers and a wretched sense of abject failure. The last time the Queensland members of the Wallaby World Cup squad had flown into Brisbane airport, the fire trucks had come out beside the runway and sprayed the plane with water by way of welcome.

'This time,' John heard Rod McCall mention to Ewen McKenzie in the row in front, 'there won't be any fire trucks.'

Exacerbating their sense of humiliation was the scene at Perth airport, which they reached after their eight-hour haul across the Indian Ocean. For there, as they exited, about 75 metres away and heading to a nearby boarding gate, was a whole posse of Australian rugby supporters, bedecked in green and gold, and on their way to South Africa. Many months before they would have booked their tickets, paid their money, with the full expectation that they would be seeing the Wallabies play in at least the semi-finals. But now they'd have no-one to cheer. John just couldn't face it, and neither could most of the others. Whether these supporters actually noticed the shadowy figures hovering behind the pillars as they passed is a moot point. Either way, John's former reckoning that he couldn't feel any worse than he did immediately after they'd lost the quarter-final to England was at that moment proven to be mistaken.

John arrived home just in time to attend the funeral of Nanna Violet Eales, who had died just a couple of days after their loss to England. It really had been that kind of month.

The World
Rugby
Corporation

Rugby is a nonsense, but a serious nonsense.

CLIFF MORGAN

Anyone who is fully informed is totally confused.

English Test hooker BRIAN MOORE, when
the fight between the forces of Rupert Murdoch
and Kerry Packer for control of
international rugby was at its height

❧

SOMETHING BIG was going down. On the eve of the World Cup
Final, between New Zealand and South Africa, the chairmen of the
three biggest national Rugby Unions of the southern hemisphere summoned the world's rugby press to the trophy room at Ellis Park stadium
to make an announcement.

Ahem. That announcement was that Rupert Murdoch's News Corporation had bought the television rights for the next ten years to a triangular
series, both at a national and provincial level, between New Zealand,
South Africa and Australia. And the amount he would paying for these
rights would be . . . $US555 million!

The response of the rugby press? Essentially stupefaction. For close on an hour, rugby reporters from all over the globe fired questions at the rugby tsars while they tried to work out the ramifications of such an enormous amount of money coming into what was still nominally an amateur code. The chairman of the South African Rugby Union, Louis Luyt, point blank denied that the announcement was a unilateral declaration that amateurism was finished, saying po-faced that the money would be going to 'rugby development'. But he may as well have saved his breath. It was obvious that such a massive amount of money was not going to be spent on buying new goalposts.

John read the news in the *Courier-Mail* and was fascinated, but there was still more staggering news to come . . .

Later that night, John watched the World Cup Final at the Brothers Rugby Club, and saw South Africa win by a breath of wind that helped carry Springbok five-eighth Joel Stransky's winning field goal, but the result was neither here nor there to him. Far more significantly, the following day around noon, John attended a hurriedly called secret meeting for Queensland's Wallabies at Tim Horan's place, where Bob Templeton addressed the gathering. Templeton had also been in contact with the men of the World Rugby Corporation and had even participated in a session with Bob Dwyer and the Australian coach of Wales, Alec Evans, whereby, at Geoff Levy's behest, they had formed up a list of the best 120 rugby players in the country. That done, they put salaries against each name as to what they would be worth on the open market if WRC could get their rebel competition up and running. Such a meeting, had it been known, would have sent the ARU into apoplexy.

Now, Templeton set out to the players the bare bones of WRC's vision. There were plans to have a professional world wide rugby competition, with three conferences of ten teams each, running concurrently and producing world champions at provincial and international levels every year. Between them, they would play 352 top-class games a year, producing 704 hours of quality television. Each team would have 30 players and five support staff, meaning WRC would require 1,000 people in all. It was all remarkably similar in concept to Super League, which was continuing to make headlines. Not the least of this were the amazing amounts of money being bandied around.

There were to be five basic tiers of payment offered, Tempo said, with the top tier of half a million American dollars a year for three years for superstars (known as the Jonah Lomu tier). After that, the next tier had key players being offered $US800,000 for a total of three years, all the World Cup squad players from the leading eight nations on $725,000 dollars, and two tiers beneath that for $300,000 and $200,000. At this point, no national union was involved, but the hope of the WRC was that, once the players were signed up, the unions would have no choice but to come on board.

John listened, gobsmacked. The other Wallabies, too, were hanging on every word. Could this *really* be happening? Templeton presently came to his conclusion.

'Men,' he said, in his best Churchillian manner, 'I think I've got to make clear my position on this. I'm a life member of both the QRU and the ARU and so I'm not going to have anything further to do with it. You fellows will do what you want of course, but if I were you I wouldn't sign with any bastard until you've at least seen what the ARU has got to offer you. Now that they've signed with Murdoch they're going to have the money to give you blokes what you deserve.'

He left it at that. The Wallabies asked a few questions, but Tempo stuck to his guns, saying he didn't know much more than what he'd told them, but he was sure the WRC would shortly be in touch with them. He had fulfilled the only commitment he had made to them, and he really didn't want to have anything further to do with it.

For John Eales, the two sides of the vice he would shortly be squeezed in — as would many other international players around the world — were now set. On the one side was the Australian Rugby Union establishment, which had just signed the deal with Murdoch and would shortly be opening negotiations with the players. On the other side was this thing called the World Rugby Corporation, a rather vague entity with an admittedly fabulous name which was offering huge amounts of money, and which by the looks of things had the support of most of his fellow players — not the least of whom was his great friend and second-row partner, Rod McCall. Just days after the meeting at Horan's house, McCall flew to Sydney to meet with Geoff Levy, and he was sufficiently impressed to return to Brisbane as WRC's chief recruiter. The WRC modus operandi was to put most of the recruiters on success fees if they delivered enough contracts, though McCall declined, saying he believed enough in the concept that he didn't want that.

By the following Sunday night, McCall and fellow recruiter and Wallaby Troy Coker were out and about in Brisbane, getting signatures on contracts. Neither was in any doubt as to who their top target was. John Eales. As McCall had told Levy, Eales 'is the best and most respected player in the country and if WRC is going to have any credibility, then we'll have to sign him'.

So it was that Rod was a frequent visitor at John's house, and an even more frequent caller on the phone. Bob Dwyer, who had also come to believe in the WRC concept, upped the ante by calling John and telling him that his form was so good he was on the top tier of payment, together with Horan and Little, a figure he fully deserved. If he signed, of course.

In fact, the contract Rod McCall dropped off to John was a little particular. For although this carefully calibrated legal document did indeed promise the second-rower $US500,000 a year for three years, a key clause — and the same clause was in every other WRC contract — said that this would be payable only if WRC was able to raise $US100 million by November. Essentially, Turnbull, Levy & Co. were taking an option on their services, telling the leading players that once they had all their signatures they would have no trouble in raising the required cash, but first they needed the players to back them.

At this point none of the players had yet heard from the Australian Rugby Union. Oblivious to WRC's recruiting, the ARU seemed to assume that it could take its own sweet time before getting the players on contract. Well, for many of the young men, this was just not good enough. The way they looked at it, their services had been bought and sold without them even being consulted, so the ARU could go and get knotted. The establishment hadn't even had the courtesy to ask the players, and yet here was the WRC promising them untold riches if they just backed them early! For many, it was no contest. They signed with McCall and Coker on the spot, just as down in Sydney they were signing with the Wallaby hooker, Phil Kearns, who was the key recruiter there.

John was not of their number. Innately cautious, and despite McCall's pressure and Dwyer's phone-call, his instinct was that he should not rush into anything. To begin with, he called his business manager, Chris White.

White was a little shocked at the highly unusual tension in John's voice and suggested he come right over to John's place. When Chris got there, John took him to the room he was sleeping in downstairs — Carmel's old room — and pulled out the contract from under the mattress. Chris flicked through it, gasping a little when he came to the offer of $US500,000 annually, and John told him everything he knew. They began to talk, and were still talking when the sun went down four hours later. White's first step was to get the contract looked at by a heavyweight lawyer, so they went to see Ian Callinan, who would shortly be appointed to the Australian High Court. This gentleman confirmed that the contract was legally sound — so long as WRC actually raised the $100 million dollars necessary.

Still, John was far from sure about signing. For the last five years he had devoted most of his energies to defending and adding to the glory of the Wallaby jersey, and it seemed that he was being asked to go in the opposite direction. Yes, the WRC in general, and Rod in particular, continued to emphasise that once the Wallabies were signed the ARU would be obliged to fall into line, but there was no guarantee of that. It seemed to John there was every chance that they would be *banned*. Outcasts!

Other Wallabies felt the same, and in all the hurly-burly of everything that was happening — all the conflicting emotions, stresses and strains — one particular episode affected John's spirit. Late one night in Ballymore car park, John had had a long conversation with his friend Brett Robinson, whom he had played with and against since school days. Robinson appreciated what the World Rugby Corporation was trying to accomplish, but he couldn't get his head around one thing. That is, that if the WRC got up and the ARU refused to bow to them, he would never ... EVER ... be able to play for the Wallabies. Robinson had not fulfilled his dream of pulling on the green and gold and was having a great deal of trouble committing to a project that would deny him the opportunity.

In long conversations with Chris White, John kept coming back to that exchange, questioning whether it was right to back a project which would deny Brett and plenty of guys like him the opportunity he had had, to play for his country.

In desperation to get him over the line, McCall tried to make John feel hard done by. 'Listen,' he said, 'you and Little and Horan have been the outstanding players for Queensland and Australia over the last few years. They've been looked after financially, but you haven't. You've been getting robbed. Just 'cause these guys can go onto rugby league they've been getting a lot of money from playing the game and you haven't.'

On that subject, Eales professed indifference. 'Look, Rod,' he said, 'I don't know about that, and I'm never going to, but either way that's not going to be the basis of my decision.'

For the record, however, McCall was partly correct in his assertion. Little, at least, *had* been on substantial contracts from the Australian Rugby Union, a long way above and beyond what the other players had received through Wallabies Promotions and Marketing. The money had been paid to him to keep him from going to rugby league.

Still, the pressure from McCall to sign never let up.

When John went to speak at a rugby dinner up at Hervey Bay, north of Brisbane, he had no sooner got to the home of his host, former Queensland halfback Stephen Tait, than there was the first of many phone calls for him. It was Rod, pressing for John to make a commitment one way or the other. Most of the guys had signed he said, but there were a few hold-outs waiting to see which way John was going to jump. Whatever else happened, the Wallabies had to stick together, because the same principle applied off the field as on it: unity was strength. To Rod's mind, the chief impediment to the Wallabies being unified at that time was John. He *had* to sign.

'But just say we can't play Test matches anymore,' John kept pressing. 'Just say the Australian team keeps going without us? I don't want to be part of it unless the ARU falls into line.'

They would fall into line with it, Rod assured him. But what if they didn't? John countered.

Finally they came to an agreement. John would sign the contract, but only on the condition that Rod would not release it to the WRC until such times as the ARU had come on board. With McCall giving that assurance, more or less, Eales did indeed sign upon his return to Brisbane the following morning — in the front seat of Rod's modest Ford, in a side street in the suburb of Stafford.

John felt sick at heart about it. All through his childhood, he had dreamed about playing for Australia. Now, he was actually doing it, but had just done something which placed that at risk. Others decided to take exactly the same risk, and in short order nearly all the Wallabies had committed to WRC, though the ARU remained oblivious to it. A strongly worded confidentiality clause in the WRC contract forbade any discussion of it and the secret held. One who didn't sign, however, was Jason

Little, for the very good reason that he couldn't — he was under a rock-solid, though secret, contract to the ARU and was not free to go to the WRC even if he'd wanted to.

IN the second week of July 1995, the ARU at last made formal offers to the Wallabies. In a conference room at Ballymore, Leo Williams, chairman of the ARU, had the floor and was setting out the figures to some of the Queensland Wallabies — $110,000, Australian, as a base payment, and then another $110,000 if they played all the Tests.

The Wallabies listened, for the most part silent, watching, waiting, but certainly doing no air punches. Finally, Rod McCall, as always the boldest of the senior Wallabies, put his hand up to speak.

'Leo, I've got a bit of a problem with that formula. You might think that's a lot, but I don't think some of these players are going to stick around for 220 grand.'

Williams would have none of it, quickly returning fire: 'When you're chairman, Rod, you can do it the way you like.'

Dan Crowley, another of the bolder Wallabies, then joined in. A tough undercover policeman who had been in the Wallabies for seven years, he was not a man to be cowed easily and waded in.

'What if we get injured, Leo, what happens to our match payments after that? What do we get of the second 110 grand?'

'Then you'll get nothing,' replied Williams evenly.

All up, it was not a performance best tailored to get the chairman into the diplomatic service, but in saying all this, Williams was totally in tune with the thinking of his rugby generation. His attitudes were formed at a time when the honour and glory of wearing the jersey was not only enough recompense, but there were literally thousands of players out there who would have been prepared to cut off their index fingers for the pleasure of wearing that jersey in battle even once.

He stood there, too, as the head of one of the two most progressive national unions in the world, which had done more to advance the cause of remunerating the players than any except for New Zealand. It was not surprising that he should have been a little nonplussed at the seeming ingratitude of the players. The problem, of course, was that the young men he was speaking to had already made the colossal leap to the point where payment for playing was not a privilege so much as a *right*.

Some of the assembled players there were sifting their way through as many as five offers — from the ARU, the WRC, Super League, the Australian Rugby League, and one or other of the many countries of the northern hemisphere that were prepared to pay enormous sums for talented, high profile players. (Though such payments also contravened the IRB's amateur regulations, it was happening on an enormous scale.)

IN the meantime, through it all, the rugby went on . . .

Michael Lynagh had now retired and neither Paul McLean nor Rod Macqueen — both Australian selectors — had any doubts as to who should replace him as captain. John Eales. The perception of both men was that the Wallabies needed someone fresh at the helm. While Phil Kearns had been a very able back-up captain to Lynagh over the previous four years, Eales was the obvious leader for the next generation.

Bob Dwyer, for his part, disagreed. Vehemently. He plumped strongly for Phil Kearns, saying there had been too much chopping and changing in the team, and what it most needed was stability. And that was the end of it. Never mind that two votes of the three on the selection panel went for Eales. In the matter of the captaincy, in the culture of the time, it was unthinkable that the coach did not get the captain he wanted, so there was nowhere else to go. Macqueen and McLean conceded to Dwyer's insistence.

Kearns it was then, who led what was still a new-look Wallabies side out in the Bledisloe match against the All Blacks in Auckland on 22 July 1995. Campese was gone, summarily dropped for his perceived lack of form in the World Cup, replaced by Joe Roff, an up-and-comer from Canberra. So too had George Gregan been made to pay the price for his own essentially ineffectual performances in South Africa, replaced by a halfback most of the Australian rugby community had never heard of, a coal-truck driver from Singleton by the name of Steve Merrick.

This was the Test match of redemption, and Dwyer was going all or nothing to win it. If they could beat the All Blacks in New Zealand it would show that they were still a major force, that what had happened to them against England in the World Cup might have happened to any team on an off day, and now they were back in the saddle again.

At one point, it looked like they might do exactly that, as they led the All Blacks 16-15 midway through the second half, but alas, alas, New Zealand quickly found the three extra gears they needed to do the job, vaulting away to 28 points by match's end while Australia remained stalled on 16 points.

That night, at the post-match function, an independent observer might have noted an unusual closeness between the All Blacks and Wallabies, gathered in little groups around the room conferring closely. Certainly there had been a growing conviviality over recent years, but this was different.

In fact the two sides were discussing the situation vis à vis WRC, each seeing where the other stood. The All Blacks had not yet signed but were committed to doing so the following weekend in Sydney, after they played the final Bledisloe Cup encounter of the year. The NZRFU still had no idea that this was the case. John had a long talk with his most direct opponent of the New Zealanders, Ian Jones, and found that the All Black had been placed in a very similar quandary to himself. He too wished to continue wearing his country's jersey in battle, but also wanted a fair return for his efforts. He too wanted the NZRFU to back the WRC proposal so rugby could enjoy the best of both worlds. He too was reluctant to stand one-out against the views of his team-mates. They parted with a warm shake of the hand around midnight, conscious that the next time they saw each other Ian would be screaming the haka at John.

The following morning John found himself sharing a recuperative hot spa with the reserve Wallaby prop, Richard Harry, who was also the son of the ARU president, Phil Harry. Because of this relationship, the men of the WRC had decided it would put Richard in a very awkward position if he was told what was going on, and though the intention was to bring him in at a later point, no-one had told him anything at all. All he knew was rumours. In the spa with John, Harry brought the subject up and John had to deny any knowledge of it as he was extremely aware of the confidentiality agreement. He hated it, and felt so low he could do the limbo under a snake's belly button, but felt he had no choice.

SYDNEY Town, Friday, 28 July 1995.

There is a special buzz in rugby towns the day before major Test matches, and on this unseasonably warm winter's day Sydney was in the full grip of it. But this time the buzz had a jarring, jangling note to it. The newspapers broke the news that something called the World Rugby Corporation had signed up most of the players due to take part in the following day's Bledisloe Cup encounter. All three, the *Sydney Morning Herald, Daily Telegraph Mirror* and *The Australian*, claimed the same thing — that the players were going, going, gone.

Many in the rugby community, and that included even at this late point some of the key administrators, simply refused to believe it. The Wallabies? The All Blacks? Signing en masse with a rebel organisation no-one had ever heard of? Pissing on their national jerseys for corporate gain? It couldn't be true! Through all the subsequent hype and hysteria, what had become clear was that the Bledisloe Cup Test was to be the last hurrah of international rugby being played in the time-honoured fashion — with players performing substantially for the pride of the jersey they wore. *Après cela, la deluge.*

The fact that New Zealand won the encounter 34-23 was practically the least significant thing that happened on the day. Far more potent were the after-match speeches. On this gently shining Saturday afternoon, virtually no-one left. First up was the ARU president Phil Harry, speaking to a crowd gripped by a strong sense of melancholy that this was the living end, that for better or worse, come what may, the essentially amateur era had just faded away before their eyes.

But if it was out with the old, the real question for the assembled rugby lovers was, just what would the new era look like? Would it be one at least run by the traditional bodies, with their rugby roots embedded deep in the rich soil of the century past? Or would it be run by a totally new group, formed maybe last Tuesday for all the crowd knew. Was all the paper talk true, about this thing called WRC?

Phil Harry, came to the microphone, and after a few preliminaries got to the nub: 'I would also like to say a few words to the spectators both here at the ground, and watching on television. This is the end of the season and in many ways is the end of an era. Let me say this . . . *That sort of spectacular, passionate game between two nations is something that money can't buy.* Thank you.'

The emphasised words were, particularly, met with warm applause from the crowd — creating the atmosphere for what came next. Wallaby skipper Phil Kearns, who like most of the Wallabies had taken Harry's last remark as a specific dig at their whole presumed involvement with WRC, was next to the podium. After a couple of preliminary comments he came to the line that would be long remembered. 'To all Australian supporters here today we thank you. It's been terrific, your support,' Kearns said, with his voice rebounding all over the still packed stadium. 'And whatever happens in the future we hope you and the union support us. Thank you.'

Around the ground, there was a stunned silence. On this lovely winter's day, after a splendid game of traditional Test match rugby, one of the most admired figures of all had just said that it was all over.

'*Whatever happens in the future, we hope you and the union support us.*'

In the atmosphere of that ground, under the circumstances of all the headlines, rumours and innuendo that had been swirling for the past few days, Kearns' words were taken as confirmation that it was all true, that the buggers had gone! Snaffled in the night by we knew not what. Immediately Kearns had finished, the crowd broke up into a series of twisted and sometimes angry knots, discussing what Kearns had said and what it meant. For most, it meant that the end was nigh. Inside the dressing room, John showered and changed with all the rest of the Wallabies, and just like them, was insulated from the highly agitated mood outside.

They would find out, though, soon enough. That night, just next to the Sydney Cricket Ground at the Hordern Pavilion, the ARU hosted a dinner for not just the two teams that had played on the day, but to celebrate the 100th Test between Australia and New Zealand. Amongst those present were past greats from both countries who had done so much to make the Bledisloe one of the foremost sporting competitions in the world. So the stage was perfectly set for the values of the older generation of rugby players to clash head-on with the values of the WRC-signed rugby revolutionaries who had taken the field that day.

In the crowded room, where some 600 were gathered, everyone but everyone was talking about the World Rugby Corporation, contracts, who'd signed what, who hadn't, what Murdoch's forces might do to counter-attack, what the Phils — Kearns and Harry — had said in their post-match speeches. John, acutely uncomfortable, tried to steer away as much as he could from the one subject that everyone wanted to talk about.

'Everything under control, John?' the former Wallaby captain Tony Shaw asked at one point, clearly inviting John to declare his hand, or at least talk to him about WRC.

'Yep, Tony, everything's fine,' John replied, admittedly a little lamely, but simply unable and unwilling to explore the subject.

The evening moved on. After dinner, and a video presentation reviewing the history of the 100 Tests between the Wallabies and All Blacks, the CEO of the ARU, Bruce Hayman, gave a thundering oration centring on the fact that 'You can't replace 100 years of fierce rivalry and national pride with created teams which lack support and purpose, and which are motivated only by the dollar.' He added that 'the older players must help the younger players through this difficult time'.

At speech's end he was met with thunderous applause from some sections of the room, and a stony silence from other sections. The battle lines of the Rugby War were clearly forming up for all to see. With the conclusion of the formalities, many of the passions that had been coming to the boil were now allowed to boil over. And this they did. Groups of people were talking animatedly all over the dimly lit room, while little huddles whispered conspiratorially. Older players from both nations tried to approach the incumbent players, meeting with mixed success. For many, the chasm was just too great to leap.

The younger generation of players, while just as honoured to wear the famous jersey, were part of the Michael Jordan generation of sportsmen around the world — not necessarily avaricious or greedy but simply wanting a fair share of the wealth that they knew they were creating, and no longer content to be fobbed off. And for the first time in rugby history, this group of players were sitting down as a rugby team opposite their administrators with what seemed like a genuine alternative before them. No longer did they simply have to accept whatever it was that their national union was prepared to give them — as the older players had had to do — they had a choice. Some players, though certainly not John, tried to explain their side of things to the older players, but only met with mixed success. All up, it was a tense evening and John was glad when the time came to go. As he left to head back to the hotel, he passed by Bruce Hayman.

'Thanks, Bruce, it was a good night,' John said, shaking the CEO's hand. It had actually been a horrible night, but John still felt it was the right thing to say.

'And that,' Bruce Hayman later told people who asked, 'made John Eales only the second player who talked to me during the entire evening.'

THINGS rapidly got a whole lot less civil. The following day, once back in Brisbane, in an effort to clear his head and remind himself what rugby was all about in the first place, John had gone down to the Brothers Oval to see the club play. It was nice to be back in such familiar and seemingly safe surrounds, the Moreton Bay figs standing as serenely as ever in the sun, whatever might be blaring from newspaper headlines. The first person he bumped into, as luck would have it, was Paul McLean — national selector, childhood hero, good friend, quasi-mentor in matters Wallaby.

'Mate, what's happening?' McLean asked. The words were neutral enough, but both men knew exactly what he meant. He meant, 'Where are *you* in all this, John? Have you signed with the rebels or are you staying true to the establishment?'

What could John say in reply? The fact was, he *had* signed with the rebels, but he had also signed that confidentiality agreement.

'Oh, I can't say too much . . . ' he replied, and looked away.

The worst part about the whole thing for John was that he couldn't confide in people like Paul McLean or Tony Shaw, both of whom he respected greatly. It wasn't simply that both were aligned with the establishment — in fact just about were the establishment — it was that John felt that if he said something he could be sued to the last dollar he possessed. True, that still didn't make an awful lot of dollars, but it was more than he was prepared to risk. When McLean tried again to engage him in conversation on the subject, John batted him off.

For the national selector and former Wallaby captain, it wasn't so much what John said as the way he said it. On the strength of it, McLean had no doubt that Eales had signed, and he said as much to John Connolly when the Queensland coach rang him later that evening. Connolly, a traditionalist to his bootstraps, was rock-solid for the establishment, and was appalled when McLean gave him his view that 'Eales is in it'.

Thus, the Queensland coach had no sooner put the phone down than he called Eales and gave him a full blast. There are few with an instinct for the jugular as sure as John Connolly's and he proceeded to go for John's. Connolly was in turn, 'appalled', 'disgusted', 'horrified' and 'amazed' that John, 'OF ALL PEOPLE', would align himself with an organisation devoted wholly and solely to destroying everything good about rugby and he wanted John to start justifying himself, and he meant NOW. And these were just his opening remarks.

In response, John was in the same bind as he had been with Shaw and McLean. He couldn't acknowledge that he had signed, meaning he really couldn't even defend himself. Essentially, he just had to sit there and take it as the coach vented his spleen. When Connolly had at last finished, Eales had no sooner put the phone down than he was calling Paul McLean.

'Mate, what did you say to Connolly?' he said. 'What did you tell him?'

Eales thought McLean had betrayed his trust by telling the coach that he thought the second-rower had signed, but McLean made no apology. Their conversation was short and intense, and it finished with McLean telling him: 'Mate, I'm afraid I can't sit around and see you go and do something like this without trying to do something to stop it.'

It was a difficult situation for both men, and entirely typical of what was happening to all the Wallabies. Everywhere, they were under attack from the wider rugby community for their perceived disloyalty. Down in Sydney, for example, when Phil Kearns' club Randwick was playing a game at Coogee Oval against their fierce local rivals, Easts, there came the usual pregnant pause in play as the hooker prepared to throw the ball into the lineout. Finally, as he brought his arm back ready to throw, a sole voice rang out from the cramming crowd.

'Throw the ball in Kearns . . . for the good of rugby.'

Kearns' shoulders were seen to slump a little as he settled himself, and then he threw the ball in, and the game continued.

John Eales escaped any such overt attacks, but still took many phone calls from older Wallabies urging him to return to the fold. Perhaps most notable of these was from Simon Poidevin, who rang John one day while he was working at the Qantas check-in counter. The former Wallaby flanker was extremely passionate on the subject, making out that John would be totally betraying everything the Australian jersey stood for if he sided with WRC. He also added that the business community as a whole would turn their back on rugby if the rebel group got up and the game would likely be destroyed. John listened to what his respected former team-mate had to say, but once again, he refused to engage.

One person who he did call, however, was Michael Watt, the man who owned and ran CSI in London — the same CSI which had brokered the deal between the rugby unions and Rupert Murdoch. Though to some this might seem a surprising source of independent advice, John had enjoyed a close friendship with the equable businessman since meeting him on the Emerging Wallabies tour of six years earlier, and trusted him. Watt did not abuse that trust, but nor did he pull his punches. According to him. The WRC simply did not have anything like the money they claimed and would sooner or later collapse. John should be very, very careful before aligning with them.

A WEEK after their angry words, John Eales and Paul McLean were brought together by circumstance, as they had been asked to present rugby trophies together at Nudgee College. McLean looked at Eales closely on the stage. The second-rower looked ragged, tired, jaded, a cold sore somehow completing the portrait of a man under enormous pressure and stress. The two went through the whole presentation, acutely conscious that things weren't right between them. At end, in the car park, McLean couldn't resist saying one more thing.

'Mate,' he called out across three car-park spaces, 'you know where I'm coming from . . . just make sure you make the right decision'.

'I'm trying to,' Eales replied.

And indeed he was . . . but it was hard.

Certain sections of the media, not faced with any agonising decision whatsoever, had gone absolutely feral pushing just one side of the argument — none more so than Peter FitzSimons on the back page of the *Sydney Morning Herald*. 'I'm losing patience with this, simply because it cannot be ridgy-didge,' he wrote:

It's one thing to make a choice for bulk money against zero money — which might have been understandable — but altogether different when they are already assured of obscene money, and are greedy enough to go after still more. John Eales take that position? Totally out of the question. Tim Gavin? I'd sooner believe that Mother Teresa runs an illegal gambling den on the sly.

Despite all this, I am prepared to concede that just possibly one or two Wallabies have signed with Turnbull. To them, let me say this: What can you be *thinking* of? Rugby is your *mother*, dammit. For the past two decades she's nurtured you, taken care of you, taught you, been proud to call you her own, and held chook raffles so that you could travel around the world. She's allowed you to walk taller down George Street than ever you would have dreamed, and now that she has come into a large amount of money you are guaranteed to enjoy enormous amounts of her largesse as one of her favourite sons.

If you make a decision that that is still not enough, that you want instead her to whore for you, too — to earn the very last buck for you she can and to hell with the consequences — then you will be deserving of your fate. And that may very well be that you miss out on the whole lot. The Turnbull thing will collapse as the rugby public rises as one against it, and your spot in the Wallabies will be taken by someone proud to wear the jersey. I refuse to believe it will come to that, though.

At their Brisbane breakfast table the following day, John and Jack Eales read the somewhat demonic diatribe one after the other, neither making a comment. Things like that worried Jack, but ultimately he trusted John's judgment. He didn't want to ask his son about it, because it was his business, and typically, John had not spoken to either of his parents about it. At that point, Jack and Rosa Eales didn't even know whether John was for the establishment or the rebels.

John sometimes wondered the same, whatever it said on the contract in Rod McCall's bottom drawer, but his thoughts when reading FitzSimons' column were clear. To his mind, it misconstrued the position of those who had signed up with the WRC and was naïve in certain respects. At the very least, the WRC offered a great vision for rugby involving all rugby countries. Apart from the money side of it, there was the thrill of maybe planting the seeds for rugby to thrive in America and the like. Plus, and this was the key, FitzSimons' column presented things as an either/or choice between the WRC and the ARU, whereas the key to the whole exercise was to bring the ARU with them. If all went well, they'd still be able to represent Australia.

As to John's failure to discuss the situation with his parents, the reality was that he barely discussed the situation with *anyone*, other than his fellow Wallabies and Chris White. Both his girlfriend Peta and his close friend Ben Perkins were quite put out that John wouldn't talk, but he point-blank refused with both.

AROUND the world, the phone calls were flying. Kearns to All Black captain Sean Fitzpatrick, Fitzpatrick to Springbok captain Francois Pienaar, Pienaar to Kearns, Kearns to McCall, McCall to Pienaar, Fitzpatrick to Springbok centre Hennie Le Roux, all of the above to various combinations of the others a dozen times over. It was primarily communication to work out just how they were all situated. There was even, in the middle of it all, something that resembled counterespionage. At one point Rod McCall in Brisbane received a frantic message that Francois Pienaar was going berserk because he'd just heard from John Eales, who'd said the whole thing was falling apart in Australia, that all the Wallabies had decided to return to the establishment and renege on their WRC contracts and WHAT THE HELL WAS GOING ON?

McCall calmly dialled Pienaar's mobile phone number and when it was answered, handed the phone over to John Eales. McCall listened to Eales' end of the conversation.

'Francois, this is John Eales . . . no, no, no, the real John Eales!'

Eales was able to assure Pienaar that whoever he'd been speaking to, it certainly hadn't been him, and in any case none of those claims was true.

So who did make the call? Neither McCall nor Eales has ever known.

IN the meantime, the ARU had identified that of all the Wallabies, John Eales was the key signing, and decided to go hard out after him to get his signature on a singularly handsome ARU contract. The person from the establishment who most dealt with John at this time was one of the senior directors of the ARU, Dick McGruther, a personable lawyer type who went back a long way with John, as he too was a Brothers man to his bootstraps. McGruther found the second-rower extremely uncomfortable during their meetings — held in Leo Williams' office in the Brisbane CBD — as if he was near torn in two by competing loyalties, but was not at liberty to say so. Though Eales never came right out and said so, he at least intimated that he'd given his word to stick with the other players and that he was committed to the World Rugby Corporation, but McGruther could clearly see he was agonising. Without necessarily trying to heighten that agony — much — McGruther kept talking to John, chipping away at his resolve. He tried to prevail upon his sense of decency and loyalty and the damage the whole WRC deal would do to the game, while also pointing out that the ARU had real cash in their coffers, as against the WRC's finances which were merely promissory. On that subject, McGruther made some extremely handsome offers for John to switch camps.

Eales was viewed as so pivotal to the outcome of the fight that the board agreed that he should be offered financial inducements over and above the standard contract. At one point, even on top of a solid offer of several hundred thousand dollars per year over three years, John was offered another $50,000 *on the spot*, if he signed then and there.

Many times in these meetings, John had to stop and ask himself if the figures they were talking about could be *real*. Was the same ARU that he had once been delighted to receive $50 a day from now offering him well over a million dollars for contracting to play the next three years for the Wallabies? (And he wasn't happy with that?!)

John held solid regardless, conscious that he'd given his word to McCall and that if the Wallabies stayed together as a unit it would be better off for the whole. He did, however, find the whole thing extremely hard. For though he had signed with the WRC, and though he did not take up the ARU's offer, he was now having what could fairly be described as second, third, fourth and fifth thoughts. It wasn't just the money matter, it was that the whole fabric of the Australian rugby community seemed to be tearing apart over the issue. People who had been his friends for years — like Paul McLean — were looking him right in the eye and telling him he was making a terrible mistake. McCall, in hour-long conversations — daily — attempted to talk him through it.

'Mate,' McCall told him one day in his home study, 'you made that decision. Do you know how many people's lives are concerned with this? You are a trump card, the game couldn't go on without you. If, when I'd asked you, you'd said "no" and given me all the reasons and stuck by it, I would have lost interest in chasing it because I don't think the game could go on without you. I would have torn up the contract I already had and forgotten about it. But you didn't say "no", you said "yes" and every-thing has fallen into place because of it. Players around the world have confidence in it, because they know you are a part of it, they've put their arses on the line because they know you're with them, that you've made your decision.'

'But I'm not comfortable with that decision,' John replied.

'Mate, it's too late. You made it, and you can't make a decision like that, that affects so many people and just walk away.'

Eales would make the point that his backing of the project was always conditional upon the ARU coming on board, McCall would reply that there was no chance of that happening if the Wallabies split up and the least he could do was not be the catalyst for that happening. It was true that a couple of the other Wallabies in Jason Little and Tim Gavin had publicly proclaimed their loyalty to the ARU, but John was the key and he should know that. At the end of one of many such conversations, the two Test second-rowers decided the best thing they could do was get all the players into the one place at the one time and decide once and for all what they were going to do.

IT was done. The word had gone out for all interested rugby players to turn up for the meeting which was to start on the morning of 10 August 1995, at 8.30 a.m. at Sydney's Park Royal Hotel, and they came in their droves. From Brisbane, from Canberra, from Sydney.

There was an obvious tension to the morning, right from the beginning. Distrust, distress, dissension and division had been the constant companions of seemingly everyone involved in the saga. This meeting was no different. Jason Little and Tim Gavin, for example, were shocked to find that Tim Kava, a sometime Wallaby team-mate, was standing at the door of the meeting room barring their way.

'Sorry, Jason, Tim,' he said, 'you can't come in. WRC players are having a meeting for an hour or so and then we'll let the rest of you in.'

So they waited. Extremely annoyed at such high-handedness — who the hell said this bloke was in charge of the shooting match anyway? — but they waited, with three or four other players who had not yet committed themselves to WRC. Downstairs, James Erskine, the head of IMG in Australia, was arriving. Buffeted by the demands of both sides, Phil Kearns had turned to Erskine for advice. The two had a professional relationship insofar as IMG acted as Kearns' agent, but the two also enjoyed a close relationship beyond that. Kearns trusted him.

Clearly, Erskine's position was a delicate one. His business relationship with the ARU was cast in concrete. In return for the guarantee of some $42.5 million, his company had the marketing rights for the union over the next five years — meaning it was very much in his interests that the ARU survive and prosper in the coming years.

The scene Erskine found on the inside was an obviously troubled one. Some 60 players were ranged around the room, together with one or two agents, and lawyers who were firmly entrenched in the WRC camp. In one corner Phil Kearns was holding a phone up, on the other end of which was the All Black captain Sean Fitzpatrick, keeping track of how things were progressing.

Before Erskine could even open his mouth, Tim Kava had jumped to his feet and broken in.

'I hope you are going to tell this group before you start, all your conflicts of interest . . . '

Erskine would have none of it. 'Listen pal,' he replied in an equally aggressive tone, 'do you want to read my speech for me or do you want me to do it myself?'

Kava backed down for the moment, but the tone was set. Erskine maintained he had planned to acknowledge his conflicts of interest anyway, and proceeded to do so. Then, after a few more preliminaries, the James Erskine Demolition Derby threw itself into high gear. For the next 90 minutes, Erskine kept hammering away at the credibility of the WRC.

His theme was that the WRC contract was based on dodgy financial premises. He told the players that he acted for athletes and sportspeople all over the world and he'd never seen anything like the contract that the Australian rugby players had signed. Didn't they understand that standard procedure in this sort of thing was for the athletes to at least receive 10 per cent down payment on the amount they were due to receive? So what had they got? Ten per cent? Five per cent? ONE per cent even?

No. They'd gone and done it, hadn't they, they'd signed themselves away and weren't getting a brass razoo in return. John, sitting two rows back, looked around. The words were clearly having an effect. From a figure as well respected in the sports business as Erskine — and whatever his conflicts of interest — the points he made seemed to be hitting home.

Well, Erskine continued with a heavy sigh, it wasn't for him to criticise, but he really just couldn't understand it.

'So maybe you don't like the ARU. Maybe you think they're pompous. Maybe you think they're old farts. Well at least there's not 57 of them like in England. I've only dealt with nine of them here . . .

'But even if they are old farts, so what? We're talking *business* here, guys. Get that through your heads. It doesn't matter that you don't like them. The thing is, they will sign contracts now that you know they're going to honour. They'll sign you to big money. Do you really think they're going to wait around to 22 November to see if WRC comes good, and then if they don't, offer you the same money they're offering you now?'

'They'll have to!' interrupted one belligerent player.

'Bullshit! It just doesn't work like that and surely you've got the brains to know it.'

It was, as the appalled McCall later described it, 'a total demolition job'.

Whatever, the job was done. After Erskine spoke, the doors of the meeting were thrown open, with Geoff Levy speaking for WRC while the director and key power-broker for the ARU, Ian Ferrier, spoke for the establishment. Neither made anything like the impression that Erskine had, and still Phil Kearns hadn't heard the most staggering thing of the day.

At the end of the meeting — where the upshot was that the players' group decided to form a seven-man committee to analyse both sides of the equation — Kearns walked out in the company of Ian Ferrier, who was now able to talk to the Wallaby captain for the first time properly all day, and unveil to him the news.

'Phil,' Ferrier said as they walked, 'we've signed fourteen of the players ...'

Kearns stopped momentarily, and turned, searching Ferrier's face for signs that he might be joking.

'Is that true?' he asked.

'It's true, Phil, we've signed fourteen of the players.'

'Well that's it then,' said Kearns, who had always maintained that the players were either one-in-all-in-or-forget-it. 'It's all over.'

AND it just about all was. While John had resisted signing back with the ARU, others had not. Around the world, players signed with the ARU and other unions, often with the promise of indemnity from possible WRC prosecution. The bottom line was that in the competition between the real Murdoch-backed dollars and the promises of greater dollars offered by the WRC, the real dollars had made enormous inroads into the ranks of the rebels. The same thing had happened all over the rugby world with key All Blacks and Springboks, particularly, returning to the fold.

Yet, as far as John knew, things were still ongoing a week later when he turned up in Melbourne to play a game for the Australian Barbarians against a David Campese Testimonial XV. The first person he ran into in the foyer was Phil Kearns, and John's first words to him were the ones used so often throughout the whole saga: 'Mate, what's happening?'

Kearns, tiredly: 'It's all over, John, the whole WRC thing is finished.'

John felt like he'd won the lottery. For all that, the combined will of the rebels had not so totally collapsed that they weren't able to use their force to gain some leverage with the ARU. After long negotiations, Ian Ferrier put his name at the bottom of what would henceforth be known as 'the Ferrier Document'.

On behalf of the Australian Rugby Football Union and its three principal provincial unions (collectively known as 'the Organisation'), Ferrier agreed that:

In Consideration of all The Players agreeing to relinquish their rights and obligations under their WRC contracts the Organisation shall:

1) Alter the Unions constitutions so that they could accommodate two players as directors on their boards.

2) Support the concept of a Players Association and make a loan of 10,000 dollars towards its establishment.

3) Guarantee a 95% share of the monies flowing from the Murdoch deal to the players.

4) Not discriminate or in any way bring retribution against any of the players who have signed a Contract with the WRC.

The final paragraph read: 'This offer shall not be revoked by the Organisation unless the overwhelming majority of The Players refuse to relinquish their rights and obligations under their WRC contracts.'

While a guarantee of 95 per cent of all the Murdoch monies from television going to the players was viewed as generous, John Eales was not at the front of the queue of those complaining. John signed a contract with the ARU to secure his fair share of those monies, and a handsome one it was too. It was later reported that Jason Little received the highest salary from the ARU — and it was said that he received half a million dollars a year over three years. Other sources claimed Eales had the highest salary. Chris White, who negotiated the contract, has never divulged Eales' salary package, though he does say, carefully, 'John was not unhappy with the final result'.

As a postscript to the whole saga, in Paris on 27 August 1995, a meeting of the International Rugby Board declared that amateurism was no more, that the central plank on which the game had been built was no longer viable in the modern era. Nick Farr-Jones, who was there when the gentlemen came out of the conference room to announce their decision, remembers that 'It looked like they had just come out of their own funeral'.

Nevertheless, love it or hate it, the advent of the WRC on top of the Murdoch deal ensured that rugby was dragged kicking and screaming into the modern sporting era — a professional era. As *The Times* declared in an editorial the day after the news was announced, 'After all, there is an ethos for every age.'

A brand new era in rugby had begun, and in only four years John Eales had gone from selling T-shirts for £5 to looking with bedroom eyes at mansions in Brisbane's more salubrious suburbs.

The Greg Smith
Era Begins

If I were a rich man . . .

FIDDLER ON THE ROOF

John Eales is a guy who can run, jump, catch, pass,
tackle, kick goals, play a square cut on the cricket field, and
post around 11 seconds for the 100 metres.

BOB TEMPLETON, 1996

IT WAS a curious sequence of events, all things considered.
Immediately after John had become one of the mostly highly paid
professional sportspeople in Australia, he went on a tour to Canada as
captain of a team synonymous with the best of the amateur ethic — the
Australian Barbarians. The team was coached by Roger Gould and managed by Ken Wright, two famous Wallabies from an era long gone, and
boasted many young players of promise such as Tom Bowman, Ben Tune,
Sam Payne and Owen Finnegan, who were being given the chance to
prove their representative mettle. They were sitting in an airport waiting
lounge in Edmonton when extraordinary news came through from
Australia, after one of the players called home. The board of the ARU had
selected Greg Smith as the new Wallaby coach.

Greg Smith!?

John, like many of the players, was amazed. Certainly it had become clear that Bob Dwyer, who had just completed his tenth and most disappointing year of coaching the Wallabies, was unlikely to hold on. But the successful coach of Queensland, John Connolly, was the one whose cab had long been at the front of the queue and few had taken Smith's candidature seriously. Smith was not without credentials, however. A successful coach with Sydney's Eastern Suburbs, he guided their Firsts to consecutive grand finals in 1990-91, and in 1992 had coached the Sydney side to beat the All Blacks by the world record margin of 40-17. On the strength of that he had taken over coaching NSW for the following three years and they had won 23 of their 33 games. Crucially, Smith's NSW team had been the victor over Connolly's Maroons in two of their last three games and had outscored their opponents, 101-52.

So it was Smith. John had never met him. For the moment, it was time to simply get on with enjoying the rest of the Ba-Ba tour. Once completed, John went on another quick overseas jaunt as a guest player for the prestigious French Barbarians who were to take on the All Blacks in Toulon. A particular delight of that trip was staying in the stylish Parisian apartment of one of his childhood heroes, Jean-Pierre Rives. The former flanker and captain of the French team in the early '80s had not only become the President of the French Barbarians, but also a successful restaurateur and artist, and John hit it off with him from the first. It was an odd kind of thing to be living cheek-by-jowl-by-towel with a fellow you had admired since you were seven, but it didn't take long to get used to. Together with the captain of the French Ba-Bas, Denis Charvet, who was also Rives' great friend and neighbour, Paris was John's oyster for four days before they all headed off to Toulon. No matter that the Ba-Bas didn't beat the All Blacks, it was a superb experience. And just as it had been when he'd first started playing, if this was international rugby, *still* give him more of it!

BUT it was soon time to return to Brisbane and get to work. Seriously. Back home in mid-November, John was at Queensland training only shortly after landing, as the Maroons prepared with unparalleled intensity for the inaugural Super 12 professional rugby competition. John Connolly, was now not merely their coach but close to being their boss and principal employer. A cliche in rugby union to that point had been for the coach to say, 'I want you guys to play as if your life depended on it.' Now it *was* their livelihoods that depended on it. One of the first things sacrificed in this new era of professionalism was jobs, as rugby administrations became less interested in their players, and *employees*, having ongoing external commitments that didn't involve boots and mouthguards. This was not a blanket ban, as John, for one, continued to do a little promotional work for Qantas, but with their heavy training commitments serious work was impossibly anyway.

Whereas Queensland trainings had usually gone from 6 to 9 p.m., three times a week, players were now turning up every day at 9 a.m. to train throughout the morning before having a light lunch . . . and then training again in the afternoon. At least their evenings were now wonderfully free, just like normal people!

Overall, there was a different *feel* in the air — a kind of consciousness that Amateur Hour was over and Big Time had begun. Some of it was subtle. It seemed there were no longer players running around in loose jerseys in the hope of hiding from the coach the contours of their stomach. Now they tended to wear tighter fitting clothing for the exact reverse reason.

Far more importantly, because the game was no longer anachronistically amateur in a professional age, the public were starting to take notice. It was put well by Joe Roff, who was interviewed in Canberra where the new Super 12 team of the ACT Brumbies had just been formed under the coaching of the former NSW coach and Australian selector, Rod Macqueen. 'I think one of the things, apart from the fact we take it more seriously,' Roff said in January 1996, 'is that the public also takes it more seriously. Before, I think there might have been some sense that we were just a bunch of blokes running around on the weekends, but now there is . . . a buzz around Canberra.'

More to the point, at least from the perspective of those who had bankrolled rugby going professional, there was also the sound of a certain *ching-ching* around rugby as the cash-registers began to turn over. For example, Canberra Milk switched its allegiance from rugby league's Canberra Raiders to the ACT Brumbies in a reputed $1.5 million deal over three years. At Ballymore, the Maroons would henceforth be turning out plastered in Bank of Queensland banners across their jersey in return for a similar fee.

The real difference, of course, was that for the first time the blue-collar-

and-jersey workers who generated the spectacle, the players, were sharing the spoils. The year before, some of players who were sweating away beside John had been scratching $20,000 annually from odd jobs. Now they were on contracts worth well over $100,000. Others, like John, had been earning around $80,000 and were now on close to half a million dollars all up, including sponsorships. It was wealth beyond their wildest dreams, one of the most staggering things that had ever happened to any of them, and yet curiously, it was rarely discussed.

In the new age, players seemed to steer clear of the subject. Discussion could only promote petty jealousies, and in that regard John had more reason than any of them to avoid it. Still, there were no rules, written or unwritten, about discussing the new car you just turned up at Ballymore in — *get a load of them wheels!* — or your new real-estate investments. And even John didn't mind discussing the Queenslander style house he had bought and moved into in the suburb of Grange, on Frome Street, set on a huge block of land with large gardens at the front and back. It was hard to believe that such a fine place could be his — or that the cheque he wrote wouldn't bounce — but no problem, in May 1996 John moved in.

ONE day, Ben Perkins was driving along when he noticed an exceptionally attractive young woman walking along the other way. Olive skin, lovely figure, nice kind of presence about her, a whole lot of *eck*, unless he was very much mistaken. Which was good, because he was feeling pretty eckish.

He stopped the car. Walked across the road. Asked her if she would like to have an orange juice with three ice-cubes in it with him, and have her palm read. She said yes. Her name was Angelika, and she was nearly 20 years his junior at just 19 years old. She proved to be a charming cafe companion on this beautiful Brissie day, and what's more, Ben liked what he read in her palm. It showed her leading a happy life, and having a child with . . . with . . . why with *him!*

And he was RIGHT!

In the early part of their courtship, Ben and Angelika sometimes went out with John and Peta. Ben had a great deal of admiration for Peta, warmed to her greatly, and he was happy to see how well she got on with Angelika. Sometimes the four of them dined together. On one occasion they went ten-pin bowling. Ben was amazed at how hard and straight

John hurled the bowling ball — it almost made him to want to issue blind-folds to the ten-pins.

John in turn was delighted to see how well Ben and Angelika went together and it made him think about his relationship with Peta. They had been going together, on and off, for well over four years, and had had some happy times together, but there were long weeks when it all seemed too hard. Quietly, he sometimes felt they were too unalike to really make a go of it. He liked being out and about with a large group of friends, she preferred quiet dinners for two; he was catch-as-catch-can, she was precise in every detail. There was more, much more, but it all boiled down to the fact that they just didn't quite fit. What particularly grated on him was when others, including those close to him, couldn't see that.

One night driving John home from Queensland training, Rod McCall started to warm to a theme that had become pretty common of late: what a good woman Peta was, and how if John had any sense he'd bloody well marry her and settle down.

'Listen Rod,' John had replied, with rare feeling as he got out of the car, 'if you feel that strongly about her, why don't *you* marry her?'

Rod was already happily married thanks, and dropped the subject ever after.

WHILE John was working harder at rugby than ever before, he was still enjoying it, and the material rewards were there for him to see and enjoy every evening when he returned home. Perhaps most importantly, he felt fitter and stronger than he ever had, and his form on the field had gone up a couple of notches. As Peter Jenkins noted in the *Australian* after a particularly impressive Queensland victory over NSW in late April,:

Eales scored all the Reds points, won most of their lineouts, made a bundle of tackles, took an intercept to prevent a try, and even tossed in a 40 m punt.

'There's only one word for him — "freak",' said his former team-mate Anthony Herbert, who had watched the game, amazed. 'A dead-set freak.'

'It got to the point where I thought Ealsey was going to kick off, catch it himself, go all the way, score the try and kick the goal,' Jason Little pitched in.

Queensland finished the regular season at the top of the table, only to lose the semi-final against Natal at Ballymore. The surprise of the

Super 12 season had been the ACT Brumbies. Against all predictions Rod Macqueen had welded together the leftovers from the two principal rugby provinces with the best of the ACT locals and turned them into a side that had beaten many far more fancied opponents, including Queensland. One of the ways he had done this was by housing all the out-of-town players in the one apartment complex, known colloquially to the players as 'Melrose Place', and they finished the competition in a highly commendable fifth place.

Beyond the success or otherwise of the teams on the field, more crucial by far was the fact that the professional Super 12 concept was gaining and keeping the interest of large numbers of people — many of them new supporters of rugby. In New South Wales, for example, a 43 per cent increase in attendances saw an average of 25,000 spectators turning up for matches at the Sydney Football Stadium — and this for a team that was not performing well. In 1994 when ACT had played NSW there had been 3,217 spectators. In 1996 there were 20,687. Five of the twelve provinces making up the competition — including all three Australian sides — posted new ground records for provincial encounters. Generally, critics were hailing the rugby played as stupendous. The new rules of the Super 12, which gave a bonus competition point to each team that scored four tries, meant that a free-flowing score-at-all-costs brand of rugby had emerged. It was sustained — inevitably — by players who had never in their lives been so fit or professionally prepared. Some thought that John might struggle that year with new lineout laws introduced by the International Rugby Board which allowed players to lift jumpers — thus closing the gap between John and less gifted jumpers — but he seemed to win the ball all the same. All up, the Australian rugby community looked forward to the international season with some impatience.

In the weeks leading up to the announcement of the first Wallaby team of Greg Smith's reign, there was great speculation in the press and rugby public as to who would be the next Wallaby captain. The captain of the previous year, Phil Kearns was injured — as well as damaged in the eyes of the ARU administration by virtue of his very public support of the WRC in 1995 — so there had to be a new anointing. Many in the media believed John Eales was the likeliest successor, but nothing was sure, particularly since John was not even the captain of Queensland. That position was held by Tim Horan. By the time of the return game against

NSW on 1 June, in Sydney — a match held outside the auspices of the Super 12 —no-one knew who was going to be the captain, even though the first Wallaby team of the season was to be announced the following day. At the function after the game, lost narrowly by Queensland, John was approached by the new chairman of the ARU, Dick McGruther.

'John, I've got something to talk to you about, would you like to meet for a coffee in the hotel cafe at 11 a.m. tomorrow morning?'

'Sure, Dick, that will be fine.'

When John told Rod McCall that he would be late for their lunch with a few of the other blokes at Doyle's famous seafood restaurant in Watsons Bay, McCall quickly gave him his expert opinion:

'You've got the captaincy.'

John was not ready to leap to any such conclusion but after a bare minimum of small talk, McGruther got to the point.

'John, I asked you here to talk about the Wallaby captaincy. The board is offering it to you. Will you accept it?'

At that instant, John had strange thoughts running through his head and was momentarily out-of-kilter. He was, frankly, surprised at the way it was done, having always thought that something like that would not be offered, as he couldn't imagine anyone ever refusing. Surmising that Dick was expecting him to think about it before answering, John proceeded to do just that.

Tick. Tick. Ti . . .

'Of course, Dick, I'd love to . . . '

The captaincy settled with a handshake to seal the deal, McGruther then warmed to a couple of other themes he'd thought about in the lead-up to this conversation. He advised John that if he was going to be an effective captain he'd probably have to be more assertive and forceful than his normal easy-going character, with which John readily agreed. Some more chat about the press conference late that afternoon and one more warm handshake later the two took their leave. If John was delighted with the honour bestowed upon him, so too was McGruther extremely happy.

Certainly, Eales' experience of captaincy was limited, in fact non-existent outside the Brothers Colts team of '89 and his brief stint with the Australian Barbarians in 1995, and yet there was a compelling argument in his favour. To this point, there was nothing in rugby Eales hadn't proved capable of. When you knew the guy had learned to kick for goal like Michael Lynagh, drop field-goals like Roger Gould, run rampaging like Mark Loane and jump like John Eales you had to figure that he'd be a good chance of learning to captain like Nick Farr-Jones if given the chance.

The one obvious disadvantage was that most of the great Wallaby captains had had a slightly narky side to their personalities, enabling them to rip into even close friends when they were not pulling their weight, and Eales had never demonstrated the slightest capacity to be anything other than straightforward friendly at all times. And yet, and yet, if he'd learned to do everything else as well as other great Wallabies, it couldn't be asking too much that he also learn to be narky like Campo.

Greg Smith had come to much the same conclusions and was happy with the choice of Wallaby captain.

BACK at Arnell Street, Jack and Rosa Eales were settling down with Nonna for a simple Sunday lunch when the phone rang. It was John, telling them the news. They were, in equal measure, thrilled and surprised. Their surprise stemmed not from the fact that John was captain — they'd always thought he had leadership qualities — but because John had actually told them before the rest of the world found out. While John still called them after every game away from home to tell them he was uninjured, when it came to major achievements or events in his rugby life, Jack and Rosa tended to read about them in the papers like everyone else. John had never been a 'Guess-what?!' kind of boy, and that part of Catholicism which teaches the virtues of humility had clearly been well learned. The fact that he was calling them now to tell them he was captain was some measure of how exhilarated he was.

AT about 1.30 on that same Sunday, Rod McCall was sitting with several other Queensland Wallabies at Doyle's, about to tuck into the main course. John was going to be a little late, he had told them a little vaguely, and should be here shortly and *hulloa!* there he was now. Hail fellow, well met, smiles all around and John took his place at the end of the table, he and McCall being granted the comfort of the end slots so they could stretch their long legs out beneath the table. McCall watched Eales closely as he sat down, looking for their prearranged signal. And there it was.

Even in the motion of sitting down, John looked to Rod and surreptitiously nodded his head. He had the captaincy.

McCall's feelings were mixed. While delighted for John, he was also conscious that there were other people at the table who would be keenly disappointed, chief among whom was Tim Horan, to his mind the finest rugby footballer he'd ever seen.

'But Tim wasn't guaranteed as starting in the Wallabies because he'd just come back from very serious injury,' McCall later explained, 'so they weren't prepared to lock him into the captaincy. They needed someone who was an automatic selection and that was John.'

THE rugby press greeted the news with warmth. As Greg Growden put it in the *Sydney Morning Herald*, 'The selection of Eales as the '96 captain, will enthuse many as he appears to be the ideal skipper, primarily because he is among the top three players in the world. He is certain to be a skipper of the John Thornett mould, being the perfect gentleman off the field, and the ideal leader by example on it.'

For his part, Eales made no bones about it when asked by the press. 'At the beginning of the year,' he was quoted as saying, 'my ambition was to be part of a successful team for a long time, and now I'm part of that team as captain, my ambition is to be part of that successful team and hopefully captain for years to come. I suppose as captain, I'm even more keen that the team do well under my leadership.'

To a certain extent the news of Eales' new leadership role was not even the main rugby story of the day for, all things considered, it had been pretty much expected. Much more intriguing was the fact that David Campese had been brought back for his 93rd cap and that, after a fairly disastrous year in rugby league, Garrick Morgan had walked straight back into the Test side to partner the new captain in the second-row. Also on the agenda was the curious structure of the team Eales had been given to lead. Just as John had been thrown into the entirely unaccustomed position of No. 8 back at the beginning of the World Cup in 1991, now several Wallabies were being tried in new positions all at once. The new coach sounded far from convincing that *he* knew exactly what he was doing. When asked at the press conference, for example, whether he thought the position of outside centre suited long-time winger Joe Roff best, Smith replied: 'I don't know. I hope so.'

In the *Courier-Mail*, the redoubtable Frank O'Callaghan went for Smith from the get-go: 'After Smith repeatedly stated that no player would be chosen out of position, the national selectors, doubtless at his insistence, have named winger Joe Roff at centre, centre Patrick Howard at fly-half, no. 8 Owen Finegan at flanker, and flanker Daniel Manu at No. 8!'

It was, by any measure, a fair point and John quietly agreed with O'Callaghan that the team seemed to have a few strange selections. But he also took the view that it was for him to captain the side that was given him, and leave it at that — though he was at least glad to see the selection in the squad of a player he had admired from the Australian Barbarians tour to Canada, in winger Ben Tune.

JOHN received the letter at home, just two days after being made captain, and it written in careful copper-plate long-hand.

3 June, 1996

Dear John,

Please accept my very hearty congratulations on your appointment as Captain of the Australian rugby team and also on your enormously successful Super 12 Series (both on and off the field.)

Next to your father, I would be the proudest 'Football Father' in Australia right now and furthermore, you have given me the 'Hat Trick' of Brothers Colts whom I signed up and went on to be Wallaby captains, namely Tony Shaw, Paul McLean and now John Eales. Thanks John,

Yours sincerely,

Merv Hazell

There were many other letters of sincere congratulations, all of which John appreciated, but the one from Merv Hazell was particularly touching. In the last few years John's appearances for Brothers had been less and less frequent — and by the end of that season they would stop altogether as the ARU and QRU insisted their employees not risk themselves in club games — but whatever else, John was a Brothers man and it made him very happy indeed to have helped make the club torch of Brothers glow a little more brightly.

As a group, the 1996 Wallabies all got together for the first time up in Brisbane, just three days after the team was announced and before they were due to play the First Test against Wales . . . and all eyes turned to Greg Smith. First meetings between Wallaby sides and new Wallaby coaches are always curious moments. For even though the new coach is the boss of the team, he is also a just-arrived immigrant, even an interloper, in Wallaby-land — traditionally a mystical place within Australian rugby culture where things are done differently and all the highways and byways are known only to a very few. It is because of this that new coaches usually feel their way early, but as the players quickly found out, Smith had other ideas. From the beginning, he was a man laying down the law, *his* law. And that first law was, if you didn't do things *his* way you were gone, and he meant GONE.

'We're going to be doing things in a different way from now on,' he told his charges, in a curious kind of menacing drawl. 'And if that doesn't suit you, that's alright, we'll just @#$% you off. If you don't perform, that's okay. There's a thousand players out there who'd cut off their finger to have a chance to do what you're doing right now.'

Generally, everyone had to understand that the days of players having solid mortgages on their Test jumpers were over. As far as Smith was concerned, from this point on, every player would have to earn his stripes every week and he didn't care who you were.

'Not even the captain has got a mortgage on his position,' he said in that first meeting, 'and I know he wouldn't want it any other way.'

Quite.

On the training paddock, John would never train harder in all his born days than during Smith's reign as Australian coach, and that started on the first day of their first camp of the year. The sessions were notable for both their length and high level of full-contact confrontation, as the coach was a believer that an ideal training duplicated match conditions. As to the way Smith wished to steer the Wallabies tactically, he introduced the team to his notion of 'sequence plays', essentially a series of pre-fabricated plays that had to be practised over and over again. Instead of ad hoc rugby which you made up as you went along in the classic fashion, this was up the other end of the spectrum. It was about constructing the unbreakable building blocks of what would hopefully be an unbeatable game. From a Wallaby scrum, for example, the call might be made for a

'B-52', which meant that the plan was for Tim Horan at inside centre to run directly at the opposing outside centre. When George Gregan was tackled, the halfback would be looking to pass the ball to the back-rowers charging through on the left, and from the ensuing ruck the second-rowers on the right. And so on . . .

It was a form of rugby that had been pioneered in Australia by Rod Macqueen when he had taken over the Waratahs in 1991 — and he had continued to use it to great effect with the Brumbies — but this was the first time an Australian coach had pursued it vigorously, and Smith wanted to try some of these sequence plays out as soon as this first Test of the season.

SATURDAY, 8 June 1996. For John, there was a great deal of satisfaction in running out at the head of the Wallabies for the first time on the holy turf of Ballymore. It was here that he'd played his first grand final, for Marist Brothers Ashgrove U/10s (*and missed the goal!*); here that he'd won his Colts premiership for Brothers; here that he'd played so many games for Queensland; here that he'd played his first Test for Australia, and that too had been against Wales. Just a little over an hour and a half later, there was no less satisfaction when he returned to the dressing room having guided Australia to a 56-25 win. In Sydney a fortnight later the Wallabies were able to double the dose with an even more handsome win of 42-3, and, after ripping Canada by 70 points the week after that, they were ready. Ready for their annual assault on Everest, beating the All Blacks.

On the way to Wellington for the First Test of the Bledisloe Cup series, sitting in the Business Class section of a Qantas jet, Greg Smith unveiled his plan to John. He did not want the Wallabies facing the haka in the tra-ditional manner, by standing facing it about five metres away, but had something else in mind . . . Privately, John was not wildly enthusiastic about Greg's plan, but again he took the view that it was the coach's call. A fair summation of what happened, however, is: It didn't work.

On a horribly wet and muddy day in windy Wellington — not entirely unknown in those parts — the two teams filed out as usual and sang their national anthems. But when the time came for the haka, the All Blacks were amazed to see the Wallabies move right down to the other end of the field and start running skill-drills, flicking the ball between them. The message the Australians obviously *meant* to send was: You guys

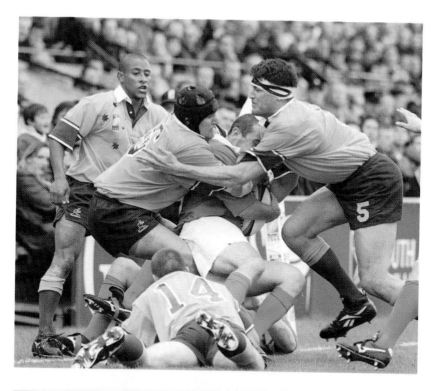

Above: Mark Connors and John stop an Irish raid during the Ireland vs Australia match, October 1999.
Photo: Tempsport ©
Action Photographics

Left: John during Australia vs South Africa at Colonial Stadium, August 2000.
Photo: Carlos Furtado
© Action Photographics

John on the burst against South Africa in the World Cup semi-final, 1999. In close support are Owen Finegan and David Giffin. The Springbok is Rassie Erasmus. © *Tempsport / Action Photographics.*

Australia celebrate victory against France in the 1999 Rugby World Cup. *Photo: Mike Hewitt* © *Allsport*

Arriving at Sydney with the World Cup, 8 November, 1999. *Photo: Scott Barbour © Allsport*

With George Gregan holding up the World Cup in a ticker-tape parade down George Street, Sydney, November 1999. *Photo : Colin Whelan © Action Photographics*

The entire Wallaby squad minutes after they won the 1999 World Cup. The man in the cap under the flash is an unknown Wallaby supporter who jumped the fence and was welcomed into the throng. *Eales family collection*

John and his eight-month-old son Elijah, 1999. *Eales family collection*

Elijah, John, Lara and the hours-old Sophia Eales on 6 October 2000. *Eales family collection*

With Ben Perkins in Coffs Harbour, June 2001. *Eales family collection*

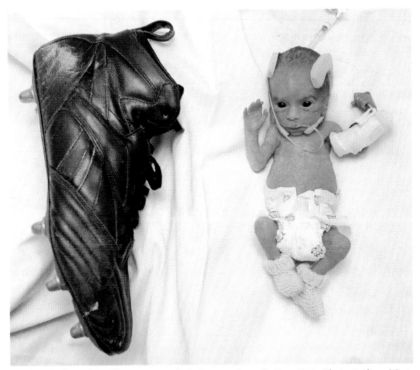

John's rugby boot alongside a premature baby born on Australia Day, 2000. *Photo: Anthony Weate © Courier Mail*

John played his hundredth game for Queensland 1 April, 2000. *Photo: Darren England © Allsport*

do what you like, we're not that interested. To many observers though, it seemed that the message that that came out was: CRIKEY! That's just too intimidating to look at front-on, so let's just fall back till we're at a safe distance.

The result was that the All Blacks were angered, and the Wallabies on the defensive from the beginning — and the combination was simply devastating. Within 90 seconds of the kick-off the hyper-charged All Blacks had stormed over the top of the seemingly somnolent Wallabies for their first try. The game was already effectively over, and things went downhill from there. The New Zealanders scored another try shortly afterwards . . . and then another, and then another. They were leading 25-6 at half-time, smashing the record of the number of points conceded by a Wallaby side in a single half of Test football. That the All Blacks showed some kind of mercy by throttling back a tad, changed not a jot the humiliation suffered by the Australians. The final scoreline was a loss of 43-6. John, who had been on the bridge of the ship when it hit the reef, *and* in the engine room, was shattered.

Certainly that is the way it looked to the newly installed Australian Rugby boss, John O'Neill, when he made his way into a Wallaby dressing room full of thousand yard stares. As he looked over at John, all the Australian captain could do was mouth the word 'sorry'.

In the wake of such a footballing disaster, there couldn't have been many upsides, but the Wallaby manager, Peter Falk, found one and related it to the stunned rugby press of two nations.

'We are trying to take the positives out of the debacle,' he said with black humour. 'The positives were that we couldn't play any worse.'

And actually, John's old friend Terry Honan squeezed out one another.

'Congratulations,' he told the Wallaby skipper over the phone, just minutes after John had arrived home, 'you've got your name on another record!'

Yep, there was certainly that. The repercussions of that game would be many. The hissing, spitting mail from the land of the Long White Cloud that landed in John's letterbox began as soon as the Wednesday after the Test and did not abate for months. The more polite ones were along the lines of: How dare you not stand and face the haka, I hope that you lose every game until you face them again. The less polite ones were a . . . lot less polite.

The letters John could have lived with, and the phone calls, but the repercussions didn't stop there. WALLABY CAPTAINCY 'NOT A BURDEN', ran the back-page headline in the *Sydney Morning Herald* above an article by Greg Growden. 'Eales' captaincy skills were criticised following Australia's record Test loss against the All Blacks in Wellington last Saturday,' the article began, 'with the main concern being that a hard-headed mongrel, rather than a softly-spoken gentleman, was required to stir up a bewildered, lost, and soon intimidated Wallaby team.'

Yes, well. John was confident in his abilities as a captain, but it there was no doubt he wasn't the hard-headed mongrel type and never would be. His style of leadership, as it had emerged, was generally laid-back. He did not lay down the law without determining first what the team thought the law should be. Many thought he took the consensus approach too far, and hungered for him to be more authoritative. Tony Daly, for example, though he did it in a good-hearted fashion, often brought the house down on long bus trips by mimicking the way John called lineouts: '19, 67, 45, 22 . . . if that's okay with everyone I mean. Any one got any thoughts? I'm quite happy to change it. Everyone's got to be in agreement with the decision.'

Haw-de-bloody-*haw*.

One who spoke to John directly on the subject was the legendary former Australian coach, David Brockhoff, and he did so in the skipper's hotel room two days before the Wallabies' next Test, against South Africa in Sydney. A passionate rugby man known for his colourful turn of phrase, the nearly septuagenarian Brockhoff asked to see John in his room at the hotel, and then proceeded to hold court as only he could. Never mind that he only had an audience of one, Brock always spoke as if he was a benign South American dictator, standing on the balcony of his palace and addressing the heaving, passionate throng below. John knew this, and kind of tried to sway appropriately, but he listened closely all the same, and appreciated the subsequent message.

'Johnny boy,' Brock began on this occasion, in his deep stentorian tones, 'we've known each other for a long time and I've always been straight with you — you know me, I'll tell it how it is. You're our captain and we *need* you to be captain, we *need* the things you bring to us as captain. But you are just *not giving* us what we need in the game, Johnny boy. You're worrying too much about being captain and what the other boys are doing and you're not getting about your own game. Get *your* game going first, be one of the pack sweeping across the field, low to the ground like maggots. The forwards must get into the South African pack like dingos among those sick rabbits beside Ayers Rock, and *you* must show them the way, Johnny.'

While John was clearly under some pressure leading up to the next Test, so too was the coach . . . and the older man did not react well to it, least of all the media criticism. One of Greg Smith's peculiarities, his charges learnt early, was a quite savage distrust of the rugby media. The old line ran that just because they diagnose you as paranoid doesn't mean they're not out to get you, and Smith seemed to follow that reasoning to the hilt. As a matter of course, he constantly brought to the team's attention every critical thing that had been written about them. In the lead-up to this Test, for example, he pointed out the most hurtful of the barbs, seeking to heighten their sense of insult, and encourage a reaction that the players were going to show the 'pernicious percillis',* as he delighted in referring to the press, that they were a lot better than described.

Outside of team-meetings and training sessions, pretty much the only place the players ever saw the coach was in the odd one-on-one session in his room. He was not a man who ate with the players, but preferred living on toasted sandwiches from room service, spooling through videos, and talking to players individually. When not in the mood to see anyone — which was frequent — he would simply put a Do Not Disturb sign outside his door.

Under the circumstances, there was never a better game than this Test against South Africa for Eales to lead from the front, and he did exactly that, playing one of his best games of the season. Just before half-time John snaffled a ball from the opposition throw-in which led to a try by Joe Roff, and enabled the Wallabies to go to the break with an 11-3 lead. The game was still evenly poised with twenty minutes to go when Tim Horan put up a delicately timed chip-kick right in front of Andre Joubert, the South African fullback. Joubert had no sooner gathered the ball in than all around went dark as if he was in a massive shadow, and the next thing he knew John Eales had tackled him right into the middle of the following week. As the Bok fullback fell, the football was coughed up

---

* The players weren't quite sure what he meant either.

and Horan swooped, scooped and *ally-ooooooped* his way to the try-line for what proved to be the winning try of the game. The Wallabies beat the incumbent World Champions 21-16, the Boks' first loss in their last sixteen Tests.

A week after their disaster against the All Blacks, the Wallabies had at least demonstrated that they were competent in the international arena, if not yet brilliant. In the dressing room afterwards, Greg Smith was all smiles as never before. Relaxed, happy, laughing.

Leading up to the next Test, against the All Blacks in Brisbane, the Wallaby coach's team-theme was that the only way forward was to beat the All Blacks and leave them with one full year to remember the result and stew over it. A fortnight later at Suncorp Stadium in Brisbane — once known as Lang Park and the very ground where John used to sneak in to watch State of Origin games — the Wallabies were very near brilliant, and undoubtedly had their finest hour on a football field for two years. Unfortunately the game went for 80 minutes, and though the Wallabies had been leading 22-9 with twenty minutes to go, a series of mistakes, mishaps and muddle-headed play on their part saw the All Blacks finish with a 32-25 victory. It had been 25-all with seven seconds to go, until the great All Black centre Frank Bunce crossed to snatch a famous victory which the New Zealand coach would ever after refer to as 'the great escape'.

Together with the other players and coach, John felt gutted and depressed in equal measure. In some ways the Wallabies were even more devastated than they had been when they were trounced in Wellington three weeks earlier. They needed that win, and in many ways deserved it, but had simply been incapable of holding on.

A loss to the South Africans a week later in Bloemfontein confirmed the obvious. The 1996 vintage Wallabies were not one of the finest drops Australia had produced. It wasn't that they were *flat* exactly, nor were they without body or bouquet, but they definitely lacked cohesion at crucial moments and seemed incapable of fighting their way out of the morass when they most needed to. At least part of the problem was clear to most independent rugby observers. That problem was that Smith had been true to his word when he said that no player had a mortgage on his Wallaby jersey, and rarely in the annals of Australian rugby had there been so many changes from week to week. After the first seven Tests of the year, John and David Wilson were the only two who had remained in the same position in the pack. Others had been dropped or switched around in their positions, and a similar lack of stability had occurred in the backs.

AFTER such an arduous year, in a strange sort of way the coming full-blown tour to Europe from the middle of October to play three Tests almost came as light relief. In those Tests they wouldn't be looking across the 50-metre line before the start of the match to see the World Champion Springboks about to charge at them, or the All Blacks, but instead would have the comparative luxury of seeing nice lads from Italy, Ireland and Wales.

On the way over to Italy, Greg Smith asked John a surprising question. 'So what's Europe like?'

John looked back at him, not sure if he was joking, but recovered in time to give a glib answer that it was fine once you got used to the conditions or somesuch. Privately though, he was staggered. There was no shame of course in being a middle-aged man without ever having been to Europe — John's own father, Jack, had had his first trip out of the country just the previous year, to see the Bledisloe Test in Auckland — but still, Smith was the only man in the team who hadn't. Most of them had been there many times, and the fact that Smith hadn't was as good a sign as any of just how far removed he was from the elite rugby mainstream, right up until the moment he had taken over the Wallabies.

The coach and captain continued to talk, as far beneath them the Middle East came and went, and the coach warmed to another theme that John had found was a constant with him: how much he was already missing his wife Janet and daughters Rachel and Alana. From their first days in camp together in early June, Greg had always said the worst thing about rugby was that it took him away from his family too much. Now, the thought that he would be away from them for the next six weeks was already weighing heavily on him.

For John, however, this tour was one he had especially been looking forward to, basically because of Nonna and St Anthony. For Italy was Nonna's homeland and, as to St Anthony, the Wallabies were due to play the Test against Italy in Padua, which was nothing less than St Anthony's home-town!

After playing their first game in Sicily, and readying to fly to the Italian mainland, John was standing with one of his team-mates making his first tour with the Wallabies, Toutai Kefu, when the Australian Rugby Union president, Phil Harry, came up. Harry had been gee-ed up by some of the Wallabies that Kefu, who was of Tongan extraction, was from a remote Pacific Island village and had only a smattering of English.

Harry: 'Tou .. tai, . . . me . . . Phil . . . Harry . . . big . . . chief . . . of . . . Australian . . . Rugby . . . Union. Fly . . . over . . . on . . . big . . . plane . . . to . . . watch . . . you . . . play. You . . . played . . . very . . . well.'

Kefu: 'Gee, thanks mate.'

All around, Wallabies were falling about in laughter, including John. Actually, Tongan Bob, as they called Kefu, had been born and bred in Brisbane and was as much a Queenslander as a XXXX beer . . .

As soon as the Wallabies arrived in Padua, John made a beeline for St Anthony's Basilica and said some prayers before the very statue of the saint on which the statuette in the Eales home was based.

Another who was delighted to be playing a Test match against Italy *in* Italy was David Campese, whose father had been born and bred in a town just 45 minutes out of Padua before emigrating to Australia in 1952. Tony Campese had flown over for the game and hosted a family reunion at the ground, with a selection of his extended relatives filling 25 seats. Making the occasion even more special was that it was to be the worthy Campo's 100th Test. Only one man had been through that barrier before, the legendary French winger Phillipe Sella.

Come the moment for the Wallabies to make their way out onto the field, the Wallaby captain told Campese that he wanted him to lead them out onto the field to fully savour the moment and let the warm Italian crowd, and his family, pay him his due. Though the winger demurred and said thanks, he really wasn't into that sort of thing, Eales pulled rank, insisted, and did one other thing besides . . .

That is, just as all the Wallabies shuffled down the darkened tunnel and out into the light, Eales stopped the team cold as Campese trotted out. It meant of course that Campese was momentarily oblivious to what had happened and was out there on his own as the crowd rose as one to acclaim him.

For all the emotion of the occasion however, the Wallabies still did not play well. Just four minutes into the second half, the locals were even leading, 15-13. That the Wallabies subsequently pulled away to win the day 40-18 changed not at all the impression that there were serious flaws in the Wallabies' attack and defence. Despite Smith's attention to sequence plays, there was precious little evidence of them out on the field, where no-one — least of all the ball-carrier — seemed sure of what was about to happen next. Many were the critics in Australia who pointed this out, but none made a bigger impact on the Wallabies than John Connolly, whose comments were carried on a Channel Ten sports program. The way John heard it from the forward coach on the tour, Jake Howard, who had heard it from Australia, Connolly had bagged the Wallabies and Greg Smith, saying they were a team divided, living in an 'atmosphere of fear' and that was why their form was so poor.

Smith was ropable, and no less so was his captain. At a press conference in their Edinburgh hotel the Wallaby coach said Connolly was as shallow as a Donald Duck comic and he was disgusted — a disgust that was heightened by the fact that there were already rumours swirling that there was a movement building at home to have him dumped as coach at the end of the tour.

John was also forthright in his condemnation. 'It is very disappointing, because it is inaccurate,' he said pointedly. 'It is particularly disappointing for me, and the other guys from Queensland, because the complaints always seem to come from Queensland.'

It was a courageous effort by Eales to put the state coach back in his box, but he was not long in copping Connolly's return fire. Early the following morning — on the day they were to play Scotland — the phone rang and it was a seriously aggrieved John Connolly on the other end of the line.

Where the hell did Eales get off, he wanted to know, criticising him when he didn't even know what he HAD SAID. And for the record, HE DIDN'T EVEN SAY THAT! On and on. Connolly even had a tape recording of the offending interview, and played it. The Queensland coach had a point. Though there was a little smoke, there was hardly the fire that John had been told about. All he could do was tell the coach he probably *had* got the wrong end of the stick, meaning the coach had got the rough end of the pineapple, and he was sorry.

THE Test against Scotland was more of the same. Despite winning 29-19, the Wallabies' manner of achieving it convinced no-one. The game had hung in the balance until the final minutes, and for a mighty Australian team against a relatively humble Scottish side, this was considered simply not good enough. At least, however, one player making his debut for Australia that day, prop Andrew Blades, played a notably fine game and there was a sense that one part of the ongoing selection merry-go-round could stop. And so to Ireland . . .

The morning after arriving at the team hotel in Dublin, Eales was having his breakfast when the ancient loudspeaker in the corner crackled into life and squawked that there was an urgent message for John Eales at the reception desk. John made his way there, but not quickly enough to prevent the message being repeated another two times before he arrived, each one more urgently.

Becoming concerned and fearing a crisis at home, he identified himself, and was quickly given a telephone.

'Mr Eales?' a thick Irish brogue came through.

'Yes!?! Yes!?!?'

'This is your 8.a.m. wake up call . . . '

As the Wallabies neared the end of their European tour, at the conclusion of what had been a singularly difficult year for the Wallabies, rumblings about John's leadership, or lack thereof, began to surface again, mostly in the media. The theme of the disquiet was the same-old: that John was too much of a gentleman to be a fire and brimstone leader of men. Still, there were signs that things were changing, and a big one came in the match against Ulster in Belfast.

Rarely in John's life had he been really angry, but this night was an exception. To begin with, the referee near blew the Wallabies off the park with his whistle, but things soon got a whole lot worse when the referee began to limp and was replaced by one of his touch judges.

Whether the newcomer was a believer in the notion that mimicry is the most sincere form of flattery, or was just a dud ref, John would never know, but the Wallabies were soon practically under siege from whistle missiles launched by the replacement ref. The bottom line was that the Wallabies were in the fight of their lives to win the game and preserve their undefeated status on tour and John Eales' mood blackened as the game continued.

Enter, stage right, from the position of five-eighth, David Knox, a man with a personality which dictated that he said what he wanted to say, whenever he wanted to say it. This sometimes worked well for him off the field when his eccentric nature and constant escapades could provide the team with hours of amusement. On the field, it could work too, when he conjured magic that only he knew was possible in the first place and was able to pass the ball into the hands of the one player capable of breaking the defensive line.

This situation, however, fitted into none of the above. The Wallabies had been awarded a penalty within kicking range. John decided the Wallabies would kick for goal and told Knox to do it. Knox demurred, saying he thought it would be better to run it. Eales said again that Knox was to kick for goal. Knox demurred again. Eales exploded.

Exactly what he said is as close to unprintable as anything he has ever said, but its general theme — expressed with great force and a lot of volume — was that Knox had better do exactly what was asked or he, Eales, would perform some extremely unpleasant acts upon him. Knox, shocked, did exactly that. Other Wallabies, standing near, were equally shocked, but also delighted — not for the humiliation of Knox but for the fact that Eales was completely in charge of the ship. Knox slotted the goal, but still Eales wasn't done.

Five minutes later when Knox again crossed his path, he gave him another blast for good measure. The Wallabies went on to win the day, the unbeaten tour tag was preserved, and the Wallabies went into their Test against Ireland at Lansdowne Road with high hopes.

The first time John played Ireland had been at the same ground in the World Cup quarter-final in 1991, when the Wallabies had made their own great escape. That game had begun with an all-in brawl after the Irish captain and flanker Phil Matthews made the unwise move of taking a massive swing at Willie Ofahengaue. Normally the most mild-mannered of men, Ofahengaue was nevertheless powerfully explosive enough to punch holes in the sides of a battleship and proceeded to do so. When the normally good-natured Matthews was asked afterwards what had got into him to take a swing at Willie like that, he is reputed to have replied 'Well you see, it was a very big game for us, and I was keen to get my retaliation in first!'*

---

* Quite possibly apocryphal, but the story *does* circulate in Australian rugby circles!

John had cause to be reminded of that story midway through the second half of the Test against Ireland when he jumped in a lineout and copped a fist in the eye so fierce that he shortly afterwards had to leave the field with a severely bruised cornea and fractured eye socket that occurred after an awkward tackle. Australia beat Ireland 22-12, and though it was shortly clear that John would have to miss the Test against Wales, there seemed little chance that they would lose to them. John was sorry to miss out on a chance to play at Cardiff Arms Park — and it was doubly painful given that his parents had just arrived in the UK to see him play — but the main thing was that the injury was not going to knock him out for a year. Instead of physios and surgeons, he could simply leave the job to Mother Nature and Father Time to sort out between them.

In his absence from the side, a young former Queensland second-rower who had moved to Canberra to play with the Brumbies, David Giffin — the last man left standing uninjured of the original second-row selections — made his debut and played very well. As it happened, though, there had been so many players making their debut for the Wallabies that year it was sometimes hard to keep track. For Greg Smith's original chopping and changing in the first few Tests of the year had continued throughout the season, to the point where it was suggested that the Wallabies would be well advised to put a revolving door at their dressing room entrance.

This, by any measure, caused an obvious lack of cohesion. When, for example, Wallaby halfback George Gregan had passed the ball to five-eighth Pat Howard in the opening action of the Test against Wales, it was only the second time it had happened in a Test match that year. And when Howard passed to inside centre Tim Horan, that too was only the second time. Bizarrely enough, for the entire year, Horan had never passed to outside centre Jason Little in a Test. Ditto to the power of two, Little to David Campese. And all of the above when Campese — who as it turned out was playing his last Test for Australia — passed to fellow winger Joe Roff on the one occasion they linked up. How could there possibly have been any cohesion? Cohesion can grow only in stability, and there simply hadn't been any this year. Certainly some measure of this had been exacerbated by injuries to such key players as Little, who had been out for most of the year, but Greg Smith could not have offered the same excuse in the case of the halfback. The season had started with

Gregan at half, who'd been dropped for Sam Payne, who'd been dropped for Gregan, who'd been dropped for Payne, who'd been dropped for Gregan!

It was, then, a predictably scratchy performance against Wales, but at least Australia emerged with a 28-19 win.

As with any tour, there were plenty of official lunches and dinners to attend, and far and away the most important one — just before they returned home — was the Lord Taverners lunch in London, a large charity affair. As captain, John was placed beside the patron of the Lord Taverners club and one of the finest cricketers England had produced in the previous fifty years, Colin Cowdrey. He was a gentle man and gentleman, and John found the 64-year-old engaging company and felt comfortable enough with him that he thought he'd give it a go . . .

'Did you enjoy the Ashes series in 1961 . . . ?' he began, fairly neutrally.

'Yes,' Cowdrey answered, perhaps a little surprised at the very specific nature of the query.

'Do you think your best inning that whole year was your 93 against us at Headingley in the Third Test?'

'Probably,' Cowdrey replied.

'And did you find Graham McKenzie or Richie Benaud our best bowler?' John continued.

'How old are you, John? How do you know all these things?'

John told him, and continued a wonderful afternoon in the great man's company.

A win over the British Barbarians meant the Wallabies finished the tour unbeaten, with twelve victories in twelve games. The critics remained as numerous as they were vociferous, but the 12/12 final result meant that the move to unseat Smith got nowhere. Whatever the critics said, however, Greg Smith could not say that Eales was not loyal to him.

'The major difference about this tour from others,' John told the press immediately after the Welsh encounter, 'is that the Test team hasn't been settled, and from game to game, Test to Test, no-one knows who is going to be in the team, which I think is a positive thing.'

HOME at last. This time, flying into Brisbane, something was significantly different for John. For the first time in many tours, Peta would not be waiting for him. Somehow or other they had drifted apart. On this tour she had turned up while the Wallabies were in Wales for a couple of weeks, and in the course of many conversations they had decided that the best thing was for them to break up. This was nothing new, particularly, as they had already broken up three times, and had always ended up getting back together again. This time, though, both knew it was definitive.

Few people in the modern age, of course, get to be card-carrying adults without having had at least one serious break-up, but if this was John's he was at least fortunate that he was not torn apart by it. In some ways it was a relief.

Just as it was a relief to see Nonna again. John always scanned his grandmother earnestly when he returned to see if she had aged at all, but the answer was invariably 'no'. She had looked very old as far back as he could remember, and she continued to look old now. Still, there were signs that Nonna was beginning to feel her mortality. Shortly after John arrived at Arnell Street he was lying on Nonna's bed with her and they began singing their favourite hymns and songs — John in his passable baritone, Nonna in what her grandson describes as 'her high pitched squealing sort of falsetto'.

After moving through 'Ave Maria', 'Oh Come All Ye Faithful' and 'Little Drummer Boy', both were in the mood to keep going, so John started in on a favourite of Catholic funerals, 'I Am the Bread of Life'.

He was just moving to the soaring chorus of '*I will raise him up, and I will raise him up* . . . ' when he noticed that Nonna had not joined in, and was in fact crying.

Wobbly
Wallabies

I'm under a lot of pressure.
Sometimes I wake up in the night and it's on my mind
and I have trouble getting back to sleep.

GREG SMITH in his own column, *Daily Telegraph*,
1 August 1997

⌇

SHORTLY AFTER Ross Turnbull had folded his World Rugby Corporation tent, he made a pertinent observation: 'When they took the game professional in Paris they unleashed an energy which they had no capacity to control.'

His thesis was that once the amateur culture of rugby administration had their high seawalls taken down, waves of hard-nosed entrepreneurial spirit would come flooding in and transform everything it came into contact with. By early 1997, it was possible to see the prescience of that comment. One of the things so transformed was the Wallaby jersey, which was relaunched in different form and with the new branding of Reebok upon it. (This was in return for a reputed increase of $1.5 million into the coffers of the ARU.) The jersey was unveiled to a highly dubious press on a hot day in late January at the ARU offices in Mount Street, North Sydney, and John acted as one of the catwalk models. He spoke to the journalists afterwards in support of the change, yet the subsequent reviews were not good, with one writer in the *Sydney Morning Herald* going particularly ballistic.

'The new Reebok jersey looks like volcano vomit on a rag,' he wrote. 'Where there used to be a lustrous gold, there is now a runny yellow. Where there used to be one predominant rich colour all over, there are now harsh triangles of green and white colliding everywhere. Where there used to be a kind of holy sheen, there is now a commercial catastrophe.'

To many, it seemed as if rugby's version of cricket's baggy green cap had been sold to the highest bidder, though John didn't necessarily see it *quite* like that. While privately he was not wildly enthusiastic about the new jersey he was also conscious that the players could hardly press the ARU to make the game professional and then not support the measures they took to provide the wages. For John the jersey still represented playing for Australia, and that was the main thing. He took a similar view a short time later when VODAFONE was plastered all over the front of the jersey for exactly the same commercial considerations.

As John readied to fly back to Brisbane on that January day, though, there was yet another sign that the game had begun to mould itself into a more commercial shape, as had his own image. For as he filed down the airbridge at Sydney Airport, there on the wall was his photograph on a huge Qantas poster beneath the heading 'The Leaping Wallaby and the Flying Kangaroo'. The text read:

John Eales is Captain of the Wallabies — Australia's Rugby Union Team. He captained the squad that toured the UK in 1996, and returned undefeated and triumphant. John is widely considered to be the most outstanding forward in the Rugby World. The connection between the Wallabies and the Red Kangaroos is more than genetic. Qantas are the official airline of the Australian team. Our support of the Wallabies is part of a lifelong commitment to Australian sport. A commitment that will continue to grow both in spirit and support as we fly into the future.

John always felt self-conscious when passing these glossy posters — and could never bring himself to so much as glance at them — but they also gave him a sense of how much the code was growing. A side benefit of his new-found profile that he was also able to put it towards helping good causes, and early in 1997 he was delighted to accept a position as an 'ambassador' to the Leukaemia Foundation. In this role John would speak at dinners, visit sick children, organise for Wallaby jerseys to be signed and given to them for fund-raising purposes, preside at the opening of new leukaemia wards and the like. It was satisfying, though he often felt guilty he couldn't do more for the families struggling with such severe illness.

For John, his own family remained the foundation stone of his existence. That 17 February, John went for dinner to Arnell Street, as he did on the same date every year. For this was Carmel's birthday and all the Eales family kept that evening free to gather and honour her memory. On this night they were all there. Jack with Rosa and Nonna. Bernadette with Tony, both besides themselves with excitement at her enormous belly and the fact that their first baby was due in less than a month. Damian, now a big shot in retailing in Sydney, was there with his new wife Tara, Rosaleen was with her boyfriend Quinton, and Antoinette was holding hands with her new romance, Robert. And there was John . . .

IT felt like the movie *Groundhog Day*. For on 5 July 1997 it was the same horror movie, same cast, same ending. After taking on the All Blacks at Lancaster Park the Wallabies went down 30-13. It was not as humiliating as the year before, when they had been buried 43-6, but the upshot was identical. Even veterans as experienced as Eales and Little had never won a Test on NZ soil, and Tim Horan had won just one from nine attempts. To critics, and they were multiplying like rabbits, it looked as though the Wallabies did not belong on the same park as the All Blacks. Sure, the Wallabies had already beaten France in successive Tests that season, but that had been expected. Two years out from the World Cup — and all thoughts were starting to turn in that direction — it was obvious the Wallabies just could not match it against serious competition.

The usual doom and gloom headlines followed their loss to the All Blacks, the usual hand-wringing over just what ailed the Australians so, and a lot of the critical commentary centred on the fact that one *J. Eales* was installed as captain.

Most damaging was a front page article in the *Sunday Telegraph* sport section on 20 July 20, just a week before the Wallabies were due to face the All Blacks again. The big bold headline read: '"SACK THE CAPTAIN" Says Wallaby legend Mark Ella'.

John had been forewarned of the attack late on the Saturday night by a phone call from John Connolly, who had told him the gist of the article and to ignore it, to 'just believe in yourself' — but it was abundantly clear that Ella didn't believe in him. Ella had not made a habit of such attacks, but after just the first few paragraphs, he slid the knife in and twisted. 'John Eales is a class player,' he wrote, 'the best forward in Australia, but it's time to recall Kearns straight away. And I'd give Kearns the captaincy because I believe Australia needs the settling influence only a man of his experience can bring to the team, especially against the All Blacks at the MCG.'

For public consumption, and however much he was hurt by the attack, Eales was typically moderate in his reply. 'Look, I don't really think this is an issue,' he breezily told reporters. 'I'm very comfortable with the captaincy and am really enjoying the role. I don't really care what Mark Ella or anyone else says.'

In response to the attack, there was hardly an outcry from outraged rugby supporters that Eales' leadership should have been called into question, as, in fact, Ella's thoughts were merely part of a widespread rumbling grumbling at the time that maybe the captaincy was part of the Wallabies' problem. The words of two people in particular, however, heartened John. One was the quiet assurance from Greg Smith that, no matter what criticism might be levelled at him being skipper, he enjoyed his coach's confidence, and *nothing* was going to change that. And the other was Ben Perkins. The two had regular long conversations on the subject, often at Ben's house in Bardon, and though Ben said nothing in particular which John fastened onto, somehow he always had the same effect on John. After talking to Ben, John always just felt better about everything. Bugger Ella!

Clearly, though, what Eales most needed at this moment — not to mention the Wallabies and Greg Smith, and Australian rugby — was a *win* against the All Blacks at that most holy site in Australian sport, the MCG. It had been a long time between drinks since the last Wallaby Bledisloe victory, going back to the Gregan tackle Test of 1994. In rugby terms, that was back in the Neolithic Age, when dinosaurs roamed the earth and the game was still amateur. Dot three, carry one, subtract two . . . the All Blacks had won no fewer than *eight* of their previous ten encounters. How much could a koala *bear* before the situation changed?

It was at least a wonderful thing to be in Melbourne. This was the first major rugby Test to be held in the sporting capital of Australia and the city seemed to be buzzing with it as people from all over Australasia, and indeed the world, streamed there to enjoy the historic occasion. Accommodation was so tight that late arrivals were taking advantage of an offer by the Crown Casino theatres to watch five movies throughout the night for $55, and the whole theatre became an informal dormitory. It all made for a wonderfully large crowd on the night of the big game. While at the first Bledisloe Cup encounter 65 years earlier there had been 15,000 spectators, and the largest crowd in the interim had been 48,900, on this balmy evening there were 90,000 spectators nearly on the button. Not for nothing did the loudspeaker play one of Louis Armstrong's most famous songs, 'What a Wonderful World'. For a person raised on the notion that rugby was the game they played in heaven, this looked about as close to heaven as they were ever likely to get on this earth.

As John ran out at the head of the Wallabies, Jack Eales watched from the stands. In his wildest of all wild dreams he'd pictured John leading the Australian team out on to the MCG pitch, and if this was not quite the way he had imagined it, with his boy wearing a baggy green cap, still it was close enough! Rosa, while also delighted, had something else on her mind. Mark Ella. Four rows down and three across, she had spied him. Though in her life she had never provoked a public confrontation with someone, on this night she was just about angry enough. Over and over she kept thinking, *How could you?*

Out on the field, alas, both the Wallabies' starboard and port engines were soon billowing smoke. After only 16 minutes, the Wallabies were behind 17-3 and the game was essentially gone. A sign of how frustrated John personally was came late in the game when he was penalised for taking an uncharacteristic swing at his opposing captain, Sean Fitzpatrick. To be fair, Fitzpatrick — the brute! — had been holding him by the jersey, preventing the second-rower from disengaging himself from a ruck, and John had simply lashed out. Yet none of the press gallery could remember seeing Eales throw the first punch on a rugby field before. By full-time the hosts had gone down 33-18. Game over.

In the wake of the Wallabies' defeat, the howling criticism aimed at the Australian coach reached a singularly high pitch, as did the calls for him to be replaced by Rod Macqueen — who had had another sterling year with the Brumbies, guiding them all the way to the final of the Super 12. Smith's contract with the ARU ran until November, but many were calling for him to give way to Macqueen immediately. In the time leading up to the Wallabies' next Test, against South Africa at Suncorp Stadium, it got so bad that pretty much the kindest thing that was said about Smith came from one of his predecessors, Alan Jones. And even then, the best Jones could muster was: 'Smith should be given the freedom to fail'.

In the face of it all, Greg Smith's behaviour became increasingly erratic, though there was likely a medical reason for this. Entirely unbeknown to him, the coach had an extremely serious tumour growing in his brain. This went a long way towards explaining his dramatic mood swings, sudden anger, sometimes disjointed reasoning and further withdrawal from the team bar the time of actual training. It is possible that this tumour had been growing for all of his Wallaby tenure. Those who had played under him at NSW level reported to the rest of the sometimes worried team that Greg was entirely different now. Phil Kearns had once said that Smith was the funniest man he'd ever met. But apart from one terrific night they'd had with him in Ireland on the tour of the previous year — where Smith had been fantastic company, warm, loquacious and indeed very, very funny — that side of him just didn't emerge.

All Smith himself noticed in terms of physical symptoms were blinding headaches that didn't seem to go away. Much later, when talking about it to a journalist, he was frank. 'At least the illness explained a lot of my very negative behaviour,' he recalled. 'I had no motivation to do anything. I thought I was pretty resilient, but it got to me. And it got to me because I was sick. The tumour was pushing into an area of my brain that affects thinking and personality. It had been affecting me for a long time, but you tend to hide things. That side of my personality just shut down . . . And it was all because of this thing that had invaded my brain.'

By the Thursday before the South African Test — a morning when Australia was grieving over a horrifying disaster that had hit Thredbo in NSW's Snowy Mountains the night before in the small hours of 30 July — the CEO of the ARU, John O'Neill, was so concerned about the way things were heading that he had a long talk with John Eales about the virtue of what he called 'player power'.

Although he did not tell the Wallaby captain in so many words that he had to take over the team, O'Neill did observe that in extremely difficult situations it needed senior players like John, Tim Horan and George Gregan to take the lead and they wouldn't be getting any problems from O'Neill if they did so. To an extent this had already happened, with John, Tim and George having asserted themselves progressively more at training sessions and sometimes organising action outside the coach's ken. A small example had been an initiative by John promulgated at forward meetings whereby, going into every Test match, each member of the pack had to have two stated goals. John's, for example, might be to claim two opposition throw-ins, hooker Michael Foley's to claim at least one opposition feed into the scrum, and so on. This was in no way contrary to what Greg Smith would have wanted anyway, but it *was* an attempt to provide direction that sometimes seemed to be lacking.

On the Friday before the South African Test, however, there was nothing Eales or O'Neill could do when it came to helping Greg Smith. For Eales it was like being firmly strapped into the front seat of a car he knew was going to crash. There he was, sitting at a fully attended press conference beside the national coach when Greg pulled from his pocket a handwritten statement which he said he wanted to read. He began to do so, and though he never named him, it was clear that one of Smith's key purposes was to make direct reply to the gathering mob who were calling for Macqueen to take over. 'Tomorrow we play South Africa in what some would described as the battle for second place in world rugby supremacy,' he began fairly neutrally, before getting to the meat and potatoes of his message.

'On the question, so often brought up, relating to Super 12 form, it is obvious to all that the Brumbies were the outstanding Australian performers. All in all, we have used 13 Brumby players, including nine who were part of the first undefeated tour to the United Kingdom, Ireland and Italy. Whilst we all believe the Brumbies had a marvellous season, in the context of their season, they played Auckland twice and were beaten twice. Auckland contained seven All Blacks. I think it is a fairly important point that some of you [the press] need to have a look at.

'I would like to ask you guys — some members of the press — if the team will receive some positive support if we beat South Africa tomorrow night. I think it is very tough on our team. I would just plead with you to give your national team some support, because I think the people of Australia want the national team to be supported. I don't think it is acceptable to Australians. If you think that it is — and that's what sells newspapers — then there's not much hope really for us.'

Eales, sitting beside Smith as he unloaded, was flabbergasted but let the press conference take its course. As far as John was concerned, this was the Greg Smith Show and he was as much a spectator as everyone else. When, at the coach's conclusion, John was asked by a stunned journalist what *he* thought of Smith's statement, John batted it off, refused to address the issue, and sat back, hoping the journalists wouldn't press him on it. Taking mercy, they didn't.

Outside, immediately afterwards, Smith himself tackled Eales.

'John, you've *got* to support me in these things,' he said. 'It's important that we present a united front, stick together as a team.'

'I can only support you, Greg,' John replied, 'if I totally agree with what you are saying. We need to discuss these issues first. I can't be going in blind on these big issues. Right now, we should only be concentrating on beating South Africa tomorrow, and not worrying about Rod Macqueen.'

Speaking of whom, in response to Smith's Pearl Harbor attack, as it would subsequently become known, Macqueen did precisely what he had done in the previous few months — that is, he said nothing, maintaining an entirely dignified silence and not getting even remotely involved.

THEY FOUND SOMEONE ALIVE! On the Saturday morning of the Test match, 2 August, the news went around the Wallabies in nothing flat. In the early hours of Saturday morning, a good two-and-a-half days after the disaster, the courageous rescue workers who had been digging around the clock down at Thredbo had detected signs of life beneath the rubble. Carefully burrowing their way down, they made contact with a survivor by the name of Stuart Diver. You bloody *beauty*. They were now delicately trying to extricate him without collapsing the whole disaster once more upon him, and themselves.

Throughout the day, even as they prepared for that night's important match, the Wallabies remained glued to the television, hoping that Diver would be pulled out okay. Late in the afternoon, just ten minutes before the team meeting, wonderful news.

They got him! He was okay! Wild cheering and great WHOOPS echoed around the hotel corridors, and the team meeting took place amid much glee. Ultimately it was one of those things that helped to put sport in perspective. While what the Wallabies were engaged in was a serious venture, it was not life and death. While people sometimes called them 'heroes,' they were *not* like the people they could see on the screen, risking their lives crawling over unstable ruins in the hope of getting someone's son or daughter out alive.

That night, at half-past seven John ran out onto the Suncorp Stadium at the head of a Wallaby side bearing black armbands as a mark of respect to the eighteen people who had not survived the Snowy Mountains disaster. Despite that, the mood of the crowd was not subdued, nor was that of the Wallabies. All there seemed glad to be alive, and as tragic as the episode had been, it was a good night to be an Australian and the Wallabies played like that. For once, passes stuck, moves clicked, tackles were made and everything worked just the way it had in training.

The Wallabies were so impressive that they received a standing ovation at half-time from the delighted crowd *and*, more importantly, full-time, when they recorded a much-needed win, 32-20 — a record, in terms of the number of points scored against the South African national team.

BUT would the real Wallaby side please stand up? Because just a fortnight later, against the All Blacks at Carisbrook stadium in Dunedin, there was another record-breaking performance, but this time it was a record against the Wallabies. Incredibly, at half-time the Wallabies were losing 36-0, and even though they were able to come back in the second-half to finish with a final score of 36-24, the clear impression was that this was because the New Zealanders had shown uncharacteristic compassion and taken their foot off the accelerator. Making the situation worse for John was the fact he'd been injured during training in the lead-up to the game, and was forced to watch the debacle from his home on Frome Street, in the company of the equally injured Tim Horan and Wallaby flanker Matt Cockbain and the just retired Rod McCall.

Could anything be worse than impotently watching such a humiliation?

Yes. Much worse was being in exactly the same position the following week, when the Wallabies played a still-smarting Springbok side in Pretoria. John sat in the stands with a strained medial ligament, and actually had some hope at half-time when the Springboks held only a slender 18-15 lead. This was before the South Africans tried the simple expedient in the second half of running straight at the Wallabies. Suddenly, there seemed to be more gaps in the Australian line than actual players. Tim Horan was still injured at the time and the South Africans ran riot. The one who John most felt sorry for was David Wilson, who had taken over the captaincy and thrown everything he had at the South Africans, but to no avail. It was far from his fault, but Wilson had been obliged to register two devastating losses in his first two games as Wallaby skipper.

The one bright Wallaby performance in the whole debacle was the young ACT player Stephen Larkham playing at fullback, who tackled himself red-raw. As admirable as Larkham's performance was, however, he seemed a mere rock in the river, while all else flowed past.

When the game was at last, mercifully over — had it been a person, there would have been a clear case for euthanasia twenty minutes before the end — the Wallabies had lost by the staggering score of 61-22. This was the most points ever conceded by a Wallaby side in a Test match, a near 50 per cent increase on the previous record of 43 points, established only the previous year in their disastrous performance against the All Blacks at Wellington.

Back in Australia, the chairman of the Australian Rugby Union, Dick McGruther, turned off the television set, appalled. Never had he seen a Wallaby side play worse. Without hesitation he reached for the phone and called John O'Neill's mobile number.

'Look, it's time to move on,' he told the ARU CEO. 'If there is an opportunity that presents itself to get Greg's resignation, you should not hesitate. I'll back whatever action you take. If he offers a resignation, grab it.'

Bizarrely after such a display, the Wallabies then spent two desultory days in Sun City, the famous casino resort two hours out of Johannesburg. Late on the Monday afternoon, they headed for Jan Smuts airport. As the rather bland South African countryside slipped by the brooding bus, Greg Smith moved around among the players and handed out copies of faxed newspaper reports from Australia he'd received. It didn't make pretty reading . . .

'The second-half performance at Pretoria,' wrote the *Herald*'s Spiro Zavos in reference to the six tries the Australians let through, 'was the most shameful 40 minutes of rugby the Wallabies have played in 93 years.'

His colleague, Greg Growden, was a lot lighter on the Wallabies than he actually felt. 'What a disgrace,' he opined. 'These Wallabies are duds, but even more upsetting is that they dudded their country. They dudded their coach, Greg Smith. They dudded the Australian rugby colours. They dudded the Australian Rugby Union, who pay their way. And they dudded those countless Australian Test greats, who ensured that for so many years the Wallaby name typified courage, heroism, and the ability to tackle adversity in its stride.'

Greg Smith's purpose in distributing such literary hand-grenades was the usual — to heighten the players' sense of *siege* and outrage — but this time he wanted to take it one step further. For shortly afterwards, as the lights of Johannesburg appeared ahead, Smith was seen to be forming up a petition on a clipboard demanding that he be retained as Wallaby coach, which he intended to circulate to the players. It was a bizarre thing to do, given that the person who would likely be the first to receive such a petition was the same John O'Neill who was sitting on the other side of the aisle from him at the time. O'Neill had no sooner discerned the coach's intention than he crushed it quickly, but it was indicative of the turbulent times.

It was clear to all that after a loss like that there would be a massive clean-out one way or another, and it was just a question of who would go and who would survive. Heading back to Australia, somewhere over the Indian Ocean, Smith divulged to his captain that he had a plan.

'I've been thinking I might go with John Connolly as assistant coach,' he said. 'What do you think, John?'

What John thought was that he was staggered. During Greg Smith's entire tenure he had constantly been at loggerheads with Connolly, and now he wanted him as his no. 2!?

'Greg, that will not work,' John replied quietly but firmly. Smith looked back at Eales, nodded, and sat back quietly — his splitting headache nearly killing him — as the four jet engines pulled them through the upper reaches of the atmosphere to what was likely going to be a hostile reception when they got back to Sydney. First, though, they had a brief stop-over in Perth to refuel. Greg Smith wandered around the airport, red in the face, seemingly dazed, his shirt out of his pants. He was wearing no tie or blazer. Whichever way he cut it, there was surely little way out for a national coach who had his signature on the bottom right-hand corner of such a debacle.

WHILE Australian rugby was going through a terrible time in the wake of the record loss, it wasn't as if the rest of the world rugby community couldn't engage in some gallows humour at Australia's expense. In New Zealand the story circulated that, on the previous Sunday night, Sydney police had been called to a big city hotel room where the body of a middle-aged guest had been found, dressed only in a Wallaby jersey and shorts. To save the man's wife embarrassment, the cops decided to dress him in women's underwear instead . . .

Few in the Wallabies would have laughed, least of all John. The fortunes of the national rugby side had never fallen to a lower ebb, and the 1999 World Cup was now well under two years away.

A DAY after arriving back in Australia, Greg Smith had a key conversation over the phone with John O'Neill, who was at the ARU offices in Mount Street, North Sydney. It was four days before the ARU board was to meet to discuss the coaching situation. Gently, gently, softly, softly, O'Neill pointed out to Smith the untenability of his position, whatever either man might think about the injustice of that.

'Do you really think the board meeting will go against me?' Smith asked.

'Yes, I do,' O'Neill replied.

'Do you think it's in my best interests to resign?'

'Yes, I do. As a friend and your boss, I think it's highly unlikely you'd survive Monday.'

Smith took a deep breath. 'On that basis, then,' he said, 'let's do it now.'

O'Neill then read out to Smith a dummy press release he had prepared against this eventuality, to see what he thought of it.

The procedure was under way, and Smith indeed resigned, just four days after the record loss to the Springboks. John's reported comment to the press provided as good an epitaph as any to Smith's Wallaby coaching career: 'It's sad to see Greg go in these circumstances, because he was a good coach.'

The Wallaby captain first heard of Smith's resignation while readying himself for some much needed R&R at the Gold Coast with a group of friends. He immediately called Greg and they had a brief, strained conversation. The older man was clearly devastated, but at least glad that it was over. He had a headache, and warmly thanked John for the call, but did not want to speak for long. John went back to packing his bags for the Gold Coast.

At the height of the rugby season it was always difficult for John to catch up with his mates as much as he would have liked, so this was intended as something of an old friends' reunion. That Saturday night they caroused until very late and John awoke late on Sunday morning to appalling news on the television. Overnight in Paris, Diana, Princess of Wales, had been in a terrible car accident and been rushed to hospital. John turned to CNN hoping for more up-to-date information that in fact her injuries were not as bad as first thought. Alas, as he sat there, stunned, progressively worse updates climaxed with the news that she was *dead*. Again, it had been that kind of week.

AN odd sort of bloke, Rod Macqueen, all things considered. Somehow, he had managed to arrive at the position of Australian rugby coach — for he was officially anointed and appointed within a fortnight of Smith's resignation — while remaining as enigmatic as the Dalai Lama to most of the rugby public and indeed to many of the Wallabies he had inherited. That is, they all knew he was out there somewhere and knew his basic background, but generally had only the vaguest idea of what sort of a man he really was. Generally his image started and finished at 'successful coach,' but as to detail, there was little.

The irony in Macqueen taking over from a Greg Smith, whose coaching career had been cut short by the devastating effects of a brain tumour, was that Macqueen had had an amazingly similar problem a decade earlier when doctors had discovered a tumour next to his pituitary gland. The tumour had been removed, but the episode proved to be a life-altering experience for the hard-driving businessman, and former successful club coach and player.

Finally out of hospital, he eased back a little in his successful graphic design business and decided to go after his long-held dream of being a representative rugby coach, where he was close to a revelation. In his first year as their coach he guided the NSW Waratahs undefeated through ten hard games. He had near equal success in the next two years, became an Australian selector, and took over a bunch of also-rans, the ACT Brumbies and guided them into one appearance in the final.

It was from this stint that most of the current generation of Wallabies knew of him. What most of the non-ACT Wallabies gleaned from their Brumby team-mates was that, unlike most coaches, Macqueen was neither one of the boys nor Hitler's little brother; he could not be categorised as a barge and bash 'em coach, but nor did he seem imbued with any particular rugby philosophy. His real philosophy, as he had first stated when making his way up the coaching ranks, was 'to win through in a well-organised, methodical manner' and he had remained true to that ever since.

All of which sounded to John, at least, like an extremely good thing. From his days as a student at Marist Brothers Ashgrove he had always responded best to being in an organised environment, with a solid structure around him. He liked certainty in his life, a routine. And Rod, from everything that he'd heard, was nothing if not systematic.

FROM the time he took over the Wallabies in mid-September 1997, Macqueen made it clear he wanted to take a very consultative approach. He telephoned John one day late that month and sounded out his views on who should be appointed as the scrum coach for the upcoming tour of Argentina and Britain.

In the last year of the Smith regime, that job had been former Wallaby prop John Griffith's, but following usual rugby form Griffith had gone the way of the outgoing coach and there was now a vacancy. Macqueen said he had in mind John's old friend — the former Wallaby forward coach who he had used at the Brumbies — Jake Howard. What did John think about that then?

It was a tough one all right. John had a high personal regard for Jake, and thought him to be one of the best in the business for sorting out scrums and getting them to the very highest notch. But some instinct told him that the time was right to bring in *entirely* fresh faces into the Wallaby coaching line-up. But could he say that, so baldly, to Macqueen? Probably, he decided. If he couldn't trust the coach to keep his confidence then they were never going to get anywhere anyway, so . . .

'Yeah,' he said carefully, 'I think Jake's great, but maybe we should look around to see if there's anyone else . . . '

'Like who?'

'Well, John Connolly's very good with the scrums. Or you could maybe try Tony Darcy, or Chris Carberry, or Tommy Lawton. Maybe you could have a chat to these people before you make a decision . . . '

At this point they moved on to other subjects, but before the conversation finished John returned to it and asked that if Rod talked to Jake about it, then he would prefer to be left out of it — or at least have the chance to speak to Jake personally. He had always had a strong personal relationship with both Jake and his son, sometime Wallaby back Pat, which made it difficult for him to be essentially advising against his inclusion at this point.

As John remembers it, Macqueen was firm in his reply: 'Mate, listen, you obviously don't know me very well, but one thing you'll get to realise is that I'm a man of my word and if I say I won't say anything, I won't say anything.'

Is everybody happy? You bet your life we are. A day later, John was in Christchurch, getting ready to speak at a luncheon, and after returning from breakfast turned on his mobile phone to find that there was an urgent message from Jake to please call him. As he was cleaning his teeth, he kept thinking about the message, and how there was a tone in the voice that he'd never heard before. The room phone rang.

John picked it up. Jake. An extremely unhappy Jake. A Jake who gave him a tirade full of anger, disappointment and *hurt* that John had not backed him. He felt nothing short of betrayed and wanted John to know that. Over the years he had delighted in John's successes, had liked to feel that he had had a small part in forming his fabulous skills, had been outspoken that John should be captain, and defended him against those who said he shouldn't, had felt that sometimes John was practically like a son to him, and now this.

John explained to the likeable forward coach the best he could that it was absolutely nothing personal, and that he had merely suggested Rod look around at other possibilities, but what he really wanted was to get off the phone as quickly as possible, to both end the agony *and* get Rod Macqueen on the phone.

Feeling totally betrayed, he was as angry as he'd been for some time and when John finally got on to the new coach he made those feelings clear.

'For us to work,' he said, 'we have to be able to trust each other. You specifically told me you would keep my confidence on this, but you didn't.'

Macqueen, perhaps shocked at the level of the Wallaby captain's fury, apologised. It had somehow happened inadvertently, and he regretted it, but it definitely wouldn't happen again.

John wasn't the only one having a few problems with Rod Macqueen at this early stage. Dick McGruther and John O'Neill were also engaged in a little hand-to-hand fighting on a particular issue. On the basis of the successful Brumbies experience, Macqueen wanted a structure whereby the Wallabies would be quite separate from the ARU, 'a kind of Wallabies Inc.' as McGruther derisively called it to O'Neill. The chairman of the ARU and his CEO were as dead set against it as Macqueen was for it, and insisted that the Wallabies remain a part of overall management of the Australian Rugby Union.

'You're not going to run the Rod Macqueen Wallabies Pty Ltd, and be off there as some kind of a satellite,' McGruther told Macqueen in some-times heated conversations, and with O'Neill's full support won the day.

A few days after their clash, John's steam over the Rod Macqueen/ Jake Howard episode remained. But still, one of Ben Perkins' theories was that a whole lot of *kal* at least made you appreciate the *eck* more. And it was funny, because even while John was feeling all this anger over the Jake Howard story he was also beginning to feel the stirrings of an entirely different emotion ...

It had begun the previous weekend when he attended the christening of Bernadette and Tony's new-born son, Daniel. One of Bernadette's close friends whom he had occasionally seen over the years was there, a petite 25-year-old lawyer by the name of Lara Khoo. John had always found her exceptionally attractive, but for some reason he had never really sat down to chat with her before. This time it was different. One of the only occasions John had ever let anyone down by not fulfilling a promised speaking engagement had been several years before, when Lara had asked him to attend a charity event she was organising, and John had had to pull out at the last minute because of an unexpected rugby commitment. He began by reminding her of the episode, repeating his apologies, and they went from there. Between coffee and cup-cakes as the christening celebration gaily swirled around them, John gently regarded Lara. Lovely. Seriously lovely. Intelligent. Warm-hearted. Worked in a law firm. Tick. Tick. Tick. Tick. Tick. *And* she was a Roman Catholic, which certainly didn't hurt any.

Of course, Lara appraised John in turn. For her, John had always been an enigmatic figure. She'd always heard he was not the stereotypical 'celebrity sportsperson', full of sweaty swagger, but she was surprised to find just how unlike that he was in person. Not only did he seem quite shy, but he seemed to listen carefully to what she was saying and to respond in kind — laughing more easily as they warmed to each other. One thing impressed her particularly . . .

A little later, observing the loving but fun way John interacted with Nonna — all joyful jest with a 95-year-old grandmother who so clearly adored him every bit in turn — Lara decided she liked the cut of his jib very much indeed. And Nonna, in turn, was delighted with Lara. When John introduced Lara to her that evening, Nonna had immediately checked Lara's ring finger and her eyes lit up when she saw that she was clearly unspoken for.

One thing led to another, and later that evening it was Lara who dropped John back home and the two ended up sitting in her car and chatting till the owls flew by. Look, Lara, it was nice catching up, and would you like to do it again some time? Good idea. Soon, then? That would be nice. I'll call you, okay? I look forward to it.

Steady Eddie, though. Careful not to appear *too* keen, John waited until the Tuesday he had flown to Christchurch before calling her at work. She did not call back that day, nor the following day, nor the following day. Booger. And there was he thinking that there had kind of been *something happening* between them.

On the following Sunday John had his first meeting with Rod Macqueen in Sydney. They discussed the upcoming tour to Argentina and Britain and continued to patch things up between them, and on the following afternoon John was back in Brisbane, showing his brother-in-law Tony over the new house he had just bought in the salubrious suburb of Hamilton. Actually, some would say 'mansion'.

A curious architectural melange of traditional Queenslander with Indian and Italian influences, the 100-year-old house was set between two quiet streets. Just as importantly, it was situated roughly halfway between the airport and the city, and was close to Ballymore. The price tag? Enough to kill a brown dog. A lot of his friends were amazed that John would, and *could*, pay such a figure, but John loved the place from the moment he saw it, had his name on a contract within days, and his house in Frome Street on the market shortly after that.

Tony was equally knocked out by the place, and invited John back home to discuss it further. When they got there, who should be pulling up outside but Lara! She had come over to drop off a present for baby

Daniel and quickly accepted Bernadette's invitation to dinner. The first thing she and John sorted out was that she hadn't got his earlier message, and as they all went inside it was clear that there was some major chemistry going on between the two. Bernadette kept looking at them thinking, 'Okay this is my brother, this is my good friend and look what's happening!'

The following Thursday, again by pure happenstance, Lara was a fellow invitee at journalist Jim Tucker's surprise 40th birthday party, and she and John ended up sitting together. The following night — neither could believe the coincidence — they again found themselves as two single guests at a common friend's dinner party. It seemed extraordinary that, after not having run across each other in years, they were at the same place as each other four times in under a fortnight. Not trusting that fate would continue to be so kind, John asked Lara out, and she accepted in a flash.

Five days later, Chris White put the key in the door of John's Frome Street home — where he was briefly staying — and came across a strange, *strange* scene.

Solo, the captain of the Wallabies, was doing a full John Travolta number, dancing around the spacious living room to the sound of REM belting out 'So Fast, So Numb' on the stereo. Step left, step right, shake your bootie, fingers in the air, and *twirl!* And again! John was so absorbed with his dancing he didn't notice Chris at first, standing gobsmacked in the doorway — this was so unlike John — but when he did it didn't really matter. He kept dancing anyway until the song was done.

'Mate,' John finally spoke, after he had turned the stereo off and Chris could again hear himself think, 'where would you take a girl on a second date?'

John and Lara decided to keep their burgeoning romance fairly quiet, as it somehow seemed easier that way, but they weren't extreme about it. One night while they were babysitting baby Daniel for Tony and Bernadette, near-neighbour John Connolly popped in to drop something off to John and chatted to the couple for all of five minutes. It was enough, and the next time the Queensland coach saw John he said, 'You'll marry that girl, John Eales. She's the one for you.'

John didn't argue. Things went so swimmingly that for the first time in his rugby career John left for an overseas tour with real regret. At least in just a little over four weeks — 31 days to be precise — he would be back.

AFTER the kerfuffle over Jake Howard, things between John and Rod Macqueen gradually sorted themselves out. One thing which helped was that Macqueen plumped for John's former Wallaby team-mate Jeff Miller for the position of forward coach. The entire team approved. Miller was one of rugby's gentlemen, and he possessed a singularly astute rugby brain. Another former Wallaby in the person of Tim Lane helped Macqueen look after the backs.

The entire team looked forward to a new start under Macqueen, and Argentina seemed likely to provide as good a backdrop as anywhere to get on with it. It is one of the world's great rugby touring destinations, with its beautiful women, exotic cuisine, wild nightlife, edgy-kind-of-*feel*. As it turned out, though, the Wallabies had little chance to enjoy any of that in the very first few days of Macqueen's reign. A lightning visit to Buenos Aires by Bill Clinton and his entourage meant that the plush hotel they'd booked downtown had been overtaken, and this first Wallaby side to tour Argentina for ten years found themselves accommodated in the Hindu Club on the outskirts of the city. It was surrounded by fields, and as the week progressed the grass grew all the greener from the Wallabies' sweat as the new coach and his staff worked them hard. His constant focus was to ensure that The Plan — 'You plan your work and you work your plan' — would indeed go exactly according to plan. One of the key features of Macqueen's blueprint for success was that all members of the team have a better than middling idea of where the ball was going to go next, and under his stewardship the Wallabies worked moves endlessly.

The new coach was not, however, a ranter and raver. An advocate of the Theodore Roosevelt view that a leader should 'tread softly and carry a big stick', he was generally softly spoken in much the same manner as steel softly shines. But when he said he 'meant business', he meant it literally. For while many a sportsman has made money by teaching the golden rules of success in sport, and how they can work equally well in the corporate world, the reality of the Rod Macqueen approach was that he did *exactly* the reverse . . .

'So what we're going to do, guys,' Rod Macqueen told them in their first serious session behind closed doors, as every player listened with the issued pen and paper before them, 'is do some SWOT analysis.'

The Wallabies looked back at him blankly. SWOT what?

'SWOT analysis,' he explained, 'is . . . Strengths, Weaknesses,

Opportunities and Threats of the opposition.'

A new Wallaby tradition had just been initiated. From then on, a few days before every match Macqueen would stand in front of the team with a big whiteboard beside him and draw up four columns. Then the team would brainstorm the Strengths of the opposition, their Weaknesses, the Opportunities that arose because of their weaknesses, and the Threats that arose because of their strengths.

Before this First Test against Argentina, for example, it was established that the obvious strengths of the hosts were their pace on the wings, their legendarily strong scrum and their superb goal-kicker. Their weaknesses were a certain lack of discipline and, most likely, a lack of professional fitness. Usually, Macqueen would already have a clear idea of the SWOT conclusions after long discussion with his management team — another new term in the Wallabies' lexicon — but the Wallabies were all encouraged to participate in the session. It all fitted in with Macqueen's general philosophy of football, borrowed from a famous Chinese warlord of two thousand years ago, Sun Tzu. It was he who had written a treatise known as *The Art of War*, and Rod often quoted to the Wallabies one of its dictums: 'Know yourself and know your enemy and in a thousand battles you'll never be in peril. Know yourself but know not your enemy, and your chances of success and failure will be equal. Know not yourself or your enemy, and in every battle you'll be in peril.' From here on in, he was clear, they were going to know both themselves and their enemy, through a lot of analysis. Get used to it.

WHEN it came to offensive patterns, Macqueen was right in his element. Just as he had done so successfully with the Brumbies, he began to inculcate in the Wallabies a different way of going about their attack, a way that was every bit as intellectual as it was physical.

'If you wanted to break down a brick wall with a hammer,' he told them in one of his first sessions, 'you wouldn't hit the wall all over with the hammer, would you?'

No, boss.

'What you would do is try to find the weakest point and then just keep smashing away at that weak point until you broke through. That is exactly what we have to do out on the football field.'

What it was about, Macqueen told them, was finding the right 'channel' to attack in. The idea of the channel was to identify the weakness in the opposition line, whether by your SWOT preparation or by reading the play on the instant. Once the weakness was identified, the plan was to pour all your resources into breaching it, with wave after wave of Wallabies pouring through that channel until the try-line was reached. In Macqueen's terminology: 'We must identify the weakness horizontally, and then attack vertically.'

Another way of forcing the weakness was to keep pounding away at a given point with the same 'sequence plays' that Greg Smith had been pushing, but whereas Smith might have had only two variations on the one sequence play, Macqueen was inclined to have as many as six. Certainly some of the things he was developing had been introduced to the Wallabies beforehand, but this was the first time it had ever been done in such a structured systematic fashion. Macqueen underlined to the Wallabies that the notion of the inherent virtues of running rugby is a nonsense — in his book it was *winning rugby* that counted.

THE first chance to prove they were good students of the Macqueen methodology would come when they played their first lead-up game to the Test, against Tucuman, in the north-west of Argentina. As they took off from Buenos Aires John gazed out the aircraft window at the extraordinary vista below. It was an amazing city, with the extremes of wealth and poverty, history and modernism, beauty and ugliness all packed tightly together in a wonderfully messy mosaic. The places rugby took you remained intoxicating to John and . . .

And a kid up in the front part of the plane was screaming to wake the dead. Screaming and screaming and SCREAAAAMING! Wouldn't stop. Eight-year-old kid, maybe ten. Screaming something in Spanish, over and over again, like a mad thing. All the Wallabies looked at him uncomfortably. John asked one of the passengers what he was saying. Deadpan, the man replied, 'He is saying the !#$%-ing plane is going to crash and we're all going to !#$%-ing die.'

Oh. Oh well then. Welcome to Buddy Holly Airways, your captain is the Big Bopper, and we hope you enjoy your flight. Happily, they landed safely, and in the blazing heat, recorded a terrific 76-15 win over the powerful Tucuman side.

Ideally, of course, after so much professional preparation and such a good start to the tour, the Wallabies would have gone out and ripped the locals in the First Test vs Argentina on that first day of November 1997, but that is not the way it happened. The Wallabies — up against a side that earlier in the season had been *smoked* by the All Blacks by a 90-point margin — were still at level-pegging 72 minutes into the Test, and had only pulled away for a try in extremis in the last minutes to post a 23-15 win. The reviews were, once again, far from sparkling. As Peter Jenkins put it in the *Australian*: 'the Wallabies might have changed their coach, but nothing much else appears to have altered since their Tri-Nations embarrassment of two months ago.'

From a personal viewpoint John had played as well as ever, taking fifteen clean catches in an overall lineout margin of 22-8, and at least the Argentina coach — the same Grizz Wyllie who had given him his Rothmans Medal in Brisbane seven years previously — was impressed. 'Eales was the difference,' Wyllie told the press. 'If you took him out of the side who knows? He just had a remarkable game. Not just at the lineout, but all over the park.'

This, however, was close to the only positive thing said about the Wallaby performance. Rod Macqueen for one was appalled — and not a little shocked — that they had come so close to losing, and said so to the team at some length.

If the coach was unhappy with how things were going in the team, so too was there a general unease within the team, part of which concerned Rod Macqueen. The feeling was that the Cappuccino Club, — as the Wallabies who had come from the Brumbies were nicknamed— were too much a team within a team, and had altogether too much influence on Rod in the way things were done. Macqueen had of course risen to the position of Australian coach on the strength of the success he had achieved with the Brumbies, so it was not unreasonable that he seek the counsel of senior ACT players such as George Gregan and Brett Robinson. So too was it normal that the Brumbies, who were used to the way Macqueen conducted such things as SWOT sessions, tended to come to the fore when player input was called for. Overall, though, a sense grew that while all the Wallabies were equal, some were more equal than others, and that the most equal of all were the Brumbies.

Some of John's unease about the direction the Wallabies were taking was apparent in his near daily telephone calls to Lara, who for the first time in her life was taking a match-by-match interest in how the Wallabies were going. John had missed her a great deal since the tour began and had mounted up phone bills that would kill *two* brown dogs, but it was worth it just to talk to her.

For the moment there was nothing for it but to get stuck in to preparing for the Second Test a week after the first. That Monday night's SWOT session was even more intense than the last, a large part of it consisting of going through all the mistakes they had made in the previous Test with a fine-tooth comb. It was a long session.

Come that Second Test, however, the Wallabies found themselves in all too familiar territory for that era. It was a complete debacle. When the curtain came down, the Wallabies had lost 18-16. Against Argentina. Against amateurs. Against all reason. They had *lost*.

How did the Argentinians, with their comparatively humble rugby pedigree, achieve their victory? By keeping it simple, stupid, and playing with great passion. Instead of intricately patterned play with the potential to break down at every complex turn, the Argentinian defensive plan could be boiled down to: if in doubt, take 'em out. In attack, their key tactic appeared to be to ATTACK, with their players elbowing each other out of the way in eagerness to get their hands on the ball to do so.

One of the greater glories of rugby is that even the strongest seeming castles can often be stormed by a team of fifteen men, strong and true, who gird their loins and *chaaaarge*, and this had clearly been just such an occasion.

To John's mind, the problem was that the Wallabies were *too* well prepared, and knew so much about the opposition that they had gone out onto the field thinking they already had the game won. It became very much a team-theme after that that no matter how much analysis you do, it's not worth, to use their vernacular, 'a squirt of goat's piss' if you don't act upon it.

In the wake of the defeat, Macqueen, in his fashion, was desperate. Before his eyes the Australian team which he had staked his reputation on turning into a champion outfit had been cleaned out by a rugby power that was meant to be Second World at best. And the worst thing of all, it seemed to the coach, as he looked around at the players at the after-match function held at the stadium, was that the Wallabies didn't seem to have an appropriate air of desperation or desolation. The side that had in their last four matches copped a record first-half deficit against the All Blacks, a record score against South Africa, a narrow win and then a LOSS to Argentina, did not seem to have one among them who was hanging his head in shame. The closest a lot of them had got to it was when they lay flat out on the ground after the game was over, without any apparent pride, which Rod found completely unacceptable. Now, it was almost as if it was business as usual — as if they had lost and lost badly but their contract money was still secure so it wasn't as if things were really grim or anything.

In short, WHAT WAS WRONG WITH THEM? How was it that they had gone out in a Test match, got thumped, and weren't devastated by it? Why was there nothing coming from them, some ideas at least, about how things could be done better? At last, though, while he was chatting disconsolately with Dick McGruther and John O'Neill came a sign . . .

Hovering above them suddenly were the captain and vice-captain, John Eales and George Gregan, obviously wanting to talk to them. At last, at *last*, Macqueen thought, a signal that there was some senior leadership in the team, capable of helping him find a way out of the debacle.

'Hi,' John began, 'We've been talking to a few of the players and there's a couple of things we'd really like to talk to you about . . .'

Yes! Yes!! YESSSSSSS!!!

'The thing is, a lot of the players aren't happy about the hotel we're staying in next being so far out of London . . .'

The other issue Eales and Gregan wanted to talk about was serious dissatisfaction within the team over the fact that nine of the 34 man touring party would not be making the rest of the trip to Britain with them, but would be going home. This had not been the case when they had left Australia, and the ludicrousness of the situation was highlighted by the fact that the reserve hooker, Brendan Cannon, had cancelled his wedding because he thought he would be going on to Britain. One of the key issues was the payment to those players, who when they left had thought that they would be paid for the entire tour, but had now been told that was not the case. However unfortunate the timing, Eales and Gregan felt that these were unresolved issues which had to be sorted out before the nine players left the following day, and it was their duty to approach management.

They may as well have saved their breath. Macqueen simply walked away without a word. McGruther and O'Neill were nearly as appalled. A little away from the rest, McGruther gave it to Eales straight: 'Mate, don't you !$%^-ing *ever* come up to us worried about bloody "housekeeping" issues when you've just represented your country and taken on a loss like that. If that's so high on your list of priorities, it's no wonder you lost.'

Macqueen's feelings were little improved a short while afterwards when he announced on the bus going back to the hotel that there would be no Wallaby Happy Hour that night, as there was absolutely *nothing* to celebrate — only to find that, after he gone back up to his room and watched the game video one wretched time through before returning downstairs, a rollicking Happy Hour seemed to be in full swing. John's view was that it was not a full-blown Happy Hour so much as a farewell drink for those tourists heading home. Macqueen's thunder did not abate when John explained these views to him.

A FEW days later, John O'Neill was in London on business while the Wallabies were preparing for the first game of their English tour in Surrey, when he received an urgent phone-call from ARU president Phil Harry.

'I think you better get up here,' he said, 'because we're in big trouble with Rod.'

Within hours O'Neill had arrived at the Wallabies' training, on a green and pleasant field, to talk with Macqueen, who was standing at one end of the field alone, while the assistant coaches ran the training. O'Neill immediately recognised a strain of deep unhappiness all around.

The problems Macqueen had were many, and not the least of them was the Wallabies' loss to Argentina which had rocked the coach to his foundations. He now wondered if it was even *possible* to turn them around. The previous day, just about the whole damn lot of the Wallabies had grumbled that Rod had wanted them to train in the afternoon, meaning they couldn't go sightseeing. As a team, they just didn't seem to get it, that they were now professionals and had to give up some of their previous amateur joys. Macqueen was also outraged at the treatment handed out by the press in the wake of the defeat, with the *Sydney Morning Herald* reporting that the Wallabies were 'spineless' and Peter Jenkins of the *Australian* characterising the Test as 'a debacle' and 'an embarrassment'. And one more thing . . .

When Macqueen had twice delayed the announcement of the team till mid-morning of the Tuesday before the Test, both Peter Jenkins and Greg Growden had blown up — it meant they would be left with only a tiny amount of time to meet their deadlines, and they had accused him of lacking professionalism. There could be few greater insults to one who prided himself on being professional above all, and Macqueen told O'Neill he would never talk to either man again.

'I just don't think I can handle this,' he told O'Neill. 'I didn't take this job to be personally attacked, nor to have attacks on my professionalism and my integrity.'

O'Neill watched carefully, at one point fearful that Rod was going to resign. Fortunately, Macqueen did no such thing, and after a long heart-to-heart the two men decided the best thing was to simply soldier on, and they would talk more when the tour was over.

The Wallabies' performance at Twickenham — John's fiftieth Test — was not one for the ages. But at least they ended up with a 15-15 draw. They might have scored a great win had John slotted a penalty goal in extra time, but there was one key problem. John wasn't kicking. He had handed the goal-kicking over to Joe Roff earlier in the game, when his own attempts had gone astray, and did not think it right to take it back. It was put best by Bruce Wilson, writing in Sydney's *Daily Telegraph*: 'When it came to kicking a longish penalty well into extra time, any thinking captain would have turned to Eales. The trouble is, he *was* the captain, and too self-effacing about his kicking to give himself the job.'

The draw meant that in their last seven Tests the Wallabies had only won two, their worst record in the last decade. In simple terms of that particular tour, the Macqueen Wallabies had been expected to win all four Tests and they had to that point won just one of their first three. Not for nothing did *The Times* rank Australia only fifth behind New Zealand, France, England and South Africa.

If the Wallabies did not have a good win against Scotland they risked the tour rightly being described as a complete disaster.

Thanks in part to another extraordinary performance by Stephen Larkham playing at fullback, the Wallabies on 22 November were at least able to finish the tour, and the year, with a good 37-8 win over Scotland. Never mind that the great Scottish fullback and captain Gavin Hastings described it as 'the worst Scotland performance I've seen', there was much from which the Wallabies could take satisfaction. It was a win, and that was what they most needed. Plus, despite the fact that they had trailed 8-3 early in the game, they had remained composed, something Macqueen had been banging on about for the previous four weeks — although oddly enough he often pronounced it 'COMPOSURE' in a quite uncomposed way.

Beyond that, though, John was glad that the rugby season was over for 1997, and no mistake.

Simon Whitehart, who was now living in Britain, caught up with him in an Edinburgh restaurant the day after the Test and was shocked by how tired and jaded John appeared.

'Look,' John said to him at one point, 'when it's all over for me, I will be so glad to walk away from it. I have just about had enough.'

Three days later and for John it was a joy to be getting home, sitting well up the pointy end of a big Qantas jet . . .

For whatever the pleasures of touring had been to a young John, the joys of getting home from them now were at least their equal. There was something about breaking through the clouds on approach to runway one and looking out to see Brissie proper sparkling in the sunshine that just got to him. Where else would I ever want to live, he sometimes asked himself when he was just back from Buenos Aires, Paris, Rome or London. Always the answer was the same. Nowhere but here. Godzone country.

Though Lara was working that day and couldn't get out to the airport, John was waiting for her the moment she clocked off, and they quickly resumed where they had left off. Things just clicked between them, and they prepared to spend a long happy summer together.

In the meantime, Rod Macqueen was not happy at all. Down in Sydney, he was forcefully putting the view to John O'Neill at ARU headquarters that it might very well be time for the Wallabies to look elsewhere for leadership. As he explained to the CEO, it was clear to him now that John Eales hadn't grown in the position, that he wasn't providing the leadership necessary to pull the Wallabies back out of their current morass. They had to start again with an entirely different culture, and the way to do that was to find themselves a new captain.

O'Neill demurred, saying things would have to be considered very deeply before making such a move. In the first place, he wasn't convinced that Eales couldn't turn into a very fine captain indeed, and in the second he reminded Macqueen that the board of the ARU had made it clear that any change would have to be approved by them, so it was ultimately neither of their decisions. The two agreed to retreat to their corners and reflect on everything they had discussed, with O'Neill at least promising to sound Eales out about just how much he valued the captaincy. If he didn't want to keep it, then the problem was solved.

A Man
with a Plan

At the international
level sport is frankly mimic warfare.

GEORGE ORWELL, 1945

There's a spirit in the Wallabies
Mere words cannot describe,
It's as if they had descended
From some legendary tribe.
There's a kinship, a tradition,
As in days so long since past,
Of crusades, of knights in armour,
And of men before the mast.

Rugby poet PETER FENTON

⤙

IT WAS LATE January 1998. And John O'Neill was on the blower. Would John like to come down to the Gold Coast for the day and shoot a round of golf? See you then.

And a pleasant enough game it was too, even if Eales habitually hit his drives a good 100 metres beyond O'Neill's. They chatted about all kinds of things, before coming onto the twelfth fairway — dog-leg, par 4 — whereupon O'Neill steered the conversation towards the captaincy.

Just how much did John value it? O'Neill wouldn't be telling him anything he didn't know by saying that Rod Macqueen had serious reservations about the way he had been going in the role. The first thing O'Neill wanted to know was, did John want to keep it?

John stood over his ball, and looked back at O'Neill, suddenly realising that this was quite serious.

He paused for a moment, and then replied with some feeling. 'It is *the* most important thing to me. I definitely want to keep it.'

That established, O'Neill spent the rest of their time out on the fairway giving John his perspective on leadership. There were already a lot of positives with John's captaincy, including the fact he was well liked by the public, had a good relationship with the media, enjoyed the respect of the players, and had generally been seen to make the right decisions on the field, but . . .

But, and this was the nub, O'Neill's view was that if John was really going to be an effective leader of the Wallabies, he could no longer be 'a creature of consensus'. As they continued to hit their shots, and O'Neill to look for his ball, the CEO warmed to the theme that John needed to step back from the fray, decide what the *right* direction was himself — irrespective of what everyone else might be telling him — and push forward from there. There was more, much more, but the upshot was that John was invited to think over his approach to the captaincy, while O'Neill promised that he would talk to Macqueen and arrange for them to get together.

That meeting took place a week later, at a cafe on Racecourse Road in Brisbane, with John Eales, Rod Macqueen and Jeff Miller present. For an entire morning, as their own little Cappuccino Club, they thrashed it out. Macqueen and Miller put forward their vision of what they wanted in a Wallaby captain — someone who would back their decisions, work hard to turn the culture around, be the 'keeper of the standards' — and asked John if he thought he could do that. Their impression, they made clear, was that in the inevitable argy-bargy between players and management on any one of a dozen different issues, John was tending to take the players' side.

John said he could be exactly the kind of captain they required, and also used the opportunity to point out to Macqueen and Miller a few areas where he thought *they* could do better. Choosing his words carefully, he said that it was no longer tenable for team management to decide exactly what was going to happen in terms of training, travel, etc. and then expect John to be their advocate among the team as to what a very good idea it was. He was happy to present a united front, but only if he was aware of the reasons behind decisions. From here on in, if he was to be captain, he wanted to be far more part of the decision making process. Fair enough. The Australian coach conceded his point, but also made one of his own — that the final decision ultimately had to rest with him.

At the conclusion of the meeting there were hand-shakes all around and a feeling that things would work better in future. Macqueen had not confirmed he would remain captain, but John certainly had formed that impression.

And so it went. If rugby could have its ups and downs — and John found himself occasionally wondering what it would be like to have a life without having to face the round eternal of trainings, meetings and video sessions — the happiest of all happy things was that his relationship with Lara was going very well indeed. John had always believed that when he found his life partner he would instinctively know that she was The One, and unless he was very much mistaken that was the feeling he had right now.

The two saw each other most days, or at least talked on the phone, and one morning in March Lara mentioned that she was feeling so unwell she had decided to take the day off work. Only mildly concerned, John sent flowers to her apartment at Red Hill and later that afternoon visited straight after training. From the first moments of entering her apartment he noticed that Lara seemed a little on edge, but that was perhaps under-standable given that she had always been absolutely healthy. Lara loved her work and was particularly enjoying her case-work in the field of commercial litigation and medical negligence. So the day off was more than a little inconvenient.

'Are you feeling better?' John asked. 'Did you go to the doctor's?'

'Yes . . . ' she replied.

'And what did he say? What's up? Is everything okay?'

'He said I'm pregnant,' Lara replied, before bursting into tears. In response, John felt waves of entirely different emotions crashing over him. *Pregnant!*

PREGNANT! His Lara! Carrying his child! But they weren't married. But he loved her. But their parents might not necessarily understand. But this was ultimately their business, and not their parents'. But they hadn't been going out together for even close to a year. But he loved her!

With a big hug, John informed her of that fact, made clear his overwhelming excitement over the news and they began to make plans. The first thing they decided was to keep the whole thing quiet for a while and not tell anyone until they had both wrapped their heads around what it would mean. One clear implication for Lara was that it would impact on her burgeoning legal career. Another was that while John was used to being a public figure, she was not, and bearing his child meant she would have to get used to a certain amount of publicity. Something they decided immediately was that Lara should move in with him. And they'd take it from there. Marriage? Quite probably, but they barely discussed it. The most important thing was that they were unreservedly committed to each other and to the baby. Besides which, a marriage would have to be squeezed into the upcoming football season, and that was not the way either of them wanted to do it. This was their baby — a baby! — and they were going to do it their way.

FOR some reason, the only emotion John felt when he told his parents the news was excitement. Some might have thought he had reason for at least a little nervousness, given how seriously he had been raised in the Catholic faith — with its narrow parameters of how a child should be conceived — but for some reason he felt none of that. His parents had also raised him to make independent decisions, live his own life, and that is what he had done.

'And so,' he said, when he finally got to the point, as his parents and Nonna waited for him to do just that while sitting at the family kitchen table, 'the news is that Lara and I are going to have a baby.'

There was a moment's stunned silence while Nonna and his parents absorbed this, and it was Nonna who broke first.

'No, no John, it's not true,' she said, 'you are not even married.'

'Yes, it *is* true, Nonna,' John replied firmly, at which point Nonna's emotions seemed to do a screaming u-turn and come roaring back the other way.

'Oh John that's great, that's great,' she said, giving him a hug. 'It doesn't matter — you don't need to be married any more, anyway'.

Jack and Rosa Eales evinced similar emotions. They had, after all, committed to each other only four months after meeting, while John and Lara had waited a lot longer. Rosa, particularly, was overcome. She tried to say something, stopped, hugged him, said 'Oh John, I love you John,' tried again to speak, failed again, and fell back once more on affirming her love for him. So it went . . .

Lara's parents took the news in similar fashion. As John explained to them, he and Lara had felt from their first weeks of going out together that they would one day love to have children together, and this simply meant that it was going to happen sooner rather than later.

Once Lara had passed the twelve week mark of her pregnancy, meaning that things looked confirmed, the couple began to tell their nearest and dearest. Of all the reactions John received, the most charming came from his old friend Garrick Morgan, when they were on a flight back from New Zealand after a Super 12 match. As the lights of Auckland faded, and they began the long haul over the Tasman sea, John told him 'by the way, Garrick, I thought you'd be interested to know, Lara is pregnant.'

Garrick looked at him. Said nothing. Looked at him again, trying to see if this was a joke . . .

'Lara?' he said. '*Pregnant?* Really?'

Really. With which Morgan broke out in an enormous grin and warmly pumped his hand.

'John, that is FANTASTIC. Geez, that is fantastic. I'm so happy for you, I feel like I just won *Sale of the Century!*'

THE news, when it broke, was quite staggering to many of John's friends.

One afternoon his old mate Rod McCall happened to be passing by John's front door and so dropped in. Gidday Rod, come in. But as McCall left the harsh Queensland sunshine to enter the coolness of the house he was immediately conscious that John already had another visitor, an attractive young woman.

'You've met Lara, haven't you, Rod?' John said.

No. No, he hadn't actually. But he was very pleased to. How are you? She was fine, and she was pleased to meet him too, after having heard so much about him.

'Lara's moving in,' John offered by way of explanation for the open suitcases and various boxes that were open all over the floor. 'We're going to have a baby.'

Riiiiiiight. McCall didn't think it good form to fall about astonished at the time, but was certainly surprised. Still, he only had to be with them for five minutes before it was obvious how happy they were together and how delighted they were to be having their baby.

WHEN the news broke to the wider public, with a photo of the happy couple on the front page of the *Courier-Mail* the general reaction was a mix of surprise and congratulations. There were exceptions to the latter, however.

One anonymous note, dropped into their letterbox read:

Doesn't worry you — more the pity.
    When you consider your Catholic education and family background (published so much.) Really an insult. Our three sons 15, 12, 10 confronted us today with the question.
    'Why doesn't John Eales have to get married to live with that woman?'
    Think about it mate!
    'What does it profit a man if he gains the whole world etc, etc,'

Signed,

'A Realistic Catholic Dad.'

Charmed, John was sure.

IF most rugby seasons produce a moment that will be locked away in the collective memory of one's team-mates, then there is no doubt which moment that was in John's 1998 Super 12 season. It came in early April, when Queensland played Auckland at Ballymore. John was standing beneath the goalposts as Carlos Spencer connected with a long-range penalty kick when the second-rower realised two things. Firstly that the ball was indeed heading over the black dot in the middle of the crossbar, and secondly that if he timed a massive leap just right, it was maybe possible he could . . .

No sooner thought than done. Before the stunned gaze of players, press and onlookers, John leapt skywards and batted the ball harmlessly away. In the dressing room afterwards, it was the talk of both teams — almost to a man they had never seen or heard of such a thing being accomplished, and there remained only one player who claimed he was underwhelmed.

That was Queensland and Brothers prop, Glenn Panaho, who maintained that far from being impressive, the episode was proof positive that Eales was losing his touch. With a straight face, he told everyone that he remembered Eales doing exactly the same thing at a club match — but on that occasion he had proceeded to boot the ball a full 50 metres upfield. This time, he noted, Eales had knocked on! What was the world coming to? What was Eales coming to? It was sad how a bloke's powers faded as he got older . . .

WITH the completion of the Super 12 season in late May — Queensland had just missed out on making the finals — in the space of six months starting from June, the Wallabies were due to play twelve Tests. It was, by any measure, a lot, and a further sign that the professional age was after a return on its money. From a purely physical point of view, it would be like being strapped to a rubber post beneath one of those huge Dutch windmills, whereby just as you were recovering from one almighty whack!, another one would shortly follow, and again, and again and again, relentlessly.

To prepare for it, though, this year there was going to be something different under the Wallaby sun. Instead of the players living their usual lives during the high rugby season of planes, trains, automobiles, buses and hotel rooms across the country, Macqueen had decided to do it differently. He wanted to establish a veritable Camp Wallaby, a base where they could do all their training day after day, in company with their wives and families if that was desired — Rod was certainly keen to have his wife Liz on site — and then return to once the Test was over. It was, whatever else, as sure a sign as any of the extraordinary distance rugby had traversed in the little over two years since the game had turned professional. In the amateur days the at least nominal rule of the International Rugby Board had been that, outside of tours, Test teams were not allowed to gather for more than three days, and yet now the Australian Test team was going to be together for months on end!

Macqueen had provisionally selected a modest kind of resort at Caloundra, on Queensland's Sunshine Coast, about an hour's drive north of Brisbane, but in April had asked John to go for a drive there with him to check it out and see what he thought. It was a small example of the new way of doing things where the captain and coach began to communicate more effectively than before. John had been impressed with the whole concept, and did indeed like Caloundra. He was happy to report as much to the team.

As a matter of fact, John was very happy with the way everything was going at that time, most particularly his life with Lara. It was a thrill to be setting up a home together, a delight to live together, a positive joy to see the contours of her stomach fill out as their baby grew. One night, late in May, after the two had been out to a Japanese restaurant at Highgate Hill, they took a blanket out into their front yard and lay looking up to the stars and chatting. After a little while, John got to the thing that he had been working his way towards.

'I have never been as happy in my life as I am right now, Lara. I love how we're going, I can't wait for our baby and I love you. I just want to spend the rest of my life with you.'

With which, he took out an engagement ring — complete with a one carat diamond that he had bought on his last Super 12 trip to South Africa — and offered it to her. Lara, crying, put it on. But the night was not over. John still had one more thing to give her. Back in the house he retrieved and then gave to Lara the crystal decanter with the World Cup motif that Joe French had given him back in 1993, telling him to 'Give this to the woman you love, and she'll be yours forever.' Done, Joe.

Lara's only regret at the time was that John would shortly be departing to base himself up in Caloundra, while she would continue her work. And so, when the Super 12 was over, the Wallabies moved into the resort at Caloundra and settled down to serious preparation for the international season. In many ways, the beachside town was a curious place to be situated, as an article in the magazine *GQ*, by writer Angus Fontaine noted:

The Queensland sun, is rising like a lazy erection from behind the bulbous mountains and canefields hemming Caloundra, a XXX-like kinda town, where sandals and socks are de rigeur and Alfie Langer could make mayor if Pauline Hanson wasn't homecoming queen. It's a strange place to hide a national sporting team, an even stranger base from which to hatch a World Cup campaign. Kamahl has a star in the footpath in Caloundra.

The resort itself lay close to the beach and consisted of many simple units with access to a common kitchen and lounge area. Single players generally shared units, while married couples with children were given bigger accommodation. The football fields were not far away, and the players were able to use bikes to get to and from training. These were bikes, mind, that the players were obliged to buy themselves. Macqueen's view was that the days of everything being laid on by the ARU, as if the players were children incapable of organising it themselves, were over. Similarly, he liked the rustic nature of the resort, compared to the often five star accommodation they had become used to in recent times. There would be no more team-sheets issued every morning telling them what was on, minute-by-minute throughout the day. Instead, they were all issued with diaries, and it was their responsibility to jot down each day whatever the manager told them was happening.

Both Macqueen and Miller made it clear that there had to be an entire change in the Wallaby culture. The way they saw it, the players had been keen to take the best that professionalism had to offer, which was money, and reluctant to take the increase in responsibility and commit-ment that must come with it.

Though not all the Wallabies were convinced Camp Wallaby was going to be to their liking, after only a week or two even the nay-sayers were starting to purr. One of the best things was that the players were able to remain with their young families for what would otherwise have been long periods away, and were the more contented for it. Players like Richard Harry, Matt Cockbain, Dave Wilson, Phil Kearns, Dan Crowley and Tim Horan all had young children, and it was a delight for them to ride back from a hard day's training to Wallaby Avenue — as their part of the resort was christened — to see all their children playing together while their wives chatted nearby.

Another new factor at Caloundra was the presence of a former rugby league international, John Muggleton, a nice knockabout kinda bloke who had always been noted for his defensive nous and who the Wallabies had briefly seen the previous year before they left for Argentina. This softly spoken former schoolteacher was there to totally overhaul the Wallabies' defensive capacity, and from the beginning it was clear he knew what he was talking about. In John Eales' early days in the Wallabies, defensive training had simply been tackling practice. This, however, was something else again, and tackle bags were the least of it. Using videos, computers, blackboards and endless analysis, Muggleton began to teach the Wallabies some of the actual science of defence.

As a small example, he illustrated how it was very common in modern rugby to have three forwards lined up beside a ruck waiting for the next wave of attack to strike. To this point the tackler of the ball-carrier was simply whichever of those three he ran at. Muggleton showed them a different way. From here on in, the man closest to the ruck was to be known as the pillar, the man next to him No. 2 while the third man out was to be known as the key.

The pillar's job was to tackle the first man from the ruck if he ran directly at him, but if the runner drifted then the pillar would let the second man tackle him, while he stayed on guard for any inside pass from the ball carrier. The second man would have to watch any outside runners off the ball carrier and any inside runners once the ball was passed to the next man. The key would be set on the ball player alone. All three could only drift out when the ball had been passed beyond the key. At all times the three men would move forward before they would move across.

It could get very complex.

The team's initial challenge of the season was against an England team which arrived with so few of their front-line players — because of contractual disputes — that it was little more than an English 'B' side. Only five in the English line-up had taken their place in the team's last Test, against Scotland at Murrayfield. The only upside to the whole shemozzle was that it generated one of sport's most widely reported quotes of the year, and it was from Dick McGruther.

'This,' the chairman of the ARU thundered to Peter Jenkins, of the *Australian*, 'is the greatest English sellout since Gallipoli. But we'll welcome them to their fatal landing here. While we wish the English well, unfortunately for them, Australians relish the opportunity to witness a Pommie thrashing and we invite them all to come out and enjoy it.'

The English rugby union had been predictably outraged, maintaining that it was not so too a *sellout*, or anything of the kind, but McGruther was never remotely tempted to apologise.

Before this match, Rod Macqueen initiated one more new tradition for the Wallabies. That is, he invited a former Wallaby of some prestige, in this case the flanker Greg Cornelsen — famous for having scored four tries against the All Blacks at Eden Park in 1978 — to present the team with their jerseys and briefly speak about what playing for the Wallabies had meant to him. In simple yet eloquent terms, which moved the

Wallabies deeply, Cornelsen spoke of his own days wearing the national jersey, what it had meant to him then, and what it meant to him and his generation to watch the Wallabies now. Every time they wore it, he said, for every *minute* they had the privilege to do so, they had to give it everything they had because, trust him, it would later seem like they had only worn it for the blink of an eye.

In response, something certainly clicked in the psyche of the Wallabies, because they proceeded to flog England like a sergeant at arms flogging a convict caught with the Governor's wife, and finished the game with an extraordinary victory of 76-0. On the day, the English had been dead lucky to get to nil. Despite all the controversy, in terms of performance from his revamped and re-tuned Wallabies, Rod Macqueen couldn't have asked for much better. The press, though, could have . . .

The front page of the *Sydney Morning Herald's* sporting liftout set the tone: 'IN 1788, ENGLAND SENT ITS LOSERS TO AUSTRALIA. 210 YEARS LATER AND NOTHING HAS CHANGED.'

There could, of course, have been no consolation for the English on the end of a scoreline like that, but they might at least have gained some grim satisfaction when the next international rugby visitors to Australia, the Scots, tumbled to humiliating defeats, losing their first Test 45-3 in Sydney and their second 33-11 in Brisbane.

For the Wallabies, the vibe couldn't have been better. In their first three Tests of the season they had scored 151 points and had only 11 points scored against them. One of the revelations of the season so far had been the form of Stephen Larkham, who Rod Macqueen had moved from being a bit-part winger and fullback to full-time five-eighth. As a child growing up on a sheep property near Yass, Larkham had been nicknamed The Phantom by his team-mates for popping up on the field where he was least expected, and so it had proved in this position particularly. Apart from a superb kicking, passing and running game, he was extremely busy around the field and it was clear to all that at least one of the troublesome jigsaw pieces for the coming World Cup campaign had been found.

Certainly, there remained within the Wallabies an acute awareness at this point that they were yet to be truly tested, but if they wanted a testing Test they certainly had it coming. The All Blacks. At the MCG. The sequel! (*Voiceover man: 'And this time, they're angry . . . '*)

Going into that Test on 11 July 1998 there was a palpable sense of steely purpose among the Wallabies. In their last seven Tests against the All Blacks they had lost every one. The last victory had been the Gregan tackle Test of 1994 which, though it had shone brightly at the time, had fallen back in the dark ages. Failure by the Australians to do the right thing by the nation on this occasion, and WHUP those All Blacks but good, would likely see yet another dark pall fall upon the Australian rugby land. Now, surely, at such a venue as this, it had to be time to trouble the scorer for a win of their own. One of the many things the Wallabies had in their favour at this point was their growing sense of cohesion and stability. For this encounter, the selectors picked the same team they had on the three previous occasions, the first time this had occurred in Wallaby history. The contrast with the way Greg Smith had done things couldn't have been greater, and it didn't stop there. For in the lead-up to this, Rod Macqueen's first time in charge of the Wallabies for a Bledisloe Cup encounter, he unveiled to John his plan to deal with the haka, the perennial problem faced by Australian rugby coaches.

John listened, and nodded in firm agreement. In many ways, it was typical of Macqueen, for he had come up with a well-thought-out response which essentially solved the problem before they got to it, and gleaned maximum advantage for the Wallabies.

And so it all came to pass . . .

Just as Macqueen planned, when the teams ran out into the middle of a roaring MCG, the Wallabies stood up and faced the haka, as per normal, with the difference that they remained wearing their tracksuits. Then, after the haka was finished, the Wallabies pulled in tight into their own circle and spent a minute going over their own things before removing their tracksuits. They had, thus, paid their due respects to the New Zealand war cry, but also provided a suitable buffer between the haka finishing and the game beginning. The All Blacks had reached their climactic moment but were then left hanging around impotently while the Wallabies, for a nice change, set the agenda as to when the game would start.

From the start, no-one played better for the Australians than Stephen Larkham at five-eighth, where it looked for all the world as if he had been born in that position, so relaxed and natural was his style, so fluent was his passing to his outside backs. In the Wallaby forwards, they simply kept grinding the All Blacks down in every facet of play. The transformation in the way the Wallabies played on this occasion from the way they had played at the same venue against the same opponents the year before, was nothing short of extraordinary.

And John Muggleton could take no little credit for this transformation. Instead of waiting for the marauding All Blacks to come on to them, for example, the Wallaby backs went straight to them on the charge and cut them down like wheat — wheat that the forwards then merrily waltzed all over like it was some pagan fertility rite previously lost in the mists of time. Again and again it happened just like that, with no-one enjoying it more than the Australian captain. Though Lara, with her now enormous belly and sitting in the stands with Daniel Herbert's fiancée Serena Frisby, probably ran him a close second.

Though the All Blacks had gone to an early lead, the Wallabies closed the gap to make it 8-8 at half-time and 40 minutes later emerged victors by the wonderful score of 24-16. At the final whistle, the Wallabies fell about in ecstasy, hugging each other, punching the air, acknowledging the roaring crowd with handclaps above their head. As they got to the sidelines, Ben Tune was so excited he jumped into the arms of Cameron Lillicrap. Even further buoying the Wallabies was good news from Sydney's Prince of Wales hospital. The previous Tuesday night, Greg Smith had collapsed and his tumour was removed in an emergency operation the following morning. The word now was that he was going to be all right, and the team had many heartfelt drinks to his health that night.

ROLLING now, gaining confidence! Even when, a week later, the Wallabies lost by a bare, hungry, sniffin' point to South Africa, 14-13, it did not dent the growing feeling that they were onto something special. That loss, while regrettable, taught them something valuable. In the final minute of play, when a field-goal would have turned the game, they had not taken the option. Much of the subsequent Macqueen debriefing focused on that fact, and when they returned to their Caloundra base — as they now did after every Test — a lot of time was spent trying to rectify that problem. The obvious thing was to follow the standard pattern and have Stephen Larkham practise his field-goals, but because he hadn't put one over in a game since the U/9s, most of the work centred on moves that would allow the accomplished Tim Horan to slot them. And of course they worked endless other moves, particularly in the backs.

Under Macqueen, the Wallabies worked on what the coach called a triangular basis. That meant starting the year with dozens of moves and then eliminating them as they went along, until for every Test they'd put in the ones that they not only knew worked, but which had the best chance of working against a particular opposition.

AND sometimes in rugby, it's like that. Games start well and just get better from there. Just seven minutes after the opening whistle of the Second Test against the All Blacks on the first day of August at Christchurch's Jade Stadium, Wallaby winger Jason Little made a burst down the right touchline. When caught by the cover defence, he managed to bounce a ball infield in a hurl-and-hope exercise, or Hail Mary, pass. Eales' new second-row partner, Tom Bowman, picked it up on the burst, turned the mighty Jonah Lomu's defence inside out and raced 25 metres to score. As the Wallabies' analysis had shown, while in attack Lomu was a freight train in ballet shoes, in defence he could be a mere siding you passed in the night.

The Bowman try was superb, but there was better to follow. In one extraordinary passage of play, the Wallabies controlled the ball for no fewer than eighteen phases, lasting 3 minutes, 10 seconds — and they might have managed more except for the fact that the sequence was terminated by a try to fullback Matthew Burke. The Wallabies kept hard at it, and though the All Blacks were themselves magnificent in their unwavering resolve, the Australians kept beating the beggars back until by game's end they were on the right side of a 27-23 scoreline. It was Australia's first Bledisloe Cup series win since 1994, their first away victory against the All Blacks since 1990, and after the first of the tumult had died down a little Eales gathered the team to him and called for complete silence.

'Listen!' he said. And they did. And there, quite clearly discernible among all the carrying on, could be heard a full-throated rendition of 'Waltzing Matilda'. In the southern part of the ground 400 massed Australians, gaily bedecked in green and gold scarves and the like, had held the fort of support throughout the game with Blackness all around and encroaching, and were now celebrating, ' . . . *you'll come a Waltzing Matilda with me! WALTZING Matilda, WALTZ-ING Mat-il-da . . .*'

'*That* is what it's all about,' Eales continued, nodding in their direction. 'We keep going from here. This is still just the beginning. Stay humble, stay focused. We're going to do these blokes 3-0 in the series.'

Shortly thereafter, John Eales, Wallaby captain, was holding the Bledisloe

Cup above his head and thanking the All Blacks for a wonderful series so far, and his team for their efforts. He didn't say it, because it would have been rubbing it in, but a booking had already been made for a First Class seat on the Qantas flight home, in the name of 'Mr B'. There was no way known such a prized possession as the Bledisloe Cup was going to travel in the hold of the plane, or, God forbid, a luggage rack.

In the dressing rooms afterwards, it was Jeff Wilson, the All Black winger, who best put his finger on it. 'Today,' he said, 'Australia just gave us an old-fashioned hiding.'

They had that.

Back home in Australia, for John it was hard not to compare the reviews his captaincy was getting now, with the calls for his dismissal that had been made just 12 months earlier.

Andrew Dawson, in the *Courier-Mail*: 'When Eales bounded on to the field after half-time on Saturday he was an authoritative figure. Eales called the team into a huddle, holding up the restart of the match for almost a minute as he addressed his players.'

Assistant Wallaby coach, Jeff Miller: '[John] has handled everything extremely well and his own game has not suffered. He has taken three or four steps up in his leadership.'

More heartening still were the quoted comments of his fellow players.

Andrew Blades: 'Ealsey was trying to keep a lid on the emotions. Ealsey is a great captain.'

Matt Cockbain: 'He is a great leader. If he is off the field, we would struggle.'

THE circumstances of the next Test were to be forever memorable for John. Now mid-August, Lara was over seven months pregnant. On the morning of the day John was due to leave for South Africa for the final of the Tri-Nations series against the Springboks, he accompanied her to see her obstetrician for a routine check-up. There was no particular drama about the visit, as everything had been going fine, but half an hour after the examination had begun the obstetrician had news for them. They were going to have their baby, *today*. The medical reasons were involved, but the bottom line was that their baby needed to be out in the fresh air as soon as possible, and Lara would have to undergo a Caesarean section that very afternoon!

Both were stunned, but Lara was heartened by John's attitude: a mixture of solicitude for her and excitement that they would be holding their baby in their arms within hours. Rather than give the impression that they were in the middle of a medical emergency, he projected a sense that this was the greatest day in the history of the world.

But first things first. From the surgery, John made a quick phone call to the Wallaby manager, John McKay, to tell him that he simply would not be able to make the flight that afternoon. He'd try to catch a flight in a couple of days time, he said. He'd be in touch. Thanks. (*Click.*) There was, of course, not the slightest hesitation in making such a call, and nor would there have been if the birth of their child had coincided with a Bledisloe Cup Test match. (A World Cup Final, John might have *thought* about!) In any case, Rod Macqueen was very good on that sort of thing, having always told his players, 'Your family comes first and the Wallabies second.'

So it was that at 5.21 p.m., about four minutes before the other Wallabies flew out of Australia, John was in the operating theatre of Wesley Hospital when the surgeon made a delicate incision in Lara's abdomen and shortly afterwards put his gloved hands through the cut to pull out ... out ... a SON! At the obstetrician's invitation, John stepped forward and cut the umbilical cord.

It was 14 August 1998. In the white corner, weighing in at just 1.97 kilograms, the baby was not a big 'un, but he was a beauty! John reeled. In all his days he had never felt anything so profound as the feelings that rushed over him at that moment, love for Lara, love for the baby, gratitude for the medical staff who had brought his family — *his family!* — through to this point.

John positively ached to hold his boy even for a moment, but as the little one was six weeks premature and there were already signs of some minor problems with breathing, in half a flash the white-coats had moved in to whisk the tiny baby away for all the tests premature babies undergo. In the absence of being able to hug his son, John embraced Lara and then headed out to the waiting room to hug all of the assembled Eales and Khoo families who had gathered in force, awaiting the news.

Not wanting to be away from his family for even a moment, John bunked down that night on a camp bed next to Lara. Somewhere near midnight when she dropped off to an exhausted sleep, he knew he still had one thing left to do. In the quiet of their hospital room, he prayed long and strong that his son would have a healthy, happy life and know the love of God.

The following day, one of the first visitors was Ben Perkins. Over the years his friendship with John had continued to deepen, a friendship that Lara now shared, and he was close enough to the couple to give them a list of five possible names they might like to consider for their boy. Top of the list was Elijah, and both John and Lara took pause from the moment they saw it.

They both recognised it as a name from the Bible and when John looked it up — 1 Kings Chapter 18 — and was reminded that it was the prophet Elijah who had spoken to God on Mount Carmel, that just about sealed it. For John, the link to his late sister Carmel was important, and as Lara also loved the name, that was that. For a second name they chose Anthony because there was surely nothing that would please Nonna more, just as nothing had pleased her more than when John's parents had given him the second name of Anthony.

Three days later John ever so reluctantly kissed both Lara and Elijah goodbye, and headed off to Johannesburg for the Test against South Africa. While much of the three days leading up to the Test was spent in training and analyses — as ever — John also spent a lot of time on the phone back to Australia and in George Gregan's room, where he kept trying to download a few grainy photos of his son over the Internet. South Africa's shaky telephone system defeated them, but on the morning of the Test John awoke to find a fax under his door. There was the tiniest of all tiny footprints silhouetted on it. Elijah's. With it was a note, in childish scrawl.

Dear Dad,

Good luck for the big game! I love you and want you to come home. I'm getting better very quickly so you will be very proud of me and so I will be bigger than you one day (believe me, there's enough milk here!!) Please win for me!

I love you,

Elijah.

Every Test match has its own context — the surrounding tableau against which it could be judged — and in this Test that context was clear. Revenge. Redemption. Restoration of pride. A year before, Australian rugby had tumbled to its most humiliating defeat against South Africa. But then they were weak. Now they were strong. Then they had little confidence and barely the semblance of a structure from which they could organise their talents. Now they felt they could withstand the best the Boks could throw at them, and still give them plenty to think about in return. The situation was perfect. It would not, of course, be easy, but the Wallabies approached the match with great confidence, none more so than their skipper.

Alas, they lost, 29-15, in a match blighted by terrible behaviour from the spectators, including the throwing of cans, oranges and bottles onto the field. That aside, the upshot was there on the front page of the *Johannesburg Times* the following day: 'SOUTH AFRICA FIRMLY ON TOP WITH A YEAR TO GO.' And it was true enough. Just twelve months away from the 1999 World Cup, the Boks had not only beaten Australia twice in a row, but also won their last fourteen Tests, equalling the record set by the World Cup winning side of '95. Clearly, they would be the team to beat in '99.

FOR John, it was a strange thing indeed, to be flying back into Brisbane at last, and into his house at Hamilton, where by now his fiancèe and one-week-old son were waiting for him. This exact same time last year, not one of the three had been in his life, and yet now they were all central to it. It was reminiscent in a way of the Talking Heads song, where a man suddenly wakes up and says: *'Is this my beautiful house? Is this my beautiful wife? Is this my beautiful boy?'*

Just one year before, he had never set foot in this house, never kissed Lara, and never even conceived of a child. Yet now they were all there, all waiting for him, and he couldn't have been happier about it.

THE finest of all feelings in rugby? It's not necessarily scoring a try, making a bone-rattling tackle, or receiving a man of the match award, winning the game . . . or even the brawl. They're all fine, but mostly the pleasure is transitory. The real joy, the one that can still warm the cockles of your soul decades after, is when you are able to give it but good to the all black boogers who have previously given it to you! So it was for the Wallabies when they took on the All Blacks at the Sydney Football Stadium on 29 August, before a capacity crowd. By winning the first two Tests 2-0 the Wallabies had assured that the Bledisloe Cup would come to Australia, but this was an historic chance to go up 3-BLOT!

Bring it on, the Wallabies were ready.

Though at half-time the All Blacks were winning 11-0, the Wallabies had not panicked and simply poured it on in the second half to play superb rugby against a wilting All Black side — *More! More! More!* — and emerged 19-14 victors to record the first Bledisloe Cup clean sweep for Australia since 1929. The victory had been built not just on a Matt Burke try where he broke his shoulder in the process of scoring, or the fact that at one point Stephen Larkham had successfully charged down an Andrew Mehrtens attempt at conversion. John Eales had also contributed to the scoreboard by way of slotting five goals from five attempts. After the match, the Wallabies did a lap of honour as the crowd roared. John felt in a complete daze, trying to comprehend what they had achieved. All up, it had been an extraordinary turnaround. Last year the Wallabies had gone down 3-blot in the Bledisloe, and now they had triumphed by the same extraordinary margin.

'How John Eales can get up off the bottom of a ruck and win lineouts and kick goals is remarkable,' the losing coach, John Hart, said afterwards of the man of the match. 'When you talk about the best in the world, Eales is up with the best of them.'

The mood in the side, looking towards the following year's World Cup, was better than ever.

'There is enormous potential here which is bubbling to the surface,' Tim Horan told the crowding press men in the dressing room. 'We have to push on with it, but there is something special emerging.'

'The side has new confidence,' Ben Tune added. 'It knows how to win.'

Heading to the after-match function on the bus that night, John sat beside Tim Horan, who summed it all up perfectly.

'Y'know,' he said to the skipper as the darkened streets of Sydney swished past in the early evening, 'the best part about this is that every Australian who's been copping it season after season for years from Kiwis — and everybody in Australia works with a Kiwi somewhere in the joint — can finally go to work or to the club on Monday morning, find the New Zealanders and give them both barrels.'

Eales nodded vigorously. That really was a lot of what it was about. It was a great thing to be a part of a great team, but the best thing of all was the connection with your supporters, and the times like this when you could deliver to them what they had long been hoping for.

As part of the World Cup qualifying procedure, the Wallabies now

racked up three successive, massive wins over Fiji, Tonga and Western
Samoa — the Fiji game being notable for John kicking nine conversions,
which equalled Matt Burke's record. As much as John continued to
begrudge time spent away from his family, before the year was done there
was still a job o'work to do.

For the latest development in international rugby had been to go
from a hotch-potch mosaic of encounters to an agreement between the
ARU and the two strongest rugby countries in the Five Nations —
England and France — to play one-off annual encounters in each other's
countries. It was for this reason that in mid-November the Wallabies had
to go to Europe to play both countries. Under the pressures of an already
full-to-bursting rugby calendar, the days of six-week tours culminating
in two Tests were over — too much time for too little return — and at
least this tour would be only three weeks long, with the Wallabies playing
the French and English on successive weekends. For John, however, this
tour was far different from any other he'd been on. Now, he would be flying away, leaving his fiancée and child behind. At least with Lara he
would be able to talk to her on the phone every day, but leaving Elijah was
different. His gloomy thought as he boarded the long-haul jet at Sydney's
Kingsford Smith airport was, 'I am going to come home and he won't
even know who I am.' The one comfort was the certain knowledge that
both Lara's family and his own would provide her and Elijah wonderful
support while he was away.

IT is a strange thing to fly out of the clouds after a long haul around the
planet and return to terra firma in different parts of the world. Stranger
still on this day, to have left an Australia enjoying the first hot breaths of
an early summer and then to land in France where the grip of winter was
just starting to take a stranglehold. Gathering their baggage, the Wallabies
wearily piled onto their bus, and headed north towards Lille, where they
were to play their first game. The mood on the bus was tired and withdrawn
— it had been a long flight, it was a bitter day outside, and all looked
forward to getting into the warmth of their hotel room and relaxing. As
they pushed on into the misty morning, John wondered how Lara and
Elijah were getting on without him, before he slowly drifted off to sleep.

Eight decades previously, another young group of Australians had
slogged north along much the same route, and their thoughts too must

have been of home. But instead of footballs and tackle bags, they were carrying guns and ammunition and materials for a long military campaign. And they were rushing, these men of the 36th Battalion, trying to stop the marauding German Army from pushing through to the Channel ports in their last desperate throw of the dice to turn the tide of the First World War. That group of Australians came to grips with the Germans on the Western Front in the town of Villers-Bretonneux on 4 April 1918. That morning, the men of the 36th fixed bayonets and charged, forcing them to retreat a kilometre. The Australians were then responsible for holding a 25 kilometre front against the Germans who were angry and regrouping. On 17 and 18 April the Germans launched gas attacks against the Australians, and a week later attacked with overwhelming force, re-taking Villers-Bretonneux.

But be buggered! On Anzac Day, 25 April, the survivors of the 36th, together with another three Australian brigades *counter*-counter-attacked, and by virtue of another bayonet charge and savage house-to-house fighting over the next three days, liberated the town — for good this time. The British Brigadier-General G.W. Grogan later described it as 'perhaps the greatest individual feat of the war'.

That victory was singularly hard won, and when it was over 1,300 sons of Australia would lie beneath the soil they helped liberate forever more.

No matter how luxurious the bus, how comfortable the heating and plush the seating, there is always a lurching moment when it slows down and then stops which tends to wake even the deepest sleeps. The Wallabies roused themselves. Where were they? Oh . . . that's right, their manager John McKay had mentioned that they were going to stop at some place called Villers-Bretonneux where Australians had apparently fought in the First World War, and this must be it. They looked out the misty windows, where a cold, driving sleet was howling down upon a graveyard where row upon row upon row of white crosses filled a lonely field. Usually, when the Wallabies stopped at some tourist attraction or other, a fair number of guys would stay on the bus and read or listen to their tape-players . . . but not this time. This was not a mere tourist attraction, and every member of the Wallaby squad got out of the bus and walked through the cemetery situated about a kilometre to the north of Villers-

Bretonneux. Each wandered among the carefully tended gravestones, and all were glad to see how carefully it was looked after, with freshly mown grass, neatly trimmed hedges, and no weeds on the graves. A memorial on which was writ large *'N'Oubliez Jamais l'Australie'* (Never Forget Australia) showed the reverence in which the cemetery was held, and that the sacrifice of the Australian soldiers had not been forgotten. There was also an Anzac Museum nearby and the streets in Villers-Bretonneux were named after many Australian towns.

John instinctively kept to himself, not wanting to speak to anyone, and yet everyone clearly felt the same because the only sound as the Wallabies wandered was the wind. And John could tell by looking at the faces of his team-mates that they were thinking what he was thinking: how young a lot of these guys were when they died! From Geelong, an 18-year-old; from Dubbo a lad of only 19, from Townsville, another 18-year-old, while the bulk of them were between 22 and 30 years old. What must it have been like for them, in those times, to be fighting on a day like today, carrying rifles, fixing bayonets and charging, and being charged at in return, all so far, far away from the sheep station they once knew, the city office, the family dairy. And now here they were, just six feet away, much the same age as the Wallabies, separated by life and death and opposite ends of the century, but also bound tightly together.

It was exactly as the song said: I am, you are, we are Australian.

The climax to the visit came when the reserve Wallaby second-rower John Welborn — who had located the grave of his great uncle whom he knew to be lying there — lay a wreath on the memorial, on behalf of all the Wallabies. All bowed their heads, and had a minute's silence.

AFTER the successful lead-up game in Lille the Wallabies fairly easily dispatched France in the Test match in Paris, 32-21, but then came a far harder encounter, against the *real* English side. There were only three survivors of the team that had been trounced by Australia in early June, and this time the English defence was not the same rusty sieve. In a dour match, the Wallabies found themselves on the losing end of an 11-9 scoreline with eight minutes to go, when a penalty was awarded to the Australians 41 metres out, on the angle. John, who had already landed three out of four possible penalty goals, stepped up. And slotted it.

After that, the Wallaby defence held and Australia emerged 12-11 victors. In a match where they had not scored a single try, against England's one, the Wallabies had 'won ugly', as the vogue expression of the time ran, but the key thing was they had won all the same.

There could be no argument. Though it had been a fairly drab ending to an otherwise glorious year, the prevailing sentiment among the Wallabies was that they could look towards the World Cup a year hence with some confidence. Eleven wins in thirteen Tests was not a bad platform to launch from.

ON the late afternoon of 29 January 1999, John kissed Lara and Elijah goodbye and went back to sleep on the lounge at Arnell Street. He would have slept in his old bed, but the weight of numbers of friends and family who had travelled from all over meant the lounge was all that was left.

Nonna was beside herself with excitement not just to have her John back home, but also over the fact that he was to be married on the morrow.

She whipped up her usual fabulous pasta meal for John and his grooms-men, Damian and Terry Honan, as well as best man Simon Whitehart, while Lara was with her bridesmaids back at their Hamilton home. Jack joined them, while Rosa retired to the bedroom to finish wrapping the family's wedding present — a washing machine — and writing a card that would deeply move both John and Lara. It read: *'To dear Lara and John, Wishing you a long and happy life and marriage together. All our love, Mum, Dad, Bernadette, Carmel, Damian, Antoinette and Rosaleen.'*

The following morning dawned hot, bright and clear, and that afternoon at 3 o'clock, in the chapel of Lara's old school of All Hallows, in Fortitude Valley, Lara walked down the aisle towards the beaming John, with Rosa carrying baby Elijah behind. In attendance were such rugby luminaries as Jason Little, Tim Horan, David Wilson, Rod Macqueen, John O'Neill, Matt Cockbain, Brendan Nasser and John Connolly, all with their partners. As well, of course, there were from John's side all of the old gang of Chris White, Patrick McGrath, Rupert McCall, et al. A clear sign of how important Ben Perkins regarded the occasion was that he gave up his regular afternoon at the racetrack to give one of the Bible readings.

JUST a fortnight after the wedding — and freshly back from a honeymoon at Lizard Island just off the coast of Queensland — John was quickly back in the full swing of training in this singularly important year for the

Wallabies. On the third morning back, he was working out with reserve hooker Brendan Cannon in Brisbane's Centenary Pool Gym, and doing an exercise designed to increase upper body strength. That is, he was doing a series of dips on the parallel bars, essentially gripping both bars and then lowering and raising his own body weight. The first five such dips went perfectly. On the sixth one, though, with his arms just beginning to vibrate under the strain, something went wrong. Deep inside his shoulder, something suddenly went clunk, followed immediately by a very sharp pain. What worried him most was that it was the same shoulder he'd broken back in 1992 against Llanelli, and it was exactly the same pain as he'd had back then.

Again, the feeling was remarkably out-of-body, in that John was almost able to watch what happened next, and listen to what was being said as urgent calls were made, physios were consulted, grim faces gathered all around, the pain continued, and within hours he was in Peter Meyer's surgery once more, just as he had been at the beginning of 1993.

This time, at least, the news wasn't quite so bad, and tests and consultations revealed that if John had immediate surgery he might, just might, be able to make it back in time for the World Cup. The rest of the rugby season was shot to pieces, of course, but it was not a bad upside to have . . .

In all the subsequent gloom and doom that was generated by his injury, it seemed only one person had something positive to say about it, and that was Lara. 'It's unfortunate, but I'm probably the only person who is not entirely unhappy about this matter. It will mean more time with Elijah and me,' she told Channel Seven. 'He has told me I have to keep telling him to stay positive and that he will get better and he has said he will hate me while I'm doing it. But all will be forgiven.'

The two proceeded to do exactly that, and John was at least able to enjoy having more time at home as, after the operation, he embarked on much the same rehabilitation program as he had in 1992. Again, he embarked on a delicate exercise regime; again he had targets to reach, again he slowly, slowly felt the strength beginning to return, as Elijah sat gurgling happily on a blanket in the front room while his father went through all manner of strange movements.

A letter John received immediately following his injury was particularly touching. It came from the man who might be expected to be the

With Lara, December 2000. *Eales family collection*

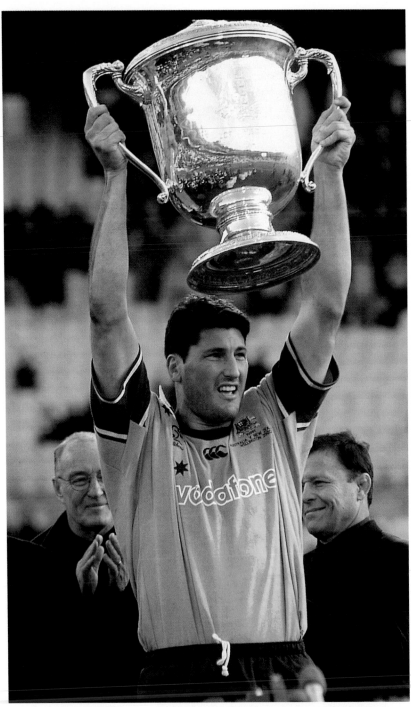

With the just won Bledisloe Cup, minutes after kicking *that* goal in Wellington, New Zealand, August 2000. *Photo: Scott Barbour © Allsport*

Left: After victory over South Africa at Colonial Stadium, August 2000.
Photo: Carlos Furtado © Action Photographics

Below: After victory over Argentina, June 2000.
Photo: Carlos Furtado © Action Photographics

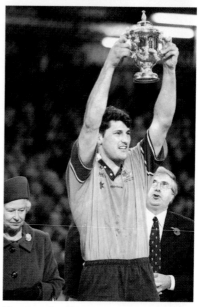

Lifting the Hopetoun Cup after beating Scotland at Murrayfield, November 2000.
Photo: Matthew Impey © Colorsport

The pinnacle of his career. Lifting the World Cup he has just received from the Queen, 6 November, 1999 at Millennium Stadium.
Photo: Tempsport © Action Photographics

With fellow Wallabies Jim Williams and Joe Roff at a South African township, August 2000. *Eales family collection*

Showing off his kicking form in the Test against Argentina at Bruce Stadium, Canberra, June 2000.
Photo: Carlos Furtado© Action Photographics

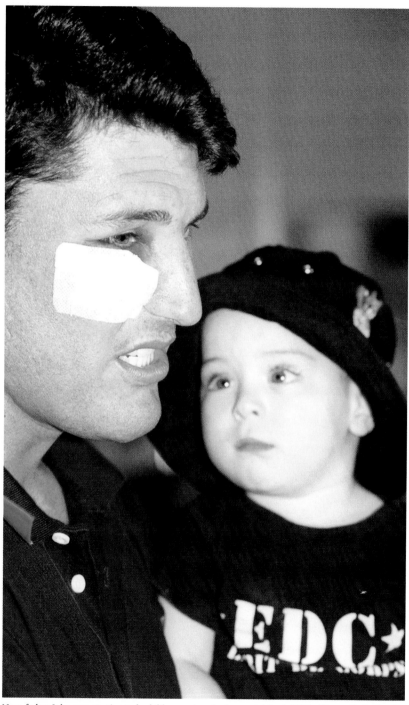

Now, father John was starting to look like a real rugby forward, March 2000. *Photo: Giulio Saggin*
© Courier Mail

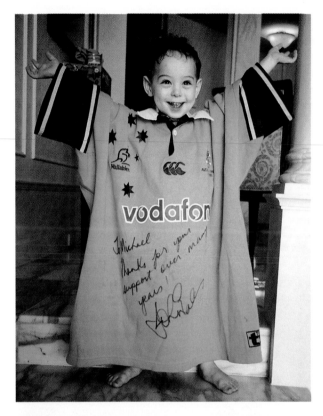

Elijah Eales in John's
jersey, 2001.
Eales family collection

The extended Eales family at Arnell Street, Christmas 2000. *Eales family collection*

most delighted at his misfortune — All Black coach, John Hart. 'I was extremely saddened to hear of your untimely injury,' Hart wrote, 'and wanted to send to you my best wishes for a speedy recovery . . . I have long admired the outstanding commitment and talent you bring to the game and I sincerely hope that you are back on the field sooner rather than later . . . '

The Chairman of the NZRFU, Rob Fisher, sent a letter similar in tone. It began: 'I was devastated to hear the news that you had suffered a serious shoulder injury. Helen joins me in wishing you a speedy recovery if not for the Tri-Nations, then certainly for the Rugby World Cup.'

Sincere messages from good and decent men. The pleasures of being part of the international rugby fraternity were ongoing and many.

If there was one notable difference in John's comeback campaign this time, it was that whereas on the last occasion he had dropped out of the Wallaby scene altogether, that option was now out of the question. As the Wallaby captain in a World Cup year, he and Rod Macqueen felt it crucial that he stay tightly involved.

Another in a similar position was Stephen Larkham, who had cruelly injured his knee in a Super 12 game against Canterbury in early April and had also undergone an immediate operation. Many rugby pundits said that the chances of the Wallabies in the World Cup depended on both of them being fully fit, which was as maybe . . . Both pressed on, one eye on the mirror to see for themselves what kind of movement they were getting, the other on the calendar as the countdown to the Cup continued.

As fate would have it, even in John's most extended lay-off from rugby in seven years, he had never garnered so many awards. On Australia Day, 1999, he received the Order of Australia for services to rugby and the community, most particularly his work for the Leukaemia Foundation. In May he was named in Queensland's Team of the Century and in June the *Sydney Morning Herald* named him as the Wallabies' best forward of the century. All the awards were most pleasing and a great honour, but his central feeling was that they were things he could enjoy later, when his Wallaby career was done. For the moment, all he wanted to concentrate on was getting himself in shape in time.

Though still unable to do any contact work with his shoulder, at least John was able to put a lot of work into keeping fit. At Ballymore, he often trained with the Queensland conditioner, Jason Weber, who was a former team-mate from their days in the Australian U/21s. Three times a week just the two of them would meet and do a series of 300 metre sprints around the lonely oval: 100 metre walk, 300 metre sprint, 100 metre walk, 300 metre sprint and so on. John hated every single moment of such sessions and didn't mind saying so. But it was precisely because of his full-blooded embrace of that which he so detested that Weber's respect for him deepened. This far into his professional training career, Weber knew the difference between a player who was putting in and one who was keeping something in reserve, and John was putting in as much as any player he'd ever worked with.

THERE is a special piquancy to Tests in World Cup years. More than a self-contained sporting contest in its own right, each Test is endlessly examined as to what it likely means for the coming contest. Who is in form, who is out of form; is this tactic working, should we unveil this move now or keep it fresh for the Cup; we might have lost this one, but it's the winner of the Final in November that everyone will remember. The Wallabies began the season with four reasonable wins over Ireland, England and South Africa.

John stayed close to the team throughout, attending all the games in Australia and many of the training camps. In the middle of July, in the lead-up to the first All Black encounter he was watching one such session when a significant thing happened. The Wallaby physio and his old friend and team-mate Cameron Lillicrap was kicking a ball around to pass the time while the Wallaby forwards did lineouts, when the ball sheared off the side of his boot and headed right towards John, about half a metre above his head. Without thinking about it, John reached up to catch it, meaning that for the first time in six months he pushed both arms above his head.

Lillicrap paused, stunned and appalled in equal measure at the risk John had taken — and the consequences if there was damage. For an agonising second he waited to see if John would scream in agony, or even wince, but there was nothing. Early days, certainly, but it was the best indication yet that the healing was actually working and the Wallaby captain might be able to make it back in time for the World Cup. Some more confirmation that things were coming along nicely came in curious fashion about a week later, in the middle of the night.

It wasn't quite that Elijah was falling, fallingg, fallinggggg towards a very grave injury and John had hurled himself in heroic fashion to the foot of the cliff to save him, but that was what it felt like. In a singularly powerful dream John had indeed had a vision of Elijah's plunge and had thrown himself like Australian wicket-keeper Ian Healy far to his right to catch him. Howzzzzzzat? Got him, yes! He was safe. It's all happening here on the Eales' bedroom floor, Bill Lawrie.

John awoke, still wrapped in half of a sheet flat out on the bedroom floor, conscious that he had just had quite a hard fall. He felt his shoulder gingerly, acutely aware that he could have wrecked everything. Though it was a little sore, it was basically okay, and he climbed back into bed more confident than before that he was going to make it back in time for the World Cup. It would be a few weeks yet before he'd put it to the test with some contact training, but it was a great start.

FINALLY it was time. After six months solid of rehabilitation exercises and watching the Wallabies in frustration from the stands, the moment came for both John Eales and Stephen Larkham to put their bodies to the test, if not *the* Test. It was time to see whether or not they were worth the price of an air-ticket to Britain for the World Cup and the game selected for them was a clash between the Australian Barbarians and Fiji on a cold August night at North Sydney Oval. If Eales and Larkham failed to make it through the game, then Australian rugby would have to revert to Plan B — hoping against hope.

Successive losses to New Zealand and South Africa — 34-15 and 10-9 — had highlighted just how much the good ship Wallaby needed Eales in the engine room stoking the fires, and Larkham at the wheel setting course through all the dangerous shoals to be found on the international rugby field.

Against New Zealand, the lineout had gone to hell in a handcart, the scrum had imitated a squeaky shopping trolley on a bad day, rucking was non-existent, and it looked for all the world as if the entire pack were getting bonus payments every time they wantonly turned the ball over or gave away kickable penalties. (All Black five-eighth Andrew Mehrtens slotted a world record nine out of nine possible penalty goals.) The Wallaby backline was little better and there seemed to be no actual construction of successful attacking movements. Occasionally they occurred, ad hoc, but the Wallabies were clearly a long way behind where they had been a year before when they routed the All Blacks 3-0.

On the weekend of the South African encounter, John had taken and passed his first test by playing his first game for Brothers in three years. Happily, he had gone reasonably well — but it was one thing to test his shoulder out in the Brisbane club arena, and quite another to test its hardness in the furnace of an international against the Fijians.

At first it seemed strange to be back out there in the middle of the threshing throng, and if John started a little slowly, his game was a lot more solid in the second half when his confidence grew that he could actually take the hits. Ditto for Stephen Larkham.

While the Barbarians finished the game with a slim win, both Wallabies finished with a major victory in that they had emerged essentially unscathed. Rod Macqueen congratulated them but gave fair warning that he was unlikely to pick them for the Bledisloe Cup encounter ten days hence. He was satisfied that they would be right for the World Cup, and he simply did not want to risk them in a Test against the All Blacks which — however important at the time — would be no more than a footnote to what the Wallabies were going to be remembered for in 1999.

For the All Blacks were clearly the in-form international side, not having lost a Test all year. They were undoubtedly going to be the ones to beat in the coming tournament. Down at the other end of the spectrum were the French, who had lost to the All Blacks 54-7 in Wellington in July, their eighth loss in ten Tests, going into the World Cup.

'The French side's confidence is completely gone.' Henri Bru, the correspondent for France's *L'Equipe* told *Time* magazine in October. And amen to that. That would be one less side for the Wallabies to worry about as they set off in pursuit of rugby's Holy Grail, the William Webb Ellis Trophy, otherwise known as the World Cup.

World Cup
1999

⁀

IT WAS IN the last week of September 1999, and all up, it was a curious beginning to a World Cup campaign. No sooner had the Wallabies landed at their digs in Ireland — Port Marnoch Hotel Resort, about half an hour out of Dublin — than they had a game of golf and followed up with an extremely rare thing in the Rod Macqueen era. That is, they all sat around and got on the plonk, as the expression goes. Usually, Macqueen took a stern view about excessive drinking, but on this occasion he turned a blind eye, made all the blinder by the plonk he was himself knocking back! The coach's feeling was that what he and the team most needed at the end of an already long year was to blow some steam out, and then they'd get into it. The following day there was no training, and the Wallabies were encouraged to sleep off their excesses of the night before and relax. Then it really did begin in earnest, as they began to train hard and get ready for the world's last major sporting event of the twentieth century.

It was as always a great pleasure for the Wallabies to be back in Ireland, as they once more gloried in the friendliness of the locals. This warmth was not remotely tempered by the fact that the Wallabies' second pool game — the twenty teams in the tournament were divided into five pools of four teams for the preliminary rounds — was against Ireland in Dublin. The Irish, as was their way, spoke as if it was a given that the Wallabies would win that encounter, and in the meantime why not have a Guinness?

One of the things John most enjoyed about the set-up was that the Wallabies seemed well removed from so much of the World Cup hype that was sweeping Great Britain. It meant the Australian players were able to stay relaxed for longer, and focus on the task at hand. Other teams did not necessarily seem to hunger for this quiet approach.

Just after the Wallabies had arrived in Ireland, John was interested to see on the evening news footage of the All Blacks arriving at Heathrow in their own Air New Zealand 747, which featured a giant painting of front-rowers Carl Hoeft, Anton Oliver and Kees Meuws all over the side. The mood the New Zealanders seemed to project was that they had come to claim what was rightfully theirs, the Rugby World Cup, and they didn't care who knew it. (And no matter that they had in fact recorded a loss in their last Test against the Wallabies at Sydney's Olympic Stadium — that was no more than a kink!)

Good luck to them. The Wallabies trained on. Amid all the intensity of their training travails, however, there remained room for jocularity. These Wallabies were nothing if not a tight group of friends and, as had been the case in 1991, often spoke to each other in a kind of shorthand. Since that last successful World Cup campaign, John had been in three generations of Wallabies, and over that time some of the slang words had survived while others had disappeared, replaced by newcomers — much in the fashion of the team itself.

For example, these days, if one Wallaby said to another, 'I was fair dinkum going to Hubble him,' it meant 'I was going to punch him,' à la the Australian boxer Gary Hubble. If he said, 'I think we're going to have to do a Rex this morning,' it referred to a fitness session that is just about going to kill us. This derived from the term 'to be monstered', which was transformed to be 'Tyrannosaurus rexed' which in turn was shortened to 'rexed'. Simple really.

'I think I've Mudanged myself' meant 'I think I've got a groin injury,' in the fashion of the ACT player Murray Harley who often suffered from such ailments, and just as he suffered the nickname of 'Mudang.' And so on . . .

On the subject of nicknames, John continued to be bemused by the airplay one of his own supposed nicknames received. As Wallaby captain, he had been getting at least his fair share of press coverage in the lead-up to the Cup, and the international rugby journalists delighted in reporting that his nickname was 'Nobody.' The gag was that he was called this because of the cliché, 'Nobody's perfect . . . ' and it really would have been pretty funny and pertinent, except for one thing. Nobody had ever called him 'Nobody'. Not once. Not ever. Nobody. *Never.*

Nevertheless, it had been printed once, and such is the way of these things it had assumed a life of its own. Journalists had succumbed to the temptation of repeating it, sometimes even after John had *specifically* denied that it was true. Whatever . . .

If you had to have a false nickname in the eyes of the press, it was at least a lot better than some of the true nicknames John had seen ascribed to rugby people over the years. These included a coach known as Tow Truck because he was always on his way to a breakdown; a fellow Wallaby who went by the sobriquet of Showbag because he was fat and full of crap; Phil Kearns who was called Lightning because as a lineout thrower he never hit the same place twice; and a rugby administrator called Mirrors because he was always going to look into something. In John's early days as captain, when he probably had swayed too far towards being a creature of consensus, he had even been affectionately known to the team as City Ford because he said 'Yes' more often — after a television advertisement that used that as its slogan.

For a large part of that lead-up to the Cup the only two names that John could think of, over and over and over again, were Lara and Elijah.

For the duration of the World Cup, John kept a day by day diary, and one of his first entries, for 1 October, read: 'I go through varying stages of homesickness. During last week I felt particularly low. In a sense you worry more about your child than your wife because you know that your wife won't forget about you. You get very jealous when you hear about other people hugging and kissing your son.'

At least Lara would be coming over from the quarter-finals on, but the one-year-old Elijah would have to remain back in Australia in the care of his grandparents. For now, though, what John most focused on was the opening match of the tournament, against Romania at Ravenhill Park, Belfast on 3 October. Much of John's time off the field was spent with the team physios Greg Craig and Cameron Lillicrap, putting in some last-minute work on strengthening his shoulder for the coming ordeals, and when he ran out at the prow of the Wallaby team on that opening day — for the first time in nearly a year — he did indeed feel confidence.

PLUS ça change, plus c'est la même chose . . .

Back in the early 1980s, at half-time of an English rugby Test, England's captain Bill Beaumont was in full cry, exhorting his troops to ever greater efforts, when he was famously interrupted by his goggle-eyed halfback: 'Oi, Bill, there's a girly running across the field with your bum on 'er chest!'

The entire team looked around, and there indeed was the fabulously well-endowed Erica Roe running in the bollocky across Twickenham. With twenty minutes to go in the Test against Romania, something very similar happened to John. The Wallabies had already scored seven tries and were gearing up to run in their eighth, when from the northern end of the ground two streakers — a male and a female — jumped the fence and were performing some fairly acrobatic cartwheels down the pitch.

Not to worry, the Wallabies kept their concentration and when the smoke had cleared had scored a 57-9 win, with nine tries run in of which three had been scored by the rampaging No. 8, Toutai Kefu. John's form had been solid without being spectacular — which was also a fair summation of how the Wallabies played in their next Test.

Against Ireland at Lansdowne Road in front of nearly 50,000 people, the Wallabies beat a valiant Irish side 23-3, and the best thing that could be said was that the Australians hadn't 'wasted their card'. History showed that all World Cup champions must play at least one World-Class Test for the Ages along the way, and it was as well that the Australians hadn't wasted theirs by laying their ace on the table too early, when a mere McScratch and Win card would have done.

Though both the coach and the press were reasonably happy with Eales's form, the man himself was not.

As he noted in his diary that night:

Sunday, 10 October: Even in the six months that I had off, the role of a lock [as second-rowers were now called] has changed so much that often I've wondered if I am still up to it as I once was. Everything seemed so much faster. Still, there was no choice but to simply persist, keep at it, in the hope that my old form would return.

One of the things that had changed seemed to be the physical dimensions of his opponents. After the new lineout laws had come in allowing lifting, tall and athletic jumpers like John were no longer at a premium. Generally, the new model second-rower was only reasonably tall, but capable of doing damage around the field. The point was that if John was going to be of true worth to his team, he would have to concentrate on being more effective in hitting rucks, making tackles and taking the ball up.

Frankly, John didn't feel he'd been doing that as well as he might, and his regular phone calls back to Ben Perkins in Brisbane confirmed as much. In his gentle way, Ben said that John seemed off the boil. It was for this reason that John consulted one of the Wallabies' key forward specialists on board for the duration, Alec Evans, who was there to assist Jeff Miller. The night after the game against Ireland the two slowly spooled through a tape of the game and Alec pointed out where John might do better. John was trying to hit every ruck, whereas what he had to do was hang back a bit and only hit the rucks he could be effective in. Otherwise he would be better advised to put himself in either the defensive or attacking line.

Monday, 18 October: Alec's attention to detail is superb. The main thing that we identified with my game was my reaction time and anticipation. They will become my goals for my next game. I know that I have been improving from game to game but such sessions show me just how far I have to go. I will make the effort after each game to have a similar session with Alec. I have to have more effect from breakdown to breakdown. It is a change of thought not to go to every breakdown but it is the way of the future.

John was rested for the game against the fairly lowly USA — the only World Cup game he had missed for Australia in three World Cup tournaments — and the Wallabies had no trouble in beating the Americans, at Thomond Park, Limerick, 55-19. This put the Australians in the quarterfinals against the resurgent Wales side, at the site of the World Cup Final, the newly built Millennium Stadium, on the land where Cardiff Arms Park had once stood.

On the Thursday morning before the match, the first fax John retrieved from under his door was from the Prime Minister of Australia, John Howard. On prime ministerial letterhead, it read:

Dear John,

Best of luck to you and the Australian team in the quarter-final against Wales. Here at home we will be cheering you on enthusiastically.

Kind regards,

John Howard

The Prime Minister was a long-time supporter of the Wallabies, often coming into the dressing rooms after games, making phone-calls of support, and John took it as an honour to receive such a letter from the holder of the highest office in the land. Or should that be second-highest? Under the Constitution, the Queen's representative in Australia, the Governor-General, had the highest office, and therein lay a furious debate that was then raging across Australia. The question was, should Australia become a republic, and if so, what kind of republic should it be? It was going to be put to the Australian people in a referendum on 6 November, the day of the World Cup Final. This would of course give the game added spice should there be a repeat of 1991, with England playing Australia. Personally, John was in no doubt where he stood on the issue, and had said as much when the Wallabies had put in their absentee votes at the Australian Ambassador's residence in Dublin.

'It would be good to play England in the final,' he had mentioned in passing to a journalist. 'That way we could stuff them in the vote, and stuff them on the field.'

The remark had taken off and been reprinted in many newspapers, both in Australia and Britain, to the point where it was now almost an issue, and many journalists henceforth either touched or focused on the subject when they interviewed him.

On the Friday morning before their quarter-final against Wales, on 23 October, the Wallabies had a team meeting at their hotel before heading out for the traditional 'skipper's run' — a light training run always commanded by the captain alone, just as it would be on the field. (And John was a captain, incidentally, who in this Test would surpass Nick Farr-Jones' record of 36 Tests in charge of the Wallabies.) At this meeting, John asked Tim Horan to address the team about what a World Cup quarter-final was like. Horan, whose father Mike was a notably articulate National Party MP in Queensland, got to his feet and, in eloquent if earthy prose, gave it to them straight.

He was here to tell them, he said, that he had been involved in two World Cup quarter-finals, both of which had been extremely tight, one of which had occasioned great ecstasy and the other great agony. What they had to expect was that this match would be every bit as hard as playing Ireland in '91 and England in '95 had been, but there was to be *no question* of them losing like they had in '95. He could sense that the team was already starting to focus on their likely game against South Africa in the semi-finals, as if the victory over Wales was already assured, but that kind of thinking had to stop, and STOP NOW. The Wallabies, a little shocked at seeing the usually jocular and knockabout Horan speaking in such intense fashion, hung on every word.

Each and every one of them, Horan continued, had to imagine, *now*, what it would be like to lose to Wales tomorrow and find themselves on the plane back to Australia on Sunday night. Could they imagine the anticlimax, the letdown it would be to the supporters and themselves? If you hadn't lived through it you couldn't possibly imagine how shattering it was, but there were a few of them there who knew, and none of them wanted to go through it again. They were NOT going to go through it again, because we ARE going to win tomorrow.

Once again, listening to him, John was thankful that the team he captained had such a bloke as Horan in it, with all his experience and leadership on call. Another whom he regarded with similar gratitude was the vice-captain, George Gregan. From the moment he had taken over as vice-captain on the tour to Argentina in 1997, John had always found Gregan to be totally supportive, a superb player who could keep his head in a crisis and help provide leadership in so many other areas. He and Horan were particularly good men to have on your side of the equation in a campaign such as this.

GAME time. The Millennium Stadium beckoned. On the way into the ground the feeling was electric. All streets in the city were closed to traffic and jam-packed with people. As the Wallaby bus passed, there were those who would applaud while others gave them the two-fingered salute. During the national anthems, John did what he had always done since playing his first Test eight years before. That is, he picked out at random a single face in the crowd, and zoned in. The funny thing about this particular face was that, far from having the usual anonymous contours — a face he'd never seen before and would never see again — he quickly realised it was a face he knew! It was Jean-Pierre Rives, sitting with two other of John's friends from the French Barbarians — with whom he had the honour of playing in 1995 — Dennis Charvet and Serge Kampf. It seemed extraordinary that of the 72,000 faces in the stadium at the time, he should have picked out Jean-Pierre, but it was true. Amazingly, even at a distance of some 75 metres, Rives realised John was looking straight at him and clenched his fist and smiled in a kind of bonding gesture. John nodded in return to signify that he had seen him, and for whatever reason felt oddly invigorated by it.

In the course of John's rugby career he had played some singularly ordinary Welsh sides, but this one was different. Having been revitalised in recent times by their accomplished coach Graham Henry, a New Zealander, the Welsh kept coming on strong to the Wallabies and refused to bow to their possibly superior pedigree.

Although Joe Roff scored for Australia after only five minutes and Matt Burke converted, taking the Wallabies to a 7-0 lead, the Welsh five-eighth Neil Jenkins soon struck back. Not for nothing had he recently surpassed Michael Lynagh's old record of 911 points scored in international matches, and in the first half Jenkins smoothly potted three penalty goals as the Welsh crowd roared its approval. Their boyos were *competing* against the mighty Australians, and doing them proud! Could a major upset be on the cards? Thanks to a Matt Burke penalty goal, Australia went into half-time with a 10-9 lead, but it was clear they had a major fight on their hands.

Back in Australia, the game was being listened to far and wide. As had happened in 1991, the success of the Wallabies to this point had meant that interest in their fortunes extended far beyond usual rugby circles, and Channel Seven was breaking new records for ratings achieved for rugby games. Most of sporting Australia was watching the game, with one notable exception . . .

In Sydney it was a howling wet night, and the society wedding of the decade, as it had been touted, was taking place between the heir to Australia's largest fortune James Packer and his swimsuit-model girlfriend Jodie Meares, the reception taking place in a series of interconnected enormous marquees erected on the lawn of Kerry and Ros Packer's estate at Bellevue Hill. Such was the occasion that televisions would not have been appropriate and guests who were rugby followers were seen to huddle in the corners around people with mobile phones, who were getting updates from people watching at home. This included the Prime Minister, who kept his promise to John Eales to be cheering the Wallabies on from home, but even he was obliged to head to the dark corners for the latest update. For many, the result was far more interesting than listening to Elton John as he belted out his greatest hits in one of the many marquees.

In the entire compound, only one man actually spent any time watching the game, and that was Kerry Packer — who now and then ducked back to the house to get an update from the television in his study. Though Packer had not loved playing the game at school, his grandfather, Herbert Francis Bullmore, had actually won a single cap for Scotland.

With the resumption of play, there was some cause for concern as the Welsh continued to swarm, but the break came in the 16th minute when Steve Larkham put through a grubber kick and Ben Tune gathered it in to score, taking Australia to a 17-9 lead. Late in the game, the entire Wallaby scrum was counting together — *one! two! three! four!* — in a manoeuvre designed to coordinate their angled shove, and yet on this occasion it was not actually moving the Welsh pack. At one point one of the Welsh forwards yelled out, 'Where do you think you're $%!&-ing going?' in a biting kind of way. From the second row, John Eales spoke up, and all fifteen other men in the scrum heard it: 'To Twickenham son, to $%!&-ing Twickenham!'

And indeed they were. When George Gregan ran in his second try just before full-time, the Wallabies ran out victors, 24-9, putting them in the semi-final the following week at Twickenham against the winner of the England v South Africa quarter-final in Paris, due to be played the following day.

That night, at around midnight, John took sleeping pills. Long experience had taught him that after most Tests, and especially night Tests, his head would be so filled with thoughts of what had gone right and wrong etc. that it was the only way he would be able to get to sleep before 3 or 4 a.m. (At other times, he could have slept for Australia.) Even with the pills, however, he was wide awake at six the following morning, which was a good sleep, all things considered. Often during the World Cup he woke at five and nothing could get him back to the land of nod, as his mind began whirring with what lay ahead for the day, the week and the campaign.

On that day, before they left their hotel for their next port of call, John saw some highlights of the quarter-final between South Africa and England, which the Springboks won essentially on the strength of five field goals by their fly-half, Jannie de Beer.

What most arrested John's attention was when de Beer attributed his extraordinary success to the fact that he had given over his life to God, while as a team the Boks had joined in a circle and publicly prayed. John watched, fascinated. Such public commitment to his faith had never been his own way — as he had always felt people sometimes took such statements as a proclamation of your own perfection — but he certainly felt it every bit as much as de Beer did.

In the other half of the draw, New Zealand and France both won their quarter-final matches, against Scotland and against Argentina, meaning they would play in the other semi-final.

ON the outskirts of London, the Wallabies settled in to the Burnham Beeches Hotel, a Georgian Manor with 82 rooms, not too far from Windsor Castle, and classically situated in five hectares of landscaped gardens surrounded by woodlands. It was the kind of place where, after playing croquet on the front lawn till dusk, you could then warm yourself in front of any one of a dozen roaring fires and be served cognac by a platoon of liveried servants. John's suite was the most magnificent he had ever occupied. Big enough to have its own postcode, it had a massive double bed with separate toilet, shower, bath, lounge room, dining room and board room. By this time both Lara and John's parents had arrived in Britain, and it did feel rather grand to show them around. (The only person John wasn't keen to show it off to was Rod Macqueen, on the reckoning that once Rod saw it he would realise there had been a mistake and it was probably meant for him!) It was particularly wonderful to have Lara in Britain — with baby Elijah at home in the care of her parents, Margaret and Hin Khoo — and though he was hard put to spend a lot of time with her, it was somehow comforting just that Lara was around.

Just as had happened in the World Cup of '91, everything kicked up a gear now that the Wallabies were in the semis. And the pressure was intense. Whereas at the beginning of the campaign the international media and the focus of the rugby community had been spread around twenty teams, it was now narrowed to just four, and there were as many as 50 media at each of their training sessions. There was also a far greater sense of urgency in the air, and the team began to be honed to a nice edge.

For John, now that the preliminaries were over, it also meant that home was not quite so far away.

Monday, 25 October: The positives in the cup now are that it is nearing the end and there is a definite end time. I can't wait to see Elijah. Now it is only 2 weeks. When I think too much about him it makes me quite sad. I really feel that I am missing so much. I really was very lucky with the time off that I had throughout this year. My ideal life when retired from rugby will entail being able to take Elijah and any other kids we have to school each morning, go straight to work then pick them up after school each afternoon. I want to be able to work really hard in the time they are at school and then spend some time with them each afternoon. I will have to assess this possibility depending on what suits our family when I retire.

For the semi-final against South Africa, there was something of a surprise when Rod Macqueen announced the reserves bench, with both Dan Crowley and Tiaan Strauss left out. The man John felt most badly for was Strauss, who had played one of the games of his life in the win over Wales but had not even made the bench against the country he had once captained. Against the monster Bok pack Toutai Kefu, who had just made his way back from a two-match suspension, had been preferred. It was tough for Tiaan, but it all went back to one of Rod's favourite sayings that he kept drumming into them: '"We" not "me"'. Team before self.

The night before the semi-final, John did what he always did the night before big matches on tour. He attended Bible study in Wallaby team doctor John Best's room. Mostly it would be just the two of them talking over a particular aspect of the Bible, and John found that both as a man and a footballer, on the eve of battle it helped him. Calmed him. Focused his energies. In his room, a little later, he would pray. First and foremost he would pray to play to the best of his ability, and that there were no injuries to either side. Sometimes he would pray to win. This night was a night like that.

The following morning there was an inspiring fax under the door:

Attention — The Wallabies — John Eales

To The Team,

The momentum is building, you can see it and feel it and so can the opposition. The whole country is behind you guys, so just get out there and back yourselves because we all are. There's only one thing better than beating the Springboks and that is tying with them and then beating them on a countback. Don't make it too easy, tease them and then nail them in the dying minutes just to show them who the greatest country in the world is.

Play Well — Trust Yourself.

Steve Waugh

Eales and the Australian cricket captain — who had successfully guided his side to a World Cup win the previous year, at the expense of South Africa — had established a friendship over the last couple of years, after first meeting at a sportsman's charity dinner. John took the fax with him to show the rest of the team, and in the breakfast room saw an extremely sobering sight. The star back of the Wallabies, Tim Horan, looked like death warmed up. He was the victim of a vicious stomach bug and had spent most of the previous day and night vomiting. Though that for the moment had stopped, Tim was unhappy to report that he felt as weak as a sick rabbit.

Over breakfast — heaped fruit for John, delicate nibbles of dry toast for Tim — the captain said not to worry, Tim might be able to do a Dean Jones and play the game of his life. When Horan asked him what he meant, John told him the story of how the Australian batsman had played the finest innings of his life in the famous tied Test of 1986 at Chidambram Stadium, Madras, despite suffering from a terrible combination of dysentery and vomiting and feeling like he was going to faint. The temperature was simmering around the 40 degree Celsius mark, the humidity in excess of 90 per cent, and at one point Jones had thought he was going to collapse.

'Mate,' the Victorian had told his batting partner and captain, Allan Border, 'I'm going to have to go off, I just can't go on, I'm too crook.'

You could have hit Border's eyes with a sledge-hammer right then, and it was the hammer which would have cracked.

'Sure mate,' he said in reply, his voice dripping with a particularly acidic kind of sarcasm, 'and when you go back in, can you ask them to send an *Australian* back, because that's what we need out here.'

Jones stayed, and went on to score 210 runs.

JUST before the final team meeting, Rod and John followed their usual custom of having a chat about what each was going to say —to make sure they were singing from the same song sheet. They also followed the custom they had lately developed of deciding in what manner they would celebrate a victory if it occurred. Before the Welsh Test they had planned to skaal a double bourbon that night, and did so. The previous year in Christchurch they had decided that they would sing Christmas carols. (No, really.) Now, though, Rod suggested they buy a bottle of the hotel's best champagne and, if they won, drink it out on the front lawn of the hotel with their wives later that evening.

And so to the meeting proper . . .

John had the floor first, and did not take long. Speaking with great force, he warmed to a theme.

'At some point in the match we as a team are going to get an opportunity to win this Test. It is up to each of us individually to take that opportunity if it presents itself to us. Be ready for it. It may come in the form of a match winning tackle or in the form of a steal in the lineout. It may be Bladesy identifying a weakness in their scrum. As a team we have to be prepared to MAKE the difference. Don't wait for someone else to. Do it yourself.'

Rod Macqueen then spoke and, typically, covered every last detail that might make the difference, right down to mentioning that if the scores were level at full-time the players should know there would be two ten-minutes halves of extra time played. If they were still level the Wallabies would win because the Springboks had had a player sent off earlier in the tournament.

AT Twickenham the ground was in perfect nick. A strong wind was blowing up the ground from the south. John lost the toss, and South Africa chose to run with the wind at their backs. Tim Horan indeed proceeded to play the game of his life, in John's mind probably just a notch above the Test he had played against South Africa in 1992 when he had been so devastating in both attack and defence. Dean Jones would have been proud: scything tackles, brilliant breaks, passes to his outside support that continued to put them in space, the lot! So too did the Wallabies as a whole play well, but although the Springboks seemed to be outgunned they simply refused to bow to their masters and matched the Australians blow for blow.

With just two minutes to go, and the score 18-15 in the Wallabies' favour, both teams were on the edge of exhaustion when the referee blew shrilly on his whistle in that particular fashion known to rugby players the world over: PENALTY! But whose? It is the way of such things that only rarely will an international side know automatically which side has transgressed, which particular action in the massed maelstrom has so offended the referee that the game must be stopped and one side punished — and both sides looked fearfully towards him.

!#@$% HELL! He was lifting his hand towards the South African side, meaning it was the Wallabies who had committed the foul. The Bok captain, Joost van der Westhuizen, threw the ball to Jannie de Beer and signalled that he wanted him to go for goal. To the Wallabies, it scarcely seemed credible. The rain was falling. The wind was swirling. He was shooting from near the touchline at a distance of some 40 metres. Even allowing for the fact that after the Boks' previous game de Beer had thanked his Lord and saviour Jesus Christ for guiding his boot so accurately, he surely had to be only a one-in-ten chance of slotting it now. If he did so, the game would go into extra time, and South Africa would still be a chance of retaining the World Cup. If he missed, Australia would be in the World Cup Final! Alas . . .

He slotted it.

Never in his captaincy career had Eales provided stronger leadership. For even as the ball went over the crossbar to tie the score at full-time, the skipper did not betray the slightest negative emotion. Not a grimace, not an oath, not a single wasted movement of his hands to hold his head in anguish or the like. He simply put his hands out wide and in a positive gesture hustled the players back into the sheds.

From this point, the Wallabies didn't wander off the field like Brown's cows, they *jogged* into the dressing-room, just as Macqueen had always insisted they do. It was not a matter purely of having extra time in the dressing room to sort things out, it was a standard to be reached, a professional thing. Once in the dressing room they slipped straight into the routine that Macqueen had also established — a routine designed to divide the precious time available into its most efficacious blocks.

First port of call was to the medical staff, with players receiving treatment for everything from the onset of cramping to troublesome abrasions. John then had his turn to speak quickly. The players, sucking on their water bottles, crowded in. The theme he warmed to was simple. Stick to our guns. We are outplaying them in most departments, and even though the definitive break has not yet come, it will come so long as we stick with it. We must not panic, must not push passes, must not move out of our natural rhythm, must keep our composure. Play for field position and the break will come. Then George Gregan spoke briefly, followed by Rod Macqueen. Though the coach did not waste any time castigating the Wallaby forward who had given away the penalty which had put them in this situation, he did emphasise that every further penalty they gave away stood every chance of being remembered every morning for the rest of their lives. NO PENALTIES.

Finally, conditioner Steve Nance took them through two minutes of a re-warm-up, before in the final minute the whole team on their own stood in a circle running through the moves and the calls.

Just as they were about to go out again, Tim Lane tapped five-eighth

Steve Larkham on the shoulder and told him straight out: think about a field-goal. Larkham nodded a little vaguely — he still hadn't kicked a field-goal since the U/9s — and then they all trotted out the door and out into the tepid light of a late English autumn afternoon as the Twickenham crowd roared . . .

For the next seventeen minutes or so, the two sides went at it, scoring a penalty goal apiece. In the stands, Lara Eales could barely stand it and said to Jack Eales beside her, 'I'm going to go, I just can't bear to watch.'

Jack Eales told her firmly: 'If you go, Lara, you'll miss it, and regret it forever.'

She stayed.

With two minutes to go, like most of the players on the field from both sides, it was all John could do to hold on. Never in his life had he been obliged to play 100 minutes of football, let alone Test football and he began to wonder if he would in fact make it to the end. His legs were cramping up, and the fear was that at one point his body would simply refuse to run any further. Shan't. Shan't. *Shan't!*

Back in Brisbane, at this time, Ben Perkins was alone in his living room, aware that it was time for desperate measures. 'HUUUUUUUUU!' he sang longer and louder than ever before. 'HUUUUUUUUUUUUUUU! **HUUUUUUUUUUUUUUUUUUUUUU!'**

It took some time, but at last the spirits seemed to be pleased enough with his efforts to give him some reward. For with the score locked at 21-21 and the 72,000 spectators at Twickenham as tense as cats on a curtain . . . it happened. From an Australian ruck, 45 metres out from the South African tryline, George Gregan scooped the ball out to five-eighth Stephen Larkham on the fly. The Wallaby backs were outside him, hungry for the ball and screaming for him to pass it when, suddenly, Larkham propped, turned, sweetly dropped the ball in front of him and sent his right leg swinging through as smoothly as a Greg Norman drive down the middle of the Augusta fairway on the first day. The ball shot forwards and up-wards, turning end over end, and sailed above the despairing hands of the mounting Springbok defence, over the head of the referee, above the South African fullback, who watched it pass over him like a satellite skimming past a high veldt full moon . . . *and through the goalposts 48 metres away!!!* It was all reminiscent of the famous South American com-mentators at the Soccer World Cup the year before: GOOOOOOOOAL!

Of the moments immediately afterwards, John Eales would long remember two things: the joyous look on Larkham's face and the immediate sense that the moment was gone, and that the Wallabies now had to switch on and concentrate for the rest of the match. There was to be no succumbing to the fatal temptation once elucidated by former Wallaby coach Alan Jones of taking a snapshot of a great move and crowding round to look at it while the game went on behind them. They had to get straight back into it and play down in their half.

A Matthew Burke penalty goal shortly afterwards emphasised the point and when the referee Derek Bevan blew the final, blessed whistle to beat all final blessed whistles to bring the curtain down on a 27-21 win to Australia, several things were touching. The first was that the 70,000 strong crowd immediately gave a thundering standing ovation, notwithstanding the fact that maybe 25,000 people in it were rabid South African supporters who had just seen their side suffer defeat. Whatever people's national colours, the ovation was an acknowledgment that all had been privileged to be present at a Clash for the Ages. Both teams seemed to feel it, too, with each side — for the first Test in anyone's memory — spontaneously lining up in two single files as all had done in the U/12s and shaking each other's hand as they walked past.

The Bok perhaps most effusive in his congratulations was also the one likely to be the most cruelly disappointed, five-eighth Jannie de Beer, who had come so close to guiding his side to a historic victory but simply couldn't match Steve Larkham's extraordinary drop goal.

But were they really the official winners? Up in the official stand at that moment, John O'Neill was in a blind panic. Sitting just a row behind the chairman of the International Rugby Board, Vernon Pugh, O'Neill had distinctly heard Pugh say a minute before the final whistle 'the Australians have just brought back on a player who had left the field; they will be disqualified.'

In a mad scramble, he now chased Pugh down.

'What did you say?,' he asked the chairman.

'Oh nothing, John'.

'I heard you say Australia is going to be disqualified — why?'

'Well that last interchange — where Ben Tune came back on for Daniel Herbert — unless it was a blood bin you can't bring a man back on.'

'Who would know whether it was a blood bin or not?'

'The referee and the fourth touch judge.'

(In rugby a blood bin is the term used to describe taking players who are bleeding temporarily off the field until the bleeding is stopped, whereupon they may return to the field. The fourth touch judge is the official who ensures that all is done correctly.)

Like a mad thing, O'Neill bolted down the stairs, burst into the referees room, where the fourth touch judge was just taking off his boots. The man looked up, wondering what on earth was going on. Before he could utter a word, though, O'Neill burst out: 'That last replacement, between Herbert and Tune, was it 'blood bin'.'

'Yes . . . ' he replied, quizzically, still wondering what was happening.

'You @#$!-ing BEAUTY!' O'Neill replied.

When O'Neill arrived in the dressing room, Rod Macqueen was quietly moving among the players, shaking each by the hand to thank him for his efforts and saying a few words about 'next Saturday'.

O'Neill would have joined him, but remained a man on a mission. Taking Dr John Best aside, he said very quietly, 'Was Herbert a genuine blood bin?'

'Yes,' Best replied, 'he had a nick on his eyebrow, and he also had cramps.'

Relieved, O'Neill went to have a close look at Herbert. There was indeed a nick there, with some blood apparent but, just to be on the safe side . . . he had a word to him, and another to John Best.

O'Neill then went and put his arm around Rod Macqueen and congratulated him, only to have the usually ultra-controlled coach return the hug with spades, even as he let out a sob of relief. The coach composed himself again quickly enough, and apologised for letting himself go — despite O'Neill's protestations — but it was the barest glimpse of how much Macqueen had been looking into the abyss of horrible defeat only to find that he was still on the path to the Promised Land. The Wallabies lived, to give it a go!

A beaming Daniel Herbert walked by. He had three newly installed stitches in his eyebrow.

BACK in Brisbane, the Eales siblings were making feverish plans. Two days before the semi-final, John had called and told all of them that if the Wallabies beat South Africa he would shout them all a trip to Britain for the final on some cheaper tickets he was going to get through his association with Qantas. To John's mind, it was little enough recompense for the wonderful support they had provided over the years. As it happened, Antoinette and her partner Robert were already living in London, so the others could use their place as a base. As to Nonna, it was sad that at her advanced age of 96 she would be unable to make the trip, but John felt that she would be there in spirit. As would Carmel. As always, during such tense times, John strongly felt her presence.

THE following day the Australians settled down to watch the other semi-final between the All Blacks and the French team — a game they knew to be all but a formality in rubber-stamping New Zealand's passage through to the final. Certainly the French were not without their arguments — they had played the All Blacks seven times in the previous ten years and recorded three victories — but on the last occasion they had met New Zealand emerged as 54-7 victors. Thus, as everyone knew, it wasn't as if the French could actually *beat* the New Zealanders, but the main hope was that they would make a game of it, and at least weaken the All Blacks for their coming encounter that Saturday. Highlighting New Zealand's confidence was a minor blue that had broken out back in Wellington as to who should pay for the tickertape parade after the All Blacks returned triumphant from the World Cup.

With all that in mind, the Wallabies watched closely . . . and saw undoubtedly one of the greatest rugby games ever played. Though the All Blacks dominated early and skipped to a 24-7 lead ten minutes into the second-half, the game was far from over. After a long *rrrrrrrrumble*, Volcano France — thought extinct — exploded! For the next twenty minutes the men of Gaul ran the ball from everywhere, playing attacking rugby even from behind their own goalpost, and in defence stormed ashore and swarmed all over everything that moved in a black jumper, even while their five-eighth slotted field-goals and penalty kicks from everywhere.

When the volcano had finally ceased its terrible eruption and the smoke had cleared, France had won, 43-31. The Wallabies were amazed with the result and the way the French had played, and even slightly trepidatious as the knowledge dawned that they were the ones who were going to face them next. In a World Cup Final! Ultimately, what the game established was that the World Cup was not the travelling Tri-Nations Show after all. France's ascension meant that the final would be contested between teams from the southern and northern hemispheres, and the ensuing surge in atmospheric electricity straight after the semi-final was palpable. When the charismatic French captain Raphael Ibanez had been asked how on earth such a victory had been possible, he replied with a superbly Gallic shrug and said, 'Ehhh, we are French . . . '

And therein lay a tale.

For not only were they French, but also the most lethal kind of French, a team that had achieved *le feeling*, a kind of deeply emotional state whereby the fifteen of them were bound together as tight as a drum and with the impact of a sledgehammer. As an example of the unorthodox way the French went about things, in their lead-up to the semi-final they had not bothered with sports psychologists, gone through 'mental rehearsals', got out their slide-rules to assess their proper angle of attack, or warmed up their computers to calculate their desired ball retention rate in the first quarter. Rather, they had kept to themselves in the build-up to the game, talking to each other about what a victory would mean to them and to their country. And when they had warmed up prior to the game, each player had worn a T-shirt upon which were written one or other of the names Cali, Tom, Lievre, Pierrot, Carbo — the nicknames of all those players who had started the campaign with them but were no longer there because of injury or suspension.

'We did it,' recounted Abdelatif Benazzi, 'because we wanted absolutely to think of them because they are a part of ourselves.'

Quite. And then in the minute preceding the match, after the anthems and the haka, they put themselves in a tight circle and . . . and sang 'La Marseillaise' again.

'It was just for us,' explained Ibanez, 'to remind us what this was about, for what we were playing. Preparing to play the All Blacks is like preparing for *la guerre*, and sometimes before a war the soldiers sing, and so did we.'

THE highest commander of the opposing army, General John Eales, wrote in his diary the following morning:

Monday, 1 November: Well it is going to be a nervous week. Last night I couldn't sleep before midnight and I was up by six am. Thoughts are just constantly going through my mind. I have to be able to channel this energy. I will resolve now that whenever I get nervous then I will think about a few specifics of our match. I will positively use the energy.

One of the key specifics of the match that the Wallabies would have to deal with was to try to find a counter to the often outrageously nefarious methods the French used to put their opponents off their game. As the Wallabies looked more closely at the French game, and talked to other internationals who had played them — particularly the All Blacks, who they ran into all over Cardiff — this theme of French foul play kept recurring. John heard from several All Blacks remarks along the lines of 'Look we haven't said much, but we were constantly eye-gouged and had our balls and hair pulled.'

Certainly there no lack of precedent for this approach. Not for nothing did the old joke run . . . **Q:** Why do they call it 'rugby'? **A:** Because 'assault and battery' was already taken.

This was no joke, though. On the Tuesday after the All Black game a snatch of video had emerged which appeared to show the French prop Franck Tournaire biting the All Black captain Taine Randell. At the least, Randell was seen flinching after contact was made by Tournaire. The All Black skipper then jumped up and shoved Tournaire in the chest while the television microphones picked up an anonymous voice from the ruck shouting: 'He's biting me. He's biting me.' How to counter such acts?

The instinct, of course, was simply to belt the bejesus out of the perpetrators, but in terms of winning the final, this would have been counterproductive. As Macqueen made clear in the first team meeting that week, the reason the French would be doing that was to put them off their game. They wanted to commit acts in the darkness to encourage retaliation in daylight, and then it would be the Wallabies who were penalised. The only way to avoid this, he said, was to be totally disciplined, not retaliate, and report it all immediately to the referee, the South African Andre Watson. That, at least, was the theory . . .

In all the business of preparing for the match, all the trainings, meetings, press conferences, video analyses and all the rest, there was still time for some relaxation — Macqueen was very strong on the fact that players needed to have some down-time — and Tuesday was a case in point.

At Tim Horan's behest, that night all those in the squad who had been a part of the 1991 World Cup win — Tim Horan, Jason Little, Dan Crowley, Cameron Lillicrap, Greg Craig, Jeff Miller and John — went to a Thai restaurant in Cardiff, where they toasted their 1991 victory, eight years to the day before. Greg Craig had brought along a scrapbook which *Courier-Mail* journalist Jim Tucker had lent him, full of clippings from that campaign. All delighted in poring over it and reliving old memories. There was Greg Craig when he had hair, there was John when he was still built like a thermometer, there was Dan Crowley presenting a XXXX football to the Queen just before the final. On the strength of it, John suggested that Dan had to do something similar this time or it would be a bad omen.

Gentlemen, a toast! To the 1991 Wallabies and their World Cup win! And to absent friends. As one, the players responded to Tim Horan's gesture, and then John made another toast. To the 1999 Wallabies and their World Cup win!

Hurrah! John's primary thought as he clinked glasses was how special it might be, some years down the track, to have two World Cup Winning Wallaby reunions four days apart:

Wednesday, 3 November: Once again I was up early, this time at around five thirty in the morning. So many thoughts are constantly racing through my head but I feel quite relaxed. The key really is to focus on the specifics of what we have to do, not the end result. That in itself is not an easy thing to do because the end result of Saturday's match is final. There is no tomorrow. We live with it for the rest of our lives. If we play well and lose then we can live with that. Not easily but we can. If we don't play to the best of our ability and lose then that would be hard to come to terms with.

The final three days before the final went by in a blur.

One of the issues that kept popping up was John's earlier comment about the republic. Both Britain and Australia were of course following very closely the twists and turns on the way to the coming referendum and it was only natural that John would be identified as one of the leading advocates of Australia divesting itself of the Queen. If this put John in the unfamiliar territory of being slightly controversial, then so be it.

Back in Brisbane, though, John's friend and business manager Chris

White was concerned enough to send John an email advising him to back off on the issue. He said he was surprised that John had such strong views and that he should make damn sure he knew what he was talking about, because people get very polarised by politics — which was what he was dabbling in, make no mistake!

John replied that he was *very* sure of his opinions, that for him it was cut and dried, and he didn't mind people knowing that he thought the monarchy had no relevance to Australia any more.

True, this republican sentiment in his breast did not extend to agreeing to an Australian journalist's request that he wear a 'YES' badge while wearing the Wallaby jersey — the resulting photo of which would have appeared on the front page of the Saturday *Sydney Morning Herald* — as he felt it would be a misuse of both his position as captain and a misuse of the jersey. But he still would have loved nothing more than to go down in history as the last Australian to have received a trophy from the Queen of England as one of her loyal subjects.

In fact, John later learned that his comments had not offended the man representing the Queen in Australia, Governor-General Sir William Deane, who was also patron of the Australian Rugby Union. At a reception in Canberra the following year, Sir William, while making clear that he was not expressing any official view on the issue, said to John quietly: 'I had a smile at your comments on the Republic before last year's World Cup Final.'

Friday, 5 November: As I write it is late on the eve of the World Cup Final. The team is still in a very relaxed mode and has been for most of the day. Tomorrow is the realisation of our destiny. The end of the road if you like. It is a life altering day. The most important thing no matter what the result is that we are able as individuals and as a team to hold our heads high and treat whatever the outcome in the same way. We will be the same people whatever the result.

On 6 November 1999, when John got up, there was a pile of faxes under his door. The first was from the Lillicrap clan wishing him all luck for a great game and wonderful result for the team. The last one was from Elijah. The one today, as was also the case the previous year, brought an immediate tear to John's eye.

'He (John) will go ahead . . . strong and mighty like the prophet Elijah'
    (Luke 1, 17).
Condemning the French to eighty minutes of rugby hell. . . . . . .

Go for it Dad and have the game of your life! I love you and miss you and
Mummy and can't wait till you come home. Give Mummy a big kiss and
hug from me.
    Lots of love to you both.
    Elijah.

Well, maybe it wasn't from Elijah himself, and more likely from
Margaret Khoo, who was looking after him back in Brisbane, but somehow John felt that if his beloved boy really could talk then that is what he
would say to him. As John readied himself to go to breakfast that morning,
just seven hours before kick-off, and counting, he found his thoughts
going constantly between Elijah and Carmel — his son for inspiration
and his sister for calm.

'It is amazing how much strength that Carmel can give me in difficult
times,' John wrote in his diary. 'Today I will have the strength of both her
and Saint Anthony to carry me through the match.'

At 10 a.m. John had his usual match-day meeting with Rod Macqueen
in the coach's room and followed usual form by exuding an air of barely
contained *excitement*. It never ceased to amaze Rod how John seemed to
retain a sense of wonder and privilege that they should all be lucky
enough to be involved in a Test match, even though he was a veteran of
68 Tests, about to play his 69th. Other players got very world-weary
about it all, and even confided that they couldn't wait for it to be over,
but John was never like that. He could hardly wait for it to begin.

John, in turn, looked at the coach with a discerning eye as they sat at
the desk in Rod's room going over last details. The Wallaby coach was
very calm and cautiously confident, but maybe too on this morning there
was a hint of difference. Maybe, just maybe, in the way Rod was kind of
oddly sparkling, he was a man who was right on the point of fulfilling a
dream. Twice in the 1980s Macqueen had guided his Warringah club side
all the way to a grand final, only to be denied. Once in the 1990s he had
managed to get the ACT Brumbies into the Super 12 Final but had fallen
short. Now he was on the edge of a possible World Cup win.

As always, the two went over what they were going to say in the team meeting, and just before they finished they discussed, as always, what they would do to celebrate if they won. This time, they decided, once back in Australia they would take their wives for a picnic on the half way line at the Caloundra field where they had done so much of their training for this moment.

BUT to the team meeting proper, in a conference room on the first floor of their hotel in downtown Cardiff. Rod and John both spoke about the game plan for the day. Generally, they wanted to keep it simple in the first part of the game, and eliminate the errors from which the French had been able to make so much capital against other opponents. Specifically they wanted to do such things as constantly run the ball straight at the fire cracker French flanker Olivier Magne, and exhaust him early as he had been their main match-winner in previous games.

When the captain and coach had finished their address, the climactic moment came . . .

The former Wallaby with the great honour of presenting the jerseys to the Wallabies before the World Cup Final was the former prop and now Channel Seven commentator, Chris 'Buddha' Handy. After a long discussion between Eales and many of the players, and in consultation with Rod Macqueen, Handy had been selected because he had been a total supporter of the team for a very long time — a guy who had defended them through the dark times and should be right in the middle of them in the good times.

Standing in front of the Wallabies, Buddha spoke, in a low, deeply strained voice, that was compelling to listen to for the simple reason that — apart from his well-chosen words — he gave the impression through the entire speech that he was just a hair's breadth away from bursting into tears with the emotion of it all. Buddha's voice was shaking with passion.

'I'm here today,' he said, 'representing all the Wallabies who have gone before you, all the Australian supporters that'll be there today, all the Australian supporters at home and scattered around the world who will be watching on TV and desperately wanting you to win. If they could be here now, they would tell you what I am going to tell you: we are very, very proud of you already, and know you'll do us proud today. We know you are going to make it a big day and you'll go onto the field with all our best wishes going with you. But we also want to ask you one more thing.

Please come out of this game absolutely exhausted knowing that you could not have given one more bit of yourself for Australia.'

His final words were well considered, well delivered, and emphasised the point.

'Whatever else happens out there,' he said, 'Please, *please* don't leave any gas in the tank.'

With which he turned and with a strong handshake he presented John with his Wallaby jersey, plus a bottle of 1991 Grange Hermitage. 1991, he explained, was a great year for rugby in Australia and also for Grange. His hope and dream was that the 1999 team would be remembered in the same light as the 1991 side and that at the end of the match they could all partake in the swilling of the bottle of red.

Following tradition, one of the Test Wallabies, this time Andrew Blades, rose to thank Handy for his words, and then himself made a superb speech during which he too struggled to keep emotional control. He noted that he was going to retire at the end of this game and high-lighted what playing for the Wallabies had meant to him over the years. He finished his speech brushing the tears from his cheeks, and he was not the only one. When John, sitting up at the front of the room, looked around it was clear that there was not a dry eye in the room, least of all his own.

To the bus, and let's do it.

As the Wallabies left their downtown Cardiff hotel — through a crowd of Australian supporters who'd gathered to sing 'Waltzing Matilda' and cheer and clap them onto their bus — there was a hiccup. Two vans were blocking the exit from the car-park and their drivers were nowhere around. Problem, what problem, officer? The Wallabies eight reserves plus Chris Handy simply got out of the bus and — one, two, three and heaaave! — lifted the vans out of the way. Let's roll.

In the Millennium Stadium dressing room just minutes before they went out, the Test team had their usual time of quiet reflection and last minute rituals before Rod Macqueen gathered them into one corner of the room. Now was not the time for talk of game plans, or tactics, or exhortations. All of that had been done. Instead, Macqueen referred to a story he'd told them in the team room, a story from the trip they'd made the previous year to Villers-Bretonneux. It concerned an Australian lieutenant by the name of F.P Bethune, a clergyman at home, who found himself in charge of twenty Australian soldiers in a particularly bloody battle. In March of 1918, it fell to Bethune's platoons to hold the line against the marauding Germans. The Australians were clearly outnumbered and outgunned, and nearby British forces considered their position suicidal. But it was crucial to the rest of the Allies that they at least try to hold the line, and the only way out was total resolve. If one man wavered they were lost. Lieutenant Bethune gathered his men and gave them written orders.

'And the orders went like this,' Macqueen said, clearing his throat, and trying to keep his own emotions in check as he read from the piece of paper in his hand.

'"This position will be held, and the section will remain here until relieved. The enemy cannot be allowed to interfere with the program. If the section cannot remain here alive, it will remain here dead, but in any case it will remain here.

'"Should any man through shell-shock or other cause attempt to surrender, he will remain here dead. Should all guns be blown out, the section will use Mills grenades and other novelties. Finally, the position, as stated, will be held."

'And guys,' Macqueen finished. 'They held their position.'

From the moment of Rod finishing, not another word was spoken. The Wallabies got up and went out the door, out into the thundering roar of a World Cup Final . . .

FAR away, in East Timor, the modern-day heirs to the Anzac tradition, the men and woman of the Australian Defence Forces, let out their own roar as Wallabies ran onto the pitch, as the game was beamed in live via satellite to their barracks. The soldiers were then engaged in a difficult operation to preserve East Timor's independence, and their commanding officer Major-General Peter Cosgrove had sent the Wallabies a warm message of support on their behalf. The Diggers are with you. Go get 'em.

THE French five-eighth, Christophe Lamaison, struck first inside two minutes with a penalty goal to make it 3-0 to la *crème de la crème* of northern hemisphere rugby, and Les Bleus were full of fire from the first. The Wallabies at least were able to douse much of that fire with smothering tackles and a resilience that never wavered, but it was clear from the first that Volcano France was not going to be dormant. For John, an extraordinary thing had happened early in the game when, feeling himself held from behind in a lineout, he had simply slapped the hand away from him and been promptly penalised by Andre Watson . . . who held up a yellow card. This was an official warning that the referee judged the offence serious enough that if John did it again, he would be sent from the field!

In the stands, Lara was sitting with Jack, while Rosa sat with the rest of their children and their partners in a different section of the stand. None of them could believe it. *John* being designated as the most dangerous man on the field at that time? *John* the baddie? Rosa, always the most emotional of supporters, found it particularly galling.

'There must be a mistake!' she near shouted. '*Not John.*'

The irony of the warning was that what John was accused of doing was as nothing to what had been going on all around from the moment the game began. For in the hidden world that lies at the bottom of sixteen massed men piled on top of each other, it was proving to be every bit as ugly for the Wallabies as they had feared. As the game progressed, first Richard Harry, then hooker Michael Foley, then John himself had their eyes gouged.

Lying at the bottom of a ruck, the Wallaby captain suddenly felt a searing sensation in his right eye as a finger pressed in. Alas before John could grab the hand doing it and so trace it up the arm to the French bloke doing it, it had been snatched away. John reported to Andre Watson what had happened and asked him to take action.

In reply, Watson made a fair point. He couldn't penalise what he couldn't see. Watson had already warned the French about dirty play, and could do little more until he actually witnessed an atrocity.

At least, despite it all, the Wallabies had edged ahead on the scoreboard in the bitter battle. A fourth Matthew Burke penalty goal just before half-time gave Australia a 12-6 lead as Watson called an end to what, in terms of a spectacle, had been a disappointing first half. (A small historical point is that the 12-6 scoreline to Australia at that time was the way the World Cup Final had finished in 1991.)

In the second half, John's innate sympathy for the referee in no way diminished the growing anger he felt towards the French as the eye-gouging continued. With just 25 minutes remaining in the game — with the Wallabies leading 18-12 — David Wilson received a gash in his chin from what had seemed to be a wayward French boot and the Australian captain had had enough.

At a halt in play, he turned to the referee and said, 'Look, this is ridiculous. I fear for my team's safety. If this continues, we will leave the field, we will just leave the field.'

Unbeknown to John, the last part was picked up by the microphone on Watson's lapel and broadcast around the world.

Again, Watson was two parts agitated to three parts frustrated. 'What do you want, what do you want?' he replied. He still hadn't been able to witness any nefariousness, nor had his touch judges.

At least, though, at this point Watson pulled the French captain Raphael Ibanez in, and indicated that enough was enough. Eales took the opportunity to have a word with the massive French second-rower Abdelatif Benazzi, who he had met on several occasions, a guy he liked and respected, and who he knew spoke a basic kind of English.

'Abdel,' he said with some force, 'this is a disgrace. You've got to get them to stop doing this, because this is not what it's all about, this is *not* rugby.'

In response, Benazzi nodded, turned to his team-mates and let loose a volley of extremely rapid French, the essence of which completely escaped John. Nevertheless, perhaps the combination of the referee's warning and Benazzi's words really had an effect, because the French seemed marginally better from then on. With twenty minutes to go, the Wallabies were nine points clear — with both sides only having kicked penalty goals — and the risk was that the match would drift to another tryless contest, like the 1995 final and Australia's semi-final victory over South Africa. Still, with the Wallaby waves continuing to crash on French shores, the hope remained that one of the landing party might plant his flag on their beach. The moment came . . .

After clever lead-up work by George Gregan, Owen Finegan and Tim Horan, Wallaby winger Ben Tune received the ball at full pace on the right flank and noted that the only thing between him and the line was the exceedingly fragile French fullback Xavier Garbajosa — who a week before had appeared to dive out of the way of Jonah Lomu the way one would away from a runaway lorry. Well, Tune might not have been driving a truck quite that big, but he still fancied his chances and put his pedal to the metal to run straight at Garbajosa, the one back on the ground who had dyed hair (always a good sign.)

It proved an astute decision. The fullback's ineffectual tackle barely hindered Tune and he was able to get the ball down for a try. The Wallabies were clearly on top, and keen to keep pouring it on — something made easier by the fact that with victory all but assured, Rod Macqueen emptied the reserves bench onto the field to ensure both that fresh Australian legs would be brought into play and that everyone would have a part in that victory.

Six minutes into injury time, after a John Eales lineout win, George Gregan sparked the second try. An extremely clever inside flick pass sent Owen Finegan on a 30 metre run, leaving six defenders in Finegan's wake, and with another three of them hitching a ride on his back for the final five metres he scored a try to seal the game.

Ask not for whom the final whistle blows, it blows for thee . . .

Andre Watson blew his whistle with that particular peal that means so much to exhausted rugby players. It was over. In the green and gold corner, weighing in at a combined total of 1512 kilograms . . . the new world champions . . . *Australia!* The final, historic score was 35-12. Almost as one the Wallabies lifted their arms in triumph before dropping them to embrace each other, and many a tear was shed in the tumultuous scenes that followed. And not just on the ground. Up in the Channel Seven broadcast box Chris Handy, his voice breaking, said, 'It doesn't matter if you're a stunned mullet, a young dingo or a vintage red — give them a cheer, Australia, they've done you proud.'

EIGHT years before at this moment, the primary emotion felt by Eales had been one of relief. This time it was joy pure. Last time he had been no sooner in the team than they had won the World Cup. This time, he'd been through the ups and downs, travelled the valleys, got lost in the jungles, and now appreciated the view from the summit as never before. Standing right at the pinnacle, as the captain of the Wallaby World Cup champions, it had never felt better.

Back in Australia, the republican referendum had been lost, but on this occasion instead of obliging the Australians to climb to her in the stands as she had in 1991, the Queen came down to them on the field. When the moment came to receive the trophy, John stepped forward, a smile as wide as the Great Australian Bight.

'Thanks very much, Your Majesty, it's a very special moment,' said the Wallaby skipper, before turning and lifting the trophy in triumph, the moment he had long dreamed about.

After everything, when the Wallabies had received their medallions and drunk deep from the Cup that was now overflowing with champagne that had magically appeared — Australian champagne, of course, rather than French — the squad gathered in a circle around Bill, as they referred to the William Webb Ellis Trophy, linked arms and belted out 'Advance Australia Fair'.

A long and luxurious lap of honour followed, as the crowd continued to roar its congratulations. Over the thirteen minutes it took to complete the lap, a Wallaby fan complete with green and gold scarf who had jumped the fence kept bouncing around the players and went nearly the whole way around with the men in gold jerseys. Yes, the security guards kept putting him back on his side of the fence — three times! — but when he kept coming back and it was clear that the Wallabies didn't mind, they gave up and let him go. It was that kind of ramble.

As they went, John at the prow with the Cup being passed around between them, fireworks went off and confetti rained down from the stadium roof. As the team continued its circuit, the Men at Work song, 'I Come From the Land Down Under' boomed around the stadium, and many of the perhaps 20,000 Australians who had travelled to Cardiff for the game danced on their seats. So too did Lara Eales as, by now right down to the front fence with Jack, she saw the transparent joy of her husband from just 50 metres away. There was no way, of course, he would see her and Jack in the throng, but she just wanted to kiss him. And suddenly there he was!

Breaking from the pack, John sprinted the distance between them and embraced them both warmly, kisses for Lara, a hand shake and a long hug for Jack. For all Jack's wonderful warmth as a father, it was one of the few times they had embraced this way and both men noted the occasion. Physical contact was not common in Jack's original family and it had carried through to him.

'I was conscious of the handshake and the hug as something exceptional,' Jack says, 'something out of the ordinary. I felt very good about it, very happy about it.'

'I loved it,' John says simply.

After one more kiss for Lara, John turned away to rejoin the team, entirely unaware that his mother, who had been with the rest of the siblings and their spouses, was even then charging down the stairs to embrace the son she never wanted to play rugby. She just missed him, alas. Back in Australia, Nonna was still dancing around the room with joy, together with her son Henry and his wife Margaret who had moved into Arnell Street with her while the rest of the family was away.

When the triumphant team at last reached the sanctuary of their Millennium Stadium dressing room they were able to renew the celebration rite begun eight years previously. John Eales led. As each of the Wallabies passed the Cup along the line to once again drink deep, the rest of the team shouted each other's names, with their newly hard-won title — 'Steve Larkham, world champion!' . . . 'Matt Cockbain, world champion!' . . . 'David Giffin, world champion!' and so on.

When they came to those for whom this was their second World Cup, the refrain moved up a key: 'Tim Horan, *double* world champion!' . . . 'Jason Little, *double* world champion!' . . . 'John Eales, *double* world champion!'

It was a perfect moment, the moment for which they had all worked so hard for so long, and the moment John particularly had been envisioning for the last four years, the fulfilment of the dream.

The running gag among the Wallabies had been that the World Cup was the best vessel in the world to have a drink out of, and so it proved when in the dressing room the Wallabies continued to pass the trophy between them and drink deep of the champagne within. This was washed down by the contents of Chris Handy's bottle of 1991 Grange which was evenly shared into 40 plastic cups and knocked back. (This was not an occasion for delicate sips.) No wine, ever, anywhere, ever tasted so good.

John showered and changed, was soon called away for the press conference and endless round of interviews afterwards — where he played down all talk of eye-gouging — but when he got back to the dressing room it was to find that Jason Little and Tim Horan had stayed luxuriating in the hot baths, sipping beer, smoking cigars and clearly in no hurry at all to get ready for the huge official dinner that awaited. Neither of them, clearly, wanted the moment to end, and both were conscious that once they left the dressing room the experience would be over, and they would have to rely on something so ephemeral as memory to properly savour it.

John joined them, and it was another hour before the three finally got moving. ('PUT HIM IN THE BOOK!' Theirs had been a long sporting journey, and by this time they were all in the book.)

In all of the accolades that came John's way in the wake of the win, one was particularly notable for its graciousness. It came from Phil Kearns, and appeared in *The Times*. John read it at the front end of a big Qantas Jumbo taking him home to Elijah the following day, and was touched.

'How much higher can John Eales go?' John's predecessor in the Australian captaincy asked. 'When he started as captain, I wondered how good a job he would do . . . But he has become an exceptional leader over the last two years, and in the semi-final and final in partnership with David Giffin the real John Eales stood up, a towering presence.'

On their way home, the world champions offered all their fellow passengers a victory drink from their holy grail. David Wilson, Steve Larkham, Matt Cockbain and Dan Crowley took the trophy and went up and down both side of the cheering plane until everyone had had their fill.

LATE, late. Late on the Monday night John finally arrived back at his Hamilton home and softly put the key in the front door. He was alone, as Lara had been unable to get a booking on the same flight and was even then somewhere over the Middle East.

Lara's parents were waiting for him, warmly embraced him and congratulated their son-in-law, and then John went down the hall to the nursery, and quietly, quietly, tiptoed in. There was his boy, asleep in his cot. He'd grown in the eight weeks since he'd seen him last. He looked fantastic, sleeping peacefully. Then he stirred, rolled over, looked up, saw John. John picked him up, held him tight, kissed him. Elijah looked back at him, seeming to examine the contours of his father's face. The one-year-old kept looking, neutrally, almost as if he was puzzled. A car quietly swished by in the darkened street outside. John sat with Elijah on the chair, and the two continued to look at each other. John kept smiling at Elijah, talking to him, stroking his cheek. Still nothing. Elijah didn't try to move away, and was not at all uncomfortable, but continued to look at John's face. Ten minutes passed. Slowly it dawned on Elijah. As John kept softly talking to him, before his very eyes Elijah started smiling, *beaming* at him!

John cried.

THE following day, John took Elijah to the airport to pick up Lara and his parents and they all went back to Arnell Street for lunch. Nonna was waiting for them in the driveway when they pulled up. As John got out of the car, she came up to him and, with an enormous smile, kissed him. Once, twice, three times.

'*Il campione del mondo,*' she said. The champion of the world.

THE next month was a complete whirlwind of interviews, celebratory dinners, tickertape parades, handshakes and back-slaps all around. Through it all, John remained humble, helped at least a little by an episode which occurred at the nearby beach hang-out of Byron Bay, which kept things in perspective.

About a fortnight after getting home, John and Lara had taken Elijah down there for a break from the madding crowd. Still, it wasn't as if it was a complete break, and the two were hard put to go to any restaurant or cafe without John being asked to leave the talisman of our time — his signature — on a paper serviette or whatever they might have handy. John always obliged, and was happy to do so, but he would have been less than human if such things didn't slightly turn his head. So it was that two days after arriving the couple were standing in a supermarket queue in downtown Byron behind an elderly gentleman when two kids ran up and asked John for his autograph. As he obliged, the old fellow turned around and looked up, way up, at John.

It turned out he had a stutter...

'Are you w-w-w-with the w-w-w-w-w-w ...?'

John helpfully broke in, 'Am I with the Wallabies?'

The fellow looked perplexed.

'No, no, no, are you w-w-w-w-w-with the w-w-w-w-Wiggles?'

AS to the Eales family, they were as delighted for John's success as ever, in their usual understated way. But, well, he had captained the Wallabies to a World Cup win after all, and maybe this was an occasion to actually make an overt gesture of acknowledgment. Damian and brother-in-law Tony Byrne organised it. On Christmas morning, when the entire Eales clan gathered at Bernadette and Tony's place in Ashgrove, John was presented with a long rectangular box. On the top side was glass, and inside lay a cricket bat, facing up. At the bottom of the bat on the left was a photo of John holding up the World Cup. Beside it was a photo of Sir Donald Bradman! Above the two photos was written, in the great man's careful copperplate:

Dear John,

In recognition of your contribution to Australian sport,

Don Bradman

And fair enough too. John Eales was a good man.

Epilogue

∽

Scenes from a Life Since...

*I actually don't think we would have won the World Cup
if it wasn't for Greg Smith. Though it was very difficult in his reign to
have so many players coming in and out of the team
all the time, it was precisely because of that that the net was spread
very wide and we are able to discover a lot of young
players who got experience early, who by 1999 were just starting to peak.*

JOHN EALES, early in 2000,
reflecting on the previous year's triumph

Old rugby players never die . . . They just look that way.

JOHN EALES, 1996

∽

IT WAS EARLY July 2000, three days before the Wallabies were due to play the Springboks at the Melbourne Cricket Ground.
John was driving back home from Caloundra on a Wednesday afternoon — ready to catch a flight to Melbourne that night — when his mobile phone rang. It was Jack Eales, and John immediately felt something bad was coming. Somehow or other, the way things worked out, it was usually Rosa who rang if she wanted to chat about this or that, and then she might

hand the phone to Jack. But when Jack made the call it meant something serious had likely happened.

'It's Nonna,' Jack said to his oldest son, without preamble. 'She's in Royal Brisbane Hospital and it's not good. I've just spoken to your mum and she is pretty distraught. I think Nonna is dying . . . '

John, usually a careful driver, shifted the car into top gear, pointed it towards the hospital and called Wallaby manager John McKay on the way, telling him he'd be unable to make the flight to Melbourne that night, and he would get back to him.

Damian had already been informed, and was on his way from Sydney. Antoinette, also, who was living in Singapore and working as a nurse, had jumped on the first flight to Brisbane. Still, when John got there, it was all eerily reminiscent of his last hours with Carmel. Nonna was unconscious, the priest was in attendance, the family gathering from all corners. They all prayed, held Nonna, said their goodbyes. It was unclear whether the near-97-year-old would die that night or linger for days, but it was clear that her long life was nearly over. As John looked at her, so many memories came flooding back. Nonna running after him as he took off from preschool. Nonna waking him in the morning, and making his breakfast. Nonna wearing his Wallaby gear in the front yard. Nonna and John singing hymns on her bed. She had always been special to him, and somehow he felt he had always been special to her.

Somewhere near midnight, John kissed Nonna, then drove home, with the plan to return first thing the following morning. There were, to be sure, many things to be thankful for at this point. Whatever else, she had lived a long and extraordinary life, and known many great joys, and John was particularly thankful as he pulled the car into his driveway that she had seen him happily married, known and loved Elijah, and that he had many photos of them together.

The phone call came at 4 a.m. It was Jack again, and John knew what was coming before he said it. Nonna had passed away peacefully, just minutes before.

AT Melbourne's Colonial Stadium two days later, John was out on the ground before the game when he was approached by John McKay.

'John,' McKay, began, 'the players are going to wear armbands to honour your grandmother. I thought you should know.'

John was greatly touched, but quick with his response.

'That's very kind, John, but really they don't have to do that. I'm going to do it, but they shouldn't feel any obligation . . .'

'Well they're going to do it,' McKay gently interrupted. 'George [Gregan] has organised it, and they all want to do it anyway.'

Many of the Wallabies had met Nonna over the years, and even those who hadn't knew how much she meant to the Wallaby skipper. In the dressing room, John looked around at the team before they ran out, each indeed wearing a strip of black insulating tape around his left biceps. He looked at Gregan and nodded his thanks. Apart from everything else, it was a gesture that his mother, who had lived in the same house as Nonna for all but eighteen months of her life, would greatly appreciate.

The Wallabies went out and ripped 'em. Playing with steely commitment against a South African side trying to prove they were better than the world champions, the Wallabies finished the game with a 44-23 victory. The Springboks had been in front with only twelve minutes remaining, but Stephen Larkham then did what he did best — which is to personally put South Africa to the sword — by gliding left, shaping to offload, and then straightening up to cut through the bamboozled defence and score a wondrous try. This burst the dam, and three more tries to Australia quickly followed for the handsome win, their tenth in succession, the largest number of points scored against South Africa.

On the Monday morning, Nonna's funeral was held at St William's, at Grovely and was well-attended by all of the Eales and many of their friends and neighbours who had come to know Nonna over the years. John gave the eulogy, and after recounting the story of her life, came to his conclusion:

'Of all the memories I have of Nonna,' he said, 'one of the most enduring will always be of Rosa talking to her in hospital the night she died. Mum was speaking to her in Italian, telling her that soon she will be up in heaven and she will finally be able to meet Saint Anthony in person. Nonna is at peace now and I know that she is enjoying catching up with all her old friends and family, particularly her parents Angela and Enrico, all her brothers and sisters, and her grand-daughter Carmel.

'Death has ended Nonna's life here on earth but it does not end our relationship with her.

'Dear God, Carmel, Saint Anthony and Nonna, Nonna has touched the lives of everyone here in a very special way. Please look after us all and help us to learn from the example that Nonna set us and please guide us to join you all again in the future.'

Then they all sang, 'I Am the Bread of Life'.

AND now, on this first Saturday of August 2000, it had all come down to this, as the referee awarded the Wallabies a penalty against the All Blacks in Wellington. There were 30 seconds left on the clock, and the score was 23-21 in favour of New Zealand. Several times in the previous few minutes, it had seemed like the game was lost for Australia as the All Blacks threatened to score and put the game beyond reach, but the Wallabies had kept clawing their way back — and even won two lineouts on All Black throw-ins to put themselves in this position. John hauled himself up from the bottom of a ruck and indicated to the referee that the Wallabies would kick for goal.

Some 30 metres out from the tryline and fifteen metres in from touch, it was going to be a difficult kick in the swirling conditions, but the Wallaby winger and goal-kicker, Stirling Mortlock, had been in fine form that day and John had confidence he could do it. Needless to say, there was a lot riding on it . . .

Three weeks previously, the Wallabies had played in the first of the Bledisloe Cup Tests, and narrowly missed winning what was widely described as 'the greatest game ever played'. After just eight minutes of that game, played before a world-record 109,000 spectators at Sydney's Olympic Stadium, the Wallabies had been losing a staggering 24-0 — but had fought their way back to the lead, only to finally lose 39-35 after Jonah Lomu scored in the corner for the All Blacks.

The upshot was that if Stirling could kick this, the Wallabies would even the series and hold on to the Bledisloe Cup, as they had won it the previous year. If he slotted it, they would also be every chance of winning the Tri-Nations Trophy for the first time, so long as they beat South Africa the following week. John picked up the ball and prepared to hand it to Stirling . . .

Stirling? Where *was* Stirling? Unbeknown to John, the winger had left the field a few minutes previously with bad cramp and was stranded on the sideline, unable to come back on. It was hooker Jeremy Paul who articulated the obvious: 'Stirling's off, John. You're up.'

Quite.

John placed the ball on the tee and began to go through his pre-kick ritual that he had worked on so many times with Ben Perkins, who was himself watching it on a bookies' television at a Brisbane racecourse, and barely daring to breathe. Nor were All Black coach Wayne Smith, Rod Macqueen, or indeed most of the rugby communities of two nations who watched, stricken with hope and fear, as John started to take his precise three steps back from the ball, and then two-and-a-half across. Lara, now nearly eight months pregnant with their second child, was sitting in front of the television at home with her mother and the two-year-old Elijah, and could barely bring herself to watch.

Up in the press box at the Wellington Stadium, Bruce Wilson thought the game was gone. A week before he had seen John attempt five such kicks in training from almost exactly this position, and he had missed all five. At least one person off the field felt that John would definitely kick it, however. In front of the television in the living room of his Auckland home, Grant Fox, the former All Black kicking maestro who had first instructed John in the finer points of goal-kicking in 1993, turned to his wife and said, 'I just know the bugger's going to kick this.'

Certainly, the pressure was as great as any footballer had likely faced at any time, but as John reminded himself — based on Fox's teachings nearly a decade previously — the ball didn't know that. It just wanted to be kicked sweetly, and John cleared his mind and focused on the goal-kicking mantra he had developed over the years, the one which had always provided sanctuary in the storm: 'Head down, slow, follow through to the posts . . . '

With his *head down* to help keep his eyes on the spot, John moved towards the ball with *slow* and deliberate steps, brought his right foot into contact on exactly the right spot, and *followed through . . .*

The ball sailed over the crossbar, just like it had done all those many times straight over the Hills hoist in the Arnell Street backyard when he had imagined exactly this situation. The Test was won, the Bledisloe Cup was theirs, and John lifted his arms in triumph as he was swamped by his team-mates. Outside of winning a World Cup, it just didn't get any better than this.

It was for the two coaches to sum up at the press conference.

Wayne Smith, of the All Blacks: 'They aren't world champions for nothing.'

Australian coach Rod Macqueen said: 'It was pretty fitting it was John. He's a great captain and it was just another example of the things he can do.'

IT was 2 June 2001, and after a Super 12 season which saw Queensland win its last five games to make it into the finals against all odds — only to lose to the ultimate champions, the ACT Brumbies — John moved up into the new version of Camp Wallaby at Coffs Harbour. This international season offered a particularly meaty challenge in the form of the British and Irish Lions, who had arrived that day on their first tour to Australia since 1989 to play a three-Test series against the Wallabies. After that there was the Tri-Nations tournament, and after that . . .

After that, *what*? Just how long was John going to keep playing? When was he going to retire? It was a question he had been asked many times every day since the beginning of the year, when speculation had first appeared in the press that this was to be his last year. In response, John had always replied with the truth. He just didn't know.

It was probably Malcolm Muggeridge who said it best: 'Few men of action have been able to make a graceful exit at the appropriate time.'

'Graceful', he felt he could manage, when the time came. But judging 'the appropriate time' was an exceedingly difficult thing to do. On the one hand his form on the field was as good as ever and he still loved playing representative rugby. On the other hand, there was just about nothing rugby could offer him that he hadn't already experienced, and he sometimes hungered to throw his energies into different challenges, perhaps in the corporate world.

Certainly, he still loved the camaraderie of being with the team, but then again his family at home was growing — his beloved daughter Sophia had been born in October — and he looked forward to the time when he wouldn't be constantly kissing Lara and the kids goodbye and leaving for extended periods.

Many of his oldest rugby friends sagely told him that 'you're a long time retired, John' and if he was still enjoying it and earning his spot in the team he should stay with it; others gently indicated that a career such as his deserved to finish on a high note and he should make a clear announcement that his last game would be against the All Blacks at the Olympic Stadium in Sydney on 1 September. There would surely never be a better moment for him to leave the stage . . . other than, of course, leaving that same stage in late October 2003, after the Wallabies had successfully defended the World Cup against all comers. Physically, John felt capable of doing exactly that, and he knew he had the support of the ARU and the Wallaby selectors if he wanted to go on.

Late on that Saturday afternoon, he took a phone call from his biographer, who had decided to press him for an answer one last time. The biography was nearly at the presses, he was just writing the epilogue, and he was wondering if John had yet made a decision as to what he was doing.

'No,' John replied. 'The answer is yet to come to me. I know that it will come at some point but it hasn't yet. If it hasn't come by the end of the year then I will keep playing.'

Amen.

Acknowledgments

ON THE EVE of the 1999 World Cup final in Cardiff, I was interviewing John Eales when it occurred to me that I was well-placed to write his biography. After all, John's rapid rise to the Wallaby second-row had an uncanny coincidence of timing to my own equally rapid descent from the same position, and we had first got to know each other a little when passing on the ladder in late 1990. I had also written the biography of the last man to captain the Wallabies to a World Cup win, Nick Farr-Jones, soooo . . .

'So on the reckoning that you'll surely do the same tomorrow, whaddabout it, John?'

Oddly enough, the Wallaby captain seemed to have other things on his mind at the time, but he called me a couple of months later to say the idea had grown on him and I got stuck into it shortly afterwards. These words are written eighteen months after that beginning, and it has been a long and often arduous journey, but I am proud of the result and wish to record my gratitude to all those who helped.

My warm thanks, first and foremost, to John himself. Within the parameters of his many commitments, he was still able to cobble together the time I needed from him. Certainly this meant we were frequently meeting in airport waiting lounges to snatch an hour or two together, or making phone calls to each other at midnight, but we were always able to keep the project moving. Both he and his wife Lara were kind hosts when I went to stay in their Brisbane home, and I particularly thank Lara for never begrudging the precious family time that I was cutting into. I hope, among many other things, that their children will enjoy reading this book when they are older.

To the Eales family generally, and John's brother Damian especially, my deep appreciation. Throughout, Damian was a valuable source whose slightly different perspective from John's helped put everything into context.

Inevitably, writing someone's life story means also telling at least some of the story of other lives close by, and it was a happy circumstance for me that so many of the people populating John's world proved to be only too willing to help me get John's story right. A lot of his friends went a long way above and beyond the call of duty to help with this book, and I cite particularly Chris White, Rod McCall, Tim Horan, Simon Whitehart, Rupert McCall, Patrick McGrath and Ben Perkins.

So successful has John's career been that from its beginning it has been examined and documented by rugby journalists from around the world, and this book owes their collective work a great debt. Time and again I would return to their original articles to get a feel for what happened in a particular episode, before putting their account up against John's memory and proceeding from there. I especially owe a dipping of the lid to the work of Greg Growden (particularly the Toutai Kefu, David Knox and Wiggles stories), Peter Jenkins, Spiro Zavos, Terry Smith, Jim Tucker, Andrew Dawson, Mark Oberhardt, Adrian Warren, Wayne Smith, Mike Colman, Bruce Wilson and Michael Blucher. I also note how invaluable a resource Peter Jenkins' *Wallaby Gold*, and Max Howell, Lingyu Xie and Bensley Wilkes' *The Wallabies: A Definitive History of Australian Test Rugby*, were, in terms of providing easily accessible information on particular Tests. In terms of rugby information that I could not find easily — particularly concerning John's career with Queensland — my friend Jim Tucker of the *Courier-Mail* in Brisbane either already knew what I needed, or was able to retrieve it without trouble, and I express my appreciation here for his generosity in sharing it with me.

My source for the brief passage in Chapter 9 concerning New Zealand second-rower Ian Jones came from his autobiography, *Ian Jones — Unlocked*, written with Bob Howitt. I cite that here because I did not wish to break the flow of the passage by citing it there. Ditto, my information about the action at Villers-Bretonneux, much of which came from research provided by the Australian War Memorial, which Rod Macqueen kindly passed on to me.

To Evan Whitton, of *The Australian*, my special thanks. I sat beside him at a rugby dinner at the Sydney Hilton in 1983 and he was the first one to encourage me to pursue journalism — taking the time a week later to follow up with a letter encouraging the same. I owe you, Mr Whitton.

The *Sydney Morning Herald*, bless its cotton socks, first published a rugby article by me on 26 May 1986, and I have covered most of the significant occurrences in Australian rugby since, both for the *Herald* and in various books, including *Nick Farr-Jones: The Authorised Biography, and The Rugby War*. While writing this biography, thus, I often found myself having to give accounts of significant episodes I had previously covered. Usually, I wrote it afresh. Sometimes, though, if I felt I could only lose by re-writing the same thing in another way, I simply wove my original account into the body of the text. On the other hand I have sometimes quoted verbatim a particular 'Australian rugby writer' — as in the description of the new Wallaby jersey being 'volcano vomit on a rag' — when I was in fact the writer concerned, simply because it would have been tiresome to quote my own articles too much.

This is my twelfth book. In the last few years I have developed a trusted team of people who have been able to provide me with great support. My principal researcher has been Kevin Brumpton, and he was as quick as ever in coming back with answers I needed to queries on such varied things as the history of

Catholicism, the street lay-out of the Brisbane suburb of Grovely and the history of the Lord Taverners Club in London. My thanks, too, to my transcriber, Margaret Coleman, who was nearly always able to turn my long and sometimes garbled tapes — poor microphone technique! — into accurate transcripts. I equally record my gratitude to my friend and colleague at the *Sydney Morning Herald*, Harriet Veitch, who frequently went home on a Friday night with one of my draft chapters and returned at weekend's end with detailed suggestions as to how I could straighten out twisted sentences and have (sniff) a closer approximation to correct grammar. In terms of the structure, tone, and feel of the book, my wife Lisa and I would often be discussing that at 1 a.m., after she had spent the previous five hours — after we had put the kids to bed — reading the chapters and making her own notes. This book is a lot better for her valued advice.

Finally, my thanks to ABC Books, in particular Matthew Kelly who commissioned the book, senior editor Stuart Neale who was the man I most dealt with after that, Deborah Brash who worked practically around the clock to get it out on time, and most especially Carl Harrison-Ford who edited the manuscript with minute attention to detail. I have worked with many editors over the last decade, and he is one of the best two.

All up, I hope I have done John's story justice, and feel it was a privilege to write it.

Peter FitzSimons
Neutral Bay, June 2001

Appendixes

Appendix 1: Statistics

John Anthony Eales (b. 27/6/70)

Brothers, Queensland, Australia

Australian Test Career Statistics

Debut: 1st Test vs Wales, Ballymore, July 21st 1991. Aged 20 years 24 days.

International Test Match Career Results Record: Australia 1991-2000

Opposition	Played	Won	Lost	Drawn	For	Against
Argentina	7	6	1	-	239	103
Canada	2	2	-	-	101	20
England	8	5	2	1	221	100
Fiji	1	1	-	-	66	20
France	5	5	-	-	140	80
Ireland	6	6	-	-	171	81
Italy	3	3	-	-	83	45
New Zealand	18	9	9	-	348	413
Romania	2	2	-	-	99	12
Scotland	7	7	-	-	238	75
South Africa	11	7	4	-	260	202
Tonga	1	1	-	-	74	0
Wales	5	5	-	-	223	46
Western Samoa	3	3	-	-	107	19
Totals	**79**	**62**	**16**	**1**	**2370**	**1216**

International Test Match Career Captaincy Record: Australia 1991-2000

Country	Year	Matches	Won	Lost	Drawn	For	Against
Argentina	1997-2000	4	3	1	-	124	64
Canada	1996	1	1	-	-	74	9
England	1997-2000	5	3	1	1	147	54
Fiji	1998	1	1	-	-	66	20
France	1997-2000	5	5	-	-	140	80
Ireland	1996-1999	2	2	-	-	45	15
Italy	1996	1	1	-	-	40	18
New Zealand	1996-2000	9	4	5	-	191	253
Romania	1999	1	1	-	-	57	9
Scotland	1996-2000	5	5	-	-	174	50
South Africa	1996-2000	9	6	3	-	216	172
Tonga	1998	1	1	-	-	74	0
Wales	1996-1999	3	3	-	-	122	37
Western Samoa	1998	1	1	-	-	25	13
Totals		**48**	**37**	**10**	**1**	**1495**	**794**

International Test Match Career: Analysis by Position 1991-2000

Position	Matches	Partner	Period	Matches	Results		
					Won	Lost	Drawn
Lock	77	R.J.McCall	1991-1995	21	17	4	-
		G.J.Morgan	1994-1997	13	10	3	-
		W.W.Waugh	1995-1997	7	4	3	-
		J.P.Welborn	1996-1998	3	2	1	-
		D.T.Giffin	1997-2000	17	15	2	-
		M.J.Cockbain	1997	1	-	1	-
		O.D.A.Finegan	1997	1	1	-	-
		J.F.Langford	1997	2	1	-	1
		T.M.Bowman	1998	12	10	2	-
Number 8	2	V.Ofahengaue & S.P.Poidevin	1991	1	1	-	-
		B.P.Nasser & J.S.Miller	1991	1	1	-	-
Totals	**79**			**79**	**62**	**16**	**1**

International Test Match Career: Analysis by Opponent 1991-2000 (Minimum 5 Tests)

Position	Opponent	Country	Period	Matches	Results		
					Won	Lost	Drawn
Lock	I.D.Jones	New Zealand	1991-1998	15	7	8	-
	R.M.Brooke	New Zealand	1992-1998	12	5	7	-
	M.G.Andrews	South Africa	1995-2000	9	5	4	-
	K.Otto	South Africa	1997-2000	5	3	2	-

John opposed the pairing of Ian Jones & Robin Brooke in 11 Tests for a 4-7-0 record.

International Test Match Career Points: Australia 1991-2000

Opposition	Matches	Tries		Conversions	Penalty Goals	Points
		4pt	5pt			
Argentina	7	-	1	-	-	5
Canada	2	-	-	-	-	-
England	8	-	-	-	5	15
Fiji	1	-	-	9	1	21
France	5	-	-	4	13	47
Ireland	6	-	-	-	1	3
Italy	3	-	-	-	-	-
New Zealand	18	-	-	4	7	29
Romania	2	-	-	5	-	10
Scotland	7	1	-	3	2	16
South Africa	11	-	-	1	3	11
Tonga	1	-	-	2	-	4
Wales	5	-	-	1	-	2
Western Samoa	3	-	-	2	2	10
Totals	**79**	**1**	**1**	**31**	**34**	**173**

Most points in a single Test: 21 vs Fiji, World Cup Qualifier, 1998, Parramatta Stadium, Sydney

International Career Highlights

★ Most matches as Australian captain (48) and third on the all-time list behind Will Carling (England 1988-96) — 59, and Sean Fitzpatrick (New Zealand 1992-1997) — 51.

★ Most capped Australian lock forward (77) and third on the all-time list behind Willie John McBride — 80 (Ireland & Lions 1962-75) and Ian Jones — 79 (New Zealand 1990-1999).

★ Fifth highest international career points tally for Australia (173), one of only 12 Australians to score 100 or more career points and the only forward to do so.

★ First on the all-time career points scoring list for forwards. John is one of only two forwards to score 100 or more career test match points. The only other forward to achieve this milestone was Jean Prat (France 1945-55) — 139 points in 51 tests.

★ Most capped Australian player in internationals against Scotland (7) and equal highest against England (8) and Argentina (7).

★ Only one of five players (Dan Crowley, Tim Horan, Phil Kearns and Jason Little) to win the Rugby World Cup on two occasions.

★ In twelve international matches at his home ground of Ballymore, from 1991-98, John never played in a losing Australian test side.

Queensland Career Statistics

Debut: vs Canterbury, Christchurch, May 6th 1990. Aged 19 years 313 days.

Queensland Career Results Record: 1990-2001

	Played	Won	Lost	Drawn	Tries	Conversions	Penalty Goals	Points
Super 12	46	28	17	1	6	66	80	402
vs Int'l XVs	7	5	1	1	2	-	-	8
Other	59	43	16	-	2	42	42	218
Totals	**112**	**76**	**34**	**2**	**10**	**108**	**122**	**628**

Most points in a single match: 22 (5 conversions and 4 penalty goals) vs. Canterbury, Super 12 Round Robin, 1996, Ballymore, Brisbane.

Queensland vs New South Wales

	Played	Won	Lost	Drawn	Tries	Conversions	Penalty Goals	Points
Super 12	5	4	-	1	1	1	12	43
Other	13	7	6	-	-	8	13	55
Totals	**18**	**11**	**6**	**1**	**1**	**9**	**25**	**98**

Queensland Career Captaincy Record

Period	Played	Won	Lost	Drawn	Win %
1999-2001	19	13	6	-	68.4%

Brothers Old Boys (Brisbane) Career Statistics

Debut: vs Queensland University, March 24th 1990. Aged 19 years 270 days.
Played 44 First grade games during the period 1990-2001.

Prepared by Matthew Alvarez, June 2001

Appendix 2:
Rugby Code of Behaviour

The following appendix has been included at John's request ...

In an effort to address problems sometimes generated by people losing their perspective on what Rugby is meant to be about in the first place, the Wellington Rugby Football Union recently developed a Code of Behaviour. It has been so successful in providing much-needed compass points that it has been translated and duplicated around the world, as well as adapted for many other sports. Here it is ...

Parents' Code

1) Do not force an unwilling child to participate in rugby.

2) Remember, children are involved in rugby for their enjoyment, not yours.

3) Encourage your child always to play by the rules.

4) Teach your child that honest effort is as important as victory so that the result of each game is accepted without undue disappointment.

5) Turn defeat into victory by helping your child work towards skill improvement and good sportsmanship. Never ridicule or yell at your child for making a mistake and losing a game.

6) Remember that children learn best by example. Applaud good play by your team and by members of the opposing team.

7) Do not publicly question the referee's judgment and never his/her honesty.

8) Support all efforts to remove verbal and physical abuse from children's rugby.

9) Recognise the value and importance of volunteer coaches. They give up their time and resources to provide recreational activities for your child.

Coaches' Code

1) Be reasonable in your demands on the young players' time, energy and enthusiasm. Remember that they have other interests.

2) Teach your players that the rules of the game are mutual agreements which no-one should evade or break.

3) Group players according to age, height, skill and physical maturity wherever possible.

4) Avoid over-playing the talented players. The 'just average' players need and deserve equal time.

5) Remember that children play for fun and enjoyment and that winning is only part of it. Never ridicule or yell at the children for making mistakes or losing a game.

6) Ensure that equipment and facilities are appropriate to the age and abilities of the players.

7) The scheduling and length of practice times and games should take into consideration the maturity level of the children.

8) Develop team respect for the ability of the opponents, as well as for the judgment of referees and opposing coaches.

9) Follow the advice of a doctor in determining when an injured player is ready to play again.

10) Remember that children need a coach they can respect. Be generous with your praise when it is deserved and set a good example.

And, finally, guidelines for the young player. Forget all the really serious stuff you often see on TV-there'll be plenty of time for that when you get older. For now, the following code is one that contains a lot of good sense in it. It may not be the way we adults always behave, but it's at least the way most of us started out.

Players' Code

1) Play for the fun of it, not just to please your parents or coach.

2) Play by the rules.

3) Never argue with the referee's decisions. Let your captain or coach ask any necessary questions.

4) Control your temper. No mouthing off.

5) Work equally hard for yourself and your team-thus your team's performance will benefit, and so will your own.

6) Be a good sport. Applaud all good play, whether by your team or by your opponent.

7) Treat all players as you would like to be treated. Don't interfere with, bully, or take unfair advantage of any players.

8) Remember that the goals of the game are to have fun, improve your skills and feel good. Don't be a show-off or always try to get the most points.

9) Co-operate with your coach, teammates and opponents, for without them you don't have a game.

All up, ENJOY IT!

Appendix 3:
'Our Destiny Is In Our Hands'

The following is the text of a single page that was handed to all the Wallabies on the morning of Monday, November 1, 1999, just five days before the World Cup Final. It was written by one of the Wallaby assistant coaches, Alec Evans, and is spliced with quotes from a book he was reading at the time, by an American Olympic rower.

The Wallabies 1999 – Our Ultimate Destiny.
Winning the World Cup.

Good day. We are privileged to live another day in this magnificent Rugby World Cup. This week will be the ultimate test.

Over this week: 'You must approach this test with the seriousness and passion that you would use to prepare to challenge your death. You must prepare — not to die — but to battle for your life in each moment, with every faculty and power available to you.'

When compared to the ordinary concept of winning and losing, 'battling for my life' requires a whole different level of conciousness.' Be reassured that the work we have done has been about preparing to be the best rugby players in World Rugby, with every faculty (ability, aptitude, inherent power and rugby intellect) and physical power to be the World Champions.

'You must purge yourself of all thoughts of self importance, and all inclination to judge either yourself or others. You must go to power with humility and deep respect.'

Humility. Where the hell does humility come from? We have people who have trained a dozen years, through a hundred wins and losses, and yet they were no more humble than people we all know whose egos are greater than their ability. For some of us, humility does not come easily. A concious effort has to be made to go after humility, to maintain respect for other players, other coaches, along with the various helpers, spectators and even prejudiced onlookers. This week we will work at maintaining respect and humility, with success.

At the opposite end of the spectrum is pride, a nasty monkey for an athlete, or anyone to carry on his back. Pride. According to Webster's, it's 'an overhigh opinion of oneself. Haughtiness; arrogance.' Stay with humility. It will serve you well.

And finally, 'You must assume full responsibility for choosing to pursue the ultimate goal. Know that you alone have chosen to be tested, and then proceed without doubt, remorse, or blame. You alone are responsible.'

Tough rule. By following this rule, we have to abandon all the usual excuses. We are totally responsible for any results in this World Cup. 'Taking complete responsibility' is the premier rule for our destiny. Being tested is directed at each and every one of us. It conjures up passion to perform and images of blood and sweat, big hits, push-tries soaring in the lineout, 's' balls, field goals, switches, starter moves, penalty goals, backs tries, running channels, taking high balls, defensive lines, place pick ups and finally, Winning.

Every day this week we will be tested, on and off the field.

'Very few people know how to win. And for some reason, most winners have a difficult time verbalising the exact path they followed to accomplish their task.'

We are fortunate to have a team with the depth of knowledge in this squad who know how to win. We have past Wallabies in their own humble and private way express with impeccable manner the pride they have in the Wallaby Jumper.

We must win for our Country, Australia.

'OUR DESTINY IS IN OUR HANDS.'

THIS IS OUR WEEK — THE EVEREST OF RUGBY.

Appendix 4: Letter from Rod Macqueen

Rod Macqueen wrote the following letter
to the Wallaby captain after the 1999 World Cup.

Date: December 15, 1999

Dear John,

Now that all the hype is dying down, I thought I might take the time to reflect on the past two years.

I remember sitting back after our defeat at the hands of Argentina and thinking how far behind we were in our standards, both on and off the field. I know we have discussed this on many occasions but it remains a check point for me at all times, to ensure our standards remain at the level we expect.

From the time I spoke to you about the responsibilities and expectations associated with coaching the Wallabies, your response and commitment to the cause have been unwavering.

The journey over the past two years has had some rough patches along the way, however there is no doubt that it has been extremely enjoyable. Your contribution and support has played a major part in our ultimate success. Unfortunately, our preparation this year was disrupted through injury, but I think this actually helped our resolve — particularly when we were able to defeat the All Blacks in Sydney. With your return from injury you brought into the team the final ingredient required to ensure we would win the World Cup.

As we head into the future and the changing cultures that go with professional sport, it is imperative that we preserve our standards, ethos and traditions, both on and off the field. It is here that you will continue to play a highly important role over the next couple of years to ensure that when you finally "hang up your boots", you will know that Australian Rugby is looking good.

Liz and I have enjoyed Lara's and your friendship and look forward to smelling the roses with you in the future. In the meantime, we wish you both and Elijah a very Happy Christmas and New Year.

Kind regards,

Rod Macqueen

P.S. Don't forget our lunch appointment at Lighthouse park — half way line.

Published by ABC Books for the
AUSTRALIAN BROADCASTING CORPORATION
GPO BOX 9994 NSW 2001

Copyright © Peter FitzSimons 2001

Statistics © Matthew Alvarez 2001

First published August 2001
Reprinted August 2001
Reprinted September 2001
Reprinted October 2001

National Library of Australia
Cataloguing-in-Publication entry
FitzSimons, Peter.
John Eales the biography.

ISBN 0 7333 1012 5.

1. Eales, John, 1970 - . 2. Rugby Union football players –
Australia – Biography. 3. Rugby Union football – Australia.
I. Title.

796.333092

Text design and typesetting: Deborah Brash/Brash Design Pty Ltd
Typeset in 10.5/14.8 pt Minion
Colour separations: Colorwize, Adelaide
Printed and bound in Australia by Griffin Press, Adelaide